# RE-SHAPING RAIL IN SOUTH WALES

The railways of Briton Ferry and district –
past, present and future

**Also by Philip Adams**

A Most Industrious Town: Briton Ferry and its People, 1814–2014 (2014)
Not in Our Name: War Dissent in a Welsh town (2015)
Daring to Defy: Port Talbot's War Resistance 1914–1918 (2016)

*Front cover photograph:*
*King* class 4-6-0 *6024 King Edward I* climbs out of Fishguard at the head of the returning *Pembroke Coast Express* special to Newport on 22 April 2006. It will later join the south Wales main line at Briton Ferry via the Swansea District line. *(Martin Davies)*

*Back cover photograph:*
Foundation works at Briton Ferry for the first road crossing of Neath River (c 1950). Here the road bridge crosses Brunel's south Wales main line and dock. *(RCAHMW)*

*Opposite:*
Nationalisation in 1948 resulted in mistakes, the biggest of which was to continue with steam traction. The *Britannia* Pacifics were a new class of main line steam locos, but their working life was curtailed by the 1955 Modernisation Plan. *(Philip Adams)*

# Re-shaping Rail in South Wales

## The railways of Briton Ferry and district – past, present and future

**PHILIP ADAMS** and **MARTIN DAVIES**

Published by Philip Adams and Martin B Davies
c/o 144 Corve Street, Ludlow, Shropshire SY8 2PG, UK
www.britonferrybooks.uk

First published 2018

ISBN 978 0 9930671 4 3

Designed by Internet@TSP, Ludlow, Shropshire
Set in Apollo and Gill Sans

Printed and bound in UK by Cambrian Printers, Aberystwyth

**A note on spelling**
The authors have avoided Anglicised versions of place names
wherever possible, except where the English version is likely to be
recognised by non-Welsh speakers. For example, *Carmarthen* is
used instead of *Caerfyrddin* but the Welsh *Cwrt Sart* is used because
it is recognisable as the Anglicised *Court Sart*. The Anglicised
locomotive names, often used by the GWR, have been retained.

**Errors**
Every effort has been made by the authors to acknowledge
copyright and to avoid infringing it. If any errors have occurred that
require correction, the lead author can be contacted in order to
amend any future editions.

**Use of photographs**
Every effort has been made to acknowledge the true source of each
photograph used in the book. When deciding which to use, as far
as possible the authors have chosen those that haven't previously
been published. However, a number of images that have been used
before are included, either because of their historical significance
or because of the dearth of alternatives. The authors have also
included photographs taken by local railway enthusiasts who are
referred to in the text. Despite the fact that some of these were
taken using rudimentary equipment, the better images were
included to paint the picture of a bygone era more clearly.

# Contents

# Dedication

The volume is dedicated on the Davies side with special thanks to Martin's wife Eiryl for her patience and understanding during the production of this book. It is also dedicated to his sons Keith and Peter, daughter-in-law Laura, granddaughter Bethany, sister Andrea, father Keith, mother Eunice and all other members of his family.

Philip Adams dedicates this book to his family and friends.

# Acknowledgements

The authors are pleased to acknowledge and thank those individuals and organisations who have helped in the production of this book. Many individuals have given freely of their time to assist with research and provided information without which this book could not have been produced.

*Some individuals deserve special mention.*
*Peter Bannister*, for making available information written by his father, Phil about his working life at Cwrt Sart shed.
The late *Jeff Beer* whose photographs have been used.
*Val Berni*, whose extensive railway career gave a tremendous insight into life on the footplate.
*Godfrey Carr*, for his reminiscences and filling in some important gaps in my memory.
*John Davies*, for use of his photographic archive and his memories of Neath and Swansea Railway Society.
*Phil Gallagher,* for his recall of memories of steam days and use of his photographs.
*Ken Harris*, for his reminiscences of footplate duties.
*Tony 'Wilbur' Griffiths*, for his reminiscences of steam days and his work in railway preservation.
*Alan Hutchinson,* for his detailed recall of steam days at Briton Ferry and beyond and lending his photographic collection.
*Hugh James*, whose second-to-none knowledge of Briton Ferry and its railways resulted in much valuable anecdotal data.
*Dorothy James,* for her perspective on the scrapping and spotting of ships and locomotives.
*Vic James*, for some interesting industrial facts.
*Jeff Jones,* for recalling steams days and for the use of his photographs.
The family of the late *Norman Jones* for use of his photographs
*Margery Lewis*, for offering her insight into a railway family's history.
*Ira Llewellyn*, whose recall of 'all things Briton Ferry' was astonishing. Happy hours were spent listening to his tales of the railway scene in the 1930s and 1940s and the personalities involved.
*Clive Reed*, for his memories of the South Wales Mineral Railway and access to his brother's photographs.
*Robert Thomas*, for his time and for his generosity in making available his unique collection of local photographs and historic railway timetables.
*David Williams* for memories of the shed in the 1940s.
*Gerald Williams*, for letting the authors benefit from his enthusiastic research into the backgrounds and achievements of local railway staff, particularly regarding Cwrt Sart shed.

*Not forgetting:*
Robert Andrew, Professors Barry and Cole, Allan Colwill, Huw Daniel, Malcolm Davies, Tom Davies, Roy Evans, Nigel Gower, Wendy Harris and the family of the late Norman Jones, Malcolm Hill, John Hodge, Carol Hutchins, Caroline Jackson, Leslie Robert John, Gail Jones, Mark Jones, Alison Kingdom, Andrea Morris, Peter Owen, Jon Skidmore, B. Stephenson, the late Alan Thomas, Richard Thomas, Grenard Tremayne, Stuart Warr, Alan Williams, Allan Williams, Glyn Williams, the late Glenys Williams; and the Baglan Boys, the Ferry Boys and the Sandfields Boys.

*And some local organisations:*
Neath Antiquarian Society, especially Keith Tucker, Robert Davies and Bob Grant; Port Talbot Historical Society; Railfuture Wales; Richard Burton Archives at Swansea University; West Glamorgan Archives

*Other important sources were:*
The Great Western Railway Society; Kidderminster Railway Museum; Ancestry UK for U.K. Railway Employment Records (1833–1956); G W Railway Magazine 1838–1943; Find My Past for Census and Trade Union Records; Wikipedia

Even with due acknowledgement to modern technology's role in affording co-authors to work a hundred miles apart, it was the diligence, interest and expertise of John Fleming and Jo Mundy of Internet@TSP, Ludlow, that really enabled the delivery of the manuscript of this work on time.

# Preface

Over the years there has been no shortage of information on railways in Britain, whether in the form of books, magazines or television programmes. As we now know from the television series *Great British Train Journeys*, Bradshaw's *Descriptive railway handbook of Great Britain and Ireland* (Bradshaw's Guide) was published as early as 1839. The guides were nonfiction, but Bradshaw's distinctive portrayal of his subject matter attracted many both to rail travel, to reading about it, and, later, to fictional film and television performances on the subject.

From Bradshaw's era onwards, the country's interest in railways has created a growing demand for material of all sorts, of both varieties. The Yellowback novels of the second half of the nineteenth century were affordable, escapist, literature designed specifically *for* rail travellers and featured writers as well known as R L Stevenson. Much of the interest in fiction has been of the nostalgic variety, particularly since the rail closures of the 1960s and the ending of steam, but the success of this genre has been due to its association with real events; the branch line closure in *The Titfield Thunderbolt* (1953) and *The Railway Children* (1906). Adults were offered such titles as *Brief Encounter* (1945), *Miss Marple: 4.50 from Paddington* (1957) and Buchan's *The 39 Steps* (1915). Perhaps it was Zola's novel, *La bête humaine*, which led to the idea of anthropomorphic children's stories, such as the Awdrys' *Railway Series*, which gave life to Thomas the tank engine and his friends. (1945–2011).

It was followed by Michael Bond's book *A Bear called Paddington* in 1958, the impact of which was so great that it was the soft toy version of Paddington that became the first object chosen by British tunnellers to pass through to their French counterparts when the tunnel link was completed in 1994.

Whilst *Re-shaping rail in South Wales* falls clearly within the non-fiction category, it is neither a Bradshaw's nor a book which converges solely on one aspect of railways, such as rail staff, locomotives, timetables, or railway maps. It endeavours to touch on most of such matters, but only insofar as they make a relevant contribution to understanding the railways of south Wales. The bonding agent between these topics, which makes the book somewhat singular, is the people of Neath-Port Talbot especially of Briton Ferry and their experiences of the town's railways within their social context.

The book covers three historical periods:

First, the general, historical narrative in Chapters One and Two covers the period from the inception of the railways until the mid-twentieth century and should provide interest for most readers. The second covers the personal reminiscences of one generation during the mid-twentieth century from 1955–1975 in Chapters Eight, Nine and Eleven. The third period, covering the last quarter of the twentieth century to the present is found in Chapter Ten.

Chapters Thirteen and Fourteen are paramount: in covering the past and future of rail transport in Britain; they form the basis for a much-needed and pivotal discussion on local public transport in south Wales.

This book's aim is, therefore, to provide interest to all readers, whether you are a rail enthusiast, member of the travelling public, transport specialist or a member of a railway family; whether you are looking for nostalgia or towards the future. As a general reader, therefore, you may wish to 'surf' over some of the more specialist rail information whereas the specialist may be less attracted to some of the nostalgic topics. No reader, however, should fail to consider the issues raised about future transport needs and how integrated transport systems, with heavy railways as their core, can contribute to the re-development and prosperity of towns such as Briton Ferry within regions such as Swansea Bay.

Chapter One

# Introduction

*The train bore me away through the monstrous scenery of slag heaps, chimneys, piled scrap iron, foul canals, paths of cindery mud, criss-crossing the prints of clogs.*

George Orwell: *The Road to Wigan Pier (1937)*

**Pre-industrial Briton Ferry**

Briton Ferry is a former industrial town in the County Borough of Neath-Port Talbot, now forming part of what is being increasingly called the 'Swansea Bay City Region'. Just like other communities in this region, the town's growth from the mid-nineteenth century was based mainly on the metals industries with railways providing an essential transport infrastructure. Geologically the town lies on heavily fractured ground near the mouth of the river Neath on a line between the upper and middle coal measures. This has resulted in a geomorphology of such beauty that it once attracted many famous painters. During the late eighteenth century, these included J M W Turner and William Daniell, whose works depicting the river at Briton Ferry are now displayed at the Tate Gallery.

However, it was Briton Ferry's marine location and neither forges, nor its indisputable beauty, nor the existence of coal in the area, that led to the industrial growth of the town. Its location was the important

Briton Ferry in 1814 – from an aquatint by William Daniell *(Tate Gallery)*

9

factor in determining its transport arrangements, both to serve of people's work mobility and the economy of the area.

Despite its industrialisation, the view of Briton Ferry from the train was not as ugly as Orwell saw Wigan. Yes, there were industrial chimneys in Briton Ferry which denuded the woodland; yes, there were piles of scrap metal and, yes, there were foul canals, but these elements were somehow hidden from the town and its surroundings in such a way that the beauty depicted by the likes of Turner was never entirely lost.

## Early industrialisation: canals, tramroads and tramways

As early as the 1660s primitive forges existed at Briton Ferry.[1] The earliest recorded railway in the area was the tram road built by Sir Humphrey Mackworth to link his coal mines on the Gnoll estate in Neath to his smelting works at Melyncrythan. This was the first ever railway to experiment with sail power! Other tram roads followed in the 1780s, most of which were short in length and rough in construction. They were built to link up with the Neath Canal, opened in 1795 to carry coal to Melyncrythan for trans-shipment to river going vessels to distribute to other parts of the country and for export. These facilities were found to be inadequate, so the canal was extended to Giant's Grave, at Briton Ferry, where it was easier to transfer the cargoes.

In 1846, the Briton Ferry Iron Works was opened on reclaimed land close to the mouth of the river Neath. The favourable location of the works facili-

Map of Lord Jersey's Estate at Briton Ferry (1815)
(West Glamorgan Archives)

tated the import of iron ore and the export of pig iron. Much of the iron produced by the puddling furnaces at the iron works could be used as a raw material for the tinplate industry so it was natural that tinplate manufacturers should be attracted to Briton Ferry by the availability of ready supplies of wrought iron.

Neath Canal at Giant's Grave in 2007 (Martin Davies)

## Industrialisation

The Vernon tinplate works, between Baglan and Briton Ferry, was the first to be opened in 1850. By the turn of the century, the accelerating industrial-isation needed to sustain the British Empire resulted in the construction of an ironworks, two steelworks and half a dozen tinplate works around a new dock in Briton Ferry. Two copper works replaced earlier works sited further up the river Neath. These works required workers and the workers were agricultural labourers who took advantage of new railways to come from the farms of rural west Wales and else-where. They required housing, some of which was provided by the rail companies. 'The railways in Wales were agents of depopulation'[2] in the country-side, but the migrants to the towns nonetheless saw their train journeys eastwards as the route to better prospects.

Some 1,362 of the 3,548 hectares of the Neath salt marsh complex were lost to industrial develop-ment and the necessary rail infrastructure, mainly on the eastern bank of the River Neath, around Briton Ferry.[3] Briton Ferry lost its sea frontage to industry but Jersey Marine, on the river's western bank, retained its frontage for a further century.

There were two reasons why industrial develop-ments occurred. Firstly, there was a growing dem-and from the rest of the industrialising world and, second, a vast accumulation of capital was available. Briton Ferry, like most of Welsh industry, depended almost exclusively on the primary processing of mineral resources, with little secondary or light pro-duction. Originally much of Briton Ferry's industries and construction were financed by local capital, although the main railways were not, but, as time went on, the Welsh economy, in general became dependent on external investment.

In 1837 the entire population of Briton Ferry was a mere 450, but the area was slowly industrialising and its population of 4,803 in 1871 had risen further to 8,456 by 1911. Many of these were rail workers.

Today Briton Ferry comprises the electoral wards of Briton Ferry East and West within the County Borough, with each ward falling neatly on either side of the railway line that has physically divided the town since 1850. In earlier times, the town was a Municipal Borough in its own right. Important though public administration has been in the history of the town and its railways, this book is about the history and geography the town's railways them-selves, and the people and industries that those rail-ways served.

## Heyday

The heyday of the town roughly coincides with the heyday of its railways, during the steam-driven industrial era which lasted over a hundred years until the 1960s. By the start of the twentieth century, the predominantly steel and tinplate town had its own Urban District Council, Public Library, and util-ities comprising a gasworks and water supplies. Gas-powered tramcars ran from Briton Ferry to Skewen. Socially and politically the town was developing, too, especially after state secondary education became compulsory in 1902. Its industrial decline did not begin until the early 1950s with the gradual loss of its metal industries.

The heyday of the town's railways was evidently unsustainable as the metal industries began to disap-pear, but its ending came from a conflation of addi-tional factors: the Beeching Report, the introduction of diesel locomotive power and a largely unplanned de-industrialisation caused by an oil crisis resulting from war in the Middle-east. The increased ownership of private cars also reduced rail passenger traffic. Freight traffic further reduced after 1980 when a planned de-industrialisation of heavy industry was to begin with a vengeance.

## Industrial decline

This book is, therefore, about the railways of a former 'most industrious town' which, today, forms a dormitory settlement for a wider employment region. Therefore, its scope cannot be confined to the two electoral wards of Briton Ferry East and West, which are effectively defined by the railway, because its railways have a wider geographical impact. This arises from the town's importance as the lowest crossing point of the River Neath, its access to the Bristol Channel and the fact that the town provides a by-passing, by road and rail, of the towns of Neath and Swansea on the route to west Wales and Ireland.

The town's importance was recently shown quite clearly by Huw Irranca Davies MP. When advocating the extension of rail electrification to Swansea, his comments[4] in the House of Commons reflected the mental image many have of the geographic extent and influence of Briton Ferry when he said:

> 'We have been talking about the economic benefits and we were told that the electrification project would be delivered to Swansea. Let us look at the developments that are happening at Swansea at the moment. There is the SA1 project and the new university campus at Briton Ferry'.

## Resurrection

It has recently been announced by the Government that the anticipated, and promised, rail electrification between Cardiff and Swansea will not take place. Whilst this is likely to reduce economic development opportunities in the Swansea Bay area, the ill-effects of this broken promise can be mitigated if the area's existing railways are better exploited than has been the case in recent times. Briton Ferry's central geographical position within the Swansea Bay region can still be an exemplar for the development of a much-needed inter-modal public transport system, based on its existing conventional rail assets.

This book is, therefore, about more than the nostalgia for the last one hundred and seventy years of the railways' motive power, infrastructure, services and people. It is also about re-shaping the ownership, operating philosophy and technology of rail within a comprehensive transport system for the needs of the people of the twenty-first century.

How this proposition for modernity can be taken forward forms the conclusion of this book in Chapter Fourteen.

### Notes for Chapter One

1. D Morgan Rees in 'Neath and District' A symposium', p 149
2. Bradley, p362
3. Mary Gilham, Swansea Bay's Green Mantle, 1982
4. House of Commons Debates, Vol 605, 8 February, 2016.

*72xx 2-8-2T no. 7235 passes Pinewood Crossing, Baglan, with a down train of coal empties, August 1964*
*(Martin Davies)*

Chapter Two

# The Railways Arrive

*Houses were knocked down ... enormous heaps of earth and clay thrown up; buildings that were undermined and shaking, propped up by great beams of wood.... The yet unfinished and unopened Railway was in progress.*

Charles Dickens: *Dombey and Son (1847)*

**Introduction**

This chapter traces the origins of the private railways in the Briton Ferry and Jersey Marine area that came together as the GWR: the South Wales Railway, the Vale of Neath Railway, the South Wales Mineral Railway and the Rhondda and Swansea Bay Railway.

**Before the railways**

Travel by land was slow, difficult and costly at the start of the nineteenth century, with horses providing the main means of transport. Turnpike roads were not well-maintained, despite tolls. For heavy loads, transport by water was better and this was indeed the case along the coast of south Wales but it was impossible to do so on many of the rivers inland because their gradients were too steep. Artificial gradients for waterways needed to be engineered, using locks if necessary, and this led to 'water roads' being built in the eighteenth century in the form of canals which followed the contours of the valleys.

Mine owners then developed a new kind of road: parallel rails fastened to the ground on blocks of stone, on which small trams were pulled by horses or men. Tramways reached places that canals could not. Several tramways existed in the Briton Ferry area in the early 19th century to serve various collieries and levels. Humphries[1] refers to a tramroad built from Eaglesbush and Penrose Colliery to Briton Ferry.

The coal ... was brought down ... by a horse-drawn tramroad which ran at the base of Tyla Morris, through the present Cricketers Field, crossing Neath Road by the lodge, over to the spot where the Briton Ferry Aerated Works now stands,

along Shelone Fields into Church Street, thence to the riverside.

This tramway predated the South Wales Railway as he also points out:

After the construction of the Great Western (South Wales) Railway it came down through the dark arch of that railway, joining the old tramroad at Shelone.

The earliest colliery in Briton Ferry itself was probably

*the Baglan colliery situated to the south of the Traveller's Rest under the Old Road, which was started in the early 18th century by the Mansels of Briton Ferry.[2]*

This was later likely leased from the Jersey Estate by Joseph Tregelles Price in the 1830s, to become known locally as *Price's Drift*.[3] Initially a pill was built from the river Neath to allow small vessels to load coal from the mine, until the coal was later moved by tramroad.

Shortly after the construction of the Great Western Railway (South Wales Railway) a tramroad was made across the clay to the river.... When the Briton Ferry Dock was made the tramroad was done away with and the coal and clay were purchased by the Briton Ferry Ironworks.[4]

After 1861, a network of tramways developed to move coal from other collieries in the Baglan area notably the *Wern Pistell*, the *Tor-y-mynydd*, the *Swan* and the *Park*. These were situated on the line of the

13

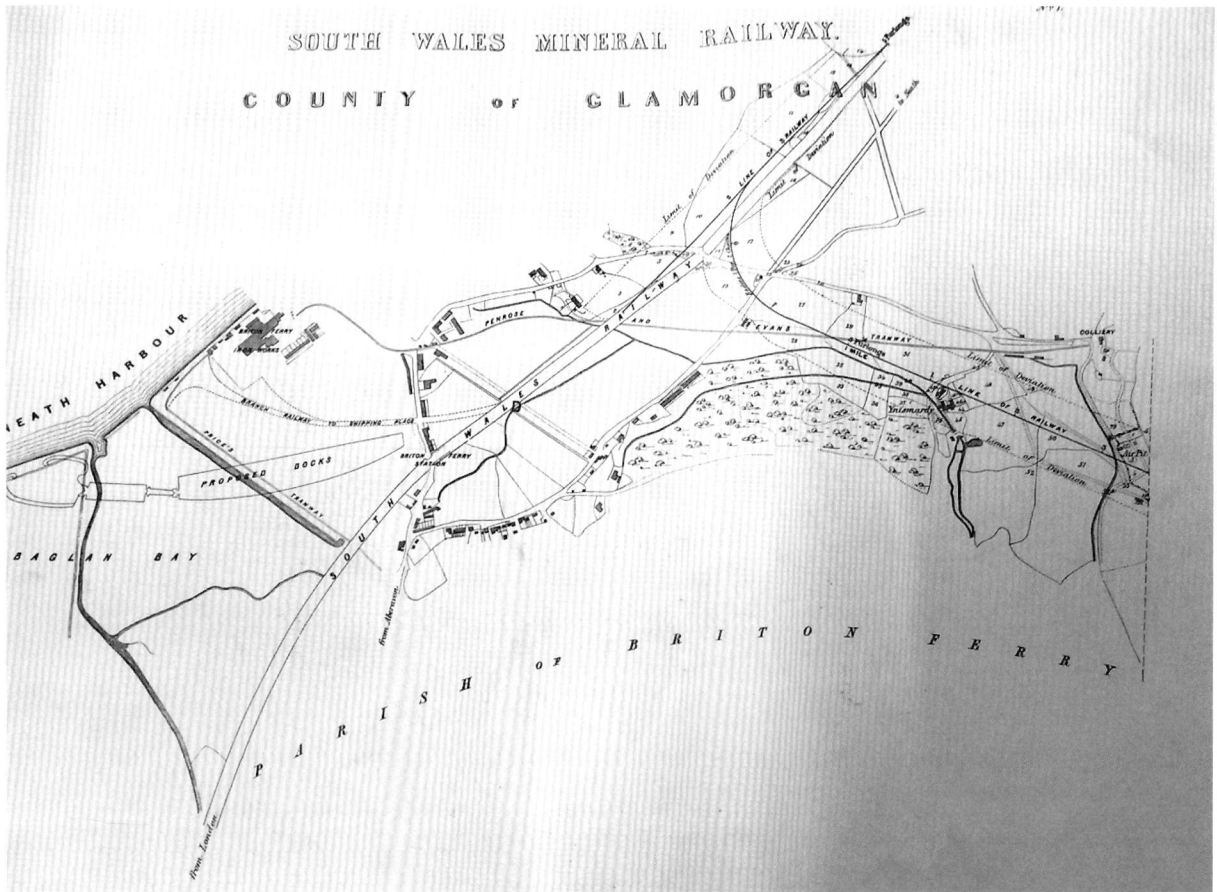

Map of 1853 (from Brunel's survey) showing Penrose and Evans tramroad and the South Wales Railway with Briton Ferry (West) station *(Clive Reed Collection - West Glamorgan Archives)*

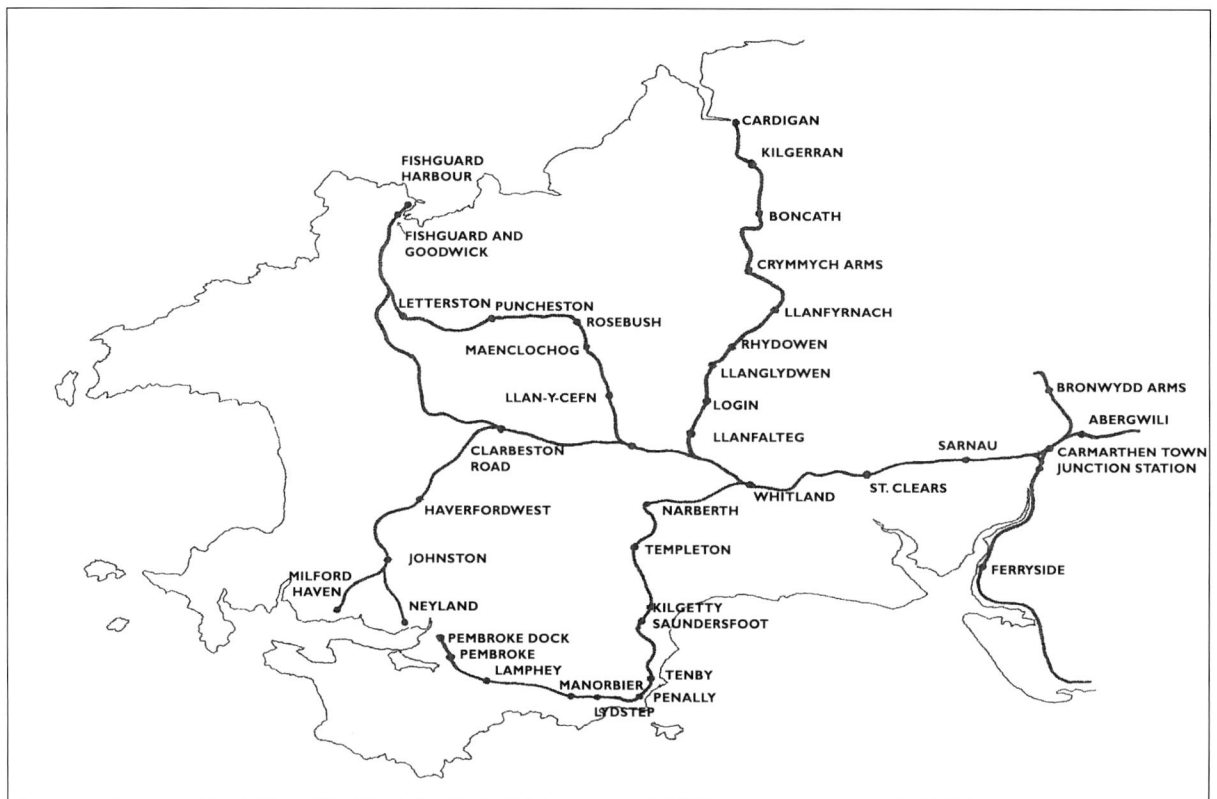

Map showing the GWR railway network in west Wales. Brunel's original plan was for a terminus at Fishguard (eventually opened in 1906) but due to economic constraints chose Neyland (which was known as New Milford from 1856 to 1906) *(J Page)*

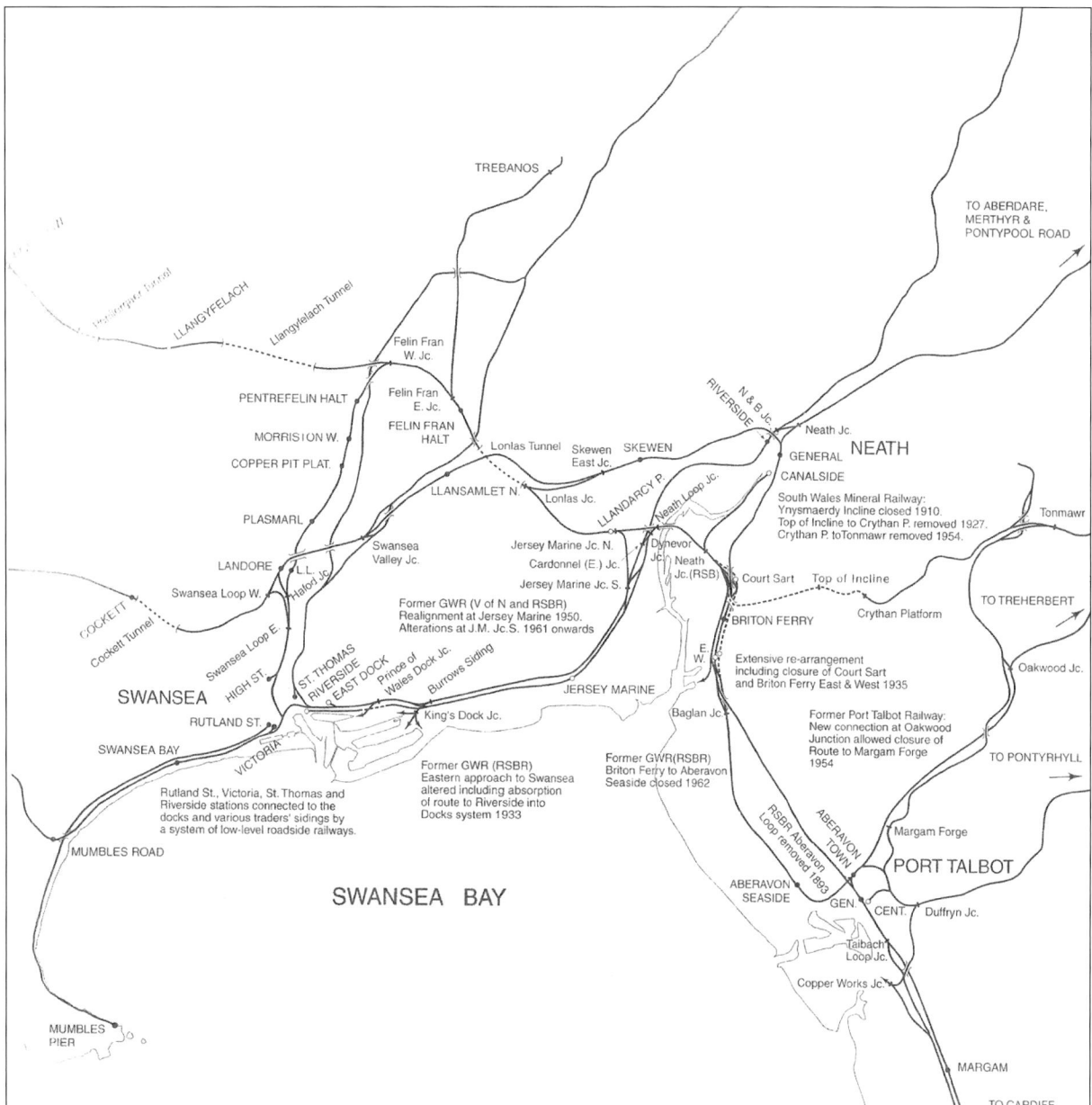

Railways in the West Glamorgan area (*Red Dragon*)

present A48 road through Baglan. Coal workings were also found in upper Baglan between Blaen-baglan and Ty Newydd farms and a tramway was built to serve Blaenbaglan Colliery. These collieries and the tramways that served them are dealt with further in Chapter Three.

Mechanical assistance soon followed on the tramways in 1804 with Trevithick's somewhat unsuccessful steam engine on wheels, running from Merthyr to Abercynon. Despite a further temporary disappointment at Scott's Pit railroad at Llansamlet in 1819, where the under-powered loco had to be withdrawn, development proceeded undeterred. Six years later, George Stephenson's *Locomotion No.1* became the first steam locomotive to carry passengers on a public railway, on the Stockton to Darlington line.

## The new railways

A quarter century later, by means of cuttings, bridges and embankments, the railways were revolutionising transport in south Wales by linking the docks, towns, mines and factories. In this way Briton Ferry had its first railway, the South Wales Railway.

It was the first of four separate private railways, constructed in the nineteenth century in Briton Ferry, that eventually came together as one, the GWR. Feeding these privately-owned, public-serving railways were the town's private, industrial rail networks. '*There used to be a rich network of railways serving Swansea and Neath*'[5] which was centred on the Briton Ferry-Jersey Marine area.

In Britain 'From the outset, railway building ... raised profound issues of ownership and control

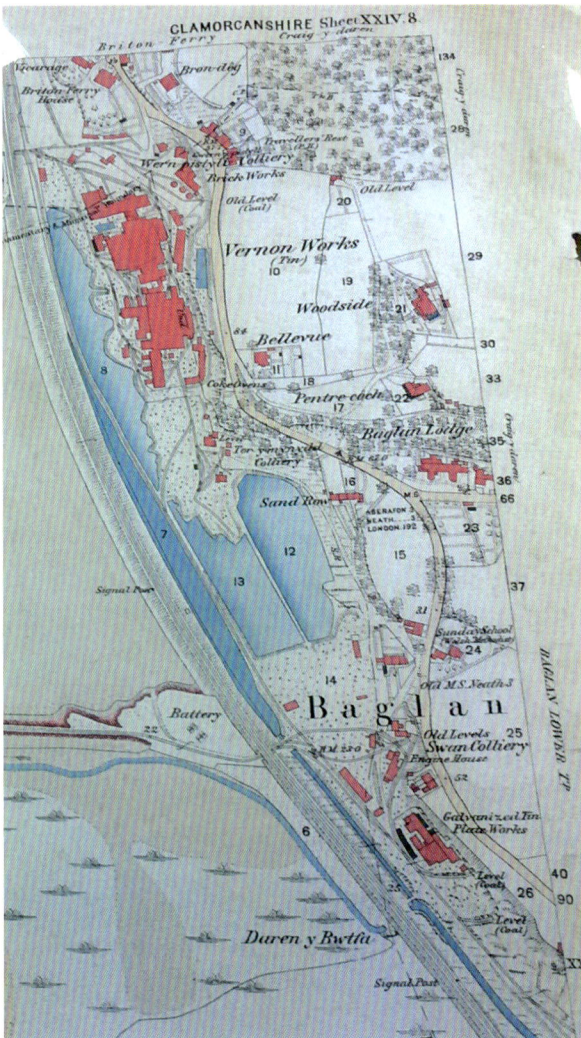

Map showing collieries and tramroads at Baglan 1875
(Ordnance Survey)

Christopher Mansel Rice Talbot
(Port Talbot Historical Society)

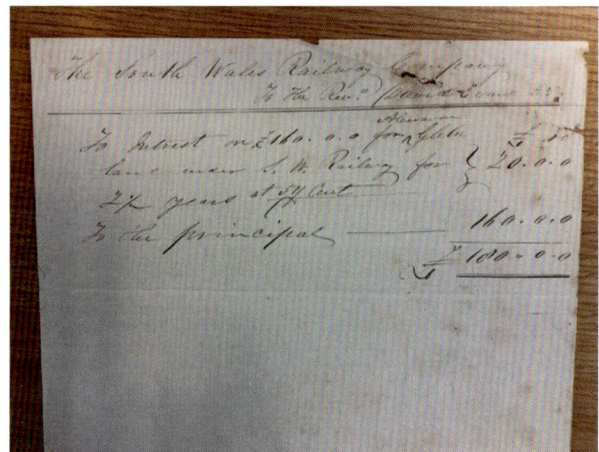

Invoice from Rev. Evans to South Wales Railway for
purchase of land (Clive Reed Collection – Swansea Archives)

over space'.[6] Briton Ferry and district was no exception, because routes were planned across land that often belonged to someone else. In Briton Ferry even some marshland had to be converted to industrial use from the spoils of its own industry. Consequently, the land was precisely charted to obtain parliamentary approval and to establish legally who owned exactly what. Network Rail is still one of Britain's biggest landowners.

The space restrictions in Briton Ferry led to three of the original railways running at different levels, but the railways' demands on the land around the River Neath were not quite as severe as that in the narrower Taff Vale, south of Pontypridd, which had to accommodate lines running at six different levels.[7]

**The South Wales Railway (1850–1863)**

The engineer of the South Wales Railway (SWR) was the famous Isambard Kingdom Brunel and its route was part of his grand scheme to link London to a great transatlantic port in west Wales. In 1836 he

Earl of Jersey (Cliff Morgan)

surveyed south Wales for a new line, but the route surveyed was not publicly disclosed. In Swansea it was rumoured that Brunel's intention was to route the railway across the mouth of the River Neath, over the burrows, and to enter Swansea from the east. This greatly concerned Neath business people fearing both a loss of trade by avoiding Neath, and concern that access to Neath port would be obstructed by a rail bridge at the estuary. John Rowland, a Neath banker was vociferous at a prospective shareholders' meeting in Neath in 1845. His intervention may have persuaded Brunel to select the route through Neath. Of this outcome, a nineteenth century pamphleteer said:

> Had Brunel's line across the burrows from Briton Ferry been carried through, six miles of journey, with all the inconveniences of Landore and its viaduct would have been avoided.

When Brunel visited the area, he stayed in a private apartment at Pyle Inn belonging to C R M Talbot of Margam Abbey, company chairman of the South Wales Railway who had family links with the Mansel family of Briton Ferry. Brunel visited Briton Ferry by horse and trap, with his horse watering at the trough on Neath Road opposite the future site of Jerusalem Chapel. On the 18 June,1850, the broad-gauge railway was opened from Chepstow to Swansea and for Briton Ferry passengers in September of that year. The SWR was also extended from Chepstow to Grange Court, near Gloucester, where it joined up with the Great Western Railway's (GWR) line from Paddington.

In 1861 a dock, also designed by Brunel, was opened at Briton Ferry to improve the shipment of coal. This soon led to the building of the series of tram-ways mentioned earlier to carry coal from pits such as Wern Pistyll and Swan Collieries at Baglan to the dock. Such was Briton Ferry's location between the river Neath to the west and the hilly woodland of Craig-y-Darren to the east that less than a kilometre of flat land was available at its narrowest for the development of the town and its railways. Although some of the marshy land near the industrial area to the south, and along the river bank, could be reclaimed, at times the demand for land almost exceeded supply.

This manifested itself in land ownership disputes between the rail companies on the one hand and the Earl of Jersey, a prominent local landowner, and a member of the Briton Ferry Local Board, on the other.

'The railway brought legally-enforced violation of ancestral ownership as broad

Location of Vale of Neath Railway's wharves (Martin Davies)

The opening of Briton Ferry Dock, 1861 *(Illustrated London News)*

acres were carved up by impassable barriers at the behest of speculative investors…but the aristocracy likewise woke up to the valuable rewards to be had from company chairmanships and directorships, which also allowed them to steer the railways' development to their own advantage'.[8]

The SWR built its station on the southern outskirts of the town, adjacent to the north end of the dock, close to Villiers Street, then a major shopping thoroughfare.

The station comprised *up* and *down* platforms. When it opened, the railway crossed Villiers Street by means of a level crossing. The station building was of mock Tudor design, typical of many stations on the South Wales line, with a signal box at the northern end of the down platform. Access to the station was by means of a series of steps which began in Railway Terrace.[9] The station wall and blocked-up entrance to the station is still visible. The GWR, took over the SWR in 1863.

Later the level crossing was replaced by a subway, which is used by traffic to this day. A similar subway was built where the railway crossed over Regent Street, further north. An 1880s map shows two nests of five sidings to the north of the station on the down side. In 1892, the signal box was replaced by another box to the north of the *down*

platform. The station, which became known as Briton Ferry West, to distinguish it from the RSBR station (called Briton Ferry East) was closed in 1935. This was part of a streamlined railway infrastructure at Briton Ferry within which a new station was built further north in Rockingham Terrace. The old Briton Ferry West station building was used as a residence until the 1970s.

**The Vale of Neath Railway (1846–1863)**

The next railway linked to Briton Ferry was the Vale of Neath Railway (VNR). Incorporated by an Act of 1846, this broad-gauge line was built to connect the collieries of its vale with Neath town and, by running powers, over the SWR to the wharves alongside the lower river Neath at Briton Ferry, replacing those upstream linked to the Neath Canal at Giant's Grave. Alfred Russel Wallace worked as a civil engineering

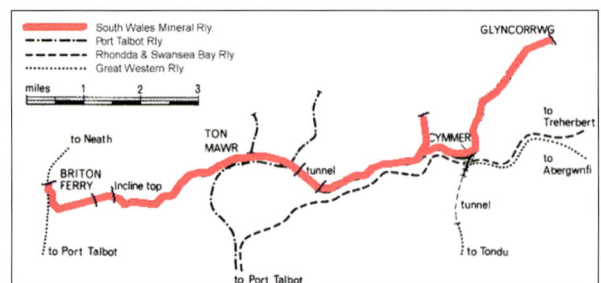

The route of the South Wales Mineral Railway *(H Morgan)*

Wagons operating on the incline at Ynysymaerdy

surveyor for the line's construction and, whilst he lived in Neath, was also instrumental, with his brother John, in designing and building Neath Mechanics Institute[10] in 1843. The line, which was opened for traffic on 23 September 1851, extended initially only to Aberdare and Merthyr, but eventually linked with the Abergavenny and Hereford Railway to form a through route to Pontypool. The extensions to the line enabled Neath and Briton Ferry to compete with the east Wales ports for the coal traffic from north Glamorgan. Indeed, it was with this traffic in mind that the Briton Ferry Floating Dock Company was opened under the auspices of the VNR in 1861.

> It was a red letter-day in Briton Ferry.
> There was the booming of guns and the
> sounds of trumpets ... and ... the place
> was fully decorated with bunting.[11]

The creation of the dock meant that the Briton Ferry riverside wharves, too, were no longer needed for this trade. However, traffic from the VNR to Briton Ferry was also short-lived, as the Swansea and Neath Railway Act authorised an extension of the VNR to the more convenient deep-water port of Swansea.

## The South Wales Mineral Railway (1861–1923)

The line was Brunel's third line in Briton Ferry and was again built to his broad gauge. It linked Briton Ferry dock with the collieries in the Afan, Pelenna and Corrwg valleys. The line was mainly for minerals, with passenger trains only operating officially above Cymmer. Its costly construction and operation

The incline bottom where it entered today's Jersey Park (R. Evans)

The so called 'Iron Bridge' which carried the SWMR across Neath Road, Briton Ferry (the present A474) near Lodge cross. The bridge remained in situ until it was dismantled during the Second World War. In the 1930s it was a popular vantage point for locals like Ira Llewellyn to watch the annual Briton Ferry carnival.
(Cliff Morgan collection, Neath Antiquarians)

Brunel's stone bridge today where the SWMR crossed the RSBR (today's SDL) *(P Adams)*

led to it becoming a 'white elephant' when its upper reaches were afforded an easier access to Port Talbot Docks via the PTR. The line was not the perfection that was expected from Brunel.

Opening in stages between 1861 and 1863, it took the shortest distance from the valleys to the port, but the route necessitated some considerable engineering works. These included the tunnel at Gyfylchi and the ambitious, one-in-ten, incline at Ynysymaerdy. Trains were locomotive-hauled for the eleven miles from Glyncorrwg along a single track, with crossing places at Cymmer and Tonmawr, to the top of the incline above Cimla. Here steam traction gave way to a rope-fed gravity-worked system. A wired cable which towed the trucks was controlled by a braked wheel at the top of the incline.[12] Loaded wagons were fed down the steep gradient and their weight used to propel the empty wagons in the opposite direction. The rope system proved unsafe at times, as witnessed in several accidents to be narrated in Chapter Twelve.

The incline passed through Briton Ferry woods to reach a level plane at its base to the east of the present A474 road, near the Lodge Cross overlooking the 'Steelworks' cricket ground. Here the reception sidings marshalled wagons into suitable trains for the journey to the docks.

A SWMR saddle tank loco *(Gerald Williams)*

The presence of today's A474 road, the SWR, and new housing in the town forced the SWMR to follow a path from the reception sidings to the north-west to the docks, instead of south, which would have been a preferable and less expensive route.

The line crossed the A474 road near the Lodge Cross by means of an iron bridge. It was then carried on an embankment to a stone bridge over Shelone Road, where Briton Ferry Community centre is now sited, and over yet another stone bridge, which is still in place, to cross the former RSBR line/*up* flying loop. At this point it was necessary to cut into the hill at Brynhyfryd, at the northern end of Shelone Terrace, to accommodate the line.

It then crossed over the SWR in a westerly direction to its own sidings before requiring a change of direction to run south, alongside the SWR to Briton Ferry dock. A small engine shed and workshop was built close to Shelone Road bridge to house the saddle tank locos used by the company.

The incline closed in 1910 following the building of the Port Talbot Railway (PTR) in 1907, which provided an easier outlet for the coal from the Corrwg and Pelenna valleys.

The SWMR's General Manager, Arthur Steel, lived at the suitably-named Corrwg House in Charles Street. 'He had multiple roles in the town and was also a member of the Urban District Council, the Briton Ferry School Board and Director of the Aerated Water Company and the Perfect Thrift building society'.[13]

Most of the SWMR was accessible to walkers up to the 1960s. Clive Reed was one:

> During the 1950s it was possible to walk the entire route of the SWMR. At that time, as we climbed the steep hill to Crythan Platform, we could see on the hill opposite an old railway carriage, it was a landmark and something to look out for on our walks. The carriage was about half the length of a passenger carriage, or possibly even smaller. It appeared to us to look like an old clerestory carriage of years ago. It remained on the hillside for many years ... but when I walked the line in 1981 it had gone.
>
> On my ramblings in the 1980s I came across a Brunel-designed, double-headed rail approximately one yard long with a fishplate bolted to one end.[14] Brunel's idea was that, once it became worn on one side, it could be turned over, thus doubling its life span. Without a flat bottom it soon worked loose and had to be

SWMR wagon workshops — Shelone Road bridge — SWMR Engine Shed

SWMR facilities at Shelone *(R. Simmonds)*

withdrawn from all passenger-carrying lines and ended up on freight-only lines. It was one of the great Victorian railway engineer's few glorious failures.

I recovered it from a gully at the top of the incline and managed to carry it about a mile to my car. This is the only large piece of Brunel rail surviving from the SWMR. Neath-Port Talbot Museum service accepted it for their collection. The only other known relic of SWMR track is a sliver, one-eighth of an inch thick, which is on display at the National Railway Museum in York.

SWMR Wagon works sidings *(Neath Antiquarians)*

RSBR coal hoists at Prince of Wales Dock, Swansea *(Page)*

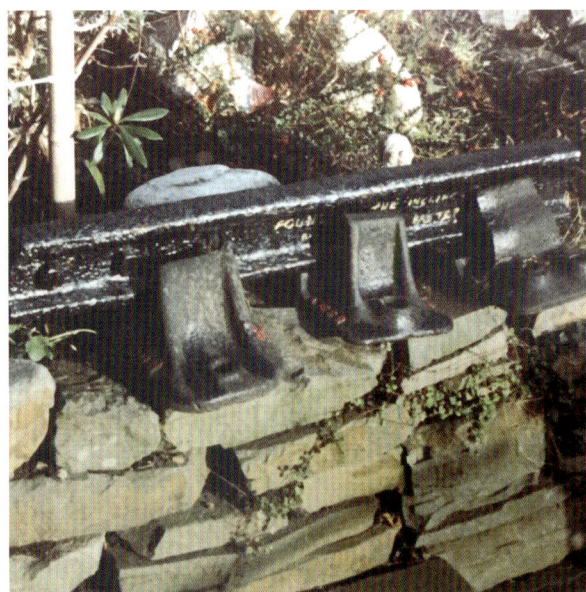

A section of broad gauge track from Ynysymaerdy incline
*(Clive Reed)*

The RSBR coat-of-arms *(Welsh Railways Research Circle)*

## The Rhondda and Swansea Bay Railway (1895–1923)

The final railway to reach Briton Ferry was the Rhondda and Swansea Bay Railway (RSBR). With Brunel's decision to route the SWR via Neath, the pressure from coal owners to bring the hard steam coal of the Rhondda on a direct route to the docks at Briton Ferry and Swansea increased enormously. At first a line was mooted from Treherbert to Cymmer, then following the SWMR but avoiding Ynysmaerdy incline, to reach the South Wales main line and Briton Ferry Dock. It was not carried through so that, by the 1880s, the pressure for such a line was so great that the RSBR was the result.

Cardiff Docks were becoming congested by the end of the nineteenth century because of the sheer amount of coal leaving the valleys. Accordingly, the Prince of Wales Dock at Swansea had been opened in October 1881 to accommodate the largest vessels of the day. Consequently, coal owners in the Rhondda and business people in Swansea became interested in an independent railway for Rhondda coal to be shipped to Swansea to avoid the bottlenecks encountered at Cardiff.

The Rhondda coal owners, who were the main driving force behind the creation of the RSBR, were prepared to battle in their desire to succeed. The story of the line's creation was a story of successive battles along its thirty-odd miles length from Treherbert in the Rhondda Fawr valley to Swansea Docks. It was double-track throughout, apart from the Rhondda tunnel which was single.

A crowded platform at Aberavon (Seaside) in the 1930s *(Port Talbot Historical Society)*

[The RSBR] practically waged a thirteen years' railway war[15] … and in 1892 a great battle was fought in the Houses of Parliament, with the result that the [company] beat the GWR all along the line and established their through connection with Swansea.

Perhaps foremost in the minds of Lord Jersey, the SWMR Chairman, and his deputy, Sir John Jones Jenkins, however, were not the legal battles, but engineering battles. The geological challenge to drive one of the country's longest tunnels between the Rhondda and Afan Valleys was the second battle and the third was the challenge to cross the River Neath.

From the southern end of the tunnel at Blaengwynfi southwards, the line's construction was less problematic than the northern end because it could use the route of the old Cwmafan Tramway part way to Aberafan. Originally there had been a plan to drive the railway through Mynydd-y-Gaer at Cwmafan and reach the coastal plain at Baglan. However,

*Baglan Hall*, the locomotive 4913 was named after the residence of the local landowners at Baglan
– the Llewellyns *(Great Western Society)*

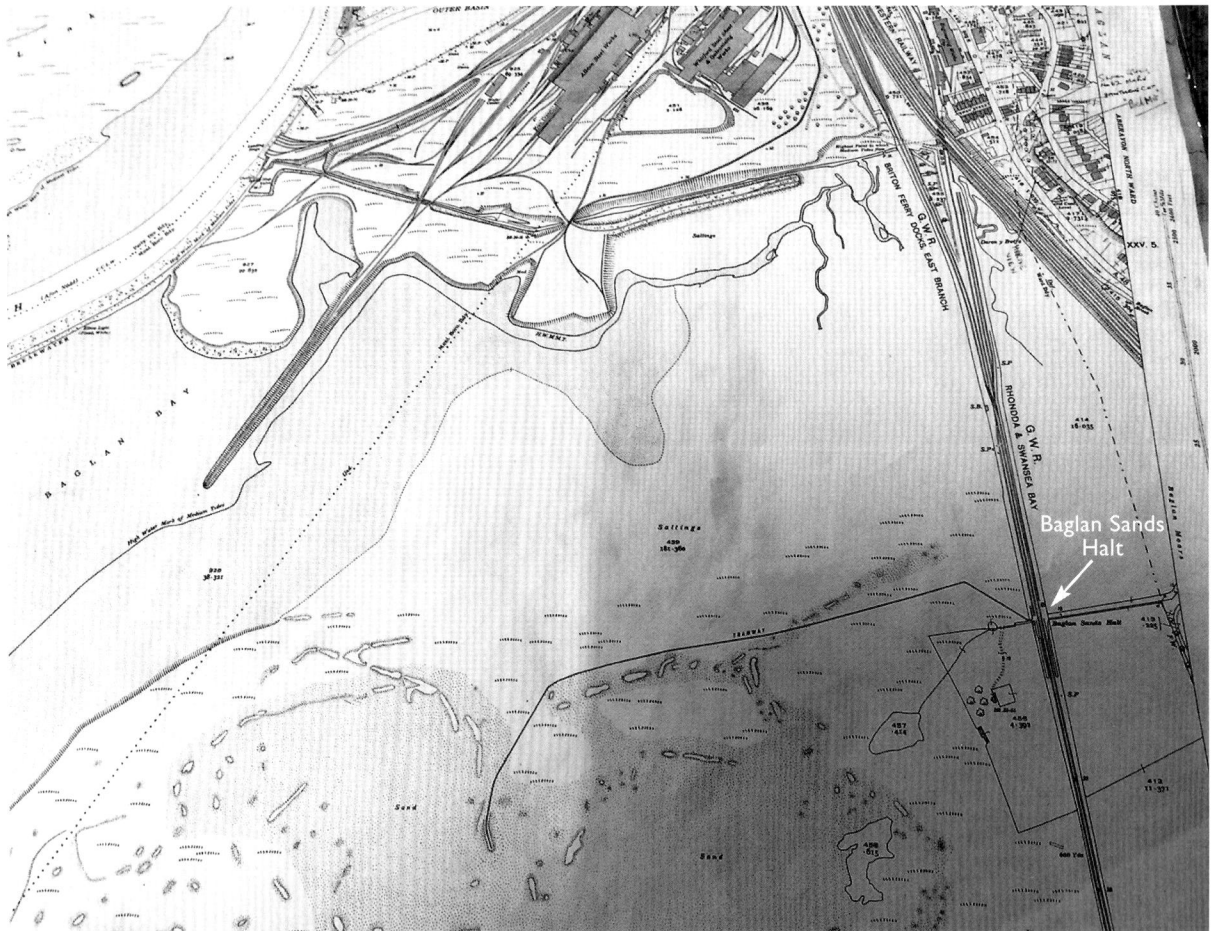

Site of Baglan Sands Halt *(OS 1937)*

RSBR bridge crossing Villiers Street near
Briton Ferry (East) station *(Cliff Morgan)*

The first battle was won in Parliament. In 1882 a proposal was made to Parliament to run a line from Treherbert to Cwmavon, then on to Baglan by means of a tunnel behind Mynydd Dinas to cross the river Neath by a bridge at the entrance to Briton Ferry dock and continue to Swansea docks. Objections were made by Neath Council and Neath Harbour Commissioners. That a battle would occur to cross the River Neath became evident from another plan proposed in an 1885 Act of Parliament. The proposal involved crossing the River Neath by means of a viaduct at the mouth of the river.

The Board of Trade considered this would interfere with shipping access to Briton Ferry Dock. Further, the board were advised:

> that the vessels trying to make the
> entrance to the Neath river would, in
> gales or wind, or in distress, be unable to
> do so, while even in ordinary weather,
> owing to the strength of the tides and the
> liability of the river to freshen, tugs
> would have great difficulty in getting
> vessels in tow through narrow openings
> without risk of damage either to
> themselves or to the bridge and its
> opening gear.

this idea was rejected on cost grounds and the described route was chosen instead.

After crossing the former A48 road by means of a level crossing[16] in Aberafan town, the railway passed over the main GWR line on the level.

It then followed the river Afan, before skirting the sand dunes to reach its station at Aberafan Seaside. This station became a hive of passenger activity in the summer months when it dealt with a great deal of excursion traffic to the seaside.

The line then crossed the coastal plain, via Baglan Sands Halt, before passing under the GWR main line at Swan Street, Baglan, near to Baglan Junction, where the branch to Briton Ferry dock diverged.

The Harbour Commissioners at Neath thought a bridge upstream would have an adverse effect on the proposed building of a harbour near the site of the bridge. Thus, an amended scheme was put forward which proposed that the line would tunnel under

RSBR Embankment at Briton Ferry after demolition of housing in the 1970s *(Cliff Morgan)*

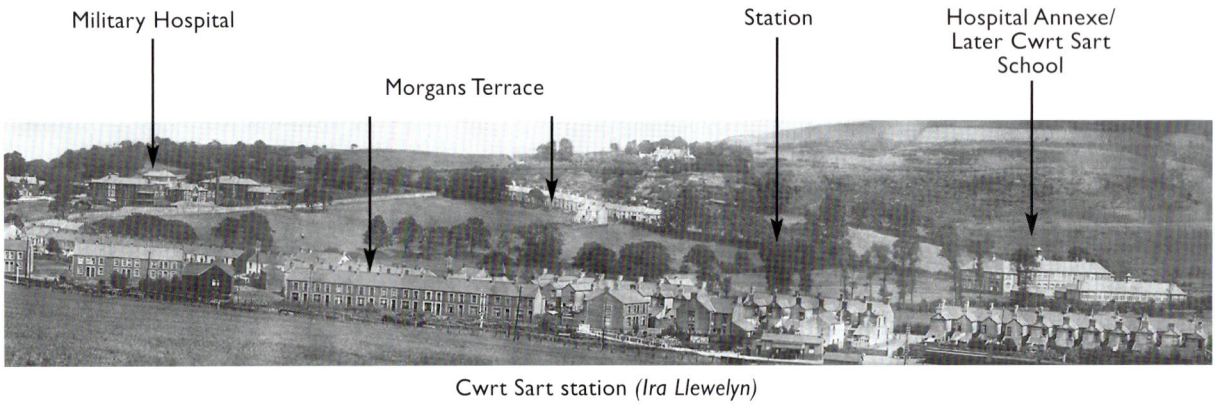

Cwrt Sart station (*Ira Llewelyn*)

Location of earthworks for proposed RSBR tunnel at Jersey Marine, 1971 (*Martin Davies*)

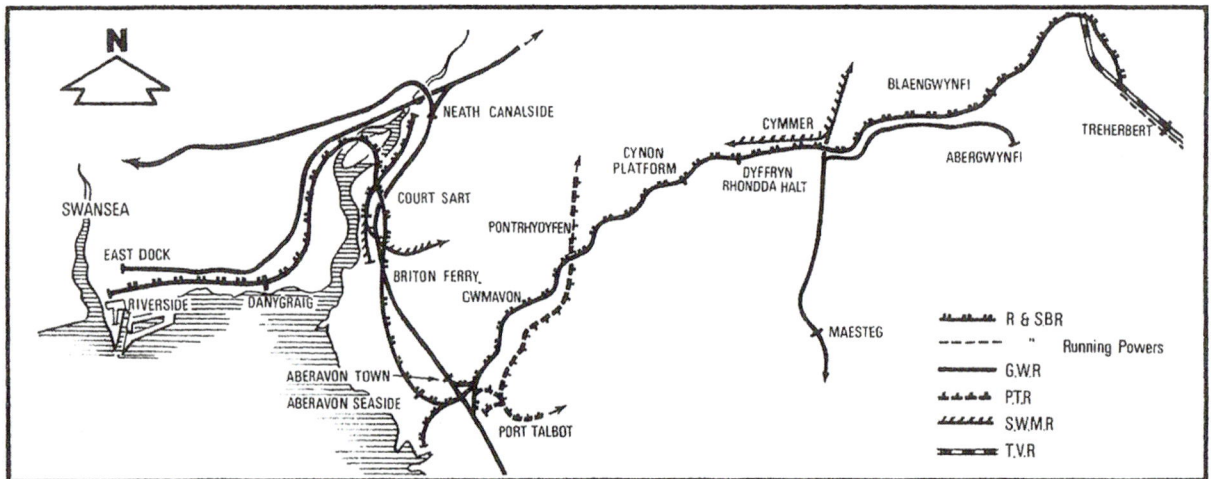

The route of the RSBR (*H. Morgan*)

the river Neath near Briton Ferry Dock. When a House of Lords committee rejected a similar proposal by the SWMR because of the bridge it proposed, the RSBR withdrew its application for a bridge in favour of a tunnel. The proposal now entailed a double track tunnel to pass under the mouth of the river Neath using brick-lined steel caissons for 764 yards of its 1,490 yards length, with the crown of the tun-

nel being 13 feet beneath the river bed. Despite further objections from the GWR, the Bill for the tunnel received Royal assent on 28 August 1883.

Work was even started on the building of the tunnel on the Jersey Marine side.

The RSBR were now faced with the problem of financing both the Rhondda tunnel at one end of the line and the Briton Ferry tunnel at the other, where

RSBR swing bridge over river, 1990s *(Robert Thomas)*

Swansea investors did not wish to do so until the tunnel was complete. The Rhondda Tunnel therefore took precedence, even though contracts for the caissons for the Briton Ferry tunnel were issued to Briton Ferry Foundry. Work on the tunnel on both sides of the river was evident until 1885, when the Harbour project was abandoned and it became possible to cross the river above ground further upstream.

The alternative location for a bridge crossing was at Dynefwr. After hearing the engineering evidence, it was stipulated in the Parliamentary bill that, if the RSBR failed to complete the work in three years, the GWR would be permitted to take it over.[17] During 1893, the GWR was, nevertheless, joined in Briton Ferry by the RSBR. The route's construction from Aberafan to Baglan had provided no real problems:

Swansea (Riverside) Station *(Michael Hale)*

the sandy and marshy land was flat, unobstructed and easily capable of being laid on a solid bed of hardcore.

In the meantime, a further battle was fought by the RSBR directors and contractor. This was both an engineering and legal battle to find a way through Briton Ferry. Much of the land needed to create a RSBR route had already been taken, both by its great competitor, the GWR, and by housing and industrial development. However, there were difficulties in routing the RSBR line through the Briton Ferry district because of the GWR and dock premises lying in its path. The most obvious route was parallel to the GWR lines in front of Railway Terrace,[18] but the route was opposed by the GWR and the Local Board. The powerful GWR got its way and RSBR had to build the line on an artificial embankment between Railway Terrace and Lowther Street where the RSBR had plans to build twelve houses.[19] [20] The author's mother recalled visiting the Assembly Rooms cinema in Lowther Street as a child in the 1920s when the whole building shook whenever a train passed by on the embankment. The RSBR line, therefore, crossed over Villiers Street by means of a bridge before reaching its own station, situated on the embankment, parallel to the GWR station. It became known as Briton Ferry East in 1924 following the grouping.[21]

The railway continued along this embankment to cross Regent Street by means of another bridge.

After crossing Regent Street, the line ran parallel to the main GWR line to Cwrt Sart, a two-platformed station. Connecting services to the RSBR's own station at Neath Canalside ran from here. From this station, the line north passed under the main line and, after passing the GWR's Cwrt Sart locomotive depot on the right, crossed the River Neath by means of a swing bridge, about which more information will follow. About half-a-mile before the bridge a junction, near Cwrt Sart depot, took the RSBR into Neath Canalside station. Although this station closed in the 1930s, the branch was used regularly for goods traffic into the 1980s with regular trains running into the Metal Box factory.

To gain access to Swansea docks, and its own terminus at Swansea Riverside station adjacent to Swansea's 'New Cut', the line passed through Crymlyn Burrows and Jersey Marine. Swansea Riverside became Swansea's sixth separate terminus.

On 27 June 1892, powers were granted to extend the line from Briton Ferry to Swansea by means of the swing bridge[22] which spanned the River Neath at a point just above the Dinefwr Wharf.[23] It was designed by Armstrong of Newcastle as the only swing bridge in the United Kingdom both on a skew

and on the curve. Its 388 feet length consisted of five sixty-foot fixed spans and a swing section 167 feet long. After crossing the river, the line turned south and then west to Danygraig within the Swansea Harbour complex, giving mineral trains access to the Swansea Harbour Trust lines. The RSBR's own terminus for passenger services at Riverside started on 14 March 1895 and, seeking to be independent of the Swansea Harbour Trust lines, the RSBR opened its own line covering the final mile to Riverside station.

The line suffered operational challenges and was never greatly profitable, until it was arranged for the GWR to operate the line and guarantee good dividends from 1906. In conjunction with this, the GWR incorporated the line's infrastructure in widening its own lines at Cwrt Sart and at Swansea docks. The GWR saw the line as a potential golden opportunity for mail, passenger and coal traffic from west Wales.

> When the *Mauretania*[24] arrived at Fishguard on Monday the mail traffic between Cardiff and Paddington was carried over the new loop line from Llandeilo Junction to Skewen.... When the line from Skewen to Cwrt Sart is finished, the complete service will be inaugurated, saving twenty minutes (and) giving a beneficial effect on the trade of the Amman and other valleys.[25]

Astonishing as it may seem, after the RSBR had engineered Armstrong's swing bridge so brilliantly, the GWR had considered a second bridge across the river at Neath Abbey:

> There are other railway rumours afloat at Briton Ferry just now, which, if correct, will doubtless mean a big thing for the thriving little town ... the GWR, in order to minimise the distance of the Fishguard route [are] to erect a large bridge across the Neath river near the present Rhondda bridge, so that express trains would then branch off at Cwrt Sart, and on to Llansamlet, thus cutting off the rounding to Neath.[26]

The idea for the second bridge was wisely abandoned in favour of using only the Dinefwr swing bridge. It was intensively used for fifty years, but, as it was heavily dependent on buoyant coal mining activity, use of the line from the west declined sharply after 1975, with the line to Swansea docks being progressively truncated. The Rhondda Tunnel[27] suffered a collapse in 1968 and the upper part of the line closed. A short section of the original route is in use near Briton Ferry and in the Swansea docks complex.

## Passenger Tramways

From 1875 a horse tramway was operated from Neath to Briton Ferry by Neath and District Tramway company. Twenty years later, when the company faced financial difficulties, it was taken over by Neath Corporation. A decision was made to modernise the system by introducing rail-mounted gas trams, based on a design seen at Lytham St Annes. The trams ran on an extended route from the Terminus Hotel in Skewen to Briton Ferry at 8 mph, but slower up gradients. The service operated from 8 am until 11 pm on weekdays and from 2 pm until 11 pm on Sundays.

During the First World War operations were difficult to sustain due to manpower shortages and increased costs. Fares were raised to 4½d from Neath to Briton Ferry and to 3d from Neath to Skewen. This did not solve the problem, so costs for alternatives were examined. The conversation cost to electricity was £200,000, for trolley buses £70,000, and between £38,000 to £55,000 for a fleet of motor buses. The decision was taken for the latter and, on 30 July 1920, the gas trams were abandoned for the South Wales Transport Company to take over and run a bus service at intervals of 25 minutes.

Tramway being lifted at Neath Road, Briton Ferry, showing SWMR ironbridge in the background
(Cliff Morgan collection, Neath Antiquarians Society)

## Notes for Chapter Two

1. *Reminiscences of Briton Ferry and Baglan*, Humphries, 1898, p.13
2. *Baglan and the Llewellyn's of Baglan Hall*, Eben Jones, 1987, p.54
3. The site is now occupied by a Macdonalds Restaurant
4. Humphries, p.23
5. Prof Mark Barry
   *https://swalesmetroprof.blog/2017/09/15/swansea-to-cardiff-in-30-minutes-and-a-swansea-bay-metro/*
6. Bradley, p.316
7. Bradley, p.374, reporting on the position in 1911
8. Bradley, p.350
9. Railway Terrace was demolished in 1976 and re-built as today's Llansawel
10. Now the home of west Glamorgan Archives and Neath Antiquarian Society
11. D. Davies
12. The incline is a 'Scheduled Monument'.
13. *A Most Industrious Town*
14. The grid reference for the site is Ordnance Survey map SS69/79 755952.
15. *Evening Express* 15 March 1895
16. In later years the crossing became a traffic bottleneck
17. *Cambrian* 12 August 1892
18. Today's Llansawel
19. Between today's Llansawel and Hunter Street
20. Rhondda and Swansea Bay Railway; S. Richards p.45
21. A government-inspired amalgamation of rail companies
22. Rhondda and Swansea Bay Railway Act 1892
23. *Western Mail* 15 March 1895
24. It was launched in 1906
25. *Carmarthen Weekly Reporter* 5 June 1914
26. *South Wales Daily Post* 28 April 1910
27. The Rhondda Tunnel Society was formed in 2014 whose aim is to link the Rhondda and Afan Valleys with a cycle path through the 3,443-yard tunnel.

Chapter Three

# Stations

*The names of the stations begin to take on meaning and my heart trembles. The train stamps and stamps onwards. I stand at the window and hold to the frame. These names mark the boundaries of my youth.*
Erich Maria Remarque: *All quiet on the Western Front (1929)*

This chapter explains the origins of the area's stations during the periods of competition between rail companies and why later consolidation of ownership and infra-structure was necessary. The outcome of the consolidation in terms of train movements, routes, signalling, loops and marshalling are examined. Chapter Four will deal with the passengers who used the stations.

### A plethora of platforms

No fewer than ten stations have served Briton Ferry and District at different times and in different places since the railway came to Briton Ferry in 1850. Five stations were in the town, with the others in the district. To understand why the town had such a plethora of stations it is necessary to examine the origins of the various lines and how they were located and re-located. The illustration below shows the GWR and the RSBR lines through Briton Ferry. These companies had stations both within the town, on the eastern side of the river, and in the district on the western side. It also shows the line which had no official stations, the SWMR.

The GWR's stations were *Briton Ferry*, which was re-named *Briton Ferry (West)* before being replaced by *Briton Ferry–Rockingham Terrace*, and *Briton Ferry Road*, in Jersey Marine. The RSBR's four stations were: *Baglan Sands*, *Briton Ferry East*, *Briton Ferry–Cwrt Sart* and *Jersey Marine*. *Baglan* and *Briton Ferry–Shelone Road* were introduced in 1994 as part of the *Swan Line*, with Shelone Road replacing Rockingham Terrace.

Briton Ferry's first station in broad gauge days *(Cliff Morgan)*

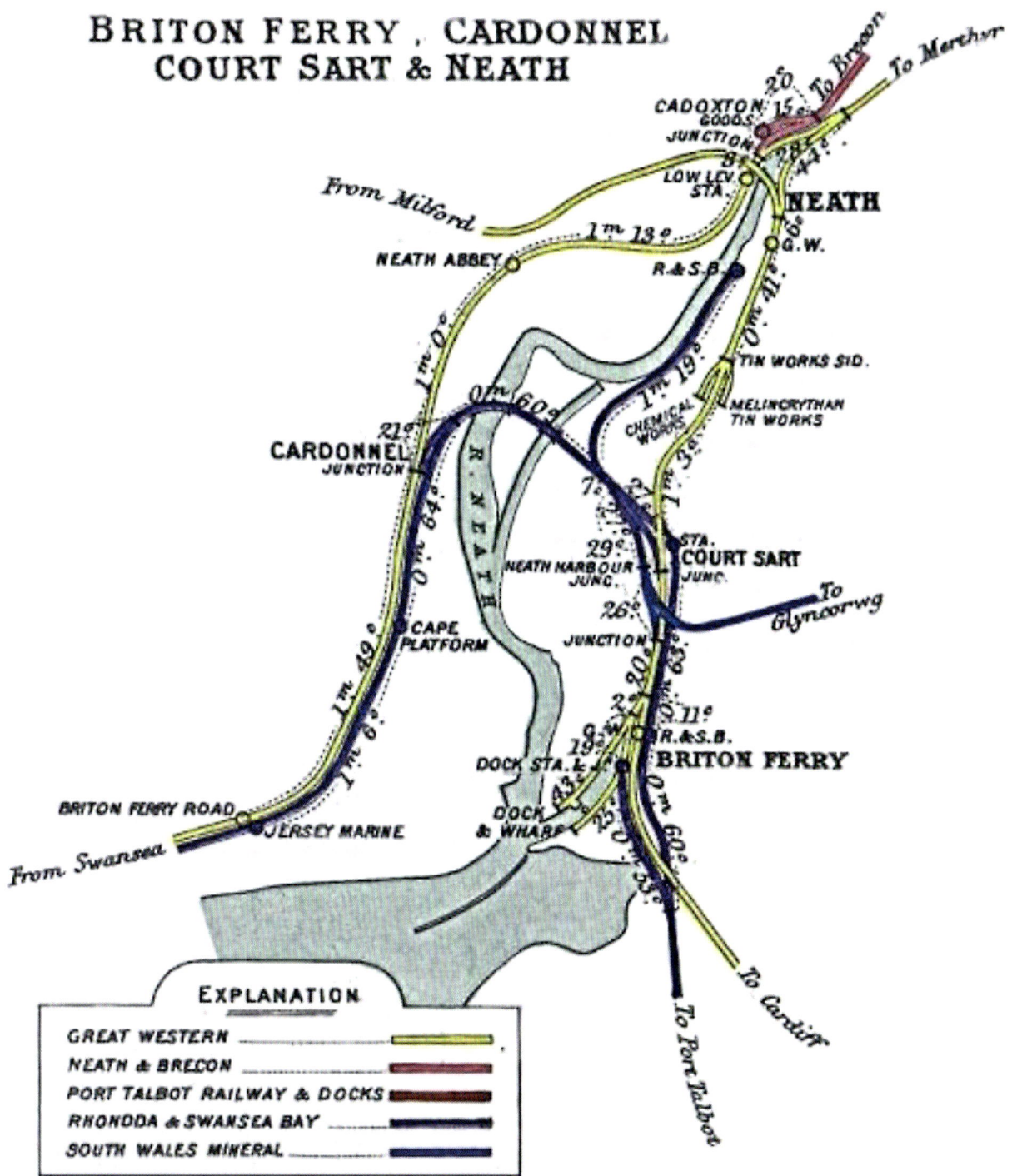

# BRITON FERRY, CARDONNEL COURT SART & NEATH

The lines through Briton Ferry *(Railway Clearing House)*

## The early days

The provision of services and facilities at Briton Ferry's rail stations have not always been up to the standard demanded by the townspeople. One of the first complaints regarded facilities:

> A fire at the goods booking office in 1870 raised the demand to the GWR for 'better accommodation in the shape of a new station, waiting rooms etc ... instead of

the wooden huts that ... are a disgrace to the place.[1]

Local representatives called a public meeting at the town's Assembly Rooms to discuss the matter, with the intention of petitioning the GWR's directors, saying that the 'present building is inadequate to meet the requirements of this thriving town.'[2]

The plan worked; some good news was soon forthcoming concerning improvements:

31

A 1920s *down* express passes Briton Ferry West with *Star* class 4-6-0 *(Cliff Morgan collection. Neath Antiquarians Society)*

This much-needed public convenience is likely to be completed early in June and will be a rock stonework building with freestone facing.[3]

## Briton Ferry (1850–1924)
## (later Briton Ferry West 1924–1935)

The town's first station, opened in 1850 by the South Wales Railway, was rudimentary. Bradshaw[4] mentioned its existence, but that was all. It lacked a public convenience until 1871, after the aforesaid fire, when one was 'erected on a liberal scale and likely to be completed in the summer. It will be a rock stonework building, with freestone dressings'.[5] It was built in Brunel's typical 'mock Tudor' style as a two-platform structure with a signal box. The replacement station was opened on 12 September 1871, 'amid the booming of guns,' at a ceremony addressed by Henry Davey, manager of Briton Ferry Ironworks. A 'feu de joie' ushered out the first train on the day the town enjoyed an extra holiday.[6]

Mr Barker was the original stationmaster, but by 1875 the GWR appointed both a station master (Caleb Nicholas of Railway Terrace) and a goods agent (George Scale of Neath Road). Mr A. Morgan, was given the added responsibility of dock-master.[7] The station was called Briton Ferry until 1 July 1924, when the GWR made it known as *Briton Ferry West*. The station's signal box, opened in 1873, was called *Briton Ferry East*, and was located a short distance to the south of the down platform. It had fourteen levers but was replaced by a new one in 1883 on the south end of the platform. This was followed by a newer box immediately to the north of the *down* platform. Another signal box, called *Briton Ferry West*, was positioned in the sidings to the east of the running lines.

From time to time the station yard was used for unusual activities, for example, in 1878, it was used to distribute coal donated by the Earl of Jersey to the poor of the town.

'The liberality of the Earl of Jersey' was a newspaper's description of a Christmas gift of thirty tons of coal from the 'right honourable Earl' to the poor of the town which was distributed at Briton Ferry railway station.[8]

In 1896 a traveller complained in a letter to a newspaper[9], under the signature of 'not a grumbler' that the District Council, the Chamber of Commerce and the GWR needed to look after the town's trading interests by providing a passenger shelter on the *down* platform.

> On this platform, there is a miserable open sort of cabin with a fireplace at one end, round which three people may stand, and thus prevent any others seeing the fire. There is a waiting room on the down platform, but for every one that waits on the up platform there are thirty on the down. I am compelled frequently to go to Swansea by the train due at 7-30 pm, and one night was there at 7-25, the place was full, and I, with perhaps fifty others, had to stand on that bleak platform in a piercing wind and hailstorm ... this was long enough to give me a bad cold ... I have with scores of others waited there for twenty, thirty and forty minutes on bitter cold nights.

As late as 1898, Councillor Gwynne of the District Council requested the GWR to cover the platforms at the station.[10] Rock stonework notwithstanding, in 1899, thirteen-year old Rees Rees of

Briton Ferry West looking northwards
(The RSBR station known as Briton Ferry East is to the right of the station building) *(Lens of Sutton)*

Shelone Road was charged at Neath County Police Court with breaking and entering the GWR station where he was employed as an errand boy. He smashed the office window with a stone, climbed in, broke open a drawer with a pair of tongs and 'took out about 4s 6d or 4s 11d.[11] Next morning, he went to Neath by motor car and then took the train to Cydweli[12] to see his uncle. He went into the White Lion Hotel for some 'pop' which he took with some fairy cakes he had bought from a grocer. That was how the money was spent and when his father fetched him home he had 8d left. The bench ordered defendant to receive twelve strokes with the birch and his father to pay the cost of the case.'[13]

The station also experienced the odd bout of violence. One such incident was described in newspapers as a 'Brutal Affair'. In May, 1890, two Briton Ferry men, puddler Jenkin Thomas and Francis Nicholas, were charged at Neath county petty sessions with assaulting police constable Lewis; being drunk and disorderly and with obstructing signalman David Thomas in the execution of his duty at the GWR box.[14] After a scuffle which resulted in PC Lewis drawing his staff and having it used against him to strike him to the ground, injuring an arm, the defendants tried to enter the box. Signalman Thomas had seen the first defendant trying to open the cross-

ing gates to cross the line before he warned the second defendant not to do so because a train was coming. One managed to cross. But both defendants later climbed up the steps to the box, threatening to throw signalman Thomas into the dock. Thomas managed to lock the door to the box just in time.

Constable Lewis had suffered an injured arm in the incident, so PS Protheroe arrested the defendants. When arrested, one asked PS Protheroe: 'Is he dead? 'On replying 'No' the defendant said: 'I do not care a xxx then.... We have killed a xxx sight better than him in Egypt.' The outcome of the case was three months' hard labour for assault; £5 plus costs, or two years' hard labour, for obstructing the signalman and ten shillings and costs for being drunk and disorderly, or fourteen days' hard labour. Their sentences would not run concurrently.

Perhaps the change of name from Briton Ferry station to Briton Ferry (West) in 1924 was to erase these earlier events from public memory. In any case it was closed in July 1935 following the opening of a brand-new station at Rockingham Terrace.

Fifty-eight staff were employed at Briton Ferry West and East stations in the 1930s.[15]

Ira Llewellyn, born in 1927 and living in Vernon Street at the time of writing, had travelled by train from Briton Ferry West station to Port Talbot and

Briton Ferry West station
in the 1970s
(Martin Davies)

Cardiff as a small boy. His father made frequent use of the old station and Ira would also make great use of the new station.

> Before the war, when the station was still open, my father and his friends who were fanatical Neath supporters would travel to Cardiff to see them play. I remember him saying that an excursion to Cardiff cost three and nine pence return and a day-trip to Llanelli cost one and seven pence return.

After closure, the station house was used as a residence with the waiting room and the ticket office being used as part of the house until the mid-1970s when the buildings were demolished. The outside wall of the station and the steps up to the platform are still in place today.

### Briton Ferry East (RSBR)

Briton Ferry East station was built on the embankment between Railway Terrace and Hunter Street, parallel to the GWR's Briton Ferry West station. Neither the RSBR line nor its station was in an ideal position between these houses; it was so located because of objections to its originally proposed route, parallel to the GWR line along Railway Terrace.

The first stationmaster for this RSBR station was Mr B Price who was unfortunate in that the primitive station became an early target for breaking and entering when it was reported that 'Thieves abound ... during the early hours of a Sunday morning the

booking office of the RSBR was broken into. Using the poker, the thieves smashed every drawer and cupboard and went away with about 14 shillings.'[16] In 1897 Mr W A Morris took responsibility for both this basic and, more elaborate, Cwrt Sart stations.[17]

Briton Ferry was also a noted centre for political and social debate in the first few decades of the twentieth century and played host to many nationally and internationally-known figures, many of whom would arrive by train. Grandfathers related stories of visits to meetings at the Public Hall by Ramsey McDonald, the MP for Aberafan constituency which included Briton Ferry. In the days before he formed the National Government, MacDonald would be mobbed by people as he travelled from Briton Ferry East station to the venue.

During the depression years of the 1930s it became common for many of those who were unemployed to congregate under the RSBR bridge in Villiers Street and to discuss the important issues of the day. As politics was high on the agenda, the area in and around the bridge became known locally as Parliament Square.

Barbara Llewellyn, Ira's wife, born 1927, lived in the adjacent Railway Terrace as a child and recalls the awkward situation that arose when a train stopped in the station and its passengers were able to look down into the kitchens and bedrooms of the nearby houses. Residents made sure their curtains were pulled tight until each train pulled away from the station. Young Barbara also made the very short journey to Aberafan Seaside. Her home and the station were conveniently close to the Assembly Rooms in Lowther Street and the busy station. The Assembly Rooms was used as a cinema until the Lodge Cinema was opened in 1938

Briton Ferry West and East stations. This view shows the GWR's Briton Ferry West station facing Railway Terrace and Briton Ferry East station of the RSBR *(R Simmonds)*

to overcome the former's great disadvantage. 'The whole building would vibrate whenever a train passed by on the embankment'.[18] The station's disadvantages, too, ended with the rationalisation of 1935 when services were transferred to the new station in Rockingham Terrace and Briton Ferry East station demolished. Despite the demolition, during the Second World War, the arches under the railway near the station joining Railway Terrace and Lowther Street were used as impromptu air raid shelters. The embankment remained in place until Railway Terrace was redeveloped as *Llansawel* in the 1970s.

### Briton Ferry–Cwrt Sart (RSBR)

The RSBR station at Cwrt Sart was very busy in its heyday, with connecting rail-motor services to Neath Canalside and through trains between Treherbert and Swansea. Nevertheless, this, the RSBR's second station at Briton Ferry, was also closed during the rationalisation programme of 1935, leaving an MoT testing depot on the site today. The *up* and flying loops are still in use but other lines serving it were taken out of use, except for the two retained as sidings until 1964.

The station's proximity to the First Western Military Hospital at Penrhiwtyn was why it was used both as a receiving point for battlefield casualties during the First World War and, sometimes, to treat casualties. At railway stations such as this, the British public got closest to the war. The towns-

Railmotor as used on Canalside branch
*(Neath Antiquarian Society)*

people gathered there to wave off those who had joined the army but, all too often, went back to see them return in ambulance trains. The first trains were greeted with crowds, red carpets, brass bands and local dignitaries, but pomp and pride were quickly replaced by sorrow as battered and broken men were unloaded onto the platforms.

The Cox family of Cwrt Sart Terrace[19] watched the incoming trains for sight of their son. Cyril Cox was due for leave from the navy, but he had exchanged his leave period with another so that he could be home for Neath Fair in September. The consequence of his leave change, was that he was killed in service at end of August 1918. Nearby in Cwrt Sart Terrace, the four young Parry girls provided cups of tea to wounded soldiers being transferred from Cwrt Sart sidings (which faced their parents' home) to the hospital.

Cwrt Sart station on the RSBR: the 13.57 Swansea to Treherbert on 14 May 1919
*(Cliff Morgan collection/NAS)*

RSBR stationmaster's hat *(R. Grant)*

Hospital Train *(Didcot Railway Centre) (Martin Davies)*

Cwrt Sart's guard, George Cox *(Alun Hutchinson and Margery Lewis)*

William Evans, of 12 Middleton Street, joined the RSBR as a shunter in 1914 at the age of fourteen. He, too, worked at Cwrt Sart station where his duties involved the careful transportation of injured soldiers to the hospital. Nothing in his many duties deterred him, so it was no surprise that when he retired over forty years later it was as foreman shunter at Briton Ferry Yard.

Cwrt Sart featured once again during the Second World War when a series of explosive bombs fell near to the station, and a few fell on the Old Road, killing members of the Curtis family.

The first bombs, not incendiaries…. A stick of nine was dropped early in 1941; the first two dropped on the railway

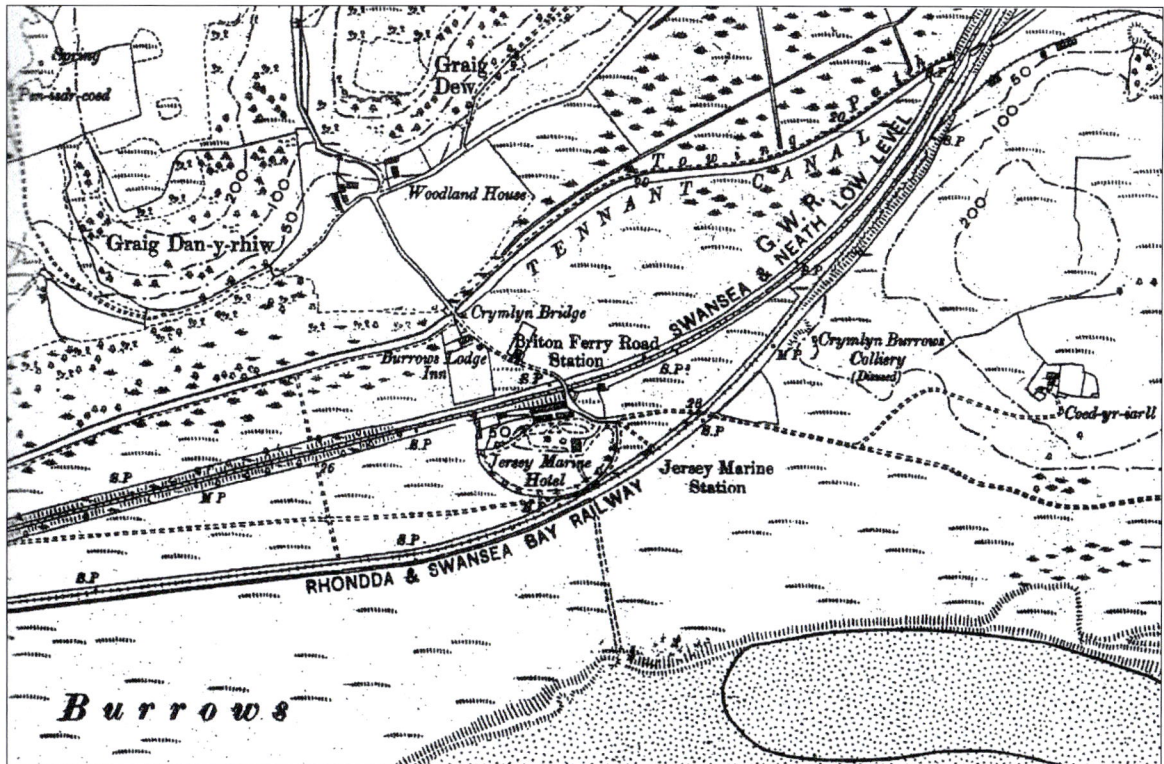

The track layout at Jersey Marine showing the locations of Briton Ferry Road (former Neath and Swansea Railway) and Jersey Marine (former RSBR) stations

workers' allotments between Tucker Street and Short Street, about twenty-five yards apart, the next two on Shelone Terrace near where I lived, the fifth and sixth on the rugby field next to Cwrt Sart school, the seventh and eighth landed on Mrs Curtis' house killing her and her husband and their son. The final bomb was dropped higher up the mountain and killed a cow. (Ira Llewellyn)

**Briton Ferry Road (GWR) (1863–1936)**

Briton Ferry Road station was one of two stations at Jersey Marine. The other was the eponymous RSBR station *Jersey Marine*. It lay just north of today's Tower Hotel and Spa, once known as the Jersey Marine Hotel, and Jersey Marine station, just to the south of it. Both were two-platformed seaside stations which enjoyed much excursion traffic. One of the most tragic accidents on the railways of Briton

Briton Ferry Road Station (*The Great Western Trust*)

37

Site of Jersey Marine station *(Michael Hale)*

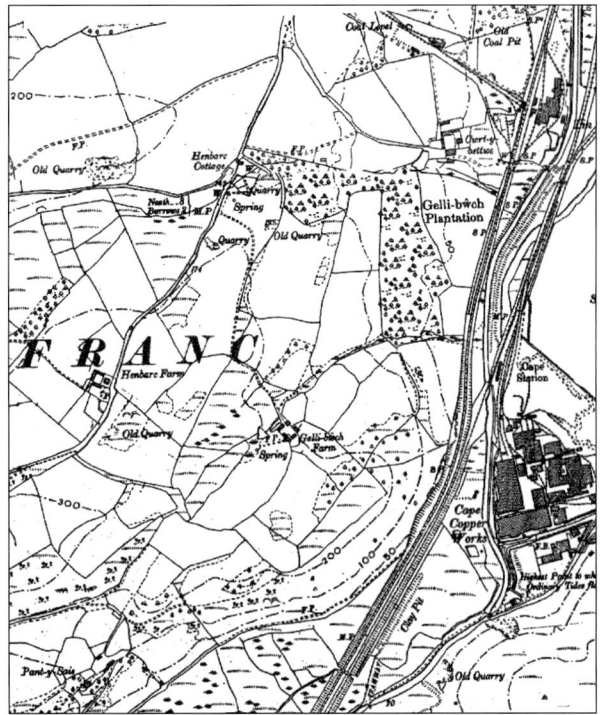
Location of Cape Platform to the north of Cape Copper
Works *(Ordnance Survey 1900 map)*

Ferry and district occurred at this station during a seaside excursion. It is reviewed in detail in Chapter Seven.

The station was also used by workers at nearby works in Jersey Marine such as Briton Ferry Chemical Works and Dawnay structural engineers. Rollerman Tom Thomas,[20] of Jack y Du Road, Briton Ferry, was one of many who used the train from Cwrt Sart to get to work at Baldwin's Elba tinplate works. The availability of the train service, and a special workman's return ticket, at two and a half old pence,[21] meant he did not always have to take the ferry across the River Neath to get to and from work. Steam-powered railcars numbers 47 and 49, based at Cwrt Sart shed were used on this line in the 1920s between Swansea (East Dock) and Glyn Neath.

### Jersey Marine Station (1894–1933)

This was a short distance from Briton Ferry Road station and the Tennant Canal to the north, but separated by the Jersey Marine Hotel, which lay between them. It was opened in 1894 on the RSBR line for the company to share both in the lucrative Rhondda coal and passenger excursion traffic mentioned above. A typical excursion to Jersey Marine Station was the running of two trains by the RSBR for Jerusalem Church and School of Llwynypia. All children were given free meals and transport with

> loads of cake, bread, milk cans and a complete set of children's roundabouts and special ice cream vendors … the day being spent on the sands and adjacent fields and woods where a variety of games were indulged in to the childrens' hearts' content.[22]

Jersey Marine was known, too, for its golf links, but Neath Free Church Council frowned upon the Sunday golf being played there and protested vociferously. The station was closed in 1935, not because of the Church Council, but because of the GWR's network rationalisation.

Briton Ferry station, from Rockingham Terrace, 1960s *(B Brooksbank)*

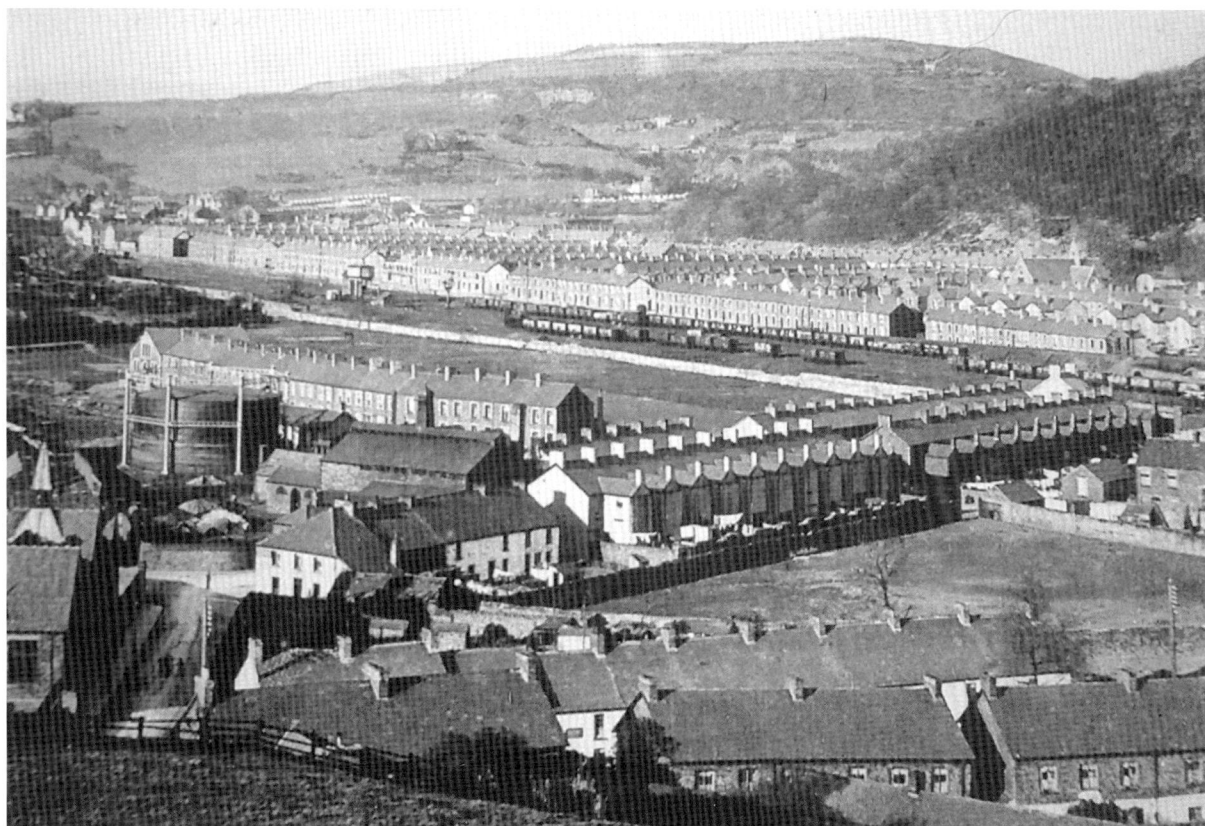

General view of Briton Ferry showing railway infrastructure before new station in 1935 *(Cliff Morgan)*

Briton Ferry Station under construction
*(Gerald Williams collection)*

## Cape Station[23]

This long-forgotten RSBR halt was positioned about one mile north of Jersey Marine and lay on the eastern side of the Tennant Canal, near to the Red Jacket Pill which connected the canal with the river Neath. The passenger lines at the halt served the workers and the goods sidings serviced the works of the Cape Copper Company,[24] Red Jacket Company and the adjacent Briton Ferry Chemical and Manure Company's works. The Cape Copper works closed in 1926 and the halt in 1936.

## Briton Ferry–Rockingham Terrace (1935–1964)

This station had long been mooted:[25]

> There are other railway rumours afloat at Briton Ferry just now, which, if correct, will doubtless mean a big thing for the thriving little town … rumour has it that a large station, combining both the Briton Ferry and the Cwrt Sart station is to be erected between the two points and which will form a junction for the old and new routes. Certain it is that a great deal of surveying is being done at the points mentioned.

## The 'Ferry' Station

Do you remember the Ferry station?
Not the one that's there today,
But the one from the sixties,
With twenty trains either way.

Yes, I remember the Ferry station,
It seemed so big to our, young eyes,
Four long platforms and a footbridge,
A junction too, so no surprise.

*Up* express passing through Briton Ferry 1950s *(Norman Jones)*

It had its own station master,
Porters too, and a booking clerk,
In the nearby ,busy, goods yard,
Wagons shunted in light and dark.

Do you remember the Ferry station?
Close to most, not out of reach,
Queues all the way down Rock'n'ham,
For the trains to 'bravon beach.

We took towels and things to swim in,
To spend the day on beach and tide,
Packed together in the guard's van,
For this twenty minute ride.

Do you remember the booking office?
With Norman Jones's smiling face,
Handing out cardboard tickets,
Neath, Port Talbot, or any place.

Clambering over the wooded footbridge,
Sweet smell of steam in the air,
Waiting on the open platform,
Till the Swansea train got there.

We saw the fish trains and the cattle,
Whitland milk tanked up for the morn,
Early evening twas a goods rush,
To get to London before the dawn.

*6847 Tidmarsh Grange* on a Cardiff to Swansea stopping train at Briton Ferry 1960 *(Norman Jones)*

*4-6-0 No 6024 King Edward I passes Briton Ferry in 2011
on a return excursion from Fishguard to Bristol
(Martin Davies)*

> There were the stoppers and the fast trains,
> Pembroke, Pullman, Red Dragon too,
> They flashed by with 'Brit' or 'Castle'
> We remember, I'm sure we do.

*Martin Davies 2018*

A quarter-century later the GWR indeed rationalised the railway layout and in the process closed both Briton Ferry East and West stations. It replaced them with a larger, more modern, station 465 metres north at Rockingham Terrace, opening on 8 July 1935 as simply *Briton Ferry*. This catered for the increased passenger traffic, with twenty trains each day calling at the new station. Cwrt Sart station was also closed and all RSBR trains were diverted on to the GWR main line to Swansea.

In Briton Ferry's heyday, the role of station-master had been most important, both because of the numbers of passengers using the station, but also because the post holder was nominally 'dock-master', being responsible for the traffic using Briton Ferry Dock and the rail crossings in the locality. After 1935, it became important again.

The station comprised two island platforms, with the *up* and *down* main lines passing between them, and the *up* and *down* reliefs along their outer faces. An *up* avoiding line from the RSBR ran through the eastern part next to the station buildings. They were on Rockingham Terrace and comprised a station-master's office, a booking office, a ladies' waiting room and a parcels and storage area. The buildings were connected to the platforms by a lengthy footbridge. Each platform had a waiting room. Briton Ferry had a stationmaster, until its closure to passengers on 4 November 1964, and goods on 6 September 1965.

Water columns at the departure end of each platform served both main and relief lines. These were frequently used to replenish the smaller tank locomotives such as the 'push-pull' *64xx* pannier tanks[26]

on the Swansea to Porthcawl services in the 1950s. Sidings to the west of the station comprised six *up* and four *down* loops with the *up* and *down* goods lines running between. The Glyncorrwg Colliery Company's engineering and wagon workshops nearby, built for the SWMR were demolished during the station construction.[27] Ira Llewellyn remembers the workshops in use when he was a small boy growing up in Shelone Terrace. The steps to access the workshops are still in situ, hidden behind a bricked-up gap in the wall around the site of the former railway yard.

When Port Talbot station was totally rebuilt in 1961 its parcels traffic was transferred to Briton Ferry in an extended storage area. An unusual parcels train called every Saturday night, hauled by an ex-LMS loco from Shrewsbury such as a *Jubilee*, but one evening a *Patriot,* 45515 *Caernarvon*, worked the train. It had 'dropped a plug' en route to Swansea and needed to be taken to Neath shed for attention. Tony Griffiths saw the loco on a visit to Cwrt Sart shed on the Sunday morning and was keen to tell his schoolmates about this most unlikely sighting. No one would believe him until his story was validated by another rail enthusiast.

The station witnessed the passing of royal trains when members of the Royal family travelled to west Wales, but only one occasion was recorded where the Royal train stopped at Briton Ferry. This involved a return trip from west Wales after the Duke of Edinburgh had opened a refinery at Milford Haven in 1960. It was recorded by Hugh James, who lived opposite the station at the time.

> The train stopped at Briton Ferry to take water. It was hauled by the last *Castle* built, 7037 *Swindon* ... the standby loco was 5004 *Llanstephan Castle*, which waited in Briton Ferry yard in case it was required.

Sometimes more prosaic consignments were despatched from the station. As a 'common carrier' the station was duty-bound to do so. Such was the obligation fulfilled when Eaglesbush (South Road) Pigeon Club wished to avail themselves of the station to send pigeons to such southern destinations as Castle Carey, Weymouth and Poole. (Andrew Adams)

Briton Ferry was sometimes pressed into emergency use as a change-over point for locomotives on trains arriving from west Wales, if there were problems on the main line between Swansea and Llanelli. Trains from Carmarthen then ran over the SDL to Briton Ferry.

Station staff at Briton Ferry in the 1960s with porter Dick Durnell on the left, and his colleague *(Neath Antiquarians)*

The *Pembroke Coast Express* normally came from Carmarthen to Swansea hauled by a *Hall*, *Mogul* or *Manor*. At Swansea, additional coaches were attached, including a restaurant car, before the train left for London. It normally left Swansea at 3.45 pm and sped through Briton Ferry at 4.05 behind a Landore *Castle*. (Hugh James)

### Staffing at Rockingham Terrace station

The first stationmaster was a Mr Russell who, like most staff, lived near to the station.

Mr Russell, was a big man, but rather ungainly as he had bad legs. His daughter, Mary, married Reg Cohen the cricketer. One of the key members of staff working at the station in the 1940s and 1950s was Lodwig Jenkins of Rockingham Terrace. The lad porter was David Evans, who became a lecturer in English at Neath Technical College where he worked from the 1960s to the early 1980s. In the ticket

office was Mrs Hayes of Grandison Street. Then there was Mr Rees, a porter who helped Mr Hancock, the Lodge Cinema manager in his spare time. Dick Durnell was another well-known member of the six or seven staff working there during the 1950s and 1960s. Many others worked in the goods department. (Ira Llewelyn)

Another well-known character to work at the station was Norman Jones, who lived nearby in Rockingham Terrace. He came from a typical 'railway family', his father having been a stationmaster's clerk. Initially starting work as a booking clerk at Briton Ferry, he was subsequently promoted to a similar position at Neath station. There, his knowledge of railway services and his friendly manner endeared him to the travelling public and railway fraternity so much so that he earned the nickname *Mr Neath Station*. Robert Thomas was a friend:

Norman was a very persuasive character with a booming voice. Although he was never more than a booking clerk you had the feeling that he ran the show. When

Norman Jones (second from left) with his colleagues at Neath Station in the 1970s *(Norman Jones)*

Neath Station was rebuilt in the 1970s, he successfully petitioned for the installation of a kitchen in the booking office. Norman Jones died in his forties.

George Lewis, another resident of Rockingham Terrace, was part of the Rockingham Terrace station complement. He delivered parcels from Briton Ferry and other stations in the area to local businesses. The author's uncle, Tom Davies, remembers George as:

> the driver of the flat backed lorry that children used to hang on to for a ride. I can't imagine that happening today! The other thing I remember about George was that he played a saxophone in a dance band that used to play in the Public Hall'.

Would his repertoire have included *Chattanooga Choo Choo*, *Tuxedo Junction* or *Night Train*? Overnight, George parked his Commer lorry on open ground near Tony Griffiths' house in Hunter Street. Tony had no need for an alarm clock for school in the morning, because he was frequently disturbed by the sound of George starting the lorry to begin his daily rounds.

The staff working at the goods department at Briton Ferry sometimes attended work-related social events, despite the GWR's parsimonious reputation for never spending anything.

> Briton Ferry goods staff held their second annual dinner and 'get together' at the Graig-y-Eos Hotel, Ogmore-on-Sea. The aim of these gatherings is to give staff of all departments and those from the district offices a chance to become acquainted and to meet people from industrial undertakings in the town to whom in the ordinary course of business they are just 'voices on the telephone'[28]

The GWR's frugality continued after the formation of British Railways. In the 1960s, it was still common for travellers to be issued with ex-GWR tickets even though it was twelve years since nationalisation. Hugh N James, the well-known Briton Ferry councillor and Mayor of Neath-Port Talbot, was employed by British Railways at Swansea. He reports that his three-month season ticket covering the period June to September, 1962, from Briton Ferry to Swansea was still a GWR ticket, no 449, costing ten shillings and

*6876 Kingsland Grange* at Briton Ferry – on an inspection special, one of the last steam-hauled trains to stop at Briton Ferry, 1964 *(Martin Davies)*

George Lewis (front row, fourth from left)
in his role as saxophonist with the Ambassadors Dance Orchestra 1949 *(Briton Ferry Photographic and Internet Technology Group)*

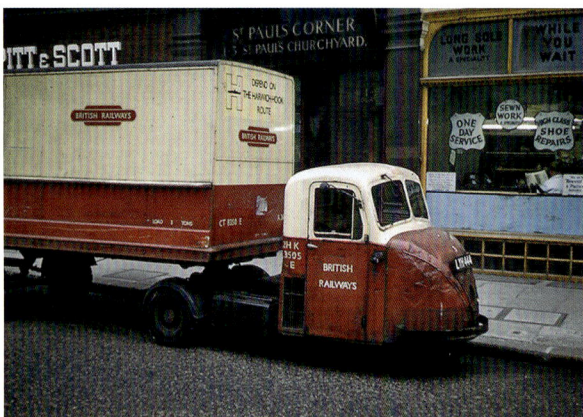

Scammell lorry *(Wikipedia)*

sixpence.[29] A single ticket from Briton Ferry to Port Talbot in the same year cost 8d.[30]

Unlike the relatively high inflation of the 1970s and 1980s, the 1940s, 1950s and 1960s saw stable rail-fares with only minor increases. During the period of Ira Llewellyn's National Service, between March 1946 and February 1948, the price of a return ticket from Neath to Reading remained at 27/6d. Similarly, in 1960, a half-fare return ticket to Cardiff from Briton Ferry was two shillings and three pence[31] and had only risen to two shillings and seven pence by 1967.[32]

Rockingham Terrace station closed in November 1964 and lay derelict until demolished in 1966, despite an unsuccessful attempt to purchase it by a young railway enthusiast, Robert Holwill. Fortunately, some remnants survived. Much of the memorabilia went on sale. Joe Cox, of Neath Road, a friend of Ira Llewellyn, purchased a station totem to adorn his garden wall. Joe was an old friend of the authors who spent many happy hours in his company at the Crown, the Assembly Rooms and the Puddlers' Arms in the 1960s and 1970s. Joe was an English graduate who found that the teaching profession was 'not his cup of tea' so he worked as a supervisor at the Albion Steelworks. A man of many talents and interests including music, art, piano-playing, cricket and, of course, railways, Joe was a ready wit.

The falling number of passengers using the local main line stations such as Skewen and Briton Ferry

View north westwards of Briton Ferry showing operating sites of RSBR, GWR and SWMR at different times (c.1931)
*(Author's collection)*
*Left:* Approximate sites of Briton Ferry West (GWR) and Briton Ferry East (RSBR)
*Centre:* Rockingham Terrace station (future)
*Right:* SWMR workshops (in picture). Briton Ferry–Shelone Road (future)
*Off to right:* Cwrt Sart station (RSBR)

meant that these also lost their train services in November 1964. Steam lingered on in south Wales until 1965. Neath locomotive shed closed in June and by the end of the year steam workings had ceased. Briton Ferry station was demolished and the superfluous railway tracks were lifted.

### Briton Ferry–Shelone Road (1994–present)

Of the ten stations that have served Briton Ferry and District at different times and in different places, this is the only station that exists. It is sited at Cwrt Sart junction where the *up* Swansea District line meets the south Wales main line. It is an unmanned station with two platforms accessed from Shelone Road. The platforms are offset from each other, with the up platform extending further towards Port Talbot, and the Swansea District line emerging on its left-hand side. The station opened on 1 June 1994 to serve *Swanline* trains.

Derelict Briton Ferry station building *(N Jones)*

### Baglan Sands Halt (1931–1939)

This two-platformed structure was opened on 1 May 1931, on the former RSBR route between Aberafan and Briton Ferry. In the 1930s the GWR and RSBR encouraged the public to make greater use of local stopping trains by erecting many halts, often adjacent to well-used tourist areas. Baglan Sands halt is an example: platforms were made of recycled railway sleepers and an equally rudimentary shelter was provided for those waiting for trains. The long stretch of golden sands was reached by foot through the marram grass-covered dunes. It was a popular place for families to picnic during the summer months: elsewhere the usual attractions such as funfairs and sweet shops needed money to be spent. This halt was well used during the depression years of the 1930s when a large proportion of the working population found themselves out of work. Baglan beach was aptly nicknamed 'the unemployment beach'.

Ira Llewellyn lived in Shelone Terrace in the 1930s and travelled to both Baglan Sands Halt and Aberafan Seaside stations from Cwrt Sart station. Val Berni, of Cresswell Road, Neath, also used the station as a child. His journey was an interesting one: from Neath Canalside, he changed trains at Cwrt Sart to alight at Baglan Sands Halt for his day at the beach. Tom Bowen[33] was a tinplate worker who often found himself without work during this period, so he made the best of the time by taking his wife and four daughters to the beach. Although the family were relatively poor, his daughter, Eunice, always

An *up* train of coal empties, passing through the new Baglan station, behind a class 37 diesel *37906* 19th January 1998
*(Robert Thomas)*

regarded these as happy times because families and friends would meet up and enjoy each other's company. Tom's family walked, but those who were a little more fortunate travelled by train. However, the outbreak of war brought much needed employment and, therefore, an end to Baglan Sands Halt's usefulness. It was closed on the 25 September 1939 and never re-opened, except for the use of one its tracks to store excursion coaches.

## Baglan Station (1994–present)

The station is accessible by foot from Seaway Parade's B4286 road bridge and by subway from the old A48 on Baglan Road. Both these roads terminate at the roundabout which also gives access to southbound junction forty-one of the M4 motorway. It is a two-platform structure which was opened in the 1990s as part of the Swanline. It is in an increasingly important location because of its proximity to Baglan

Two local passenger trains pass at Briton Ferry station in the mid 1990s. *158841* on the 11-07 Bridgend to Swansea and *143618* on the 11-00 Swansea to Cardiff 15th October 1994 *(Robert Thomas)*

*Up* oil train from Swansea Docks hauled by 2-6-2T 7226 leaves Briton Ferry on the loop line, with the RSBR line to Aberafan Seaside on the right. In the background is Brondeg House and Cavalli's café, now the location of McDonalds.
*(R Reed)*

Energy Park, which expects to generate a total of 3000 jobs, a major hospital, a school and many retail outlets. Trains presently call here every two hours in each direction.

These stations were not:

> 'extensions of the Swindonisation of the High Street that began in the 1980s … when we stopped being passengers and became customers. Sock Shop and Tie Rack appeared, the gist being that the only people who had any business travelling were people travelling for business.... In Europe what you hear on trains is minimal and informative: you get told your destination and the stops as they approach. In Britain it's a relentless patter of pseudo information aimed at pseudo customers by people running a pseudo business. You don't 'read' the safety instructions, you take some time to familiarise yourself with them. Your belongings must always be 'personal' and in case you were wondering, as you neared your 'station stop' what to do with them, you are 'advised to remember to take them with you'.[34]

## Sidings, signalling, land and routes

The paths of both passenger and freight, trains to, from and through the area needed to be controlled safely, and efficiently and. This required the best use of a complex system of track layout including main lines, passing loops and sidings. Effective signalling, routing and marshalling of trains was essential to achieve this.

Two pannier tanks, 9617 and 9716 run light engine past Pine Tree crossing, Baglan en route from Margam to Cwrt Sart shed in 1964 *(Martin Davies)*

*6832 Brockton Grange awaits the road at Briton Ferry signal gantry (Martin Davies)*

The line from London approached Briton Ferry along the coastal plain from Port Talbot via Baglan. Its double track eventually proved inadequate to accommodate the increase in traffic following the rapid growth of the Swansea Bay area during the second half of the nineteenth century. Loop lines had to be constructed, under the control of a new signal box at Baglan, where freight trains could be held to give priority to passenger trains on the *up* and *down* main lines. This busy box was adjacent to the *up* loop line near the Evans Bevans playing fields. From there it marshalled the succession of freight, parcels and empty stock trains to free the main line for passenger trains. Near Swan Street, the main line and loops crossed over the RSBR line. Both *up* and *down* RSBR lines passed under the bridge before the layout was altered in 1935. Baglan junction, situated near Swan Street, allowed trains from Aberafan to run parallel to the *down* loop line.

There were five sets of sidings alongside the main line which served the Albion Steelworks, Baglan Bay Tinplate Works, the Whitford Galvanising Works and, later, BP Petrochemicals at Baglan Bay. A substantial signal gantry with seven separate signal posts was necessary to control all movements in and around Briton Ferry station and the lines alongside the docks. The gantry was positioned near Briton Ferry dock above the *up* and *down* mains, *down* loop and the line from Aberafan seaside. Operations were controlled by the important Briton Ferry signal box opposite the original Briton Ferry station site.

Before the rail network was pared down to today's configuration it was possible, in the event of incidents, to use diversionary routes. A particularly disruptive incident took place in July 1957 whose impact was ameliorated by using one of these routes:

> An accident occurred at Baglan loop, when loco *7200*, a large 2-8-2 tank, became derailed. It took up half of the track and caused a blockage of the main line, which was on stop for some eight hours. Trains to Cardiff were stacked-up in Briton Ferry yard. They took a diversionary route using the RSBR line – running to Aberafan Seaside then reversing on to the connecting line to Port Talbot station, where another locomotive was attached. This optional route was often used on Sundays when there was engineering works being carried out on the main line at Baglan. All trains would then need two locomotives, one at each end, to get to Port Talbot station. (Hugh James)

A pedestrian subway led from today's *McDonalds* roundabout under the railway lines to give access to those working at the works around the dock. It followed the route of an old tramway which had been used to move coal from *Price's Drift* mine, near the Old Road in Baglan, to the dock.

The loop lines originally ran from Baglan to the site of Briton Ferry West station but were extended to a length of one-and-a-quarter miles to the new Briton Ferry station in Rockingham Terrace during the remodelling of the mid-1930s. The signal box at Briton Ferry commanded a clear view of the many lines in the vicinity. With 120 levers, it was one of the busiest on the main line from Cardiff to Swansea,

Railway network at Briton Ferry Docks in 1935 *(Cooke)*

BRITON FERRY DOCK (1935)

WHITFORD STEEL SHEET
& GALVANISING Co.
To GROVESEND STEEL &
TINPLATE Co LTD P2A 2.4.1940
To R.T. & B. LTD 8.10.1947.

ALBION STEELWORKS

BAGLAN BAY
TINPLATE WORKS
P2AT 7.12.1952

SEE PAGE 114

TRAMWAY

No 3

D O C K

VICTORIA
TINPLATE
WORKS

GWALIA
TINPLATE
WORKS

BRITON FERRY
STEELWORKS
R.T. & B. LTD.

P. WAY ON IRON ORE STAGE REMOVED EARLY 1944
IRON ORE STAGE REMOVED 1944
(? WHICH ONE)

WALLEROO
CROSSING

49

A substantial signal gantry with seven separate signal posts controlled all movements in and around Briton Ferry station and the lines alongside the docks *(Hugh Daniel)*

controlling several junctions and a host of sidings.

The work of some signalmen could be quite solitary at times and those on duty welcomed the chance to talk to others during their working day. One was a keen 'birdwatcher' who usually had a pair of binoculars to hand to observe the wildlife in and around Shelone Woods. He consistently referred to the woods as *Hill 60*, apparently referring to a battle site in the Korean War. On a few occasions in the early 1960s a group of train-spotters were even invited to

the box and given a crash course in the art of signalling. Their course skills could not be used because the box closed in March 1965 following the introduction of MAS.[35]

Raymond Williams wrote one of the best fictional depictions of the signalman's life at Glynmawr box in *Border Country* (1960). It was based on his father's real-life experience as a signalman on today's Marches Line at Pandy, between Abergavenny and Hereford. Signalmen, especially in more remote areas

Port Wallaroo crossing *(Robert Thomas)*

A *down* perishable train passes the signal gantry at Briton Ferry East behind Goodwick's *5039 Rhuddlan Castle*, June 1963 *(John Davies)*

where there were relatively few trains often filled the time in between official duties by performing other tasks such as watch repairing, growing vegetables and barbering. Neville Granville recalls some of the other expedients to pass the time: 'Some took up barbering, others grew tomatoes ... some mended boots, made jewellery, did council paperwork; others read books or simply spent the long hours in deep thought'.[36]

Passing train crews would often make time in their daily working routine to pop into the box for a 'short, back and sides'. John Morgan, who worked for many years as a signalman in the Afan valley recalls his time working at the Lower Cynon signal box: 'it was a very quiet box, seeing very few people. To make my time more interesting I did a Signalman's Correspondence Course and made myself a crystal set

as, at the time, (early 1950s) portable wirelesses were quite big and the batteries didn't last long.'

Branching off the *down* loop line near the signal box was *Port Wallaroo* branch line, named after the public house of that name at its crossing in Church Street. This line carried the SWMR to the dock. Nearby a well-known Briton Ferry business, *ERG Saph, (Ironmongers and Ships Chandlers)* supplied Keith Davies[37] with his plumbing supplies for many years.

> I regularly visited there as a teenager to pick up daily supplies of 'Kontite' and 'Yorkshire' fittings, being served by Lionel Saph or Ernie Jones. The atmosphere created by the Two Ronnies in their 1980s *Four Candles* sketch was reminiscent of Saph's store. (Martin Davies)

Up freight passes the site of Briton Ferry West station in 1963 behind 2-6-2 tank no 4108 *(John Davies)*

The important Briton Ferry signal box (left), opposite the original Briton Ferry station. 0-6-0T no. *8414* from Swansea Docks is passed by 2-6-2T no *4106* on a Swansea–Porthcawl train. *(Hale)*

*Port Wallaroo* was the name given to the pub by its first landlord, George Truscott, an ex-Cornish tin miner. He had emigrated to Australia, with his family to work in the copper and gold mines at Port Wallaroo. Following the death of his wife and two children, George decided to return to Britain, to work in the new Vernon Tinplate Works. He disliked the hard work in the Vernon so he left, bought the *Cupola* pub and renamed it the *Port Wallaroo*.[38]

The *Port Wallaroo* branch line served the works on the west side of Briton Ferry Docks: the Briton Ferry Iron Works, the Briton Ferry Steelworks, the Gwalia and Villiers Tinplate Works and the Cambrian Coke Works. A nest of sidings alongside the docks accommodated the goods wagons serving the works. A spur of the branch curved around the base of the Warren Hill and ran along the eastern bank of the river Neath to Giants Grave to serve the Wern Works and Ward's shipbreaking yard. In the 1960s this spur was used to move withdrawn steam locomotives to Wards' yard, where some 150 engines were dismantled. Although all the works on the eastern side of the docks had closed by 1959, the branch to Giant's Grave remained open well into the 1980s.

A shunter's cabin near the Port Wallaroo crossing provided facilities for the docks shunters and the foot-plate staff who parked their 'dock pilot' loco outside the cabin between duties. When the busy rail crossing was in use, pedestrians had to use the footbridge alongside the crossing. Here, too, the narrow-gauge railway from the Briton Ferry Iron works to the slag tip at Baglan Bay crossed the Wallaroo track at ninety degrees.

On the eastern side of the dock was a clutch of lines which serviced the Albion Steelworks, the Baglan Bay Tinplate Works and the Whitford Works and a siding running into a goods shed which, was covered when the new Briton Ferry road bridge was built.

Briton Ferry goods yard comprised eight sidings, in addition to the *up* and *down* goods lines. Here trains were marshalled to serve the needs of all the local factories. A pannier tank locomotive was stationed outside the cabin awaiting yard pilot duties. After the closure of Briton Ferry station in 1964 the track layout in the vicinity of the former station was simplified. The *up* avoiding line and the *down* relief line were both removed in November 1968. After that slow trains heading west would use the *down* goods line. Rationalisation of the track layout at Briton Ferry continued in the 1980s when three sidings were taken out of use and the *up* loop was cut back at the south end before joining the *up* main.

To the north of today's Shelone Road station, bridges crossed the main line allowing the SWMR from Tonmawr to join the GWR tracks to gain access to Briton Ferry Dock. The stone bridge that remains was for the SWMR to cross what became the Swansea District line's flying loop. The SWMR built an engine shed on the Brynhyfryd side of the line which was in use from 1877 until 1910. Towards Neath, the Neath Harbour Railway had built a junction in 1874 which was intended to take trains to the proposed Neath Harbour. The intended line was never built, but in 1894 the RSBR constructed its line to Swansea Docks passing under the main line to Neath, just to

Briton Ferry Station yard pilot. The wall was a favourite viewpoint for train spotters. *(R Reed)*

the north of Neath Harbour Junction. A connecting line was built in 1903 from the unused junction on the GWR to the RSBR along with a signal box named Cwrt Sart Junction.

In 1914, following the opening of the Swansea District line, a new layout was installed at Cwrt Sart. An *up* flying loop was constructed from the RSBR line, avoiding Cwrt Sart station, then running alongside the RSBR to join the GWR to the south of the SWMR overbridge. At the same time a *down* flying loop was built from the site of the former Neath Har-

bour junction running into the down RSBR line. A new signal box, sited closer to the SWMR over-bridge, was also opened at the same time.

From time to time the complexities of ownership of the rail sidings serving the rail companies and private industries provided difficulties for all concerned.[39] On one occasion, the ownership of a broken rail on the branch line running into several works could not be established, 'preventing a large number of trucks loaded with pig iron, steel bars and tin plates from reaching their destination'. Eventually

View towards Cwrt Sart from Shelone Bridge *(R Thomas)*

the serious consequences resulted in two sets of men arriving to do the repair, one gang already at work when the other arrived.

A year later 'a somewhat singular scene is reported to have taken place on the GWR at Briton Ferry'. The GWR had an arrangement to connect their line with the RSBR's. The GWR paid the RSBR for the right to do so but had not done it. The RSBR, under the personal direction of its Engineer, Mr Yockney, decided to take matters into their own hands by making the connection. 'A gang of workmen employed by the GWR were standing near, and immediately threw back the earth as fast as it was removed from between the sleepers.' Mr Yockney's gang subsequently withdrew.'[40]

There were also land disputes with Lord Jersey[41] who had been RSBR Chairman. One such saw 'railway magnates at Briton Ferry':

> The express train which normally passes through Briton Ferry at 3.30 pm stopped at this station on Friday afternoon for the convenience of Mr Wolfe Barry, Engineer; Mr Henry Lambert, General Manager of the GWR; Mr J J Leaning, District Superintendent, Mr Sims, Goods Superintendent and Mr E H Lloyd, Engineer, for the purpose of inspecting the piece of land in dispute.

Two years earlier[42] at the Court of Appeal, the court dismissed the appeal by the GWR. Sir Horace Davey QC, for the Earl of Jersey, won the case to restrain the GWR from acts of trespass and to force them to meet their obligation to make up a road which had been the condition of some land transfer to the GWR. When the RSBR wanted to build their line through Railway Terrace road and not at the back of the Railway Terrace houses,[43] it was the GWR which objected. So, too, did the ratepayers who sent a deputation to the GWR Directors at Paddington to support its objection. The GWR protest succeeded and the originally authorised route was adopted.[44]

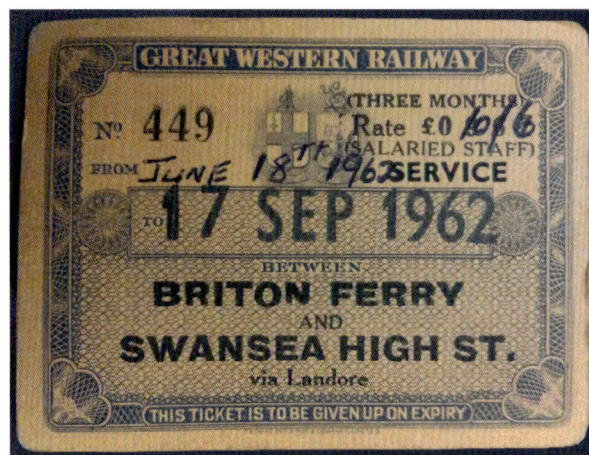

## Notes for Chapter Three

1.  *Western Mail*, 19 March 1870
2.  *Western Mail*, 30 March 1870
3.  *Western Mail*, 10 March 1871
4.  *Bradshaw's Descriptive Railway Handbook of Great Britain and Ireland*, 1860
5.  *Western Mail*, 10 March 1871
6.  *Western Mail*, 13 September 1871
7.  Phil Bannister, who for many years worked at Cwrt Sart locoshed, and grew up in Briton Ferry recalls that in the 1920s the dock-master was Mr Virgo and his deputy a Mr W. Daniels.
8.  *Cardiff Times*, 28 December.1878
9.  *South Wales Daily News*, 7 April 1896
10. *South Wales Daily Post*, 4 September 1896
11. About £28 at 2017 values
12. Kidwelly
13. *South Wales Daily News*; *South Wales Echo*, 30 September 1899
14. *South Wales Echo*, 10 May 1890
15. *Branch Lines Around Swansea* – Mitchell and Smith
16. *Cambria Daily Leader*, 19 March 1897
17. Humphreys
18. Eunice Davies, Martin Davies' mother
19. Now known as Morgan Terrace
20. See 'Briton Ferry: A most Industrious Town' for more about him
21. At 1930 prices the equivalent today would be £0.62
22. *Rhondda Leader*, 6 July 1901
23. The 1888–1913 6" Ordnance Survey map's name.
24. Cape Copper and its predecessor, Red Jacket Copper, used the *Welsh* process of extracting copper from its ores. The process was also used at Wallaroo in South Australia.
25. *South Wales Daily Post*, 28 April 1910
26. Such as 6412 (now preserved in South Devon)
27. He was born in 1927
28. *British Railways Magazine (Western Region)*, June 1950
29. £10.75 in 2017
30. £0.61 in 2017
31. £2.25 in 2017
32. £2.66 in 2017
33. Grandfather of co-author, Martin Davies
34. Patrick McGuiness: *Diary* in *London Review of Books*, 2 November 2017
35. A system of infra-red train detection and signalling
36. *Fifty years Within Station Limits*; John Morgan, p.46
37. The co-author's father
38. Peter Harris, Hampshire, *Rootsweb*
39. *Evening Express*, 10 March 1893: 'The right to a railway rail'
40. *South Wales Daily Post*, 2 March 1894
41. *South Wales Daily News*, 5 January 1895
42. *South Wales Daily Post*, 13 July 1893: 'The Earl of Jersey v The Great Western Railway Company'
43. Subsequently demolished and re-built as today's *Llansawel*
44. *South Wales Daily News*, 9 and 22 February 1894

Ticket 1 (527): Gt Western Ry | Gt Western Ry — NEATH GEN'L NEATH GEN'L — TO — ABERGAVENNY G.W. — via Caerleon — THIRD CLASS — 7/8 C Fare 7/8 C — Abergavenny G.W Abergavenny G.W — FOR CONDITIONS SEE BACK (W.L

Ticket 2 (2962): GtWesternRy — CHEAP — For day of issue by trains as advertised — COCKETT to — NEATH GENERAL — THIRD CLASS — SEE BA... W.D

Ticket 3 (1152): Gt. Western Ry. | Gt. Western Ry — H. M. FORCES ON LEAVE. — NEATH GEN'L NEATH GEN'L — TO — BRITON FERRY — THIRD CLASS — BritonFerry BritonFerry — FOR CONDITIONS SEE BACK (W.L

Ticket 4 (197): Gt. Western Ry. | Gt. Western Ry. — Return Excursion | EXCURSION — SALOON and Third Class | Third Class and SALOON — Douglas I.of M to | Neath to — NEATH | DOUGLAS I. OF MAN — By the Isle of Man Steam Packet Co's Boat Liverpool Landing Stage W side F.y Wrexham | Via Wrexham W side F.y Liverpool Landing Stage and Isle of Man Steam Packet Co's Boat — W.H See back | W.H See back

Ticket 5 (170): Gt. Western — MONTHLY RETU — Morecambe to — NEATH GENERAL — Via Preston Crewe Wem Saloo Hereford & Caerleon — FIRST... — FOR ...TIONS

Ticket 6 (3800): Gt. Western Ry. | Gt. Western Ry. — Return Excursion DAY TRIP | EXCURSION DAY TRIP — STAPLETON Rdto | Neath General to — NEATH GENERAL | STAPLETON ROAD — via Ashley Hill &S. Tunne | via S. Tunnel & Ashley Hill — THIRD CLASS | THIRD CLASS — A.I. See back | A.I. See back

Ticket 7 (640): Gt Western Ry | Gt Western Ry — Neath General | Neath General — TO — SWANSEA H.ST. — FIRST CLASS — 2/1 C Fare 2/1 C — Swansea H.St. Swansea H.St — FOR CONDITIONS SEE BACK W.£

Ticket 8 (456): B.R. (W) CHEAP — For day of issue by trains as advertised SERIES (B) — NEATH to — MUMBLES — via Swansea .&S.M. Rly — Passengers to find their own conveyance across Swansea — THIRD CLASS — SEE BACK (W.L

Ticket 9 (1442): Gt Western Ry | Gt Western Ry — HALF DAY EXCURSION RETURN TICKET — ST.FAGANS ST.FAGANS — TO — BARRY ISLAND AND BACK — Via Penarth Curve — THIRD CLASS — Barry Island Barry Island — FOR CONDITIONS SEE BACK

Ticket 10 (7830): Gt. Western Ry. | Gt. Western Ry. — Newport H. St. | Newport H. St. — TO — BRITON FERRY — 3/11½ PARLY.(3rdCls) 3/11½ — Issued subject to the conditions and regulations set out in the Company's Time Tables Books and Bills. (C.G) — Briton Ferry Briton Ferry

Ticket 11 (3344): Gt. Western Ry. — H.M. FORCES ON LEAVE — NEWPORT H.St. to — NEATH GENERAL — THIRD CLASS — SEE BACK A.I.

Ticket 12 (012): British Rlys (W) | British Rlys (W) — Return Excursion DAY TRIP | EXCURSION DAY TRIP — Issued at Newport 7. | Issued at Newport — Newport TO Cardiff | Cardiff TO Newport — Via Marshfield | Via Marshfield — First Cls. Fare | First Cls. Fare — FOR CONDITIONS SEE BACK (W.L | FOR CONDITIONS SEE BACK (W.L

Ticket 13 (958): Gt. Western Ry | Gt. Western Ry — WORKMAN'S TICKET — Court Sart | Court Sart — TO — BRITON FERRY ROAD — THIRD CLASS — 2¼d Fare 2¼d — FOR CONDITIONS SEE BACK

Ticket 14 (264): Gt. Western Ry — MONTHLY RETURN — Norwich(L.N.E) to — NEATH GENERAL — via Liverpool St & Padd'n — Exclusive of conveyance betw'n London Termini — THIRD CLASS — Fare 66/... — FOR CONDITION...

Ticket 15 (3162): Gt. Western Ry. | Gt. Western Ry — CHEAP RETURN | CHEAP TICKET — For day of issue by trains as advertised | For day of issue by trains as advertised — NEATH on Gt. Western Ry. TO BRITON FERRY | Briton Ferry to NEATH on Gt. Western Ry — Via | Via — Third Cls Fare | Third Cls Fare — E.B. SEE CONDITIONS ON BACK E.B

Ticket 16 (1436): Gt. Western Ry. | Gt. Western Ry — Return Excursion EVENING | EXCURSION EVENING — PORTHCAWL to | Briton Ferry to — BRITON FERRY | PORTHCAWL — THIRD CLASS | THIRD CLASS — FOR CONDITIONS SEE BACK (W.L)

Ticket 17 (3862): 2nd-SINGLE SINGLE-2nd — Briton Ferry to — Briton Ferry Briton Ferry — PortTalbotGeneral PortTalbotGeneral — PORT TALBOT GENERAL — (W) 8d Fare 8d (W) — For conditions see over For conditions see over

Ticket 18 (1121): Gt Western Ry | Gt Western Ry — Cymmer Afan | Cymmer Afan — TO — NEATH GENERAL — Direct or Via Pt.Talbot — Passengers to find their own conveyance across Port Talbot — THIRD CLASS — 2/2 C Fare 2/2 C — Neath Gnl Neath Gnl — FOR CONDITIONS SEE BACK. (W.L

Ticket 19 (4938): 7 | 8 | 9 | 10 | 11 | 12 — 8.47 GREAT WESTERN RAILWAY — SWANSEA H.ST. — The holder is prohibited from entering the Company's Trains. Not Transferable. — Admit ONE to PLATFORM — Available ONE HOUR on DAY of ISSUE ONLY — This Ticket must be given up on leaving Platform — 1D — FOR CONDITIONS SEE BACK — 1 | 2 | 3 | | 5 | 6

Chapter Four

# Passengers

*Railway termini are our gates to the glorious and the unknown. Through them we pass out with adventure and sunshine. To them, alas! we return.*

E M Forster

## Introduction

Memories of steam traction still exist in the minds of many over-65s and this chapter will evoke memories for those in that age group. But it is not written merely for wistfulness: it is written, too, for the train enthusiast and the general reader, especially younger readers. It aims to explain too, how well, or not, our railways were managed in the past and how technical and social changes have affected the railways. Readers may note parallel events between the substantial changes that occurred in the railway system with those that occurred in the coal and the iron, steel and tinplate industries a half a century ago.

It recounts the train services from, or passed through, Briton Ferry and district to serve the needs of the towns from the early days of steam railways to the present. It portrays the townsfolk's views and expectations of the services offered, with anecdotes concerning some unusual passengers and atypical train services in both peacetime and war.

## Passenger services

Direct services to and from London were available from Briton Ferry station seven days a week in the 1870s, with two trains in each direction on weekdays and one on Sundays. Journeys took much longer than today. The April 1877 timetable[1] shows that journeys to London were via Chepstow, Gloucester and Cheltenham because the four-mile, 624-yard Severn tunnel was still in the third year of its thirteen-year construction. The quickest trip was the weekday mid-day from Paddington which took seven hours and fifty-five minutes to arrive at Briton Ferry, but most journeys to London lasted over nine hours. Passengers could avail themselves of first, second or third-class seats. Mail trains ran every day, but they did not stop at Briton Ferry. A Saturday 'market train' also left Swansea at 6.45 pm for Port Talbot, stopping at all stations.

No doubt officialdom, if not the public, was so pleased with progress on the station facilities that

April 1877 *up* timetable from New Milford to London *(Great Western Society)*

they felt comfortable enough, in October 1889, to welcome to Briton Ferry station the Sirdar of the Egyptian armies, Sir Francis Wallace Grenfell and Lady Grenfell. They arrived 'on a special train at 3.20 pm'[2] to meet his sister, Mrs Llewelyn of Baglan Hall. 'On the arrival of the party at the railway station they were met by a large and enthusiastic concourse.' No doubt, according to Mr Henry Gower, Chairman of the Local Board, that was because his 'skill and military judgement as general commanding the forces resulted with such brilliant success'.

Such special services were very welcome, too, for events such as Neath fair, which attracted both local people and visitors from afar, but regular services for the bustling town, however, began to be a concern:

> The poor state of the train service at Briton Ferry was discussed by Briton Ferry Chamber of Commerce in 1891 who sent a statement of complaint to Mr Leanning of the GWR. It pointed out that Briton Ferry was 'at a disadvantage compared with several other stations of

Poster for special train to Neath fair
*(Port Talbot Historical Society)*

minor importance' because no down train stops at Briton Ferry between 9.17 am and 12.51 pm; nor between 3.28 pm and 7.38 pm, the last down train; and no train stops between 10.18 am and 2.05 pm, nor after 6.23 pm.[3]

A 'traveller' wrote to a newspaper complaining about the withdrawal, after two years' operation, of the 12.15 passenger train, saying:

> It is with a shock that the inhabitants of Briton Ferry and those who visit and have business with this thriving town ... is to be discontinued.... Why this step has been taken is a mystery ... the bookings are not small as a rule ... and the train is one of the best suited to Briton Ferry ... which is served badly by the GWR in the matter of train.[4]

Things had improved somewhat by 1921 when the winter timetable for that year showed five *down* trains stopping at Briton Ferry West between 9.05 and 12.50. Fourteen *down* trains called on weekdays, two of which were London trains, of which the 1.00 am from Paddington continued to serve Briton Ferry until 1964. In the *up* direction it shows Briton Ferry West being served by thirteen trains, including the 7.00 am boat train from Fishguard Harbour to Paddington. In addition, most of the RSBR services that used Cwrt Sart and Briton Ferry East stations, had connections to Neath (Canalside).

The 1921 RSBR summer timetable showed seven trains calling on weekdays in each direction. On Mondays, Fridays and Saturdays this was supplemented by a through train from Newport to Aberystwyth, a service jointly operated with Taff Vale railway making use of Great Western tracks in west Wales. Taff Vale and RSBR coaching stock was used alternately. Saturdays saw an extra three *up* and two *down* trains between Swansea (Riverside) and Treherbert. Altogether Briton Ferry was served by about twenty trains in each direction, a level of service which was maintained until Rockingham Terrace station was closed in 1964.

Briton Ferry residents who enjoyed a Saturday night on the town were better off going to Neath, rather than Port Talbot. The last RSBR train from Aberafan Town for Briton Ferry left at 21.55, and the last Great Western service departed from Port Talbot only twenty minutes later. However, revellers could have an extra hour's pleasure in Neath's cinemas, as the last train home from Neath steamed in at 23.14.

# LONDON, BRISTOL, NEWPORT, CARDIFF,

**WEEK DAYS**—continued.

| For Local Tables see pages | | a.m. | a.m. | a.m. | p.m. | p.m. | p.m. | p.m. | a.m. | p.m. | p.m. | p.m. | p.m. | a.m. | p.m. | a.m. | noon | p.m | p.m | p.m. |
|---|---|---|---|---|---|---|---|---|---|---|---|---|---|---|---|---|---|---|---|---|
| 24 to 31 | LONDON (Paddington) .... dep. | | | | | | | | 11 50 | | | | | 11 15 | | 10 45 | | 1 16 | | |
| | Ealing (Broadway) ,, | | | | | | | | | | | | | | | 10 56 | | 1 20 | | |
| | Reading ,, | | | | | | | | | | | | | | | 11 40 | | 2 0 | | |
| | Oxford ,, | | | | | | | | | | | | | | | 11 10 12 0 | | 2 3 | | |
| | Swindon ,, arr. | | | M | | | | | | | | | | | | 12 45 12 58 | | 3 0 | | |
| 29, 96 to 95 / 24 to 31 | SWINDON dep. | | | 11 10 | | | | | | | | | | | | 12 52 | M25 | 3 5 | | |
| | Wootton Bassett ,, | | | 11 21 | | | | | | | | | | | | | 1 36 | | | |
| | Brinkworth ,, | | | 11 30 | | | | | | | | | | | | | 1 45 | | | |
| | Little Somerford ,, | | | 11 37 | | | | | | | | | | | | | 1 52 | | | |
| | Hullavington ,, | | | 11 47 | | | | | | | | | | | | | 2 15 | 3 33 | | |
| | Badminton ,, | | | 12 0 | | | | | | | | | | | | | 2 27 | | | |
| | Chipping Sodbury ,, | | | 12 13 | | | | | | | | | | | | | 2 35 | | | |
| | Coalpit Heath ,, | | | 12 28 | | | | | | | | | | | | | 2 40 | | | |
| | Winterbourne ,, | | | 12 32 | | | | | | | | | | | | | | | | |
| 72 | Filton Junction arr. | | | 12 41 | | | | | | | | | | | | | 2 47 | | | |
| | Ashley Hill ,, | | | 12 46 | | | | | | | | | | | | | 2 52 | | | |
| 24 to 31, 71, 72 | BRISTOL {Stapleton Road ,, | | | 12 48 | | | | | | | | | | | | | 2 54 | | | |
| | {Lawrence Hill ,, | | | 12 53 | | | | | | | | | | | | | 2 58 | | | |
| | {Temple Meads ... ,, | | | 1 2 | | | | | | | | | | 1 23 | | | 3 6 | | | |
| 24 to 31 | Bath dep. | | | | 12 37 | | 12a57 | | | | | | | STOP | 1M25 | | | | | |
| 24 to 31, 71, 72 | BRISTOL {Temple Meads dep. | | | | | | 12 56 | | | J 5 | | | | | 2 25 | | | | | |
| | {Lawrence Hill ... ,, | | | | | | 1 5 | | | 1 40 | | | | | | | | | | |
| | {Stapleton Road ,, | | | | | 1 5 | 1 11 | | | 1 45 | | | | | 2 35 | | | | | |
| 72 | Ashley Hill ,, | | | | | | 1 15 | | | 1 50 | | | | | | | | | | |
| | Filton Junction ,, | | | | | | 1 23 | | | 1 59 | | | | | | | | | | |
| | Patchway dep. | | | | | | 1 27 | | | 2 4 | | | | | | | | | | |
| | Pilning ,, | | | | | 1 32 | 1 34 | | | 2 13 | | | | | | | | | | |
| 96 to 99, 103 | Severn Tunnel Junction arr. | 8 55 | 9 50 | | | | | | | 2 25 | | | | | 3 5 | 3 16 | | | | |
| 144, 146, 147 | Wolverhampton (Low Level) dep. | 8 55 | 9 50 | | | | | | | | | | | | | 10 40 | | | | |
| | Birmingham (Snow Hill) ,, | 9 43 | 10 15 | | | | | | | | | | | | | 11 20 | | | | |
| 96 to 102 | Cheltenham (St. James') ,, | | 12 5 | | | | | | | | | | | | | 1 30 | | | | |
| | Gloucester ,, | | 12 30 | | | | | | | | | | | | | 2 10 | | | | |
| 96, 97, 103 | Chepstow ,, | | 1 15 | | | | | | | | | | | | | 3 0 | | | | |
| 96 to 99, 103 | Severn Tunnel Junction dep. | | | | 1 35 | | | | | 2 30 | | | | | 3 10 | 3 20 | | | | |
| | Magor ,, | | | | | | | | | | | | | | | 3 27 | | | | |
| | Llanwern ,, | | | | | | | | | | | | | | | 3 35 | | | | |
| 104 to 106 | NEWPORT {arr. | 1 40 | 1 46 | | 1 56 | | | | 2 27 | 2 47 | | | | p.m. | 3 25 | 3 46 | | 4 21 | | |
| | {dep. | 1 45 | 1 50 | | 2 0 | 2 16 | | | 2 32 | STOP | | | | 3 18 | 3 30 | 3 53 | | 4 26 | | |
| | Marshfield ,, | | | | | | | | | | | | | | | 4 2 | | | | |
| 107 to 114 | CARDIFF arr. | 2 2 | 2 8 | | 2 17 | 2 33 | | | 2 49 | | | | | 3 35 | 3 48 | 4 17 | | 4 43 | | |
| 112 | Barry Docks arr. | | 2 55 | | 2 55 | 3 19 | | | 3 19 | | | | | STOP | 4 34 | 5 2 | | 5 37 | | |
| 107 to 114 | CARDIFF dep. | | | | | | 2 45 | 3 2 | 3 8 | | | 3 25 | | | 4 5 | | | 4 50 | | |
| | Ely (for Llandaff) ,, | | | | | | | | 3 13 | | | 3 31 | | | | | | | | |
| | St. Fagan's ,, | | | | | | | | 3 17 | | | 3 36 | | | | | | | | |
| | Peterston ,, | | | | | | | | | | | 3 42 | | | | | | | | |
| 86, 108 | Llantrisant ,, | | | | | | | | STOP | | | 3 52 | | | | | | | | |
| | Llanharan ,, | | | | | | | | | | | 4 0 | | | | | | | | |
| | Pencoed ,, | | | | | | | | | | | 4 7 | | | | | | | | |
| 115, 116 | Bridgend ,, | | | | | | | | | | | 4 29 | 4 42 | | | | | | 5 33 | |
| | Pyle ,, | | | | | | | | | | | 4 37 | 4 57 | | | | | | 5 55 | |
| 116 | Porthcawl {arr. | | | | | | | | | | | 5 8 | 5 8 | | | | | | 5 15 | |
| | {dep. | | | | | | | | | | | 4 20 | | | | | | | | |
| 116, 117 | Port Talbot and Aberavon dep. | | | | | | | | 3 49 | | | 4 50 | | | | | | 5 34 | 5 46 | |
| 117 | Briton Ferry ,, | | | | | | | | | | | 4 58 | | | | | | | 5 54 | |
| 110, 116, 117 | Neath ,, | | | | | | | | 4 2 | | 4 45 | 5 6 | | | | | | | 6 5 | |
| | Skewen ,, | | | | | | | | | | 4 53 | 5 13 | | | | | | | 6 12 | |
| | Llansamlet ,, | | | | | | | | | | 5 1 | | | | | | | | 6 20 | |
| | Landore arr. | | | | | | 3 55 | 4 15 | | | 5 6 | 5 23 | | | | | | | 6 25 | |
| 87 to 90 | SWANSEA (High Street) {arr. | | | | | | 4 5 | 4 30 | | | p.m. | 5 35 | | | | | | 6 0 | 6 35 | |
| | {dep. | | | | | | 3 50 | 4 5 | | | 5 10 | | | | | | | 6 10 | | |
| | Landore dep. | | | | | | 4 0 | 4 22 | | | | | | | | | | | | |
| | Cockett ,, | | | | | | | | | | 5 20 | | | | | | | | 6 20 | |
| | Gowerton ,, | | | | | | | | | | 5 27 | | | | | | | | 6 26 | |
| | Loughor ,, | | | | | | | | | p.m. | 5 32 | | | | | | | | 6 31 | |
| 118, 119 | Llanelly ,, | | | | | | 4 22 | 4 45 | | 5 0 | 5 45 | | | | | | | | 6 42 | |
| | Pembrey and Burry Port .... ,, | | | | | | | | | 5 7 | 5 54 | | | | | | | | 6 51 | |
| | Kidwelly ,, | | | | | | | | | | 6 7 | | | | | | | | 7 1 | |
| | Ferryside ,, | | | | | | | | | STOP | 6 16 | | | | | | | | 7 10 | |
| | Carmarthen Junction arr. | | | | | | | | | | | | | | | | | | | |
| 118, 119 | CARMARTHEN ,, | | | | | | 4 49 | 5 12 | | | 6 30 | | | | | | | | 7 21 | |
| 119 | Newcastle Emlyn arr. | | | | | | 7 30 | 7 30 | | | | | | | | | | | | |
| | Lampeter ,, | | | | | | 7 11 | 7 11 | | | | | | | | | | | | |
| | Aberayron ,, | | | | | | 8 15 | 8 15 | | | | | | | | | | | | |
| | Aberystwyth ,, | | | | | | 8 25 | 8 25 | | | | | | | | | | | | |
| 118, 119 | Carmarthen dep. | | | | | | 5 0 | 5 22 | | | | | | | | | | | 7 35 | |
| | Carmarthen Junction ,, | | | | | | | | | | | | | | | | | | | |
| | Sarnau ,, | | | | | | | | | | | | | | | | | | 7 47 | |
| | St. Clears ,, | | | | | | 5 16 | 5 38 | | | | | | | | | | | 7 59 | |
| | Whitland arr. | | | | | | 5 25 | 5 47 | | | | | | | | | | | 8 9 | |
| 119 | TENBY arr. | | | | | | 6 27 | 6 58 | | | | | | | | | | | 9 8 | |
| | Pembroke Dock ,, | | | | | | 7 10 | 7 40 | | | | | | | | | | | 9 46 | |
| 91 | Cardigan (for Gwbert-ou-Sea) arr. | | | | | | | 7 55 | | | | | | | | | | | | |
| 93 | Whitland dep. | | | | | | | 5 55 | | | | | M | | | | | | 8 19 | |
| | Clynderwen ,, | | | | | | | 6 7 | p.m. | | | | p.m. | | | | | | 8 31 | |
| 94 | Clarbeston Road ,, | | | | | | | 6 20 | 6 30 | | | | 7 10 | | | | | | 8 43 | |
| | Haverfordwest (for St. David's) .. dep. | | | | | | | 6 32 | | | | | | | | | | | 8 56 | |
| | Johnston ,, | | | | | | | 6 45 | | | | | | | | | | | 9 10 | |
| 92 | Milford Haven arr. | | | | | | | 7 5 | | | | | | | | | | | 9 33 | |
| | Neyland arr. | | | | | | | 6 55 | | | | | | | | | | | 9 20 | |
| 94 | Fishguard and Goodwick .... arr. | | | | | | | 7 2 | | | | 7 43 | | | | | | | | |
| | FISHGUARD HARBOUR ,, | | | | | | | 7 5 | | | | 7 45 | | | | | | | | |

J—Change at Lawrence Hill.
M—Rail Motor Car, one class only.
S—Saturdays only.

U—Calls at Badminton to set down 1st class Passengers from London on notice being given by the Passenger to the Guard at Paddington.
V—Saturdays only. Other days leave at 2.25 p.m. via Reading.

1921 GWR timetable *(Robert Thomas)*

# SWANSEA, PORT TALBOT AND TREHERBERT.

117

**(RHONDDA AND SWANSEA BAY RAILWAY.)**

**Week Days only.**

| Miles | Station | | a.m. | a.m. | a.m. | p.m. | | p.m. | | p.m. | | p.m. | p.m. | p.m. | | p.m. | | p.m. |
|---|---|---|---|---|---|---|---|---|---|---|---|---|---|---|---|---|---|---|
| | | | | | | | SATURDAYS ONLY | | Through Train Aberystwyth to Newport (G.W.), via Pontypridd. | | MONS., FRIS. AND SATS. ONLY, July 22nd to September 26th only. | | | | SATURDAYS ONLY. | | SATURDAYS ONLY. | |
| — | **Swansea** (R. & S.B.R.) ¶ | dep. | 725 | 9 0 | 1125 | 1245 | | 157 | | ... | | 445 | 6 0 | 7 25 | | 9 6 | | 920 |
| 1 | Danygraig | „ | 7 28 | 9 3 | 11 28 | 12 49 | | 2 1 | | . | | 4 49 | 6 4 | . | | . | | . |
| 3½ | Jersey Marine | „ | 7 36 | 9 8 | 11 34 | 12 55 | | 2 7 | | ... | | 4 55 | 6 10 | 7 33 | | 9 15 | | 9 29 |
| 6½ | Court Sart | arr. | 7 43 | 9 16 | 11 41 | 1 3 | | 2 14 | | 3 52 | | 5 2 | 6 17 | 7 40 | | 9 22 | | 9 36 |
| 8 | **Neath** (R. & S.B.R.) § | arr. | 7 51 | 9 29 | 11 53 | 1 23 | | 2 26 | | ... | | 5 13 | 6 44 | 7 50 | | .. | | 9 47 |
| | | dep | 7 30 | 9 6 | 11 30 | 12 52 | | 2 1 | | . | | 4 50 | 6 0 | 7 29 | | . | | 9 24 |
| — | Court Sart | dep. | 7 44 | 9 17 | 11 43 | 1 6 | | 2 1[illegible] | | 3 57 | | 5 5 | 6 19 | 7 42 | | 9 24 | | 9 39 |
| 7¼ | Briton Ferry* | „ | 7 47 | 9 20 | 11 47 | 1 11 | | 2 19 | | 4 0 | | 5 10 | 6 23 | 7 45 | | 9 25 | | 9 43 |
| 10 | Aberavon (Sea Side)† | „ | 7 53 | 9 26 | 11 53 | 1 17 | | 2 26 | | ... | | 5 16 | 6 29 | 7 51 | | 9 3[illegible] | | ... |
| 11 | Port Talbot (Aberavon Station)† | arr. | 7 56 | 9 29 | 11 56 | 1 20 | | 2 29 | | 4 8 | | 5 19 | 6 32 | 7 54 | | 9 37 | | 9 51 |
| | | dep. | 7 59 | 9 31 | 11 58 | 1 22 | | 2 32 | | 4 10 | | 5 22 | 6 34 | 7 58 | | 9 39 | | 9 54 |
| 12¾ | Cwmavon | „ | 8 5 | 9 37 | 12 5 | 1 29 | | 2 40 | | . | | 5 28 | 6 40 | 8 5 | | 9 48 | | 10 0 |
| 14½ | Pontrhydyfen | „ | 8 12 | 9 44 | 12 14 | 1 36 | | 2 47 | | ... | | 5 36 | 6 47 | 8 13 | | 9 55 | | 10 7 |
| . | Cynonville Halt | „ | 8 19 | . | . | 1 42 | | . | | . | | . | . | . | | 10 0 | | . |
| . | Duffryn Rhondda Halt | „ | 8 24 | 9 53 | 12 23 | 1 46 | | ... | | ... | | ... | ... | ... | | 10 5 | | ... |
| 18¾ | Cymmer (for Glyncorrwg) | „ | 8 30 | 9 58 | 12 27 | 1 52 | | 3 0 | | . | | 5 49 | 7 0 | 8 26 | | 10 12 | | 10 20 |
| 21 | Blaen-Gwynfy | „ | 8 39 | 10 7 | 12 36 | 2 0 | | 3 10 | | ... | | 5 58 | 7 9 | 8 35 | | — | | 10 28 |
| 24 | Blaen-Rhondda | „ | 8 50 | 10 19 | 12 49 | — | | 3 20 | | . | | 6 8 | 7 20 | 8 45 | | . | | 10 40 |
| 24¾ | **Treherbert** (T.V.R.) | arr. | 853 | 1025 | 1255 | ... | | 327 | | 4 47 | | 615 | 723 | 8 50 | | ... | | 1045 |

| Station | | a.m. | a.m. | | a.m. | | p.m. | p.m. | | p.m. | p.m. | p.m. | p.m. | |
|---|---|---|---|---|---|---|---|---|---|---|---|---|---|---|
| | | | | Through Train Newport (G.W.) to Aberystwyth, via Pontypridd and Treherbert. | | MONS., FRIS. AND SATS. ONLY, July 22nd to September 26th only. | | | SATURDAYS ONLY. | | | | | SATURDAYS ONLY. |
| **Treherbert** (T.V.R.) | dep. | 755 | 925 | | 1116 | | 1210 | ... | | 225 | 529 | 724 | 9 10 | |
| Blaen-Rhondda | „ | 7 58 | 9 29 | | . | | 12 14 | . | | 2 28 | 5 33 | 7 28 | 9 13 | |
| Blaen-Gwynfy | „ | 8 9 | 9 40 | | ... | | 12 2[illegible] | 2 23 | | 2 38 | 5 43 | 7 38 | 9 23 | |
| Cymmer (for Glyncorrwg) | „ | 8 15 | 9 47 | | . | | 12 29 | 2 30 | | 2 44 | 5 56 | 7 44 | 9 29 | |
| Duffryn Rhondda Halt | „ | 8 17 | ... | | ... | | ... | 2 34 | | 2G48 | ... | 7 48 | 9 32 | |
| Cynonville Halt | „ | 8 21 | . | | . | | . | 2 39 | | 2G52 | . | 7 52 | 9 36 | |
| Pontrhydyfen | „ | 8 29 | 9 58 | | ... | | 12 45 | 2 45 | | 2 58 | 6 7 | 7 58 | 9 42 | |
| Cwmavon | „ | 8 36 | 10 5 | | . | | 12 52 | 2 52 | | 3 5 | 6 14 | 8 6 | 9 49 | |
| Port Talbot (Aberavon Station)† | arr. | 8 41 | 10 10 | | 11 50 | | 12 57 | 2 57 | | 3 10 | 6 19 | 8 11 | 9 54 | |
| | dep. | 8 42 | 10 12 | | 11 51 | | 12 59 | 3 0 | | 3 12 | 6 21 | 8 13 | 9 55 | |
| Aberavon (Sea Side)† | „ | 8 45 | 10 16 | | ... | | 1 8 | 3 4 | | 3 17 | 6 25 | S8 16 | ... | |
| Briton Ferry* | „ | 8 52 | 10 23 | | 12 0 | | 1 11 | 3 10 | | 3 24 | 6 32 | 8 23 | 10 5 | |
| Court Sart | arr. | 8 54 | 10 25 | | 12 2 | | 1 18 | 3 12 | | 3 26 | 6 34 | 8 25 | 10 7 | |
| **Neath** (R. & S.B.R.) § | arr. | 9 1 | 10 34 | | . | | 1 23 | . | | 3 39 | 6 44 | 8 35 | 10 19 | |
| | dep. | 8 44 | 10 8 | | ... | | 12 52 | ... | | 3 15 | 6 0 | 8 10 | 9 53 | |
| Court Sart | dep. | 8 55 | 10 26 | | 12 5 | | 1 15 | 3 14 | | 3 27 | 6 36 | 8 27 | 10 9 | |
| Jersey Marine | „ | 9 8 | 10 34 | | — | | 1 22 | 3 22 | | 3 35 | 6 44 | 8 35 | 10 19 | |
| Danygraig | „ | 9 11 | 10 43 | | . | | 1 32 | 3 30 | | 3 44 | 6 51 | 8 44 | . | |
| **Swansea** (R. & S.B.R.) ¶ | arr. | 916 | 1046 | | ... | | 135 | 3 33 | | 349 | 655 | 847 | 1030 | |

G—Saturdays excepted. S—Saturdays only. ¶—About 1 mile from Swansea (High Street) G.W. Station. §—About ¼ mile from G.W. Station.

*—About 50 yards from G.W. Station. †—About ¼ mile from G.W. Station.

**The Train Service between Swansea (R. & S.B. Railway) and Treherbert is subject to alteration. Passengers should consult the R. & S.B. Company's announcements.**

1921 RSBR summer timetable *(Robert Thomas)*

## Major changes in the Twenties and Thirties

The First World War had a big impact on railway operations in Britain and at its end many railway companies were faced with significant problems.[5] The Government of the day decided that the country would be better served by a four large railway companies rather than the many independent companies that existed at the time. When the 'grouping' of companies took place only the Great Western of the original companies retained its title. In south Wales independent companies such as the Taff Vale and the RSBR were totally absorbed by the GWR.

This seemed to have little impact at Briton Ferry initially; the redundant companies' locomotives and coaching stock were absorbed by the GWR and continued in use until standard GWR stock and locomotives were introduced, but the frequency of service remained the same.

### Passenger travel on the SWMR

Although the SWMR was operated as a freight line, it sometimes carried passengers officially and unofficially. Officially a passenger service and some dedicated trains were introduced between Cymmer and Glyncorrwg, primarily for the use of miners employed in the Corrwg valley. It lasted into the 1960s. Unofficially passengers were conveyed from Crythan platform to Tonmawr in guards' vans during the 1920s and 1930s. As, Clive Reed[6] related what his grandfather, a GWR man, and other Cimla residents told him:

> Passengers from Cymmer, Glyncorrwg, and Tonmawr were seen walking from the platform along the country lane through Cimla to Neath during the inter-war period to do their weekly shopping. On the steep return journey, many stopped part way at the Tyn y Twr Hotel on Bwlch Road[7] for refreshment after the long walk up the Cimla Hill, before continuing on their journey to Crythan platform. Cannier shoppers left their orders with the shopkeepers of Neath to have them delivered to the hotel, saving themselves a long journey down the hill and back.
>
> My grandfather frequented the inn when he journeyed from Crythan platform to work in Treherbert in the 1920s and 1930s, although his first trip on the line was as far back as 1905.

## 1930s Rationalisation

The major effect of the rationalisation of the infrastructure at Briton Ferry in 1935 was the elimination of the independent RSBR trackwork, and the concomitant closure of Briton Ferry East and Cwrt Sart stations, in favour of the new station in Rockingham Terrace.

The 1930s became a period of increased competition in service provision between the Big Four companies. Improvements were constantly made to the design and construction of locomotives and rolling stock, with the aim of accelerating train services and attracting passengers from rival companies. After certain German and American locomotives, intended for high speed running, had been streamlined to lessen the air resistance, LNER's engineer, Gresley experimented with streamlining the 2-8-2 locomotive *Cock of the North*.[8]

In 1935 the GWR followed, deciding to celebrate its centenary by adopting this latest trend in locomotive engineering, despite the company's Chief Mechanical Engineer, Collett thinking otherwise.

'orders being orders', something had to be done about streamlining. He had a paperweight model of a *King* on his desk. An office boy was sent out to buy some plasticine ... and then Collett, in a few minutes, determined the shape the streamlining should take by running plasticine down the sides of the running plate, round the cylinders and filling the spaces behind chimney and safety valve covers where eddies occur. A hemispherical 'blob' was stuck on the front of the smokebox ... a draughtsman was given the job of providing working drawings for a *King* and a *Castle*.... The locos thus decorated were *6014 King Henry VII* and *5005 Manorbier Castle*.... They were the very first British locomotives to have streamlining added to them. They preceded the *A4*s by six months.[9]

Ira Llewellyn, then eight years old, enjoyed watching trains on the embankment below his home in Shelone Terrace with friends such as Joe Cox. They witnessed this novel experiment.

Many types came through, *Halls*, *Stars*, *Courts* and, of course, *Castles* such as *Neath Abbey* and *Isambard Kingdom Brunel*, but there was one loco I remember in particular. The *bullet-nose* we called it, as the smokebox was pointed. It was named *Manorbier Castle* of Old Oak Common shed and it had a straight nameplate, unlike the other *Castles*. We'd see it pass dozens of times, but it would always cause a stir and we'd shout *Look out boys, the bullet-nose is coming!*

The streamlined *Manorbier Castle*

The modification was short-lived because Collett was never convinced of the benefit of streamlining, despite the later success of Gresley's A4 Pacifics such as the world-renowned *Mallard*. Former Cwrt Sart driver Val Berni had the privilege of firing the record breaker when it took part in the inter-regional locomotive exchanges of 1948. He was then a fireman at Old Oak Common and *Mallard* was tried out on the Paddington to Plymouth expresses.

The GWR did not entirely dispense with streamlining: in 1934 it purchased four streamlined diesel railcars from AEC. Briton Ferry played host to one of these machines when the service from Birmingham was extended to Tenby. These machines were nicknamed *Flying Bananas* because of their shape, but they proved to be very popular with the travelling public on services to Porthcawl and via Landore (Low Level) to Swansea.

## Excursions and publicity – good and bad

The term 'excursion' seems quite archaic today. The Oxford dictionary defines it as 'a journey or ramble with the intention of returning to the starting point' or a 'pleasure trip of a number of persons'. The rail companies were keen to offer excursions, especially following the reduction in the working week at the end of the nineteenth century. After a working day beyond two pm on Saturdays could no longer be forced on workers, it was often possible to make a short, daytime, excursion. One such was to Briton Ferry Road, Jersey Marine, on a May Sunday.[10] The newspaper report below was to reassure the public that such excursions were safe, despite the deaths of the Hill sisters on a previous excursion.[11]

> Excursion trains ran at intervals to this highly popular place of resort yesterday, thousands of persons availing themselves of the pleasant outing offered for the day. The strictest and most admirable precautions were taken to prevent accidents at the railway station, the immense crowds very wisely following up the arrangements made for their safety.

The GWR ran a highly effective public relations unit to encourage holidaymakers to visit places served by its trains such as the glamorously depicted *Cornish Riviera* and the *Cheltenham Flyer*. People from Briton Ferry were not slow to take advantage of the railways for both holiday travel and day trips. The railways realised that day trips, which were likely to be more frequently taken than holiday journeys, could provide a lucrative source of revenue. With a gradually declining coal trade to the docks after the First World War, much encouragement was therefore made, especially by the GWR, for the populace to taste the local offerings afforded by rail. The south Wales ports were well-served by rail for freight from the tinplate towns and mining valleys. To secure passenger revenue, it was decided by the rail companies that Porthcawl and Barry Island should feature prominently in their promotional posters to attract passengers. Similarly, it was possible to venture on day trips on the RSBR to Aberafan beach from towns such as Briton Ferry, Skewen and Llansamlet and those in the Rhondda valleys.

The RSBR also offered typical excursions for the Christmas Holiday period:[12]

> *Wednesday December 23: Excursion tickets to Aberystwyth, via Briton Ferry and Pencader, will be issued at Taff Vale and Swansea Bay stations*

An AEC railcar approaches Neath station on a local working to Porthcawl in the 1950s (*Norman Jones*)

An excursion from Briton Ferry of Jerusalem Chapel members (*West Glamorgan Archives*)

*Thursday December 24: Trains will run as on Saturdays, supplemented by Special Trains from the Rhondda Valley to Carmarthen and intermediate stations to Newcastle Emlyn via Briton Ferry.*

It is intriguing to read the descriptions of the day trip destinations. Whilst some were quite bland, such as the Gower Coast *for unspoilt natural beauty* others, like Barry, became increasingly superlative: *for varied enjoyment, the gem of the Welsh coast, the children's paradise.* For most of the year, the majority of trains on the south Wales valley lines mundanely carried coal to Barry Docks, but during *Miners' Fortnight*, particularly, it was the miners themselves and their families that were carried on those very lines with much excitement.

Tintern, Chepstow, and the Vale of Usk were some of the excursion possibilities to the east, with Porthcawl a very popular half-day destination. Indeed, British Rail was still heavily promoting Porthcawl well into the 1950s: Porthcawl *has everything, for happy healthy holidays.* Its Coney beach was Britain's brightest pleasure beach. The towns of Barry and Porthcawl therefore 'vied with each other for visitors, and it was not just the locals who came'.[13] To the west, Fishguard, St David's and Tenby were promoted, with Tenby being the choice of many '*for sunshine and unrivalled golden sands, 5¾ hours from Paddington*' (GWR).

Yet it was so much quicker from Briton Ferry or Clydach! Glenys Williams[14] joined the Sunday school excursions to Porthcawl in the 1930s:

> We climbed on board the train in the makeshift station in Clydach and packed in to the carriages for our annual Whitsun trip to Porthcawl.... Mother would carry a wicker basket full of sandwiches and cakes for our picnic.... It was always Coney Beach in the morning and then a walk to Rest Bay in the afternoon.

Dorothy James has a memory of standing in a guard's van, but can't recollect a station in Porthcawl when she made the trip from Briton Ferry in the 1950's, but adds:

> Coney Beach was considered 'dirty' so it was always Rest Bay. Quieter and more 'respectable'.

The rail companies' advertising portfolio covered both holidays and work destinations. Today people can commute to work daily from Briton Ferry to Cardiff, but the attraction portrayed by a 1933 GWR poster was to the *City of Conferences*. Was the poster really intended to attract people to Cardiff as a work destination? There could be little doubt of the intention of the Milford Haven poster: *where fish comes first* was to prioritise goods traffic. Most people in Briton Ferry knew the importance of the fish trade. The white vans that formed the trains from Milford that roared through the town daily with fresh fish for the London markets was the reason for that. The GWR also used the slogan *south Wales docks for quick despatch*, to encourage the use of its own docks for the products it carried. Swansea Docks was therefore

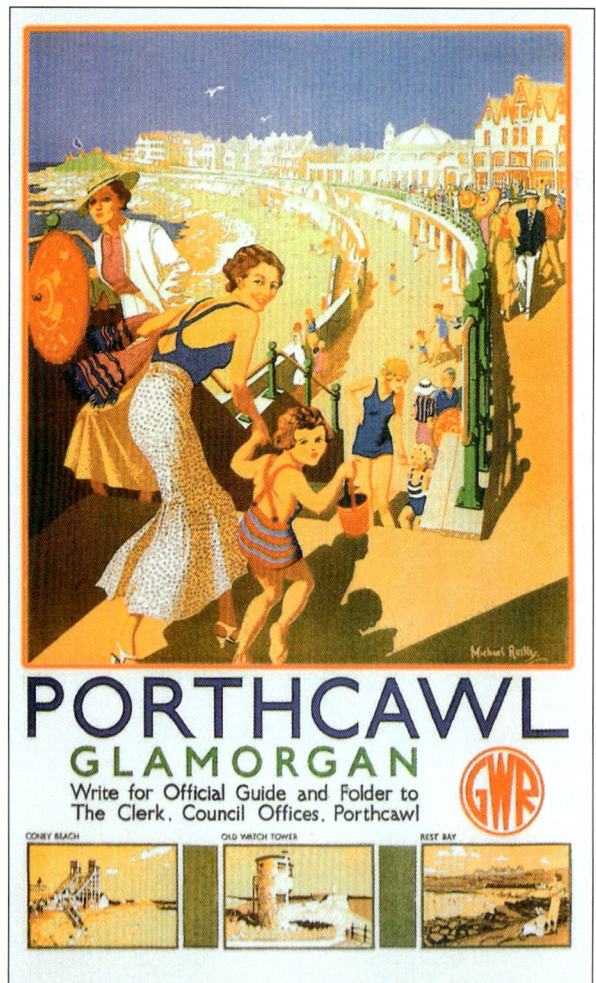

Porthcawl excursion train poster (*NRM*)

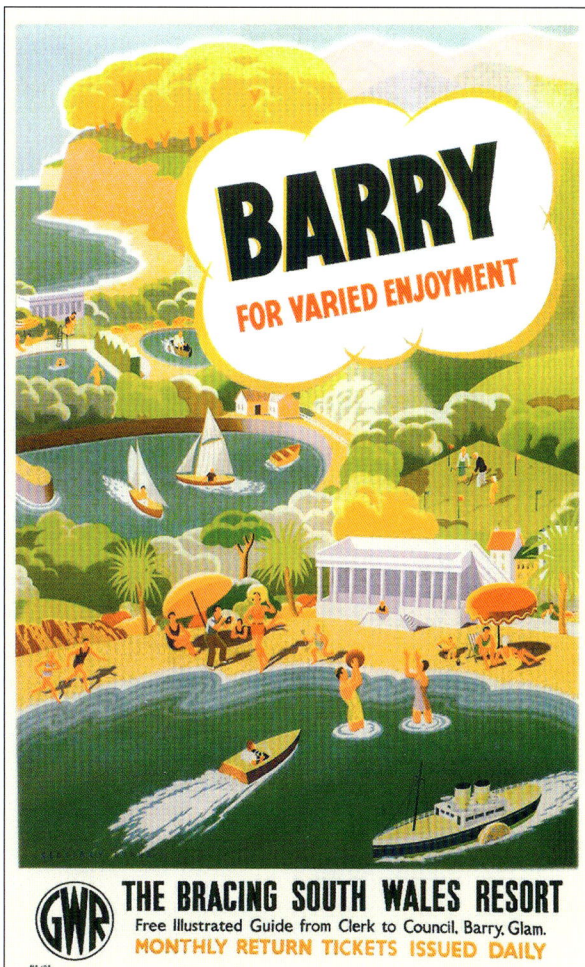

Barry excursion train poster (*NRM*)

carry a total of 114,912 evacuees from London. Each train had up to twelve coaches and up to 800 passengers. The first train involved in this 'exodus' left at 8.30 am on 1 September 1939. Ealing Broadway was the main embarkation point because of the ease of transfer from the underground system. Fifty-eight trains departed on this first day carrying a total of 44,032 passengers, with a similar number of trains on the second and third days. On the final day, there were twenty-eight trains accounting for 17,796 passengers. Some specials ran to places like Maidenhead and Newbury, but the majority headed to the West Country and west Wales, as far away from the bombing as possible.

The trains, destined for Carmarthenshire and Pembrokeshire towns like Clarbeston Road, travelled through Briton Ferry on their way west. Although several normal services were cancelled for the period concerned, the procession of trains, full of highly emotional children heading into the unknown, must have been a sight that residents won't have forgotten easily. One of the evacuees who travelled from Kent to Whitland in the second wave of evacuations in 1940 described evacuation as:

> an incredible adventure. I had never been away from my parents before ... what the others felt I do not know. I suppose my feelings were a mixture of apprehension, resignation and excitement.... It was a long journey. Passing through the more industrialised area we wondered what we were in for, but the sun glistening on Carmarthen Bay as the train went along the coast near Ferryside stirred even we boys, at an age not noted for scenic appreciation.[16]

Following the outbreak of war, people of eligible age who were classed as fit for combat were recruited into the armed forces unless they were employed in a reserve occupation. Jobs in the coal mines, steel industry, armament factories, or on the railways were so reserved. Workers too young to enlist were recruited into a reserve civilian occupation until they were old enough to 'join up'.

Seventeen-year-old apprentice plumber Keith Davies[17] was too young to be conscripted into the forces, so he was, instead, conscripted to work at a munitions factory. His journey to work was on a special train from Briton Ferry to the Royal Ordnance Factory at Tremains, Bridgend, alighting at the new station built for thirty thousand workers. It was typical of the daily journey many men and women made from towns in south Wales.

portrayed in both its industrial glory and as 'a delightful seaside resort'.

**Passengers during World War Two – evacuees and conscript workers**

The Second World War had a major impact on the day-to-day operations of the railway network, bringing changes in the number and frequency of trains and the nature of passenger and freight traffic passing through towns like Briton Ferry. In 1938, it became increasingly clear that war with Germany was a probability and thus preparations were made by the railway companies. Anticipating a possible surprise attack, on virtually the eve of the war, plans were made for the evacuation of children and many others, including their teachers and expectant and nursing mothers. Evacuations took place from London and other major cities which were likely targets for enemy bombing. On 31 August,1939, the Ministry of Health announced that: 'It has been decided to start evacuation ... tomorrow, Friday 1 September. Evacuation, which will take several days to complete is taken as a precautionary measure.'[15]

In four hectic days, the GWR ran 163 trains to

Great Western Railway

SWANSEA DOCKS

Swansea industrial poster *(NRM)*

Evacuees arriving at Gowerton *(G.W.R. at War - Bryan)*

Keith worked on the construction of the factory. It meant leaving Briton Ferry at 6.00 am to spend a gruelling day digging trenches and laying water pipes before returning home by train, still wearing wellingtons and caked in mud, to reach Briton Ferry at 7.00 pm. He never could enlist in the armed forces. Despite later passing a medical for the Royal Marines, the tuberculosis he suffered following a motor cycle accident resulted in medical conscription to Talgarth sanatorium. Visits from family members and friends during his extended recuperation meant a long and very complicated railway journey from Briton Ferry to Talgarth via the Neath and Brecon Railway. After he had made a full recovery, he became known as 'Keith the Plumber' working in his father's plumbing firm *Tom Davies and Son*. He installed many central heating systems in the 1960s and 1970s which are still working in Briton Ferry houses today.

Ira Llewellyn, too, had not yet been conscripted for National Service during the war, so he was able to observe most of the trains passing through the town:

Four trains a day called at Briton Ferry taking the workers to and from Tremains. They were non-corridor trains, taking mainly girls to and from work. The trains usually started

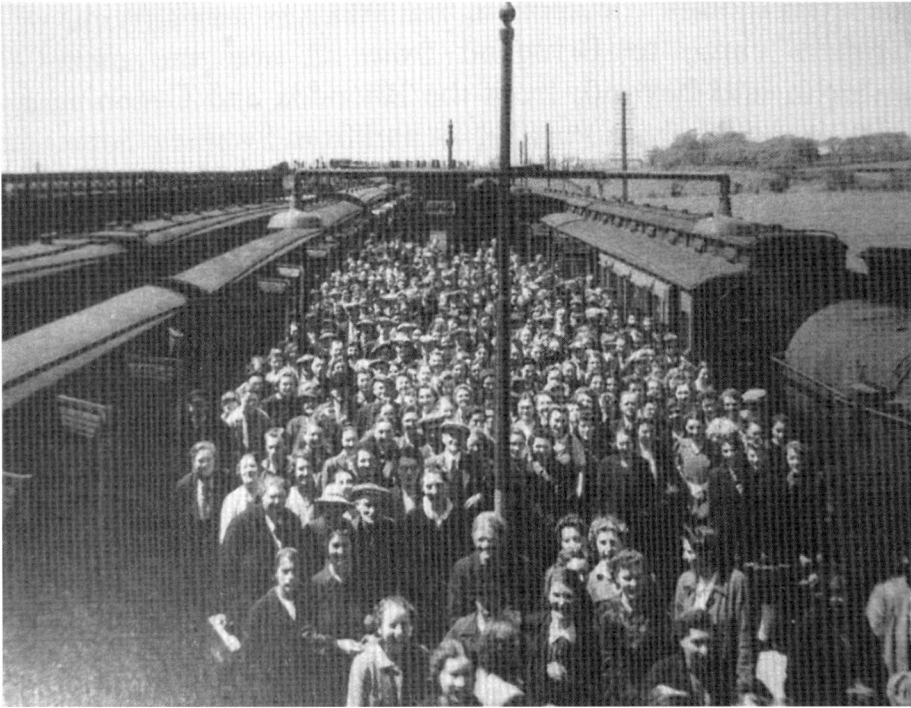

Tremains after the arrival of morning trains *(the Welsh Arsenal)*

from Swansea but stopped at all stations, picking up at Briton Ferry at 5-20 am for the morning shift. This train then returned to bring the night shift workers home to Port Talbot, Briton Ferry, Neath and Llansamlet. Another train called in the evening for the other shift change. The girls worked twelve-hour shifts. The trains were usually ten coaches long and were hauled by large *31xx* 2-6-2 tanks based at Landore.

One chap I knew well was Fred Williams who lived in Water Street.[18] During the war his sole job was on the 'Arsenal trains'. He worked odd hours, often starting work in the early hours of the morning. Fred was a regular chapel-goer and Sunday school teacher. He would often stray from the scriptures by relating stories about his daily work on the railway. Fred would tell us tales about the locos, and any unusual incidents such as derailments. As boys we found his 'lessons' most interesting and informative. He was a lovely chap, a Devonshire man.

Val Berni was a cleaner at Neath shed in 1942 and prepared locos such as an *81xx* class 2-6-2 tank, used on some of the Tremains trains. One of the regular drivers on the train was Arthur Heyward, of Neath Road. He was a top dog. His fireman was usually Tom Mills or Bryn James, who later moved to London to become drivers.

The women from Briton Ferry who worked at Tremains worked long hours but were comparatively well-paid. There was some resentment amongst men working in reserved occupations such as those in the steel industry that their wives often earned more than them, particularly those men who had less-skilled jobs. However, many of the female workforce paid a price for their daily toil. Those who filled shells with gunpowder often suffered side effects from exposure to the chemicals used. They often developed a sallow complexion with skin tinged yellow.

Keith Davies in 1939 *(Martin Davies)*

## The effects of war on train services

The GWR was the first railway company to issue a new emergency timetable in September 1939. It showed both a reduction in the number of trains run and a great increase in journey times. Main line trains often took up to two hours extra to complete their journeys, but some drivers were better at sticking to the new schedules than others. Tim Bryan[19] quotes a correspondent for the Railway Magazine who describes a journey from Bristol to London which was 'sixty-eight minutes late arriving at Paddington even on the emergency timetable.' At the other end of the spectrum he described a trip from Paddington to south Wales when the driver of the 8.55 am from Paddington 'completely forgot that there was a war on' and touched 80 mph at Pilning and, despite a subsequent signal check, still arrived in Newport at 11.39 instead of 11.50 am.

As the blitz intensified, train speeds were reduced by necessity as well as by the timetable. People were discouraged from making unnecessary journeys to enable the armed forces to be mobilised without difficulty. Troop trains were often of great length and usually double-headed. Briton Ferry frequently saw these as they made their way west to the military bases in west Wales. Conversely, the evacuation of the British Expeditionary Forces from Dunkirk, and, later, western France meant that special trains were operated from the initial disembarkation points on the south coast to all areas of the country, so the GWR was again instrumental in running special trains to west Wales for the returning troops.

Milford Haven was also used as a port for disembarkation to move troops eastward. The GWR was responsible for moving some 182,808 men, a high proportion of the total. Some idea of the tremendous strain borne by the company was the fact that 'in the five weeks ending 22 June 1940, the Company had run 1,659 special trains. This staggering number excluded a further 671 ammunition and equipment trains and another 102 special coal trains. Throughout the operation, staff made herculean efforts to ensure the whole operation passed off as smoothly as possible, often working long hours and missing meals to get the work done. The GWR Magazine paid its own tribute:

> Footplate and train men had no regard for
> their own convenience and gladly did
> their parts in taking trains on even
> though they had worked long hours.[20]

As industry got into its stride and was placed on a war footing, general goods traffic rose by fifty-one per cent while coal traffic had increased by forty-one per cent. Many of the engineering factories in the Briton Ferry and Neath area, such as the Metal Box, Taylor's Foundry and the Albion Steelworks, were directed to produce armaments and this became a regular source of traffic for the local railways. There was significant through traffic too, associated with the ordnance factories at Tremains and Pembrey. These trains often travelled at night and the 'black out' meant that as much as possible was done to reduce any possible sources of light which would attract enemy aircraft. Locomotive cab windows were replaced by metal plates and canvas sheets were put in place between cab and tender to mask the glow from the firebox. Some footplate staff went further to protect themselves by reducing the strength of the head lamps at the front of the locomotive by inserting sheets of paper into the gaps in the lamps, a practice frowned upon by the authorities which could lead to disciplinary action.

Bill Morgan was a driver at Neyland shed in the 1940s and sometimes drove ammunition trains eastwards through Briton Ferry. He was prepared to take the risk:

> whenever I found myself pulling an
> ammunition train from Milford Mining
> Depot, I decided that if a slip of paper
> might save my life, then a slip of paper I
> would use. After all you can recover from
> disciplinary action![21]

Churchill voiced the thoughts of many after the USA entered the war in December 1941 when he pointed out that 'the industrial might of the United States would lead to eventual victory … the flow of munitions would vastly exceed … anything that had ruled up to the present'.[22] The first American troops in Wales landed at Swansea Docks on 18 August 1942. All 6,281 troops were disembarked and dispersed directly from the docks to their bases within twenty-four hours by twelve special trains. Eastbound trains travelled through Briton Ferry with many GIs being billeted less than 200 yards from its new railway station. This process became a regular occurrence over the next few years as more and more troops landed at south Wales ports. Trains conveying those who had landed at Newport and Cardiff, which were headed for bases in west Wales, also passed through Briton Ferry. David Williams, then a cleaner, recalls trains of GI's passing Cwrt Sart shed, taking the District Line to Llanelli:

> I remember on one occasion a troop train
> full of Yanks had stopped on the line
> which came from Swansea, crossing the

river Neath on the swing bridge.... The Yanks threw packets of chewing gum and hard-boiled eggs at us which we pelted back at them.[23]

American troops were often deployed at Swansea Docks to assist in the unloading of shipping and in the preparations for the D-Day landings in Normandy. Some of the 370 billeted in and around Briton Ferry had arrived by train.[24]

> Some were billeted in a Nissen hut alongside the Public Hall. Today it is a Tesco store and few of the shoppers will know of its former use.[25] Others became guests of local people who had spare rooms. Laura Davies of Vernon Street became Briton Ferry's first GI bride after she became friendly with an American soldier who lodged with her family.

Sometimes the GIs found it hard getting to grips with the Welsh place names. Those based near Cwmtwrch in the Swansea Valley, pronounced the name of the local station at Gwys as *Gee Whiz* and Ystradgynlais became *Why Strangle Us?*

Due to the significant increase in freight traffic during the war Britain suffered from an acute shortage of heavy goods locomotives. The USA assisted by supplying 400 *S160* class 2-8-0 locos, built by American locomotive builders, Alco, Lima and Baldwin. They were powerful, easy to maintain, and had a high route availability. They did valuable work in south Wales, before being shipped to the continent after the invasion in June 1944. Val Berni from Neath was based at Old Oak Common during the war and fired these locos: 'they had square fireboxes and needed a different technique of firing to the western engines".

Some were serviced at Cwrt Sart. Gerald Williams, a former fitter at the shed, recalls using large steel bars, nicknamed *Yankee Bars*, to remove coupling rods from *Halls* and *Castles* in the 1960s. These bars were used for the maintenance of the massive *S160*s and were probably left behind after the war, rather than accompanying the few of *S160* locomotives that have been restored for use on Britain's heritage railways.

## High-ranking Passengers

Although security was very tight for visits to military establishments by high ranking military and political figures, both Churchill and General Eisenhower travelled through Briton Ferry during the war. Churchill and his entourage were photographed walking down

US troops disembarking at Swansea Docks *(GW at War)*

Swansea High Street on his morale-boosting visit in the aftermath of the 'three-day blitz' on the city in 1941. David Wooderson, the Kent schoolboy who was evacuated to west Wales, witnessed the visit by Churchill to Whitland that same year.

> There was great excitement when word got around that Churchill himself was to pass through. The line was cleared, a pilot loco went ahead to check that all was well, then came the train hauled by a spotless locomotive, 5040 *Stokesay Castle*. The great man got off, appeared briefly in the town square, raised his hat to the crowd and was whisked away in a large car, probably to Aberporth on Cardigan Bay, where we learnt after the war that weapons were tested, or to the anti-aircraft gunnery school at Manorbier.[26]

Churchill again travelled by train through Briton Ferry later in the war to inspect the preparations for the Normandy landings at Amroth and Wiseman's Bridge beaches, proxies for their French counterparts.

Until the ending of military conscription in the early 1960s, special troop trains were still seen travelling through Briton Ferry, but the train which headed west on 31 March 1944 was a very special train. No other train had carried such distinguished military personnel as this. Visits to Wales by the Chiefs of the Allied Expeditionary Forces were rare but, prior to the D-Day landings, General Eisenhower's train passed through Briton Ferry on a trip to inspect the infantry divisions in west Wales. It left Addison Road depot in London for Tenby, using the Swansea District line from Cwrt Sart. On board were British and US chiefs of staff, the General's staff car, jeeps motor-cycles and everything else needed by the Supreme Commander. On the return journey, he visited the US troops based at Margam Park.[27]

*S160* locomotive on a wartime freight (*G.W. at War* T Bryan)

## Wartime damage

Briton Ferry was located close to Llandarcy oil refinery and became used to the sound of overhead enemy aircraft during bombing raids. Although there was no wholesale damage to railway property in the town during the hostilities, some families were seriously affected when planes targeting the refinery, and being chased by British aircraft, discharged their bombs at Cwrt Sart.

Air raid shelters were provided for railway staff and signalmen had a special 'container' in which they could seek refuge during an air raid. Those on duty at the signal boxes at Baglan, Briton Ferry, and Cwrt Sart, not being able to abandon their work stations, would make full use of these during a period of enemy action. Bill Morgan described finding the occupant of Llandarcy signal box after an air raid on the nearby oil refinery.

> I spotted the tall metal box standing in the corner, approximately six feet tall and three feet square, with narrow letter box style slit on the sides ... (I) heaved the door. A startled face looked up at me, for all the world looking as if he was sitting on a lavatory! He held a torch in one hand and a book in the other. *Iesu Grist there's a fright you gave me*, he exclaimed in annoyance.

At the time Bill was driving a *53XX* class on the late afternoon parcels train from Neyland to Paddington, rather than the usual *Castle*. He and his fireman, Fred, would normally have worked this

General Eisenhower's train passed through Briton Ferry (Brynallt Jones)

train through to Cardiff but this time it had to be stopped short at Briton Ferry. All had been well until they reached Llanelli, but thereafter the orange air raid warning changed to red. As they steamed eastwards from Llandeilo Junction, they realised that an attack on Swansea was imminent.

> the flares continued to light up the sky ahead and the ominous sounds of exploding bombs continued to reach our ears. Our sails were well down as we rattled and swayed along, no longer conscious of the build-up of heat and humidity but only of the menace in the skies above us. We approached Llandarcy tunnel with some degree of thankfulness, at least we would be unseen and comparatively safe for a few minutes. Our

Churchill at Swansea
*(South Wales Evening Post)*

speed was restricted through the tunnel as there was a signal just on the other side. *The signal's on, Fred!* I exclaimed in surprise as we neared the end of the tunnel. Fred slowed us down just outside the tunnel, the signal was about seventy-five yards ahead – the first time I had ever seen it on.

*No sense in waiting out by here Bill, we might as well get into the tunnel until we get the road* and without more ado Fred took us back the few yards into the welcoming shelter of the tunnel. Like a tortoise's head our loco was, just tucked into its shell ... the horizon was aglow with orange fire.... The loco shuddered beneath our feet as explosion followed explosion. *That one was bloody close* muttered Fred as a particularly deafening, earth-shaking bomb exploded nearby. A screaming whistle heralded yet another descending bomb ... the thunderous explosion was ... followed by the sharp crash of breaking glass – lots of it.[28]

Realising the signal box had been hit, Bill Mor-

gan cautiously ran along the track to find the box still standing and climbed up the steps to open the door to find the signalman hiding in his shelter. Bill, Fred and their guard waited for nearly two hours while that 'interminable raid of destruction spent itself' and eventually got the right of way. They discovered later that Llandarcy had borne the brunt of the attack. They proceeded cautiously, leaving the signalman climbing back into his windswept box.

We eventually reached Briton Ferry after a slow journey at five miles an hour. Surprisingly we had met no obstruction on the line, although there were dark, shadowy craters in the fields alongside. Just luck it was. We found that we could go no further than Briton Ferry with our parcels and we were told to leave our *53XX* there and go to the cabin where jugs of hot tea were waiting for us. There were eight of us ... all waiting to reach Landore where we spent our double-home on this run, so it was decided to give us a light engine and we could all get on the footplate.[29]

69

## Post-war workers' trains

Workers' trains retained importance for a time after the war because the post-war recovery meant a significant boost for industry in South Wales. The steel industry played a major role in the reconstruction of Britain and output in the local steelworks increased steadily. In the late 1940s the Labour Government sought to modernise the industry in south Wales by closing many of the small uneconomic plants in west Glamorgan area and replacing them by larger, more advanced, works under the Steel Company of Wales. The company's Abbey Works at Port Talbot was opened in 1951, becoming fully operational two years later, and was directly employing 20,000 at its peak.

Many people from West Glamorgan and elsewhere travelled by train to Port Talbot and to a new station built at Margam to serve the integrated steelworks. Trains called at Briton Ferry before and after the shift changes. The first eastbound train at Briton Ferry was the 5.00 am departure from Swansea which called at 5.28 am, taking those people starting work at 6.00 am. Workers returning home from the night shift were accommodated on the first westbound stopping train, which reached Briton Ferry at 6.28 am. Similar activity took place in connection with the afternoon and night shifts.

Eastbound trains also took passengers to Treherbert, Porthcawl, Cardiff, Bristol, Cheltenham Spa and Birmingham (Snow Hill) and all stations en route. Trains headed west to Swansea, Carmarthen and Milford Haven. One train only from London stopped at Briton Ferry, the 1.00 am departure from Paddington. There was no equivalent train in the opposite direction, so those bound for Paddington needed to change at Neath or Port Talbot. The 1.00 am was a most appealing conveyance, having sleeping facilities as well as carrying the daily newspapers for Swansea. It took the 'Great Way Round' through Gloucester, but it was nevertheless a convenient train for those who had spent a day in the capital and had attended a West End show or concert in the evening. It reached Briton Ferry at 7.03 am.

Hugh James travelled on this train from London one November day in 1964 after a successful interview at Paddington for the post of journalist on the staff of *Rail News*, the in-house magazine of British Railways. His early morning arrival at Briton Ferry coincided with the last day when passenger trains used the station. Another passenger who joined that train at Briton Ferry was Alun E Hutchinson:

> I was determined to witness the last train
> to stop at Briton Ferry station even

though it was very early in the morning. It was hauled by a *Hymek* diesel *D 7036*. After taking some photographs, I decided to go one step further and travel on the train to Neath. I walked back home from Neath station to Briton Ferry, which we thought nothing of in those days, having taken part in what is now a historic occasion.

A blacked-out cab *(GW at War)*

As today, no London Paddington trains stopped at Briton Ferry in the *up* direction so passengers from Briton Ferry, changed at Neath or Port Talbot for their onward journey. A further seventeen trains from Paddington to Swansea and west Wales sped through Briton Ferry on their way west and an equal number travelled in the opposite direction daily.

A time-interval system was in operation for trains to make journey planning a lot easier for the rail traveller. Those to the same destination departed at the same number of minutes to the hour. Paddington to Swansea and west Wales trains left at five minutes to the hour e.g. 8.55, 9.55 and so on. Swansea to London departures were normally half past the hour, with the first departure at 6.30 am. Other trains to pass through Briton Ferry were those between Swansea and Penzance, Manchester, Birmingham and Bristol.

The empty stock of a workers' train from Swansea to Margam in the loop line at Baglan in August 1964, behind pannier tank 9464 *(Martin Davies)*

The last passenger train in Briton Ferry station behind *Hymek D7036* in November 1964 *(Alun Hutchinson)*

## The titled trains

In the 1950s the General Manager of the Western Region sought to revive the GWR's identity through several initiatives. One was to name trains and another was to repaint important coaching stock in chocolate and cream livery. The 5.55 pm from Paddington acquired the legend *The Red Dragon* as one of south Wales new titled trains.

> This was a distinctly lethargic beast, for in the *down* direction, with numerous stops it was not until ten minutes to midnight that the last of its tail dragged itself wearily into Carmarthen.[30]

The train, usually headed by one of Cardiff Canton's best *Britannias*, flamed its way through Briton Ferry about 10.03 pm. The *up* train, which left Carmarthen at 7.15 am, was also scheduled to call at all stations to Swansea. It graced Briton Ferry with its presence about 9.53 am, too late to be seen by Briton Ferry boys attending school. A *Castle* or *Hall* was booked for this leg of the journey before the train had its third engine change in Cardiff. A newly serviced *Britannia* was the usual motive power to London, but after 1960, *Kings*, displaced from the West Country by the new *Warship* diesels, were commonly used. Even the UK's last main line locomotive *Evening Star*, a freight locomotive, was used for a

short period in 1960 until the senior management decided that it must be replaced by a more 'suitable' machine.

The *Capitals United Express* was another of the newly-named trains, inaugurated in 1956. It left London for Cardiff at 3.55 pm, using the locomotive that had brought the *up Red Dragon*. The somewhat less euphonious name was reportedly the brainchild of Lord Mancroft, a Junior Minister with responsibility for Welsh affairs in the Government of the day.[31] Although the train's headboard just bore the coats of arms of London and Cardiff to symbolise its official status, it continued to west Wales, speeding through Briton Ferry at 8.55 pm. The empty stock was returned from Fishguard to Cardiff the next day by a Goodwick locomotive, frequently Mogul *6347*. It paused in the loop at Briton Ferry at 4.50 pm to allow yet an even superior titled train, the *South Wales Pullman*, to pass.

For many years passenger services between Paddington and Swansea were not particularly noted for speed. However, things changed in 1953 with the introduction of a new express leaving the capital at 10.55 am. This train was the *Pembroke Coast Express*. Within a year it had become the fastest of all the south Wales services taking just 128 minutes for the 133.4 miles from London to Newport and reaching Swansea in three and three-quarter hours. Its thirteen chocolate and cream coaches buzzed through Briton Ferry at 2.20 pm with one of Landore's finest

4-6-0 *6003 King George IV* waits to take over the *up Red Dragon* at Cardiff General Station for its journey to Paddington, 1960 *(Colour Rail)*

The South Wales Pullman at Briton Ferry (*John Hodge*)

*The Pembroke Coast Express* behind *4094 Dynevor Castle* passes Briton Ferry 27th June 1960 (*John Hodge*)

The last steam-hauled Pullman (Alun Hutchinson)

locomotives. Six of its coaches continued to Pembroke Dock, with the remaining vehicles, including the restaurant car, being detached at Swansea. The service necessitated four engine changes. The *up* train glanced Briton Ferry at 4.05 pm with another of Landore's silver-buffered *Castles* at its head. Martin Davies regularly encountered this train as he walked home from Baglan primary school in the late 1950s before dropping into Stones café[32] for some liquorice or ice cream.

The last of the four named expresses serving the Swansea area was the *South Wales Pullman* of 1955. Unlike the other railway companies, the GWR had an uneasy relationship with the independent Pullman company, the doyen of luxury train travel. Thus the GWR preferred to develop its own in-house service and introduced the *Torquay Pullman* in 1929 and a transatlantic service to Plymouth, aimed at the tourist market.

In contrast, the *South Wales Pullman*, made up

The Blue Pullman at Port Talbot (R Reed)

of eight heavy Pullman vehicles, was aimed at the business market. The growing industrial and commercial development of south Wales in the 1950s suggested that there would be sufficient demand for a luxury dining service. A special feature was the *Daffodil Bar* in the *Diamond* car with an attractive lady attendant in Pullman uniform. For many years the Pullman consisted of three first class cars which bore the names *Diamond*, *Cecilia*, and *Zena*.[33] Its five second class vehicles simply bore numbers 27, 35, 55 and 171, but the standard of comfort, hospitality and catering was second to none for both. The trains were hauled by a *Castle* in prime condition, (often Landore's finest) on the depot's 'star turn'.

Briton Ferry passengers using the Pullman needed to change at Port Talbot or Neath, where they paid a supplement of ten shillings (first class) or five shillings (second class) on top of the normal fare, to be served meals and refreshments at every seat. The *up* train passed through Briton Ferry at 4.55 pm. It was headed by one of Landore's best *Castles*. The *down* train left Paddington at 9.55 am, giving passengers the opportunity to appreciate the beauty of Briton Ferry woods as they worked their way through the lunch-time cheese course.

Altogether, in 1960, Briton Ferry was served by twenty-two *down* trains on weekdays and one train on Sunday. There were twenty-four *up* trains on weekdays, but none on Sunday. In the summer months, the basic service would be augmented by trains running to and from major holiday resorts. Some were day excursions, but others ran regularly on summer Saturdays. These enabled railway enthusiasts to make day trips to such destinations as Bristol and Gloucester, and on the Swansea to New Milton train in search of those steam locomotives rarely seen in south Wales.

The Western Region kept up with the times by investing in three eight-car *Blue Pullman* sets. One replaced the steam-hauled *South Wales Pullman* after Friday 9 September 1961, the last *down* steam-hauled *Pullman* being headed by 5048 *Earl of Devon*. The final *up* working passed Briton Ferry on the same day behind a sparkling 4090 *Dorchester Castle* of Cwrt Sart depot. Richard Burton and Viscount Tonypandy were among the well-known passengers who used the steam-hauled service.[34]

With the introduction of the *Blue Pullman*, the train workings were reversed with the Swansea train now leaving at 6.00 am, reaching Paddington at 10.15 am. The new journey time of three hours thirty-five minutes was the fastest ever recorded between Swansea and London, thirty-five minutes quicker than the steam-hauled train. The *down* train left Paddington at 4.55 pm, reaching Swansea at 8.40

pm. The trains were so well patronised it was decided in 1967 to run an additional *Blue Pullman* trip in each direction. This time the *down* train left Paddington at 9.00 am, thus passing Briton Ferry an hour and forty minutes earlier than the original steam working, with a 12.20 pm arrival in Swansea. The departure in the *up* direction was fifteen minutes earlier than the steam service to reach the capital at 7.45 pm. This pattern of service remained in place until 1973 when all Western Region Pullman workings were abandoned and the *Blue Pullman* coaching stock was scrapped at Ward's, Briton Ferry.

The new HST services from May 1973 were scheduled to operate at speeds up to 125 mph.

### Summer travel in the 1950s and 1960s

It took little more than ten minutes on foot from anywhere in Briton Ferry to reach the station at Rockingham Terrace. That suited everyone in the days before car ownership was commonplace, but it was particularly welcome during summer evenings in school term time when it enabled families and friends to escape to Aberafan beach for an hour or two. In those summers, the sun seemed always to shine. The Treherbert-bound train from Swansea arrived at Briton Ferry at 5.21pm and, by 5.29 pm, had deposited its passengers, usually mothers and young children, at Aberafan Seaside station. Robert Davies of Neath travelled as a boy with his family:

> So many people got off the train at Seaside Station that the driver and fireman had to help the guard to check the tickets, leaving an almost empty train to continue to Treherbert.

Of course, Aberafan beach and Aberafan (Seaside) were not the same thing at all. The use of the name *Seaside* was an old railway trick of giving misleading names for stations to mask their exact location. It seemed to be an interminably long walk from the misleadingly named *Seaside* station to the real Aberafan beach. The length of the walk from station to beach along Victoria Road was probably illusory: it just seemed interminable for youngsters after such a quick train journey. How ironic that the same journey cannot be made as quickly today by car.

The former RSBR line from Briton Ferry to Aberafan Seaside ran across a long stretch of marshy land and large sand dunes. The dunes were gradually disappearing as hundreds of mainly semi-detached houses were being hastily erected to house the workers at the expanding Steel Company of Wales at Margam. It seemed a shame to lose the dunes

Porthcawl train pauses at Briton Ferry behind pannier tanker *(Watercolour by Martin Davies)*

because, even as young children, one would venture there to play. They were no longer an option, but Aberafan beach was.

People from Briton Ferry made great use of the former RSBR during the summer months. In the 1950s, when money was scarce and car ownership very limited, families from 'the Ferry' and elsewhere would crowd on to platforms and pile onto the train to Aberafan Seaside. At Briton Ferry this was sometimes the 9.18 am from Neath to Treherbert which arrived at 9.23. In the early 1950s, co-author Martin Davies travelled with his mother, cousin Vicki, Auntie Evelyn and younger sister Andrea, then a baby in a pram, from the still-occupied wartime 'prefabs' in Wern Bank to the station. They travelled in the guard's van of a train full of beachgoers with buckets, spades, bags of luncheon meat, corned beef sandwiches, glass bottles of *Tizer – the Appetiser* or *Our Boys'* dandelion and burdock pop. After a day of sandcastles, ice cream and 'all the fun of the fair' they retraced their steps to catch the 6-26 pm train to Briton Ferry or elsewhere.

Aberafan Seaside station in 1960 with a DMU in the platform and a pannier tank shunting the goods yard.
*(Courtesy of the Great Western Trust)*

*5601* of Abercynon at the head of the empty coaching stock for a Rhondda valley to Aberafan Seaside excursion at Briton Ferry yard 1959. *(Martin Davies)*

Trains would normally be hauled by nothing more glamorous than a *56xx* tank engine, the sort specially designed to shift the coal from the south Wales valleys. It had no more than three compartment coaches so that you had to choose your compartment and your company before you got on, because you could not change your mind later. To open the heavy doors, you had to lower the window using a long leather strap attached to the door before turning a large brass door handle. Putting your head out of the window for just a few seconds risked receiving an unpleasant eyeful of grit from the hard-working locomotive.

Some kept away from the windows to stare instead at the net rack above the seats where beach bags and such like were stored. Below the rack would usually be a rectangular mirror or railway adverts to encourage passengers to make further visits to such faraway places as Aberystwyth. Often the woven seat covers and the colourful postcard-type adverts still proudly boasted the GWR logo. One well-known poster showed the extent of the GWR network by means of an array of red veins. Another showed a smiling, hard-working uniformed railwayman exhorting youngsters to get *a job on the right lines*. Once the beachgoers were decanted onto the platform at Aberafan, the empty coaches would travel forward to Briton Ferry, where the stock was stored in the station sidings until the trains returned in the evening, no doubt in preparation for the regular weekend excursion trains from the Rhondda.

**At the beach**

There were two beaches at Aberafan, divided by an old breakwater. Most Briton Ferry visitors went to the larger, western beach, presumably because the eastern was a little industrialised and looked onto the iron ore boats creeping in and out of Port Talbot docks.

My two friends, Malcolm John and Raymond Perrett and I made regular trips to Aberafan Beach before and during the war. On one occasion during the war, we were on the beach on a fine day, but we could see a line of clouds approaching rapidly from the south-west which would have brought rain well before the time our train was due to return to Briton Ferry. As we had no protection we decided to walk home through the sand dunes and, hopefully, get home before the rain arrived. We knew there was an army shooting range in the dunes but, as it was marked by a prominent red flag, which we were behind, we felt safe until half way past we heard bullets which obviously had overshot the targets. We flattened ourselves face down into the sand and made a dash when we judged there was a break in the firing whistling over our heads. (Malcolm Hill – *War Memories*)

Aberavon Seaside train at Briton Ferry - Note young mothers using porter's crossing *(Michael Hale)*

## A musical journey

Robert Andrew of Sandfields attended the comprehensive school. A talented musician, he played violin in the school orchestra along with the late Alan Good and Phil Ryan (of *Eyes of Blue* and *Man* fame). Joining the West Glamorgan Schools Orchestra brought him into contact with the railway.

> The orchestra met on a Friday night at the Gwyn Hall in Neath. As I lived in Sandfields it was easy for me to get to Neath from nearby Aberafan Seaside station. Alan, Phil and I travelled together on the train from Treherbert. This left the 'Beach' station about half past six and got us into Neath about quarter-to-seven. It was only a five-minute walk to the Gwyn Hall so we got there in plenty of time. After two hours of music-making we'd shoot off in time for our train home at 9.35 to get us back to Sandfields before ten o'clock.

## Summer services to and from south Wales

The summer timetable also offered a great choice of trains, especially on Saturdays. Many visited popular holiday resorts further afield, taking people on their annual holidays on the traditional 'change-over' day at hotels and guest houses. Tenby was a popular destination for west Midlands residents, where, at the height of summer one was as likely to be greeted on its beaches by the distinctive tones of a Midlander as a Welsh voice. Demand was met by a through train each weekend from Birmingham to Pembroke Dock. Travellers from other parts of the country to 'Little England Beyond Wales' could use the extra trains from Paddington to Pembroke Dock and other west Wales destinations. Conversely, south Walians could travel for their annual holidays to resorts on the south coast of England such as New Milton, or to the popular west of England beaches of Weston-Super-Mare, or Paignton, using the Swansea-to-Kingswear and Carmarthen-to-Weston services. These trains were headed by a variety of interesting locos in the form of anything that a running shed could press into service on a busy summer Saturday.

Lines through Briton Ferry station were hectic on a summer Saturday. As well as the standard return services from Swansea and west Wales to Paddington, Manchester, Bristol, Cheltenham and Penzance, extra trains were run between the regular expresses. Detailed records are available. At Briton Ferry, excluding local passenger trains, thirty-eight *up* trains and twenty-eight *down* trains passed through.

**Table 142** **SWANSEA, NEATH, ABERAVON and TREHERBERT**

**WEEK DAYS ONLY**

| Miles | | am E | am S | am | | am | am | am | am S | | am S | | pm | pm | pm E | pm | pm S | pm S | | pm | pm | pm | |
|---|---|---|---|---|---|---|---|---|---|---|---|---|---|---|---|---|---|---|---|---|---|---|---|
| — | **Swansea** (High St.) .. dep | ② | ② | **7 0** | .. | .. | 8 50 | .. | 1115 | .. | .. | .. | **1 55** | **2 10** | .. | 4 55 | **7 25** | .. | .. | **8 45** | **9 10** | .. | .. |
| 1½ | Landore | | | 7 6 | | | | | | | | | 2 1 | 2 16 | | 5 0 | 7 30 | | | 8 49 | | | |
| 3½ | Llansamlet North | .. | .. | 7 11 | .. | .. | 9 0 | .. | .. | .. | .. | .. | 2 6 | 2 21 | .. | 5 5 | 7 35 | .. | .. | 8 54 | .. | .. | .. |
| 6 | Skewen | | | 7 17 | | | | | | | | | 2 11 | 2 27 | | 5 11 | 7 42 | | | 9 0 | | | |
| 8 | Neath (General) | .. | .. | 7 22 | .. | 7 30 | 9 8 | 9 18 | 1131 | .. | 1138 | .. | 2 20 | 2 35 | .. | 5 16 | 7 47 | 8 15 | .. | 9 5 | 9 25 | 9 35 | .. |
| 10¼ | Briton Ferry | | | | | 7 37 | 9 13 | 9 23 | | | 1144 | | 2 25 | 2 40 | | 5 21 | 7 53 | 8 20 | | | | 9 40 | |
| 13 | Aberavon (Seaside) | .. | .. | .. | .. | 7 48 | .. | 9 30 | .. | .. | 1150 | .. | .. | 2 48 | .. | 5 29 | .. | 8 28 | .. | .. | .. | 9 48 | .. |
| 14 | Aberavon (Town) **A** arr | | | | | 7 53 | | 9 34 | | | 1155 | | | 2 51 | | 5 32 | | 8 32 | | | | 9 51 | |
| | Aberavon (Town) **A** dep | .. | .. | .. | .. | 7 55 | .. | 9 36 | .. | .. | 1156 | .. | .. | 2 52 | 4 23 | 5 34 | .. | 8 33 | .. | .. | .. | 9 53 | .. |
| 15¾ | Cwmavon | | | | | 8 0 | | 9 42 | | | 12 4 | | | 2 57 | 4 28 | 5 41 | | 8 40 | | | | 9 59 | |
| 17½ | Pontrhydyfen | .. | .. | .. | .. | 8 8 | .. | 9 49 | .. | .. | 1211 | .. | .. | 3 8 | 4 35 | 5 48 | .. | 8 48 | .. | .. | .. | 10 6 | .. |
| 20½ | Duffryn Rhondda Halt | | | | | 8 17 | | 9 58 | | | 1220 | | | 3 19 | 4 44 | 5 58 | | 8 56 | | | | 1015 | |
| 21¾ | Cymmer Afan | 7 33 | 7 37 | .. | .. | 8 24 | .. | 10 5 | .. | .. | 1226 | .. | .. | 3 25 | 4 50 | 6 5 | .. | 9 2 | .. | .. | .. | 1020 | .. |
| 24 | Blaengwynfi | 7 40 | 7 45 | | | 8 30 | | 1010 | | | 1234 | | | 3 33 | 4 55 | 6 10 | | 9 8 | | | | 1026 | |
| 27 | Blaenrhondda | 7 49 | 7 55 | .. | .. | 8 41 | .. | 1020 | .. | .. | 1244 | .. | .. | 3 42 | 5 5 | 6 19 | .. | 9 19 | .. | .. | .. | 1035 | .. |
| 27¾ | **Treherbert** arr | **7 52** | **7 58** | | | **8 44** | | **1023** | | | **1247** | | | **3 45** | **5 8** | **6 23** | | **9 22** | | | | **1039** | |
| 35½ | 125 Porth arr | 8 31 | 8 31 | .. | .. | 9 21 | .. | 1051 | .. | .. | 1 16 | .. | .. | 4 16 | 5 51 | 6 51 | .. | 9 51 | .. | .. | .. | 11 4 | .. |
| 38¾ | 125 Pontypridd " | 8 41 | 8 41 | | | 9 31 | | 11 1 | | | 1 26 | | | 4 27 | 6 1 | 7 1 | | 10 1 | | | | 1115 | |

| Miles | | am S | am E | am | am | am | am E | am S | | pm | pm E | pm | | pm | pm B | pm E | pm | pm | pm | pm E | pm | pm S | pm S |
|---|---|---|---|---|---|---|---|---|---|---|---|---|---|---|---|---|---|---|---|---|---|---|---|
| | 125 Pontypridd .. .. dep | 6 36 | 7 10 | .. | .. | 8 36 | 1036 | 1036 | .. | .. | .. | 1 36 | .. | 4 52 | .. | 5 28 | .. | 6 36 | .. | .. | 9 36 | 9 36 | 1040 |
| | 125 Porth " | 6 47 | 7 21 | | | 8 47 | 1047 | 1047 | | | | 1 47 | | 5 3 | | 5 37 | | 6 47 | | | 9 47 | 9 47 | 1051 |
| — | **Treherbert** .. .. dep | **7 18** | **7 50** | .. | .. | **9 30** | **1125** | **1125** | .. | .. | .. | **2 32** | .. | **5 40** | .. | **6 4** | .. | **7 20** | .. | .. | **1015** | **1030** | 1118 |
| ¾ | Blaenrhondda | 7 21 | 7 53 | | | 9 34 | 1128 | 1128 | | | | 2 35 | | 5 44 | | 6 7 | | 7 23 | | | 1018 | 1034 | 1121 |
| 3¾ | Blaengwynfi | 7 30 | 8 9 | .. | .. | 9 44 | 1138 | 1138 | .. | .. | .. | 2 45 | .. | 5 53 | .. | .. | .. | 7 33 | .. | .. | .. | 1043 | .. |
| 6 | Cymmer Afan | 7 38 | 8 14 | | | 9 50 | 1144 | 1144 | | | | 2 53 | | 6 0 | | | | 7 40 | | | | 1050 | |
| 7¼ | Duffryn Rhondda Halt | 7 42 | 8 18 | .. | .. | 9 55 | 1148 | 1148 | .. | .. | .. | 2 57 | .. | 6 3 | .. | .. | .. | 7 44 | .. | .. | .. | 1054 | .. |
| 10¼ | Pontrhydyfen | 7 52 | 8 26 | | | 10 4 | 1156 | 1156 | | | | 3 5 | | 6 12 | | | | 7 52 | | | | 11 4 | |
| 12 | Cwmavon | 8 2 | 8 33 | .. | .. | 1010 | 12 3 | 12 3 | .. | .. | .. | 3 11 | .. | 6 18 | .. | .. | .. | 7 58 | .. | .. | .. | 1110 | .. |
| 13¾ | Aberavon (Town) **A** arr | 8 9 | 8 41 | | | 1018 | 1211 | 1211 | | | | 3 19 | | 6 26 | | | | 8 6 | | | | 1119 | |
| | Aberavon (Town) **A** dep | 8 10 | 8 42 | .. | .. | 1020 | 1212 | 1212 | .. | .. | .. | 3 20 | .. | 6 27 | .. | .. | .. | 8 7 | .. | .. | .. | 1122 | .. |
| 14¾ | Aberavon (Seaside) | 8 14 | 8 45 | | | 1024 | 1218 | 1218 | | | | 3 24 | | 6 32 | | | | 8 12 | | | | | |
| 17½ | Briton Ferry | 8 27 | 8 53 | 9 0 | 9 9 | 1033 | 1230 | 1232 | .. | 2 2 | 2 25 | 3 33 | .. | 6 40 | .. | .. | 7 22 | 8 20 | .. | 8 47 | .. | .. | .. |
| 19¾ | Neath (General) | 8 34 | 9 0 | 9 7 | 9 15 | 1043 | 1238 | 1240 | | 2 8 | 2 30 | 3 40 | | 6 47 | 7 1 | | 7 28 | 8 27 | 8 43 | 8 55 | | 1140 | |
| 21¾ | Skewen | .. | .. | .. | 9 22 | 1049 | .. | 1246 | .. | .. | 2 34 | 3 45 | .. | .. | .. | .. | 7 33 | .. | .. | 9 0 | .. | .. | .. |
| 24¼ | Llansamlet North | | | | 9 28 | 1055 | | 1251 | | 2 16 | 2 40 | 3 50 | | | | | 7 39 | | | 9 5 | | | |
| 26¼ | Landore | .. | .. | .. | 9 34 | .. | .. | 1257 | .. | .. | 2 45 | 3 55 | .. | .. | .. | .. | 7 44 | .. | .. | 9 10 | .. | .. | .. |
| 27¾ | **Swansea** (High St.) .. arr | | | **9 26** | **9 40** | **11 5** | **1255** | **1 6** | | **2 30** | **2 54** | **4 3** | | | **7 21** | | **7 50** | | **9 5** | **9 17** | | | |

**A** About ½ mile from Port Talbot (General) Station

**B** Will not run from 6th November to 16th December, 1961 and 15th January to 31st March, 1962 inclusive

**E** or E Except Saturdays
**S** Saturdays only
② Second class only

**LOCAL TRAINS between Swansea and Briton Ferry, see Table 104**

**For additional trains between Blaengwynfi and Cymmer Afan, see Table 134**

A Neath to Treherbert timetable, 1961

These include express passenger, stopping trains, fish, milk, mail and parcels' trains.

The first train of the day was the *down* Mail train from Bristol to Neyland which arrived at Briton Ferry at 4.11 am. The earliest *up* train was the 3.25 am Fishguard-to-Paddington boat train, an addition to the timetable to cope with the extra passengers crossing from Ireland at that time of year. This train steamed through Briton Ferry at 5.50 am, as dawn was breaking. The regular service, the 3.55 am from Fishguard, reached Briton Ferry some thirty minutes later, hauled from Llanelli by *Earl of Ducie* and by-passing Swansea by using the District line.

The busiest period for eastbound trains was between 8.30 am and 10.00 am, when nine, mainly holiday, trains passed through, sometimes only ten minutes apart. The last *up* train recorded that day was the 8.30 pm Whitland-to-Kensington milk, which joined the main line at 10-55 pm. The last down train was the 8-30 pm empty stock working from Paignton to Swansea which steamed through in the dead of the night behind *Guild Hall*.

The motive power used on trains passing Briton Ferry on Saturday 9 July 1960 is shown in the table on page 83.

The 9.05 am Swansea to Kingswear service, which reached Briton Ferry at 9.30 am, was a convenient train for train-spotters who were heading for a day's *ferro-equinology*[35] in Bristol, enabling them to arrive there at a reasonable time without a change at Cardiff. Train-spotters travelling further afield to Bath or Gloucester departed on the 7.05 am diesel from Briton Ferry. Martin Davies' father picked up his friends from Baglan in his Commer Cob plumber's van to get to the station. They sat on copper pipes, reels of solder, and brass fittings for the journey sometimes leaving with coverings of *Swarfega*[36]. All carried duffle bags containing delicacies for the day, such as beef-burger sandwiches, with *Wilbur* carrying a large lump of salt in his glasses case to spice up his pork pie.

In the late 1950s the *Swansea and District Holi-*

## Table 104—continued

## LONDON, SWINDON, BADMINTON, BRISTOL, NEWPORT, CARDIFF, SWANSEA, CARMARTHEN, TENBY, NEYLAND and FISHGUARD HARBOUR

| | pm | pm | pm | pm | pm | pm | pm | pm | pm | pm | pm | pm | pm | pm | pm | pm | pm | | pm | pm | pm | pm |
|---|---|---|---|---|---|---|---|---|---|---|---|---|---|---|---|---|---|---|---|---|---|---|
| 61 PADDINGTON dep | .. | 4 55 | .. | .. | .. | .. | .. | .. | .. | 5 31 | 5 43 | .. | 5 48 | .. | 5 55 | .. | .. | .. | 6 55 | .. | .. | .. |
| 61 Reading General „ | .. | | | | | | | | | | | | | | | | | | 7 36 | | | |
| 61 Oxford .. .. .. dep | .. | | .. | .. | .. | .. | 5 5 | .. | .. | 5 52 | | | | | .. | .. | .. | | 6H39 | .. | .. | .. |
| 61 Didcot ........ dep | .. | | | .. | .. | .. | 6 | 6†22 | .. | 6 45 | | | | | .. | .. | .. | | | | | |
| 61 Swindon .. .. arr | .. | | | .. | .. | .. | 6 47 | .. | .. | | | | | | 7 23 | .. | .. | | | | | |
| Swindon .. .. .. dep | .. | | | .. | .. | .. | .. | .. | .. | .. | | | | | 7 27 | .. | .. | | | | | |
| Badminton .. .. .. „ | .. | | | .. | .. | .. | .. | .. | .. | | | | | | 7 56 | .. | .. | | | | | |
| Bristol (T.M.) Z dep | .. | 6 20 | .. | .. | .. | .. | .. | .. | 7L20 | | | | | | 8 5 | .. | .. | .. | 9L 5 | | | |
| Lawrence Hill .. „ | .. | 6 25 | .. | .. | .. | .. | .. | .. | 7L25 | | | | | | 8 10 | .. | .. | .. | 9L10 | | | |
| Stapleton Road .. „ | .. | 6 29 | .. | .. | .. | .. | .. | .. | 7 36 | | | | | | 8 14 | .. | .. | .. | 9 24 | | | |
| Filton Junction .. „ | .. | 6 40 | .. | .. | .. | .. | .. | .. | | | | | | | 8 21 | .. | .. | .. | | | | |
| Patchway ........ dep | .. | 6 44 | .. | .. | .. | .. | .. | .. | | | | | | | 8 24 | .. | .. | .. | | | | |
| Pilning (High Level) .. | .. | 6 50 | .. | .. | .. | .. | .. | .. | | | | | | | 8 30 | .. | .. | .. | | | | |
| Severn Tunnel Junc... arr | .. | 7 1 | .. | .. | .. | .. | .. | .. | 8 4 | | | | | | 8 41 | .. | .. | .. | 9 54 | | | |
| 179 Wolverhampton(LL)dep | .. | | 4 35 | .. | .. | .. | .. | .. | | | | 4 55 | | | .. | .. | .. | | .. | | | |
| 179 Birmingham (S.H.) „ | .. | | 5 5 | .. | .. | .. | .. | .. | | | | 5 40 | | | .. | .. | .. | | .. | | | |
| 105 Cheltenham Spa A „ | .. | | 6†19 | .. | .. | .. | .. | .. | | | | | | | .. | 7 30 | .. | | 7 48 | | | |
| 105 Gloucester Cen... „ | .. | | 6 35 | | .. | .. | .. | .. | 6s40 | | | | | | .. | 7 55 | .. | | 8 22 | | | |
| Severn Tunnel Junc... dep | .. | | 7 3 | .. | 7 28 | .. | .. | .. | 8 5 | | | | | 8 43 | 8 59 | .. | .. | | 9 30 | .. | 9 55 | |
| Undy Halt ............ | .. | | | | 7 30 | .. | .. | .. | | | | | | | 9 5 | .. | .. | | 9 36 | .. | | |
| Magor .. .. .. .. „ | .. | | | | 7 33 | .. | .. | .. | | | | | | | 9 17 | .. | .. | | 9 47 | .. | 1012 | |
| Newport arr | .. | 7 27 | 177 27 | .. | 7 45 | .. | .. | .. | 8 19 | 8 29 | 8 37 | 8 44 | 8 57 | 9 17 | | 9 31 | 9 47 | | 1017 | | | |
| dep | .. | 7 47 | 207 29 | .. | | 7 50 | .. | .. | 8 23 | 8 31 | 8 40 | 8 48 | 9 2 | 9 21 | | 9 35 | 9 50 | | | | | |
| arr | .. | 7 20 | 377 45 | .. | | Stop8 10 | .. | .. | 8 41 | 8 48 | 9 0 | 9 6 | 9 20 | 9 37 | | 9 51 | 10 8 | | 1035 | | | |
| Cardiff (General).. dep | 7 15 | 7 25 | .. | 7 48 | .. | .. | 8 20 | .. | 8 55 | | | 9 15 | | 9 30 | | 10 0 | 10 20 | 1020 | | | | |
| Ely (Main Line) .. .. | .. | | | | | | | | | | | | | | | | | | | | | |
| St. Fagans .. .. .. | .. | | | | | | | | | | | | | | | | | | | | | |
| Llantrisant ............ | 7 29 | | | | | | 8 35 | | | | | | | 9 45 | | 10 34 | 1034 | | | | | |
| Llanharan .. .. .. „ | 7 34 | | | | | | 8 42 | | | | | | | 9 50 | | 10 40 | 1040 | | | | | |
| Pencoed .............. | 7 39 | | | | | | 8 51 | | | | | | | 9 55 | | 10 45 | 1045 | | | | | |
| Bridgend .. .. .. „ | 7 45 | 7 49 | .. | 8 15 | | | 9 t 0 | | | | | 9 t48 | | 10 3 | | 10 52 | 1052 | | | | | |
| Pyle .. .. .. .. .. | .. | | | | | | 9 10 | | | | | | | | | 11 10 | 1110 | | | | | |
| Port Talbot (General) K | .. | 8 t10 | .. | 8 30 | 8 40 | | 9 21 | | 9d43 | | | 10 t 8 | | | | 11 10 | 1110 | | | | | |
| Briton Ferry .. .. .. | .. | | | | 8 47 | | 9 27 | | | | | | | | | | | | | | | |
| Neath (General) .. .. | .. | | 8 43 | 8 55 | | | 9 33 | | 9 t55 | | | 10 t20 | | | | 11 18 | 1118 | | | | | |
| Skewen .. .. .. .. | .. | | | 9 0 | | | 9 38 | | | | | | | | | | | | | | | |
| Llansamlet North .. .. | .. | | | 9 5 | | | 9 43 | | | | | | | | | | | | | | | |
| Landore ............ | .. | | | 9 10 | | | 9 48 | | | | | | | | | | | | | | | |
| Swansea (High St.) arr | .. | 8 40 | .. | 9 59 | 9 17 pm | | 9 55 | .. | 1015 | | | 10 40 | | | | 11 8 | 11 38 | 1138 | | | | |
| dep | .. | | .. | .. | 9 30 | | .. | .. | | | | 10 45 | | | | 11 14 | | | | | | |
| Cockett .. .. .. .. | .. | | .. | .. | 9 40 | | .. | .. | | | | | | | | | | | | | | |
| Gowerton North .. .. | .. | | .. | .. | 9 45 | | .. | .. | | | | 10 58 | | | | 11 f40 | | | | | | |
| Llanelly ............ | .. | | .. | .. | 9 55 | | .. | .. | | | | 11 t 9 | | | | | | | | | | |
| Pembrey and Burry Port.. | .. | | .. | .. | 10 3 | | .. | .. | | | | 11 17 | | | | | | | | | | |
| Kidwelly .. .. .. .. | .. | | .. | .. | 1012 | | .. | .. | | | | 11 29 | | | | | | | | | | |
| Ferryside ............ | .. | | .. | .. | 1020 | | .. | .. | | | | 11 37 | | | | | | | | | | |
| Carmarthen .. .. arr | .. | | .. | .. | 1030 | | .. | .. | | | | 11 50 | | | | | | | | | | |
| 146 Aberystwyth ..... arr | .. | | .. | .. | | | .. | .. | | | | | | | | | | | | | | |
| Carmarthen .. .. dep | .. | | .. | .. | | | .. | .. | | | | | | | | | | | | | | |
| Sarnau.............. | .. | | .. | .. | | | .. | .. | | | | | | | | | | | | | | |
| St. Clears .. .. .. | .. | | .. | .. | | | .. | .. | | | | | | | | | | | | | | |
| Whitland .. .. .. arr | .. | | .. | .. | | | .. | .. | | | | | | | | | | | | | | |
| 149 Tenby .. .. .. arr | .. | | .. | .. | | | .. | .. | | | | | | | | | | | | | | |
| 149 Pembroke Dock .. „ | .. | | .. | .. | | | .. | .. | | | | | | | | | | | | | | |
| Whitland .. .. .. dep | .. | | .. | .. | | | .. | .. | | | | | | | | | | | | | | |
| Clynderwen ........ | .. | | .. | .. | | | .. | .. | | | | | | | | 12 35 | | | | | | |
| Clarbeston Road 151 .. | .. | | .. | .. | | | .. | .. | | | | | | | | | | | | | | |
| Haverfordwest W...... | .. | | .. | .. | | | .. | .. | | | | | | | | | | | | | | |
| Johnston (Pem.) .. .. | .. | | .. | .. | | | .. | .. | | | | | | | | | | | | | | |
| 148 Milford Haven.. arr | .. | | .. | .. | | | .. | .. | | | | | | | | | | | | | | |
| Neyland .. .. arr | .. | | .. | .. | | | .. | .. | | | | | | | | | | | | | | |
| Fishguard & Goodwick arr | .. | | .. | .. | | | .. | .. | | | | | | | | | | | | | | |
| Fishguard Harbour. „ | .. | | .. | .. | | | .. | .. | | | | | | | | 1 10 | .. | .. | | | | |

For Notes, see page 209

Briton Ferry timetable, 1962

*day Express* ran. It picked up passengers at stations between Swansea and Port Talbot to take day excursionists to one of the local resorts. The locomotive hauling the train was quite distinctive because it had a large circular head-board that ostentatiously covered the whole of the smokebox door. A *Hall* class locomotive such as Landore's *Newton Hall* or *Garth Hall* was often used for this train.

## Other special trains

During the rugby season a procession of excursions hauled by anything from a Landore *Castle* to a Llanelli *Grange* ran from west Wales to Cardiff for the international matches, usually with standing room only from Neath onwards. If anyone from Briton Ferry was lucky enough to get hold of a match

A New Milton to Swansea train passes Baglan
*(Martin Davies)*

*Earl of Ducie (Steam in the Sixties)*

ticket, they caught a 'sardine special' from Briton Ferry. Martin Davies was indeed fortunate when the famous All Blacks team, called *The Invincibles*, played Wales at Cardiff on 21 December, winning six points to nil and featuring such legends as Colin

*Britannia Pacific 70018 Flying Dutchman* pictured at Briton Ferry in 1959. It is recently ex-works and has been stopped light engine opposite the signal box. The driver walks to the signal box to find out the source of the problem
*(Martin Davies)*

*Longworth Manor* was used for the last steam-hauled excursion to Cardiff in 1965 *(Colour Rail)*

Meads, Don Clarke, Waka Nathan and Brian Lahore. Steam locomotives were used on specials to 1965 with the last being for a Wales v England international. The Llandeilo to Cardiff special was hauled by *Longworth Manor*. Wales won by fourteen points to three, but *Longworth Manor* was lost forever a few months later when it was cut up at Bird's scrapyard in Bynea.[37]

## Dieselisation of Passenger Services

Although Briton Ferry had hosted GWR diesel railcars from the 1930s to the 1950s, and diesel multiple units from 1960, most passenger services passing through or calling at Briton Ferry still had steam haulage. Diesels were only used on Swansea to Birmingham and Bristol and Treherbert to Swansea trains.

*5919 Newton Hall* passes Briton Ferry with the *down* Manchester-Swansea train, 27th June 1960 *(John Hodge)*

A line-up of return rugby excursions at Pengam Sidings, Cardiff *(R. O. Tuck)*

*Hymek* main-line diesel locomotives were introduced to replace steam locomotives on the south Wales line in 1962. They progressively took over the steam duties of the *Castles* and *Kings*, but these diesel-hydraulic locomotives suffered from 'teething troubles'. There were many failures in the early years as Tony Griffiths observed at Briton Ferry.

I remember the first week that the *Capitals United Express* had a *Hymek* on it. Only on three of the nights did the *Hymek* manage to complete the journey through to Swansea. On the other nights,

the locos failed and had to be replaced by the nearest steam locomotive available … one night the train had a 2-8-0 *3866*, another night a 42xx tank, *4299*, running bunker first and on Saturday night I think it had the Margam banker, a *94xx* pannier tank complete with head-board!

The *Hymek* was simply not powerful enough to cope with the London trains which required the equivalent power of *Kings* and *Castles*. They were of a size suitable only to replace less powerful *Moguls*, *Manor* and *Halls*.

Steam rescues diesel! A *52xx* 2-8-0 and a *41xx* 2-6-2 tank were commandeered at Severn Tunnel to pull a failed *Hymek* and its Paddington to Swansea train onwards. The ensemble are seen at Newport station in 1962. *(Colour Rail)*

An *'Inter-City 125'* on an *up* London express passes through Briton Ferry in the late 1970s *(Robert Thomas)*

## Beeching's effect on local services

The lesson from these breakdowns was that rushing to eliminate steam locomotives was a mistake. Many of the *Castles* which the *Hymeks* were intended to replace had been taken out of storage and had to be reinstated for 1962 summer timetable. Suitably-powered *Western* class diesels replaced the *Hymeks* from 1963 onwards and soon the capable *Westerns* came to dominate the Paddington to west Wales services. However, they were non-standard designs which did not fit in with British Rail's policy and were to be replaced by the standard, ubiquitous Class 47 diesel-electrics in the late 1970s.

The Beeching Report had a sobering effect on the railways serving Briton Ferry. Passenger numbers had declined during the late 1950s and early 1960s with growing car ownership and more competition from bus services. The last passenger train from Treherbert to Neath was the 10.30 pm departure on 3 December 1962, hauled by 2-6-2 tank *4169*, a regular on this line for a several years. It crossed the last up train, hauled by a *56xx* 0-6-2 tank at Blaenrhondda, before entering the Rhondda tunnel for the last time. Services from Maesteg to Treherbert continued to use it until 1970.[38]

> 'the engine whistled its way all the way from Treherbert to Briton Ferry, and the sound of detonators filled the air,' recalled Tony Griffiths.

On 2 November 1963, passenger services from Swansea to Porthcawl were withdrawn. The resultant decline in revenue from Briton Ferry station, and the smaller numbers using main line services, put its future in the balance. The station was scheduled for closure, along with many of the intermediate stations on the Cardiff to Swansea main line. In November,1964 group members rushed to Briton Ferry station to photograph the last calling train hauled by a *Hymek* type diesel D7036.

## Passenger train services in 2017

Today's National Rail database/timetable shows ten passenger trains scheduled to stop at Briton Ferry for eastbound travel and eight for westbound travel on weekdays.[39] In addition, the timetable offers eight westbound trains which can be boarded at Briton Ferry which, by changing trains at Neath, allows for eastbound travel on trains which do not stop at Briton Ferry. Similarly, five further westbound journeys are possible from Briton Ferry which involve changes at Port Talbot or Swansea to make a westbound journey to the west of Swansea. Two questions arise: firstly, how useful are these trains, both the eighteen which stop at Briton Ferry to get to destination without change of train and the thirteen which require a change? The second question is: why does the latter incur extra costs? 'You need to buy more than one ticket for this journey', says the website. Interestingly, the extra cost applies regardless of whether the change of train involves a second

A Cardiff Central to Builth Road train passes Briton Ferry in the late 1990s headed by a Class 37 diesel *37058*
27th September 1998 (*Robert Thomas*)

train operator. Does this situation arise because of the over-complex ticketing system, or is the answer that customers are intentionally being made to pay for more for an inferior service, or both?

## Strengths and weaknesses of present timetable

The strengths and weaknesses of the present passenger timetable for Swanline services can best be assessed by asking both passengers and non-train users. In preparation for this book a limited survey of train users was completed to determine whether passengers were satisfied or dis-satisfied with the services from Briton Ferry station and the results were as follows.

*Frequency of trains*
Infrequency of trains was the aspect that most passengers disliked. They expressed a wish for an hourly service and were unhappy that no service has been provided on Sundays 'for the last four years'. One shop worker, a regular commuter to Swansea, said she was unable to work on Sundays without a train.

*Fares*
Most passengers held railcards and felt fares were reasonable. One person however, a student, felt fares were 'extortionate'. Most compared train fares favourably with bus fares, possibly implying that bus fares are more expensive. On longer distances, e.g. involving Severn Bridge tolls, one found the train cheaper than car and certainly less stressful.

*Comfort*
A general dis-satisfaction was expressed over inadequate provision of seating because of too-short trains. This was an acute problem during school holidays and at Christmas. Passengers said they could tolerate this on very short journeys only. One passenger who was otherwise quite favourably disposed to using the station had successfully claimed compensation for overcrowding. Another, a grandmother, commented that one design of train was ideal for accessing with a buggy, perhaps an indirect way of meaning that other designs were less convenient. Interviewers observed a large proportion of passengers pulling roller cases of various sizes.

*Punctuality*
This was raised as a concern by one passenger. One of the five trains included in the survey was late.

*Destinations*
The passengers interviewed used the stations for a range of destinations, near and far. One passenger's ultimate destination was New Zealand. For non-local destinations (eg Paignton) passengers welcomed the facility to be able to book seats.

The Capitals United title was one of several applied to important south Wales passenger trains in the 1950s and 1960s

*Connections*

One passenger, travelling to Haverfordwest, stressed the importance of train punctuality for connections. In her case the problem was that the last bus was from Haverfordwest was 18.10, so it was essential for

the 15.55 from Briton Ferry to be on time there.

For this reason, the inter-modal connectivity issues to be considered in Chapter Fourteen are most relevant to an assessment of the strengths and weaknesses of the present timetable.

## Notes for Chapter Four

1. *Cambrian*, 6 April 1877
2. *Cardiff Times*, 19 October 1889
3. *South Wales Daily News*, 6 November 1891
4. *Evening Express*, 27 April 1900
5. See Chapter Eleven for more on this
6. Museums Education Officer for the area in the 1980s
7. Later the site of the Cimla Hotel
8. A replica of which, the 'Prince of Wales' is being constructed at the time of writing
9. O S Nock: *Stars, Kings and Castles*
10. *Western Mail*, 30 May 1871
11. The incident and following events are described in detail in Chapter Twelve
12. *The Rhondda Leader*, 19 December 1903
13. Furness
14. Martin Davies' mother-in-law
15. Knox: *The Unbeaten Track*, 1944, p.20
16. *David Wooderson's War*: BBC Archives
17. Author Martin Davies' father
18. now Ormond Street
19. Tim Bryan: *The Great Western at War*, p.21
20. *GWR Magazine*, April 1940, p.128
21. *Behind the Steam* – Bill Morgan, p.176
22. The Great Western at War – Tim Bryan, p.162
23. *Memories of the Great Western Railway*
24. Ira Llewelyn
25. Philip Adams: *A Most Industrious Town*, p.142

26. *David Wooderson's War*: Part 4, 'Evacuation to Wales (2), BBC Archives).
27. Information accessed 26 June 2017 from *https://museumwales* re Gwyn Briwnant Jones' 1994 painting in its 'Images of Industry' collection
28. Bill Morgan: *Behind the Steam*, p.177–8
29. Morgan, p.180
30. C J Allen: *Titled Trains of the Western Region*
31. C. J. Allen
32. Once a GWR temperance bar.
33. *Zena* is now used on the special Orient Express charter train.
34. The actor, and George Thomas, then Secretary of State for Wales, later Speaker of the House of Commons
35. A humorous translation: 'The study of the iron horse'
36. Goff Carr, Jeff Beer, Alan Thomas, Jeff Jones, Alun Hutchinson, Tony 'Wilbur' Griffiths and Martin Davies were regulars on these outings with Phil Gallagher and Brian Thomas of Sandfields.
37. Robert Thomas reported this train and filmed it.
38. Alun Hutchinson, Godfrey Carr, Anthony (Wilbur) Griffiths, Alan Thomas, Jeff Beer, Jeff Jones and Hugh James, made the trip along with many other local railway enthusiasts.
39. *http://ojp.www.nationalrail.co.uk*; accessed 10 April 2017

Chapter Five

# Industrial Railways

*There is nothing in machinery, there is nothing in embankments and iron bridges and engineering devices to oblige them to be ugly. Ugliness is the measure of imperfection.*

H G Wells

## Introduction

Industrial railways can be distinguished from mainline freight traffic. Industrial railways are those operations carried out on private industrial premises using their own locomotives and, sometimes, equipment. Today's mainline freight comprises two types of traffic: intermodal container traffic, which is a post-steam era development, and trainload freight, whose origins date from the era of steam trains. Trainload freight usually carries metals, oil, construction materials and waste products. Their loads frequently originate from the industrial railways which have an interface with the public network.

Although the term 'trainload freight' was not used for industrial railways, the traffic generated by industrial railways was just that.

The railways of Briton Ferry and district were created during the age of steam power to service the steam-powered metallurgical industries. The raw materials delivered to these industries included coal to generate the steam for processing them. The transport of the end-products and by-products to their places of consumption was almost exclusively the business of the railways. The quays and wharves at Briton Ferry dock and riverside provided the site for many of these activities.

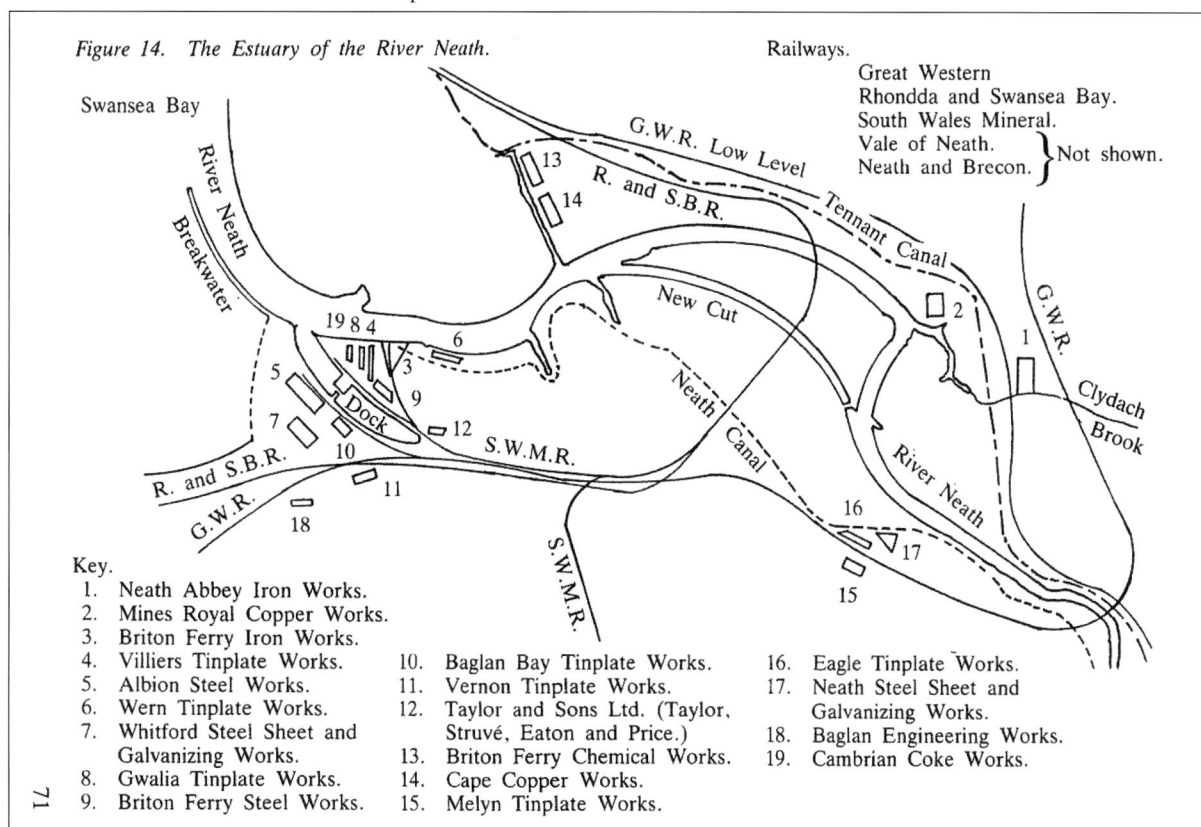

Figure 14. The Estuary of the River Neath.

Railways.
Great Western
Rhondda and Swansea Bay.
South Wales Mineral. } Not shown.
Vale of Neath.
Neath and Brecon.

Key.
1. Neath Abbey Iron Works.
2. Mines Royal Copper Works.
3. Briton Ferry Iron Works.
4. Villiers Tinplate Works.
5. Albion Steel Works.
6. Wern Tinplate Works.
7. Whitford Steel Sheet and Galvanizing Works.
8. Gwalia Tinplate Works.
9. Briton Ferry Steel Works.
10. Baglan Bay Tinplate Works.
11. Vernon Tinplate Works.
12. Taylor and Sons Ltd. (Taylor, Struvé, Eaton and Price.)
13. Briton Ferry Chemical Works.
14. Cape Copper Works.
15. Melyn Tinplate Works.
16. Eagle Tinplate Works.
17. Neath Steel Sheet and Galvanizing Works.
18. Baglan Engineering Works.
19. Cambrian Coke Works.

Industrial establishments in Briton Ferry c1900 *(Roberts)*

Briton Ferry Dock operations, 1965, showing the transition from steam to diesel *(Jeff Jones)*

Therefore most industrial railway operations in the district concerned metallurgical processing of some kind. Most of the operations no longer physically exist, nor as businesses; hence the value of reviewing them here. The following industrial railways were all related to metals processing: Briton Ferry Ironworks; Briton Ferry Steelworks; The Albion Steelworks; The Whitford Sheet Works; Thos W Ward, Giant's Grave; Baglan Foundry and Engineering Co; BP Chemicals, Baglan Bay; Taylor and Sons Foundry; Vernon Tinplate; Metal Box Company and Eaglesbush Works; Cambrian Cokeworks, and coal mining in Baglan.

This chapter concludes with some industrial railway mishaps and a review of the origins of the names of the industrial locomotives.

## The industrial rail interface with the public network

The industrial railway layout of Briton Ferry was largely fashioned in the second half of the nineteenth century by the needs of the new iron, steel and tinplate works that were created around the town's dock, built to Brunel's design. On both eastern and western sides of the dock extensive sidings served local works until the 1950s when the dock closed with its layout being much as it had been for several decades. Nonetheless, on both sides of the dock extensive sidings still served the local works. Briton Ferry's tinplate works also closed in the 1950s to concentrate tinplate manufacture at modern facilities at Trostre and Felindre in west Wales, whereas the Iron Works, the Albion Steelworks, the Whitford Works, and the Wern Aluminium Works remained in full production in 1958.

The retention of the non-tinplate works meant that most of the industrial lines remained in regular use, with GWR pannier tank locomotives used

The dock pilot pannier tank *5720* between duties near Port Wallaroo crossing *(Martin Davies)*

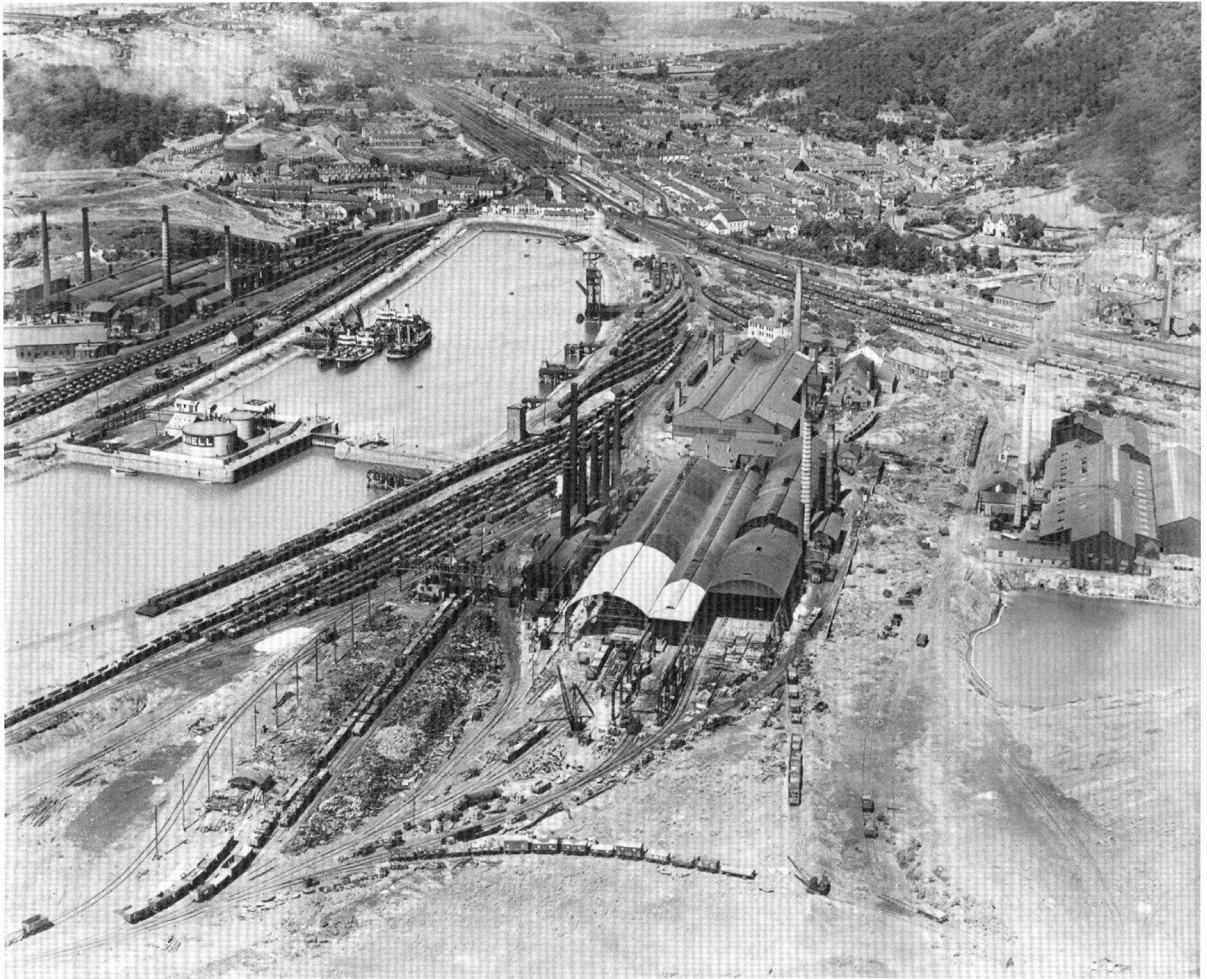

The eastern side of the dock, showing the rail system to the Albion Steel works, Baglan Bay and Whitford works from the south *(RCAHMW)*

The eastern side of the dock, showing the rail system to the Albion Steel works, Baglan Bay and Whitford works from the north *(RCAHMW)*

around the dock to shunt the sidings. Locomotives such as the 'dock pilot' directed wagons, received on the Wallaroo line, to the wharves or to the works where their final movements would be controlled by private industrial locos. The important 'dock pilot', would be parked between shifts at the shunters'

cabin, near the level crossing at Church Street.[1]

A branch line rounded the ironworks following the river bank to the Wern[2] works and Ward's ship-breaking yard at Giant's Grave. This yard provided a source of scrap steel for the Albion steelworks. A further source, in the mid-1960s, was scrap arising from the dismantling of steam locomotives phased out by British Railways. Chapter Ten has more information about the one hundred and fifty or so small tank locos that were scrapped at Giant's Grave.

**Briton Ferry Iron Works**

This was the town's oldest manufacturing enterprise of any significance, opened in 1846, just before the construction of the South Wales Railway and Briton Ferry Dock. Initially a narrow-gauge tramway was built to serve it, enabling horses to pull wheeled ladles of molten slag from the works after the furnaces had been tapped. This method was not converted to locomotive operation until 1882.

The private industrial locomotives which operated in the works of Briton Ferry were largely hidden from public view, so some locomotives were not as

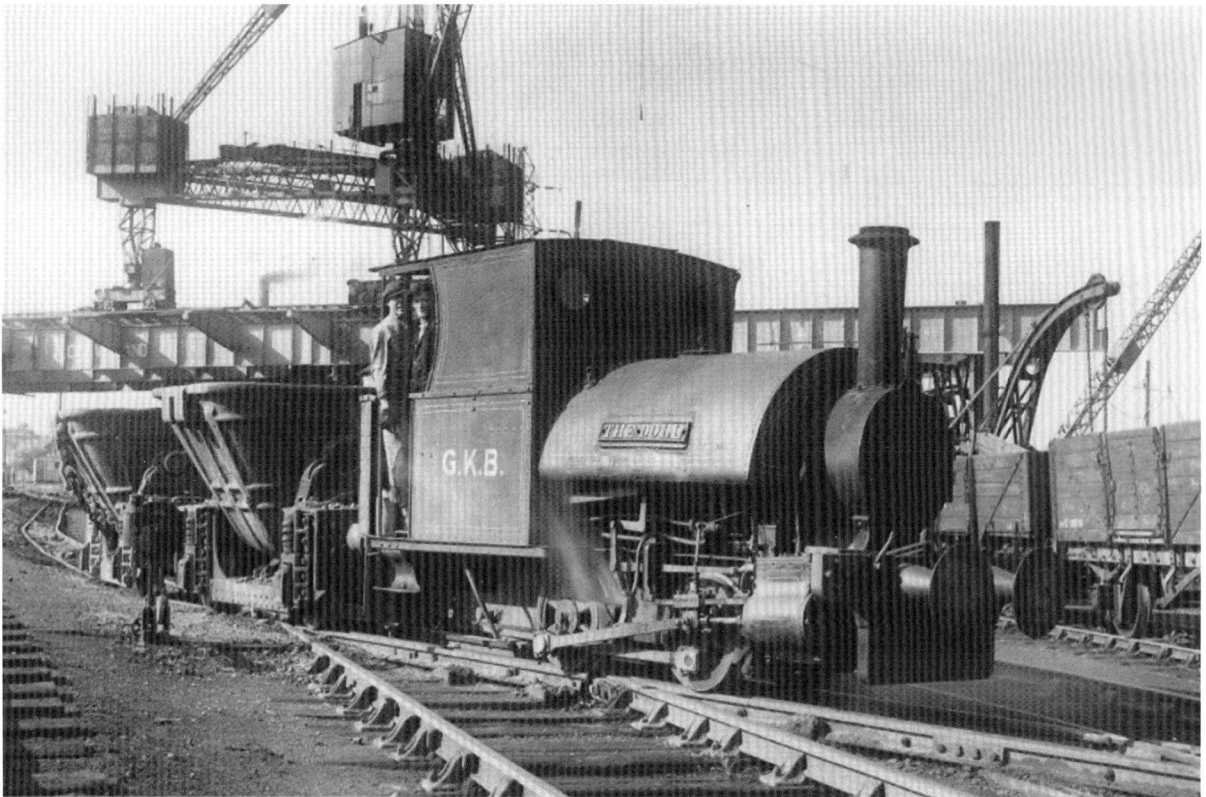

Briton Ferry Ironworks- loco The Doll takes its load of molten slag crosses the standard gauge tracks at Briton Ferry Docks en route to Baglan Bay *(Colwill)*

well known in the town as others. The two originally used for slag removal bore quaint names, one being called *The Dandy,* long before the comic of that name became popular! These were replaced early in the twentieth century by two newer locomotives.

Of these, the smaller was known affectionately to young and old as the *Doll* and the locomotive became part of Briton Ferry folk lore. The duty of the *Doll* and its counterpart was to pull truck-mounted ladles of red-hot slag from the blast furnaces at the ironworks to a desolate spot on the moors at Baglan, where they would tip their contents down an enormous bank of slag. If you stood close enough whilst it was passing, and one often did, the heat from the ladles was palpable. So too was one's nervous feeling that the ladle might suddenly swivel on its trunnions and engulf the observers in molten slag. Such accidents had been seen by the public on its tortuous route.

From the furnaces, the route passed the north end of the dock at Dock Street, visible to all. The toy-like narrow-gauge locos then bravely passed among their larger, standard gauge brethren, even crossing the RSBR lines to reach its destination. When the locomotive stopped and the crew alighted from the cab to clear the train's path at a pedestrian level crossing near the Vernon tinplate works it was a favourite spot, especially for children:

We thought of the docks as adventurous ... as we picked our way over the tangle of rail lines from the steel and tinplate works, peering into the parked trucks, stopping to watch[3] the Dolly pulling its loads.

The crossing gates shut off the Wallaroo line from vehicular traffic whereas the footbridge was for pedestrian protection from traffic on both the narrow gauge industrial line and the Wallaroo line. Martin Davies' poem, *The Ballad of The Doll*, depicts the feelings many townspeople experienced when in the proximity of *The Doll*.

See *The Doll* coming down the track,
Better step aside, better stand back,
Its ladles of slag, rock from side to side
And driving *The Doll* is no easy ride.

It chugs along as it makes its way,
From the Iron Works to Baglan Bay,
Furnace waste to reclaim the land,
Tipping slag on the dunes of sand.

Between the Old Steel and Warren Hill,
Like a toy train, but with power to kill,
Some poor souls found no way back,

BFW No 5 *(Industrial locos of West Glamorgan)*

Ironworks narrow gauge near Port Wallaroo Crossing early 1950s, prior to building the first Briton Ferry road bridge
*(Robert Davies)*

When *The Doll's* load came off the track.
Snaking round past the shunters hut,
Port Wallaroo crossing gates are shut
From the foot bridge, if you look below,
A moving inferno, a red-hot glow.

Heat is rising from the molten mass,
You're secretly glad to see it pass.
*The Doll* turns east to cross the tracks,
The ladles are still rocking forth and back.

A Coughlin driving *The Doll*, 1932 *(G Williams)*

The western side of the dock, showing the rail system to the Ironworks, Villiers tinplate and Old Steel works from the south *(RCAHMW)*

The western side of the dock from the north. Villiers and Gwalia tinplate and 'Old Steel' works *(RCAHMW)*

Around the Dock on a narrow route,
Chugging past the Albion, hear the toot,
Warning everyone, *keep out of the way*,
Near the subway at the end of the day.

The little engine with its lethal load,
Comes to a halt at the end of the road,

The ladles are tipped without delay,
And more land is made, out in the bay.

But that took place before fifty-nine,
When furnaces were tapped for the very last time,
No more iron, no more slag taken by rail,
The days of *The Doll*, now an old Ferry tale.

Ira Llewellyn's vivid memories of the *Doll* arise from his time working in the Albion steelworks:

Twice a day *The Doll* would run to the tip, once in the day and once at night. The Dolly line ran at the top of the docks. Going to work you would walk under the subway which passed under the main line near where the roundabout is today. It had a low ceiling, so you had to crouch as you walked through. The line ran past the works end of the subway. On a night shift, you'd see the whole sky light up and you'd know the Dolly was tipping.

Storage of withdrawn locos at Briton Ferry Docks sidings before scrapping *(Jeff Jones)*

Albion steelworks in the 1970s *(Martin Davies)*

Clive Reed, despite living some two miles away at Moorland Road, Neath could also say:

> When playing outdoors in the summer we could see the evening sky light up with a red glow. We knew then that the *Doll* had discharged its molten slag out on Baglan Bay.

The rail system to the ironworks followed the docks to the western side. A branch line served the Old Steel, Gwalia tinplate and Cambrian Coke works[4] from which the principal line followed the Neath river bank to the Wern works and Wards shipbreaking yard at Giant's Grave.

As well as the narrow-gauge line, the ironworks was served by a standard gauge line for removing pig iron from the works. It came off the spur from the Port Wallaroo branch, which served the coal hoists on the west side of the Dock. In the 1860s the works used *Mountaineer*, an articulated 0-4-4-0 tank locomotive, for shunting until replaced by two conventional 0-4-0 saddle tanks in the 1890s. One was named GHD, which were the initials of George Henry Davey, a well-known Briton Ferry industrialist and a director of the works at the time.

The last loco in use was a Peckett 0-4-0 *Doreen* which had been obtained from nearby, closed Briton Ferry steelworks and subsequently sold to T W Ward when the iron works itself closed in 1959. However, the rail network remained in place after the ironwork's blast furnaces were demolished – a scene witnessed by groups of townsfolk from a vantage point on Warren Hill. In the mid-1960s the lines were used to store withdrawn steam locomotives bound for the local scrapyards.

## Briton Ferry Steelworks

This independent works was opened in 1893 on the west bank of the dock close to the Briton Ferry Ironworks. The company was taken over by Richard Thomas and Baldwins, who ran it until closure in 1951. *The Old Steel*, as it was known locally, had five open hearth furnaces and was so named because it preceded the Albion steelworks on the opposite side of the dock. It too was served by the Port Wallaroo branch line from near Briton Ferry signal box, traversing Church Street at its level crossing, to run along the western side of the dock.

Shortly after the crossing, a spur ran to Giant's Grave from which the old steel was accessed. It had fourteen sidings, four of which ran inside the plant. The works opened with one locomotive, a small Peckett 0-4-0 named *Martha*, supplied new in 1893.[6] A second loco called *Roy* was obtained ten years later for the higher traffic levels generated by increased steel output. Two others, *Lindsey* and *Doreen*, supplied by Peckett and Son, Bristol, were added

*Albion No 1 (Jeff Jones)*

93

*Herbert Eccles (Jeff Jones)*

between 1912 and 1920. A fifth, *Albion No 2* was a transfer from the Albion steelworks. The restructuring of the steel industry in 1951 led to the closure and dismantling of the works.

Following the closure *Doreen* was transferred to Briton Ferry Ironworks, while *Roy* was bought by T W Ward. The others were scrapped. The works' sidings remained in use for wagon storage and, in the mid-1960s, acted as 'stop-off points' for withdrawn steam locomotives, heading for local scrapyards.

### The Albion steelworks

The Albion steelworks on the south-eastern side of Briton Ferry Dock opened in 1895 with eight open-hearth furnaces. It was acquired by Briton Ferry Steel Company in 1914 and during the war came under French Government control to manufacture steel for munitions. A new rolling mill was built in 1934 which remained busy for most of its existence. As the major employer in the town, it employed 1,050 in its heyday, becoming a wholly-owned subsidiary of Duport Steel Ltd in 1956.

*Albion No 12 (Jeff Jones)*

The works was served by a branch line which ran from Briton Ferry station yard to the east side of the dock. Three spurs came off this branch, one lead-ing to the sidings adjacent to the main line, another to the Whitford Steelworks, and a third to the Baglan Bay tinplate works. The branch then split into two tracks alongside the Albion steelworks, one for materials moving in, and the other for the outward shipment of finished steel billets. Eleven sidings were used for storage by the works, with other tracks leading into the plant itself and its locomotive shed. The sidings running to the coal hoists provided extra space for wagon storage when the dock ceased shipping coal.

The earliest records[7] of steam locomotives at the works date from 1911, even though unknown steam locos were used previously. In that year, two locomotives were delivered by Andrew Barclay of Kilmarnock, being designated *Albion No 2* and *Albion No 3*. Presumably an *Albion No 1* was previously used. In any event these were joined by a new *Albion No 1* in 1916, supplied by Peckett of Bristol.

These locos were the mainstay of the fleet until 1935, when they were joined by a new loco called *Herbert Eccles*.

*Albion No 2* was transferred to the *Old Steel*. *Albion No 1* was still in regular use well into the 1960s. The policy of naming locos after the directors of the company continued when *John Bevan* appeared a year later. Both came from locomotive builder Beyer Peacock of Manchester, the company that built the famous Beyer-Garratt articulated locomotives and, later, the short-lived Hymek main line diesels for British Railways' Western Region. After the Second World War the output of steel from the works increased and the greater volume of rail traffic meant that more motive power was required. Two new larger 0-4-0 locomotives were acquired. They were boringly called *Albion No 10* and *Albion No 12*.

Perhaps the fashion for appelation ended in 1951 because the names of private Briton Ferry Steel Co Ltd directors were no longer *de rigueur* under the nationalised Iron and Steel Corporation of Great Britain. But it remains a mystery why there wasn't an *Albion No 11* or why the numbers jumped from *Albion No 3* to *10*!

The line of promotion for railworkers within the steelworks was a simple one: from shunter to driver. Eddie Hutchinson[8] followed this line to engine driver until retirement. He represented the company's cricket club in the 1930s and 1940s being a superb fielder.

Locomotives were maintained in an engine shed by a staff of qualified fitters. Ira Llewellyn, another fine cricketer for the club, was a fitter and turner in the shed whose tasks included making small replacement parts for the locomotives.

Gerald Langham was the last driver employed at

the Albion steelworks. He was born into a railway family. Gerald started as a carpenter at Duffryn Yard, serving as part of the breakdown crew before he became a driver at the Albion until the works closed in 1978. His nephew, Jeff Jones, whose grandfather worked at Cwrt Sart shed, visited him at work in the sixties and seventies.

> He regularly worked on *Albion No 1*, *Herbert Eccles* and *Albion No 12*, but really enjoyed being at the controls of the diesel shunters which replaced the steam locos in the late 1960s. From time to time he would drive the crane to dismantle steam locos at the nearby Slag Reduction site when *Cadbury Castle* was being scrapped there, the only *Castle* to be broken up locally. He managed to save some odd pieces of equipment from the loco including the brass plaque from the cab detailing modifications to the loco such as the fitting of a double chimney. I still have this plaque at home.

In 1959 the Albion had its first diesel on trial,[9] but it was unsuccessful, so the company instead purchased two used diesels from the Steel Company of Wales at Margam and a new loco from Ruston and Hornsby. For the last few years of their existence *Albion Nos 10* and *12* ran as oil-burners as an economy measure. Although they looked ungainly with the oil tanks perched on top of their cabs, the conversion from coal to oil possibly extended their working lives until their scrapping on-site in the late 1960s. Diesel shunters were bought from British Railways to replace them, only to be transferred to Duport's Llanelli steelworks in 1978 when the Albion works closed.

## The Whitford Works

Whitford Steel Sheet and Galvanising Company Ltd was constructed in 1909 on the eastern side of the Dock to the east of the Albion steelworks. The plant was served by a spur off the branch from Briton Ferry station goods yard to the Albion steelworks. Of five sidings, two ran into the works and one linked to the Albion.

An unusual feature of the works, because it was close to the shoreline, was the three tidal pools' often used by local people as an alternative to Baglan sands. These were known as *The Cabbage* (due to its shape), *the Favourite* and *The Midnight Pool*. They were replenished by the incoming tide and, being only five or six- foot deep, were regarded as being safe for children to bathe in. Many *Ferryites* learned to swim in their waters.

Albion No 10 as an oil burner *(Jeff Jones)*

Eddie Hutchinson *(Margery Lewis)*

Albion diesel D8 *(Robert Thomas)*

*Raven at the Whitford works (Alun Hutchinson)*

Diesel picking up wagons from Ward's interchange sidings, early 1980s *(Robert Thomas)*

The works produced steel black plate and corrugated galvanised roofing sheet from 1911. With a second war impending, from 1938 to 1940, it made Anderson air raid shelters for countrywide distribution, but during World War Two itself, it was requisitioned by the government for dismantling tanks. In 1946, it returned to the production of steel sheet until closure in 1951, when most of its workforce transferred to Port Talbot's Abbey Works. Yet the works re-opened for the assembly of jerry cans and, later, rolling corrugated steel sheets. Finally, it became a stocking and processing depot for reclaiming material from Ebbw Vale Strip Mill. Its history of closure and reopening earned it the nickname locally as the *Umbrella* works!

Diesel passing Port Wallaroo crossing with Ward's wagons *(Robert Thomas)*

A Ward's loco picking up bolsters at Briton Ferry dock *(Robert Thomas)*

ROF 7 No 6 was used by Wards in the late 1950s and early 1960s *(Brian Owens)*

Alun Hutchinson stands alongside a line-up of pannier tanks at Ward's scrapyard in 1965 *(Jeff Jones)*

Four separate steam locomotives were used by the Whitford works during its existence, with one being used at any time. One of these, *Rainbow*, operated from 1874 until it was scrapped in 1933 and replaced by another Manning Wardle 0-4-0 tank named *Raven*. This locomotive, of 1910 vintage, whose name derived from its previous home at the Raven tinplate works in Glanamman, was the last locomotive and remained operative until the works closed in 1958.

*Raven* lay derelict outside the works in the early 1960s. Forlorn and out-of-use, it seemed as much a part of the landscape as the Whitford ponds nearby until it was scrapped in 1968. Tony Griffiths[10] was offered the chance to purchase the loco for the princely sum of £50! For practical reasons, he declined.

### Thos W Ward, Giant's Grave

Thos W Ward Ltd, was a Sheffield steel and engineering business which became synonymous with Giant's Grave in the twentieth century. *Wards*, as locals knew it, opened a shipbreaking yard at Giant's Grave in 1906 on a pill on the eastern bank of the River Neath which had previously been used for coal exports. Over the years this pill stored hundreds of the vessels for dismantling. When Wards needed a rail line to move the scrap arising at its yard to the sidings at Briton Ferry dock, a short branch line from the Port Wallaroo line was laid along the eastern river bank to Giant's Grave.

Over the course of its existence, Wards used eighteen separate machines, with three or four in use at any one time. They were all bought *used* off other industrial concerns, with the predominant steam loco being standard 0-4-0 saddle tanks from builders such as Peckett, Hudswell Clarke, Hawthorne Leslie, or Avonside.

At the end of World War Two, Wards took delivery of large quantities of Allied and German battle-helmets and disabled armaments. These often got into the hands of young boys in Briton Ferry who wore the helmets when playing soldiers. The truth is that boys raided the rail trucks for such trophies before they arrived at Wards.

*Doreen* was a long-time Briton Ferry resident, having been originally supplied new to the Briton Ferry Steelworks in 1920, but it was still frequently seen in the late 1950s and early 1960s, along with *ROF 7 No 6*.[11] The latter was loaned out to BR for a short period in 1965 when, British Railways found itself short of a restricted wheelbase shunting loco for the South Dock branch in Swansea after its own (51218) had been withdrawn. For a short time in 1965 it could be seen well away from Giant's Grave, crossing the bridge near the Pump House at Swansea's South Dock, or marshalling wagons at Burrows sidings.

*Doreen* met the cutters' torch when the first diesel arrived at Wards in 1962, but *ROF 7 No 6* soldiered on until being scrapped in 1968. In 1965, it was common to see a diesel loco bring the regular wagon haul of scrap to the exchange sidings and return to Giant's Grave with a quartet of withdrawn steam locos in its train. By then Wards was concentrating on dismantling steam locos, not ships. Later the company also turned its attention to breaking up coaches and wagons. Richard Thomas of Port Talbot often left his home in Cardiff in the 1960s and 1970s ostensibly to visit relatives in Briton Ferry.[12] His original motivation for visiting was because his mother was brought up in the town and his grandfather had worked in its Iron Works, but his allegiance became much stronger because of his enchantment with these rail activities. So smitten was he that his recollections are incised in his memory in quite some detail:

Moving along Ward's branch in the early 1990s *(Robert Thomas)*

RCW 0-4-0 tank *Rosyth* at Ward's in the early 1980s
*(Robert Thomas)*

What fascinated me about *The Ferry* was Wards' rolling stock dismantling business. I remember, from as early as 1964, mainly ex-GWR locos lined up on the right-hand side of the dock. There was always a constant flow of withdrawn coaches and wagons, awaiting the cutter's torch. In the mid-sixties green, Bullieid, carriages from the Southern Region were brought in and reduced en masse to standardise the fleet. So many were delivered that they were stored in the dock sidings and at Cwrt Sart. They were followed, around 1968, by Derby light-weight DMUs[13] in green and blue livery. The onslaught continued into the 1970's

when the Blue Pullmans arrived in 1974. These were partly dismantled in the iron works sidings; each chassis was removed … I think there was a fuss at the time as blue asbestos was exposed. Things still continued, though, with a further tranche of *Southern* electric DMUs in 1977. Trade seemed to peter out in the eighties with the disposal of guard's vans. To my knowledge just a few diesel locos were dealt with after that.

When Wards decided to shut its shipbreaking operations in 1983 and concentrate on its cement business, seventy-seven years of activity at Briton Ferry came to an end. Norbrit Wharfage, a company that concentrated on the shipping of scrap rather than the scrapping of ships took over the wharf at Giant's Grave, but the business inherited a small diesel shunting loco from Wards.

In the early 1980s, steam finally returned to the Giant's Grave branch when the Railway Club of Wales steamed their preserved 0-4-0 tank *Rosyth*, giving brake van rides to the public. This was steam's 'swan song' on the industrial lines of Briton Ferry. Rosyth, with its Royal Naval connotations, was an appropriate locomotive to appear at Wards. Today Briton Ferry Shipping Services operates a scrap shipment business from Giant's Grave, having taken over in 1995 without rail connection

Rail layout at BP Chemicals with diesel special, 1980s
*(Robert Thomas)*

## Baglan Foundry and Engineering Co Ltd

The foundry was established in 1894 to manufacture ingot moulds and bottom plates both for the local steel industry and for export to France and Australia. It was located between the east side of the RSBR line and the main A48 road at Baglan, with rail connection by a siding from the up line. A diesel shunter, previously used by the Vivian Sheet and Blackplate Works, Port Talbot, was used from 1953, although there are no records of previous motive power.

When the A48 road through Baglan was widened in the late 1950s, the company transferred its operations to the sites of the Melyncrythan Tinplate Works and the Neath Japan works. It used sidings off the main Neath-to-Port Talbot line, but the exchange sidings had a sharp curvature which restricted the type of main line steam locomotive that could service them. Instead, the company used its own new diesel locomotive David to marshal wagons in and out of the works.

Vic James, trainee metallurgist at Baglan Engineering Works in the 1960s:

> there was one loco called *The David*, a diesel, which was always a spotless green, and which could push in about eight wagons on the sharp curves going into the

A train of tankers leave BP works for Briton Ferry yard, behind a Class 47 diesel, 1980s *(Robert Thomas)*

works. It was crewed on a day shift by a driver and a shunter. The shunter was called Sid Townshend ... the raw material for the furnaces in the foundry consisted of scrap steel, pig iron and limestone.... The ingot moulds that were produced could be used between seventy and 100 times before needing replacement ... thus there was constant demand from the Albion and from Llanelli steelworks which, like Baglan Engineering, was owned by Duport Steel, ... flat wagons were used to take out the moulds.

The changes in steelmaking technology in the 1980s had an impact on the nature of the product made by Baglan Engineering:

> When continuous casting was introduced into the steel industry there was no longer a demand for ingots and Baglan Engineering stopped making ingot moulds and changed to making weights for fork lift trucks.

The works provided jobs for about 300 people in its heyday, but ceased railway operations in the 1970. Its loco *David* was sold to the Express Dairy Company, South Morden, London, and the works ceased production in the 1990s. Jeff Beer, who travelled on many of the *Baglan boys'* railway trips, served his apprenticeship and worked for many years as a welder there.

## BP Chemicals, Baglan Bay

Baglan Bay Works was opened by BP Chemicals in 1963 partly to benefit from the supply of feedstocks by pipeline from the nearby BP Oil Refinery at Llandarcy. It was constructed on land reclaimed from marsh and sand dunes to the west of the former RSBR line to Aberafan Beach. The operation became one of Europe's largest petrochemical plants, employing 2500 people at its peak in 1974. Its products were transported from the plant by rail from a siding off the closed ex-RSBR line. Wagons were propelled to the exchange sidings where they were taken forward to Briton Ferry yard to be formed into trains. The plant used two former British Rail diesels *D3989* and *D4003*. From 1985 until 1989, part of its loco shed was used to store the preserved pannier tank, *9642*, before it was transferred to Upper Bank works for restoration by the Swansea Vale Railway. On closure in 2004 the locomotives used by BP Chemicals were sold to heritage railways.

The site was redeveloped as Baglan Energy Park, a gas turbine power plant and a paper mill, but the trackwork remains for use today by Colas Rail to transport logs. Its activities are dealt with in Chapter Six.

## Taylor and Sons Ltd

Briton Ferry Foundry was opened in 1862 on a site between Regent Street and the main Swansea to Cardiff railway line. It changed ownership several times before it adopted the name *Taylor and Sons Ltd* in 1900 and continued to trade under this name into recent times.

Specialising in the manufacture of heavy machinery for the steel and tinplate industries it soon gained a reputation for good workmanship. Its founder was one of the privileged band who had served an apprenticeship at the Neath Abbey Ironworks, which in its day received world acclaim for the quality of its engineering.[14]

During World War One the foundry was used to manufacture munitions for the armed forces and 'one of the first shells to be made in Wales' came from this factory.[15]

Phil Bannister[16] worked at Taylor's during the World War Two.

I started my apprenticeship as a moulder at Taylor's Foundry in 1939. When the air raids started some of us employees had to stay as firewatchers. We stayed in the pattern shop ambulance room. Later, I joined the fire service as an alternative to the home guard and was on duty when the Swansea blitz took place. We had to stay in the fire station in case Briton Ferry was bombed. Someone else on duty at the time was the singer, Bruce Dargavel, who later became famous. It was nine in the morning when the crews came back to the station ... all safe and sound.

Taylor's siding on the west side of the GWR was laid in 1870 and connected with the Port Wallaroo branch. Two locomotives were used, but rail-borne traffic ceased in 1965 when the track was dismantled. Adjacent to Taylor's Foundry was a power house from Brunel's time. It housed two stationary boilers, one in use and one on standby to provide steam power to work the coal hoists and open the gates at Briton Ferry Dock. Part of the building still stands today. Cwrt Sart shed supplied the boiler in the form of a complete locomotive. In the 1950s this was a redundant Taff Vale locomotive, which still bore the number *309*.

Locomotive used as stationary boiler to provide steam to power operate the dock gates. The locos used were supplied by Cwrt Sart shed *(Neath Antiquarians)*

The Metal Box factory at Melyncrythan, Neath can be clearly seen in the background of this photo from Cwrt Sart shed showing *5055 Earl of Eldon* coming on shed in August 1964 *(Martin Davies)*

### The Vernon Tinplate Works

This was one of the earliest works in Briton Ferry, situated on land at the eastern approach of the first Neath river bridge. It began producing tinplate in 1860 using puddling furnaces, rolling mills and a tinning plant. It became The Ferry Tinplate Company Limited and operated so successfully that it was taken over by the Briton Ferry Steel Company in 1921. Martin Davies' mother, who visited the works if her father forgot to take his lunch box to work, witnessed the harsh working conditions. They remained vivid memories throughout her life.

During World War Two the works was taken over by the RAF as a storage depot. Afterwards it became a warehouse for O L Davies (Plant Hire) until it was demolished to make way for the realigned A48 road in the 1950s. Part of the site was taken over by N&C Coaches in the early 1960s. The firm was famous for its express coaches, which competed with rail passenger services between Neath and Cardiff and were known locally as *Brown Bombers* because of their livery. The Works was rail-connected from a spur off the RSBR line, but no records exist of the motive power used at the works. Movements were controlled by Vernon Junction signal box until this was closed in the 1935 rationalisation and Briton Ferry box assumed control until the sidings were taken out of use after 1953.

### The Cambrian Cokeworks and other industrial premises

Smaller works like the Vernon, Gwalia, Villiers, Wern and Baglan Bay tinplate likely used the locomotives of neighbouring firms because their activities did not justify their own motive power. The Cambrian Cokeworks, owned by Cardiff Washed Coal, Coke and Patent Fuel Co, was located between Briton Ferry dock and the river Neath. It provided Briton Ferry Ironworks with up to eighty tonnes of coke daily from its forty ovens for the Ironworks' blast furnaces.[17] It washed 300 tonnes of coal per day which were brought by train from local pits along the Wallaroo branch. A track diagram for 1898 shows five sidings associated with this works.[18] The works had its own locomotive to assist in the several train movements needed to deliver coal. Unfortunately, no records exist of the locomotive(s) used. The works was auctioned on 2 March 1905 in Cardiff.

### The Metal Box Company and the Eaglesbush Works

The Metal Box Company, colloquially *The Box*, was an important industrial concern and one of the largest employers in the local area. Its works in Melyncrythan, on a site between the Neath Canal and the GWR, opposite the Melyn Tinplate Works, was set up in 1921 to make metal containers from the

tinplate being manufactured in large quantities in the area. After first purchasing the Eaglesbush Works, at a time when there was increasing demand for canned goods, the Company built a new factory close by in 1937, but on the opposite side of the Neath Canal.

Eaglesbush was connected to sidings which ran alongside the down main line, with five lines leading into the works. The main site which housed the tin mills, the pickling and annealing plants and tin house was encircled by two sidings which probably used its own motive power. The Metal Box site was connected by rail off the Neath Canalside branch by a spur from December 1937. It fanned out into ten sidings, of which seven ran into the factory building.

Supplies of tinplate originally came from its own Eaglesbush factory and other works in the area, such as the Melyn and Gwalia, until the new tinplate works at Trostre and Felindre came on stream. A large proportion of the finished products were shipped to other Metal Box factories by rail[19], notably to Worcester. *The Worcester* was the appropriately nick-named rail working that passed through Briton Ferry from the works around mid-day.

Initially the works was designed to produce tops and bottoms of cans and to apply a lacquered coating to the inside and outside of the can, but changes in demand made it necessary to print decorative designs on the outsides as well. Production in Neath began at the end of 1937 with six units for making components. The first unit for lacquering sheets was introduced in January 1958.[20]

At its peak, in 1968, the fifty-acre factory employed 2,800 people and was one of the largest in Wales. Its products included aerosol cone ends, strip seal ends, and ring and cap assemblies. Aluminium strip was used later in addition to tinplate in the manufacture of these products.

Trains from the Metal Box were marshalled by a pannier tank and taken forward by a mixed traffic 4-6-0 from Worcester shed on *The Worcester*, usually

a *Hall* or *Grange* but, sometimes, a high mileage *Castle*. Scrap from the works was taken away for re-use at Trostre and Felindre in the form of lightweight silver trimmings which made them very visible when they fell onto the trackside. The trip freights to the Metal Box were some of the last workings in the Neath area to be steam-powered. From 1965 when Cwrt Sart shed closed until 1983, when the rail connection was abandoned, the trains were worked by Class 37 diesels.

The Metal Box's own locos moved wagons around the works site. No records exist of motive power used before 1963, probably because traffic levels up to then didn't provide enough work for an in–house locomotive. As the works expanded, a small 0-4-0 diesel shunter was purchased from Robert Stephenson and Hawthorns of Darlington (RHSD). It was replaced by a small Ruston and Hornsby machine in 1978. When rail operations were discontinued both locos passed into preservation, the RSHD going to the Industrial and Maritime Museum in Swansea and the Ruston to the Vale of Neath Railway Society, Aberdulais.

The Canadian firm *Crown Cork and Seal* bought the company in 1996 and were its last owners. Operations and workforce were progressively run down until the factory closed completely in 2016.

There were few families locally who didn't have some connection with the works. Through its links

The Metal Box's own RSHD diesel at work *(Metal Box)*

Lightweight 0-6-0 pannier tank *1645*, is seen shunting in the sidings near the *Galv* works in 1960 *(Robert Thomas)*

with the community, Metal Box was regarded as a local institution because of its sophisticated staff welfare policy. Jeff Jones of Baglan, a lifelong railway fan, and now the proud owner of an ex-London Transport bus, spent most of his working career at the 'Box', but Max Boyce is probably its most well-known former employee.

## Neath Sheet Steel and Galvanising Works

This company, adjacent to the Eaglesbush works, saw many changes of ownership during its lifetime: Briton Ferry Steel Company, Duport, the Steel Company of Wales and British Steel. It was on the site of an old chemical works which had supplied sulphuric acid to the nearby tinplate works. The *Galv*, as it was affectionately known, was established at the end of the nineteenth century to coat sheet steel with zinc in its galvanizing plant as a protection against rust and corrosion. Its five hot sheet mills were not mechanised until 1954 by using plant imported from Australia. One of the early directors was Herbert Eccles whose involvement in the Briton Ferry Steel Company resulted in a steam loco being named after him.

The works was connected by a pair of sidings, which had been used by the chemical works, with the *down* goods loop line. Under a private agreement

with the company, the GWR allowed one of its short-wheelbase pannier locos to be used for shunting.[21] It was specially kept at Cwrt Sart shed for this purpose because of the short radius of the company's lines. Railway staff working on this shunting turn were paid a special bonus by the company!

## Coal mining in Baglan

Coal mining was well-established in Baglan at the beginning of the nineteenth century. Ordnance Survey maps for 1880 show a network of tramways servicing the half-a-dozen collieries in the area: the Wern Pistyll, Price's Drift, Tor-y-Mynydd, the Swan, the Park and the Baglan Hall collieries.

The oldest was likely to have been Baglan colliery, situated near the site of today's McDonald's restaurant and operated by the Mansells of Briton Ferry from the early 18th century until the mid-19th century. Nearby, Wern Pistyll colliery was named after the stream that ran into the Neath estuary from the high ground above Baglan Old Road. This was linked by tramway to Briton Ferry Dock. Mining seems to have ceased by 1898 as the OS map for that year shows no evidence of a tramway. Price's Drift had been started by Joseph Tregelles Price in the 1830s. It was served by a tramroad with a gradient

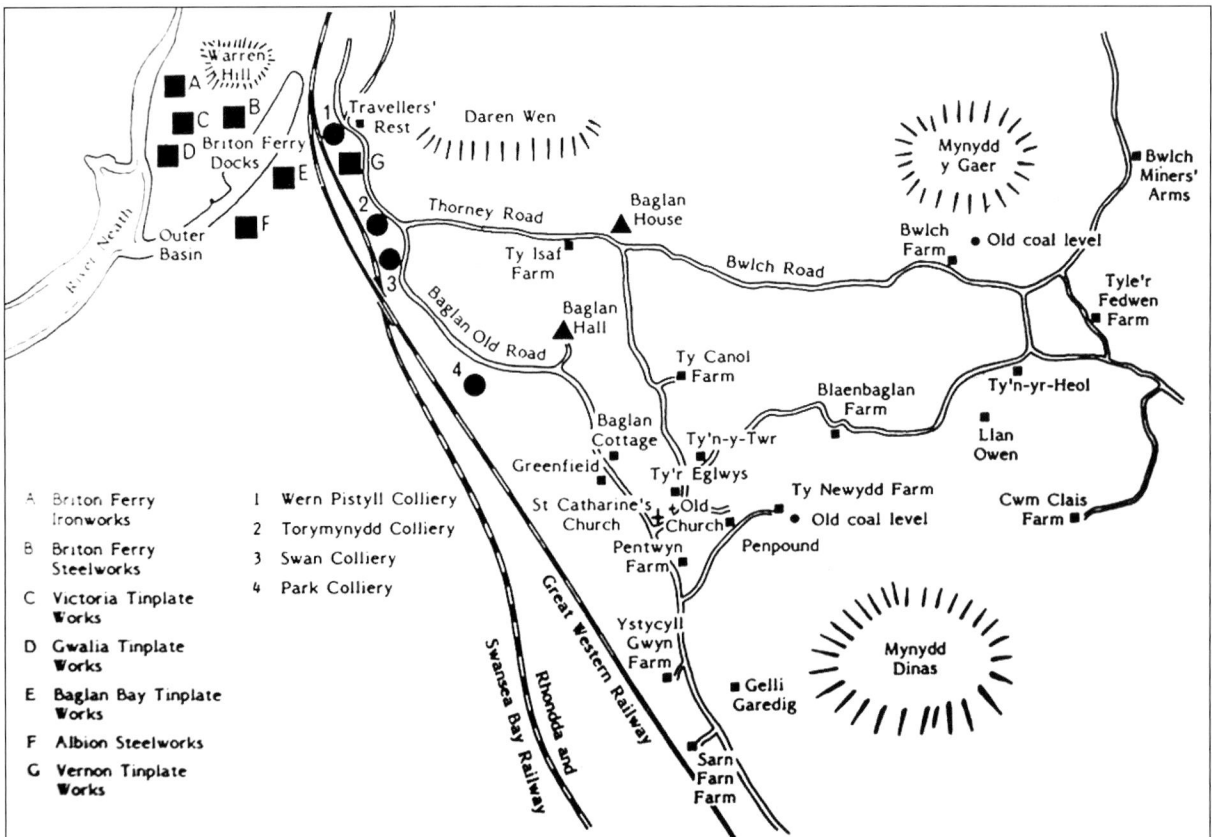

A map of the Baglan area in the late 19th century showing the various works and colleries in operation (E. Jones)

of 1 in 24. Wagons must have been rope-worked. This probably ceased working by the beginning of the 20th century. Baglan historian Harry Barnsley remembers the area from his schooldays.[22]

> 'From the age of nine I walked from Swan Street to the Vernon Place School in Briton Ferry every day. My schoolmates and I played on the disused tramway which belonged to Price's drift and which ran north to south under the reservoir of the Vernon Tinplate Works, which lay on the rock (protruding from the Old Road) which is the southern boundary of the car park of Cavalli's café.[23] We used to mount the tram chassis and- pull it up the slope to the old pulley house. Then we would let the tram run down the gradient veering to the right through the tunnel under the New Road and into the tunnel under the Great Western Railway. The surface area of Price's Drift became known as 'Phil Rosser's Yard where Mrs Anne Davies of Ty'n-y-Twr farm (known affectionately as Annie the Milk) stored her three-wheel milk barrow overnight for her daily deliveries of milk to Briton Ferry.

Tor-y-mynydd Colliery was situated opposite the cottages of the same name near Swan Street. Less than 250 yards south-east of Tor-y-mynydd, and just south of Swan Street, was the Swan Colliery. The capped shaft of the mine, which closed around 1886, was unearthed during road construction in the 1980s. Park Colliery was further east, near Willow Way in Baglan.

Baglan Hall Colliery, was set up by Thomas and Williams in 1854 and taken over by Grenfell and Sons who also owned the Swan and Park collieries. It was linked with the main rail line at Baglan by two sidings, which had a short life-span from 1874 until the colliery closure in 1888. The Baglan up loop line was later constructed on the sidings' site, with Baglan Hall signal box built directly opposite the site of the later Baglan Loop box. Records show an 0-4-0 loco of 1866 vintage being operated by Baglan Hall Colliery. All these mines were served by a tramway and linked to coal stages at Briton Ferry dock.

**Accidents on the industrial railways**

Passers-by at the north end of the dock at Dock Street sometimes saw some sorrowful incidents:

> Around the docks there was a little engine called *The Doll*; it would take slag from

the nearby works. One evening it tipped over by the level crossing and my grandmother's brother, Stanley Pearson was killed. He was the driver.[24]

W H Rowland was the traffic manager at Jersey tinplate works[25] and Secretary of Briton Ferry Fire Brigade. His misfortune in 1893 was to have a leg badly crushed due to a flying shunt being made by the works engine. The shunter had erroneously set the points to the line where Mr Rowland was sitting on a truck, and not to the empty line which was needed. The steel bars on the flying truck were driven through the truck into Mr Rowland, who was 'to receive the assistance of Dr E V Pegge'. The medic was again attending to a serious incident that year at Cambrian Coke Works. John Thomas, a weigher, was getting on a locomotive belonging to the works when he slipped, and the engine passed over his foot, crushing it so badly that it 'is feared it will have to be amputated'.

The everyday risk of assembling any type of wagons into a set could lead to a nasty outcome and the death of William Owen was one such. He was a brake man on the South Wales Mineral Railway's incline and, whilst hitching the trucks on Saturday morning, he was caught by the wheels and had his leg taken off at the thigh. He died at seven o'clock the same evening.[26]

An equally tragic outcome resulted from an incident in 1894, when fifteen-year-old Robert Beer, one of eight children of 22 Middleton Street, was run over by a travelling locomotive crane at Briton Ferry steelworks. He had only been on duty a few minutes and was 'killed almost instantly'.[27] An enquiry was held at Briton Ferry police station where 'the jury suggested that the company be asked to place a warning bell or whistle on the crane'.[28] Despite his son's death, the father, William, a carpenter, went on to become a GWR guard. Regrettably, such fatalities occurred sporadically amongst the complex rail systems of the town where the industrial and public rail operations intertwined.

In 1900, sixty-six-year-old John Williams of Neath Road, a truck discharger working for Ben Thomas, siding contractor, was applying a brake to one of the trucks when, having a spade in one hand, he tripped and fell under the truck which passed over his leg just above the knee. Dr W B Harry performed the amputation at Williams' home before the patient died. In 1916 Thomas Myerscough, a Briton Ferry steelworks foreman, 'was standing by a pile of bricks' when he was 'crushed during shunting operations'.[29] Also, in 1916, thirty-two-year old Arthur Picton, of 34 Pantyrheol, succumbed to crushing injuries sustained when passing between some wagons on a gradient.

Many industrial rail accidents were mirrored those on public railways whilst others, such as Pearson's, arose from causes specific to the industrial operation itself.

*The Doll's* nameplate at Towyn *(Narrow Gauge Rail Museum)*

## The names of the industrial locomotives

Some, such as *Herbert Eccles* and *John Bevan* were named after the directors of the works in the town, Eccles at the Vernon tinplate and Briton Ferry Steel, and Bevan at the Albion steelworks. Eccles was more than a steelworks director: as a scholarly collector and expert on Swansea porcelain he was an adviser on English porcelain at the Victoria and Albert Museum's Department of Ceramics. The ironworks loco's name of *GHD* were the initials of George Henry Davey II, Director of Villiers tinplate, Briton Ferry Ironworks and Briton Ferry Pipe and Brick. He was also a civic leader in the town. One wonders why the remaining locos were not similarly named, perhaps as *M G Roberts* or *Jenkin Hill*, in their capacities both as steelworks directors and civic leaders.

*The Doll* was undoubtedly named because of its diminutive character. *Raven* was evidently named after its original home. Six of the other named locos (*Martha*, *Roy*, *Lindsay*, *Doreen* and *David*) are likely to have been affectionate appellations of family members associated with the works concerned. Only the origins of *Dandy*, *Mountaineer* and *Rainbow* escape us. The numerous locos which were designated numerically, such as *Albion No 1* or *ROF 7 No 6*, were so named, perhaps, to give a reflection of the run-of-the-mill, prosaic, but honest, lives that these machines played in the industrial life of the town.

Some of the nameplates have survived. Alan Williams, a driving force behind the highly acclaimed railway book *The Red Dragon and other old friends*, is the proud owner of the plate from *Martha* and one from *The Doll* whose other nameplate is on display at the Narrow Gauge Museum in Towyn.

This train's title gave a more precise indication of its destination than those or other titled trains

### Notes for Chapter Five

1. A stone's throw away from co-author Martin Davies' home
2. Formerly the Jersey Tinplate Works; the railway connection was made by Lord Jersey in 1883.
3. Nicholson: 'Martha Jane and me'.
4. The Wallaroo branch
5. It also served the Briton Ferry Steelworks, Gwalia and Wern tinplate works and Thomas Ward.
6. *Industrial Locomotives of West Glamorgan*, Potts and Green, p.53
7. *Industrial Locomotives of West Glamorgan*, Potts and Green p.51
8. Father of Alun, Majorie, John and the late Audrey Hutchinson of Brynhyfryd Road
9. Manufactured by Sentinel in Shrewsbury
10. Of Briton Ferry
11. The government numbered the Royal Ordnance factory at Pembrey as number 7. The locomotive was thus ROF 7's (Pembrey), No 6 .
12. The Eynons of Thomas Street, Briton Ferry
13. Diesel multiple units
14. *Briton Ferry (Llansawel)*, Cliff Morgan, 1977, p.71
15. *Briton Ferry (Llansawel)*, Cliff Morgan
16. He later went on to work at Cwrt Sart engine shed
17. *South Wales Echo*, 10 January 1890
18. *Track Layout Diagrams of the Great Western Railway*, R A Cooke, p.20
19. Trevor Philips Ltd of Cadoxton was a road haulage contractor which transported some of the output by road.
20. *Neath and District – A Symposium*, Elis Jenkins, p.210
21. For many years in the 1950s and 1960s the loco used was No 1645
22. Quoted in Eben Jones: 'Baglan and the Llewellyns of Baglan Hall', p.56
23. Now McDonald's
24. Carol Hutchings: 'The Railway' in 'Memories'
25. Later, Wern Works
26. *Cardiff Times*, 25 March 1882
27. *South Wales Daily Post*, 16 February, 1894
28. *Cardiff Times*, 24 February 1894
29. *Herald of Wales*, 8 July 1916

Chapter Six

# Goods and Freight Trains

*Network bottlenecks and insufficient investment in catering for 9' 6" high
shipping containers currently restrict growth.*

Network Rail (May 2013)

Today's mainline freight comprises two types of traffic: intermodal container traffic, which is a post-steam era development, and trainload freight, whose origins date from the era of steam trains. Even during the steam era of the twentieth century the nature of goods traffic was quite different from today. For most of that time railways had the obligation to act as a 'common carrier'. They had a monopoly on the movement of goods and the common carrier obligation was introduced by the government to ensure that rail companies did not cherry-pick the most profitable routes. This obliged them to carry any goods offered by the public at nationally-set rates, on defined routes, without discrimination. Despite competition from road transport from the 1920s, the government did not relieve the railways of this obligation until 1962, so local rail traffic departments were still working under this obligation until well into the twentieth century.

Intermodal container traffic offers great opportunities for Britain's railways, but it also highlights some important rail engineering issues which are outlined in Appendix Six.

**The start of the twentieth century**

An undated GWR ledger containing the staffing records for the Traffic Department at Briton Ferry and Neath states that, at Neath, both Mr W A Fox, the Chief Booking Clerk, and Mr F A Willey, Chief Parcels Clerk, received a salary of £140 a year. The importance of Briton Ferry is shown by the fact that eleven salaried posts reported to Mr A E A Wheeler, Briton Ferry's Chief Goods Clerk. His larger salary of £150 a year may have been for the greater responsibility in his position than those of the Neath staff. Mr W K Parry, the Assistant Goods Clerk, also received a substantial salary of £130 for managing two accounting clerks. Mr E W New's staff of three

clerks worked from a single-storey building alongside the dock with responsibility for accounting for goods inwards and outwards. Booking and parcels duties fell to Mr W J E Watts and his staff of two.

Fred Kingdom was Chief Goods clerk in the 1960s and a local politician. His path through local government to become Chairman of West Glamorgan County Council was less surprising than his railway career to become Chief Goods clerk. This is how he became responsible for a staff of twenty-five.

> As soon as I reached my sixteenth
> birthday I went to work on the Great
> Western Railway locomotive sheds near
> Farm Road. Working on the footplate
> grades was regarded as a good job and my
> work as an engine cleaner took me into a
> new life: railwaymen were a great body of
> workers. The job entailed cleaning steam
> engines with waste-soaked in oil that
> brought out the richness in their green
> and black colours of the locomotives. It
> was shift work and I worked alternative
> weeks of day and night shifts. It also
> involved cleaning underneath the engine.
> The 'big ends' and the plate behind them
> were red in colour and had to be cleaned
> so that the engine driver did not get his
> overalls dirty when he oiled the big ends.
> We were meant to put a sign on the engine
> when working underneath, to stop the
> engine being moved. We seldom used the
> sign. Other cleaners then played tricks on
> you. They would get in the cab and move
> the forward and reverse leavers that
> caused the big ends to move to give the
> impression that the engine was about to
> move. It was frightening because if caught
> behind the big ends you could be crushed

*Castle* No *7025* Sudeley Castle of Worcester shed heads an Albion Steelworks to Tipton train of steel billets past Briton Ferry West, August 1964 (*Martin Davies*)

to death. Another job that cleaners had to do was cleaning the ash from the firebox especially over and under the brick arch. It was very hot and dirty work, so we used old clothes with our heads covered and a handkerchief over our noses.

We also had to act as call boys during the night when we went to the house of a driver to call him an hour before he was due on duty to ensure that there were no late trains. When you became more experienced and senior you were given turns to be upgraded to fireman on the footplate. My first turn was on the 03.55 Felin Fran pilot. The call boy came far too early with the notice that I was required for duty. His hammering on the front door frightened my mother who got up to wake me, but I was thrilled of course to have a firing turn. Steam engines were magnificent, and it was a joy to work on the footplate.

Unfortunately, or fortunately as it turned out for my political work, I failed the medical examination to go on the footplate as a fireman. I was then given an opportunity to become a clerk in the time office, dealing with time keeping and wages. Entrance to the clerical grades was by an entrance examination. My mother arranged for me to have coaching lessons, but before I had completed my tuition I reached the age of eighteen years and five months and received my call up papers for the army.

Eventually, in March 1957 I passed an examination held at Swansea station in the subject of Station Accounts (goods)

which was the career path that I then followed in the goods office in Briton Ferry.

Staff travelling to and from work at the goods department had to be vigilant because the Briton Ferry Iron Works tramway passed close by, taking molten slag to the tip at Baglan Bay.

Briton Ferry was a very busy centre for rail freight traffic. The earliest load carried was coal. It was brought down to the docks from collieries in the Neath valley by the VNR and, by the SWMR, from the Corrwg and Afan valleys via Ynysymaerdy incline. The collieries in Baglan area, such as Swan and Baglan Hall, used tram-roads to take coal to the docks. Coking coal was also brought in for the Cambrian Coke Works, next to the Gwalia Tinplate Works.

The development of the iron and steel, and later the tinplate industry adjacent to the docks, gave a big impetus to rail-borne traffic in the form of both raw materials and finished products. Pig iron from Briton Ferry Ironworks was shifted the short distance to the adjacent steelworks, or moved to the second, Albion, steelworks opposite. Scrap steel, the other main raw material for the steel furnaces, was readily available from the shipbreaking yard of Thomas Ward from 1906 onwards. In the 1960s additional scrap steel came from breaking up steam locos.

Tinplate works such as the Baglan Bay, Gwalia and Vernon used the steel produced at Briton Ferry's two steelworks. Much tinplate was used in the canning industry resulting in movement by rail from Briton Ferry to the Metal Box in Melyncrythan. The extensive sidings alongside the dock accommodated the wagons used by these factories. Indeed, shortly after the First World War eleven parallel roads were in place on the east of the dock, plus all the lines

*0-6-2 tank 6624* awaits the signals at the head of a freight from Margam to Aberdare, 1961 *(Martin Davies)*

feeding the individual works and two sidings to feed the coal hoists. On the eastern side of the dock were eighteen parallel sidings, four of them feeding coal hoists, together with separate lines running into the Albion Steelworks, the Baglan Bay Tinplate Works and the Whitford Steelworks.

As well as the traffic to and from the local industrial undertakings, Briton Ferry witnessed a continuous flow of through goods trains throughout the day, with Briton Ferry yard being the focal point for shunting operations.

## Coal

Trains taking anthracite coal from the Amman Valley collieries around Pantyfynnon followed the Swansea District line to destinations further east, hauled by 2-8-0s (or 2-8-2s if journeys took them into England). Similar wagon hauls of 'black diamonds' from the Neath and Dulais valley mines would use the line through Neath. This traffic was still buoyant into the 1960s, when most collieries were still working. A significant boost to the demand for anthracite throughout the country came from the installation of

A pair of class 37 diesels (*37294* and *37275*) bring an *up* merry-go-round coal train to Aberthaw from the Swansea District line through Briton Ferry, 21 April 1982 *(Robert Thomas)*

109

A block oil train from Llandarcy to Rowley Regis 'passes Cwrt Sart shed' behind 2-8-0 *2876* in 1963 *(John Davies)*

domestic central heating systems powered by solid fuel, a trend associated with greater home ownership. Indeed, co-author Martin Davies helped his father with the installation of 'Rayburn' and 'Parkray' central heating boilers.

**Oil products from Llandarcy**

Britain's first oil refinery was opened in 1922 by the Anglo-Persian Oil Company at Llandarcy. Supplied with crude oil by pipeline from Queen's Dock, Swansea, the refinery was a significant employer with over two thousand people employed at the peak of its operations. Many people from Briton Ferry travelled to work there daily, often by train, using the purpose-built Llandarcy platform from 1924 until it closed in 1956. By 1960, Llandarcy was refining some eight million tons of crude oil annually and was still the country's third largest refinery. Thus, it was an important source of trainload freight traffic with regular petroleum and tar trains heading east, usually hauled by 0-6-2 or 2-8-0 tanks.

Developments at BP's purpose-built terminal at Angle Bay, Pembrokeshire in the 1960s led to the movement of refined products by 'block trains' of 100-tonne tankers. The main traffic from Pembrokeshire was to Rowley Regis in the Midlands by trains hauled by 2-8-0s, BR 2-10-0s, *Halls* and *Granges* from Cwrt Sart shed. In the diesel era class 47s were used.

BP Chemicals built a plant at Baglan Bay in the late 1960s to exploit the proximity of supplies from

An oil train from Swansea Docks is eased off the Swansea District line on to the *up* loop line at Briton Ferry Station behind 0-6-2 tank *5623* *(John Davies)*

A pair of class 37 diesels (37294 and 37220) speed through Briton Ferry with a 'block' oil train bound for Milford Haven, 17 May 1990
(Robert Thomas)

Llandarcy oil refinery. It was rail-connected via part of the truncated ex-RSBR line near Briton Ferry dock and became the source for much rail-borne traffic for some forty or more years until the plant was closed. The rail connections remained in place and are now used by Colas Rail for its log trains to Chirk.

## Oil traffic from the west

A further source of traffic from west Wales resulted from the development of Milford Haven in the late 1950s as a major port for oil tankers. The increase in the size of these so-called super tankers, often up to a quarter of a mile in length, meant that conventional ports such as Swansea could no longer accommodate them. Hence, several companies chose to site new oil terminals and refineries on the shores of the haven, one of the world's deepest natural harbours. The first was Esso at Herbranston west of Milford Haven, which was officially opened on 2 November 1960. Initially, traffic was dealt with by general freight trains but, from September 1963, traffic levels were

such that a dedicated service of block oil trains was started. The first train was the 5.00 pm Herbranston to Coleshill tanker train which passed Briton Ferry about three hours later. Soon other oil companies found the vast waterway an attraction and Regent and BP built refineries on the opposite shore of the haven. Gulf followed and chose a site at Waterston with a rail connection from the Milford branch in 1968. Amoco followed in 1974.

## Steel

The opening of the Abbey Works at Margam and its associated tinplate mills at Felindre and Trostre led to the regular movement of strip steel westwards, with movements continuing today to Trostre. In the 1960s the steel on the 'strip coil' trains was visible, being carried in open wagons hauled by 2-8-0s and 2-8-2 tanks based at Duffryn Yard depot. The tinplate produced at Felindre and Trostre, however, was usually transported concealed in specially-fitted wagons, generally hauled by a mixed traffic loco

A strip coil train from Margam to Felindre is seen near Cwrt Sart Junction, 1963
(John Davies)

111

A van train for the Metal Box at Cwrt Sart Junction in 1963. The loco *3621* still bears the embellishments from its use on the last passenger train from Neath to Brecon in October 1962. *(John Davies)*

such as a *Hall* or *Grange*. *Hardwick*, *Poulton* and *Penhydd* were popular Granges used by Llanelli shed in the early 1960s to marshal tinplate trains at Llandeilo Junction.

When Duport Group took over the Albion steel-works, the investment in a new furnace enabled the company to fulfil increased orders for its engineering-steel billets from sister works in the Midlands for use in the car industry. Thus regular billet trains left Briton Ferry yard in the mid-1960s for the Black Country, hauled by locos originating in the west Midlands including *Castles* from Worcester shed.

The Metal Box in Melyncryddan, Neath, was a major employer in the local area, which at its height employed some 3,700 people. Its parent company was the largest user of tinplate in the country in 1964 when the Neath factory had thirty production lines making can ends. A regular lunchtime departure from the Neath factory to its Worcester counterpart was 'The Worcester' hauled by a 4-6-0 from Worcester depot such as a *Grange*, *Hall*, *Manor* or a high-mileage *Castle* to haul. The Metal Box was initially supplied with tinplate from several small works in and around Neath, but from 1949, following rationalisation of the industry its sources were the modern plants at Felindre and Trostre. Rail delivery to the Metal Box was via Briton Ferry yard and onto the Canalside branch from where it was taken forward by a pannier tank. Fitted vans full of can tops, and mineral wagons bearing scrap tinplate moved in the opposite direction.

The 3.50 pm Whitland to Kensington milk train glides on to the main line at Briton Ferry behind ex-works *Castle* 4074 *Caldicot Castle*, 1960 *(From a watercolour painting 12"x 7½" by Martin Davies)*

## Milk

Briton Ferry witnessed a daily procession of fast freights carrying perishable goods from west Wales. These had to run at speeds more associated with express passenger trains, at a sixty-mph average, to ensure swift dispatch of the food produce to the large centres of population such as the south east.

Rail-borne milk traffic was well established by the early 1900s. Its source, Carmarthenshire, an important dairy farming area, had important milk processing plants at Whitland, Johnston, Aberystwyth, Llangadog, Newcastle Emlyn and Felin Fach. Until the 1930s, milk was collected in the familiar churns which were seen on many railway platforms. This meant that milk trains had many pick-up points or milk traffic was simply added to passenger or other perishable traffic. To overcome the inconvenience of this the GWR, along with other companies, introduced dedicated bulk milk trains in the 1930s to cope with the volumes to be moved. By the 1960s, four trains each day were needed to transport the milk sent from Carmarthenshire to London. The heaviest of these was the 3.50 pm Whitland-to-Kensington, usually consisting of fifteen or so glass-lined tank wagons, each carrying 3,000 gallons and each weighing about twenty-eight tons when fully laden. Each train carried enough milk to satisfy the needs of 160,000 people.

Such a heavy load required haulage by a *Castle* or *County* class 4-6-0, which on weekdays involved a Swindon locomotive. The attraction of this train to railway observers was that it was often used as a 'running-in turn' for locos fresh from overhaul at Swindon Works. The loco employed could, therefore, be from some distant depot on the such as Wolverhampton or Penzance. Such rarities in south Wales usually galloped through Briton Ferry at around 6.00 pm. Two other milk trains, the 5.15 pm and 8.30 pm departures from Whitland, were lighter trains and had less glamorous motive power such as a *Hall* or *Grange*. However, the 6.45 pm from Carmarthen, which included tanks from the other milk depots mentioned above, was also hauled by a *Castle* from Carmarthen depot. These trains reached London in the early hours of the next morning with the milk empties returning from Kensington or Wood Lane later that morning.

Val Berni worked from Old Oak Common shed from 1942 to 1949 when he often worked the milk train from Felin Fran to London:[1]

> We used to come down from London with the parcels, on Monday, Wednesday and Friday, and stay the night of course. On a Saturday, instead of working the parcels back we'd work the 5.50 pm milk from Felin Fran. We'd take the engine, usually a *Castle*, off shed at Landore tender first, then reverse down to Hafod Junction. From there we'd then go engine-first along Morriston branch through Landore Low level and Morriston to Felin Fran. We'd wait by the signal box for the train coming from Whitland. This was a very heavy train, with eighteen milk tanks. We'd drop some off at Wootton Bassett, and then carry on to the milk depot at Wood Lane with the others.

## Livestock

Significant traffic in livestock came across the Irish Sea with the opening of New Milford as a ferry port, business that was transferred to the new port of Fishguard Harbour after 1906. A regular working in the 1950s and 1960s was the 3.35 pm freight from Fishguard to Paddington which largely consisted of cattle wagons. The wagons had partly-open sides so their speed could be affected by considerable side draught. This train was rostered for one of Goodwick depot's *Halls* to Cardiff. *Abberley, Knowsley,* and *Moreton Hall* were the regular locomotives that passed through Briton Ferry at about 6.30 pm in the early 1960s with Irish cattle.

## Fish

Milford Haven provided another source of perishable goods for the railway in west Wales. It was one of the main fishing ports in the country in the post-war period and three daily fish trains left the port, one bound for Severn Tunnel Junction, one for the Midlands via Carmarthen and the Central Wales line, and another for Paddington. The first of these left Milford at 3.20 pm and reached Briton Ferry about 6.45 pm hauled by one of the *Counties* based at Neyland.

Bill Morgan worked from Neyland to Gloucester on the fish trains in the 1930s and 1940s. An enterprising soul, he found a way of supplementing his income by supplying a chain of well-cultivated 'customers' along the route with fresh fish, including his landlady at his lodgings in Gloucester. All these goods trains from west Wales used the Swansea District line and gained the Swansea to London main line at Briton Ferry. No doubt Bill Morgan had sold out well before Briton Ferry.

The afternoon Fishguard to London goods train which included many cattle wagons in its load passed Briton Ferry in the early evening. Here engines are changed at Cardiff Canton in 1960 as Goodwick's *5908 Moreton Hall* is about to uncouple to make way for a fresh *Hall* for the onward journey (*R O Tuck*)

## The Fifties and Sixties

It was fascinating for youngsters to sit on the parapet of the bridge at Shelone Road and watch the movement of the trains. Sometimes we would be there from dawn till dusk ... even at night in bed one could listen to the whistling of through-trains and to the clanging of wagons being shunted. The freight trains carried billets from the Albion for the Black Country mills, steel coils for pickling and finishing at Trostre and Velindre, tinplate scrap from the Metal Box, milk trains to London, cattle and fish trains from west Wales, petroleum and tar trains from Llandarcy, mail, stone and, above all, coal and pit-props to and from the Amman, Swansea and Neath Valleys.[2]

In the 1950s and 1960s the afternoon Milford Haven fish train was regularly *County* hauled. *1001 County of Bucks*, seen here at Neyland, was a favourite for this turn.

In 1963 the train was dieselised. *D1015 Western Champion* passes Briton Ferry docks late that year *(John Davies) (this loco is now preserved)*

## Changes in freight traffic after 1970

Additional trainload oil trains were run to destinations previously not served from Pembrokeshire. These were to Sighthill and Polmadie in Scotland, and to Albion, Birmingham, Bromsgrove and Kingsbury in the Midlands. When the smaller capacity tanks were replaced with 100-tonne (gross laden weight) tank wagons some lengthy trains resulted, requiring haulage by a class 47 diesel or sometimes double-headed by two class 37s.

During one week in November 1974, forty-two block trains were worked out of the three refineries and for each of these there was a corresponding back-working of empty tank wagons, but the highest ever number of trains was fifty-two, achieved in January 1977.

All these trains passed through Briton Ferry at intervals during the day but, from 1976, so great was the volume of traffic that more trains were run through the night to ensure best use of the line. Decline in oil traffic started in the 1980s with the clo-

sure of the Esso and Gulf refineries. Rationalisation of oil refining facilities during the recessions of the 20XX decade followed. The last refinery, operated by Murco, closed in 2015. It was purchased by Puma Energy for use as a petrol storage and distribution terminal and now sends oil products by rail through Briton Ferry both to the Puma depots purchased from Murco and to Puma's existing UK depots.

## Automotive

In the 1970s when Ford Motor took over the Jersey Marine premises formerly used by Prestcold to make refrigerators, their camshafts, con rods and crankshafts became another source of regular rail freight movement. Block trains from Jersey Marine made their way to Ford's engine plant in Bridgend via Briton Ferry, until the Jersey Marine plant was run down in the 2000s with this traffic ceasing and the plant eventually closing under the ownership of Linamar in 2010.

Pannier tank shunting in Briton Ferry yard *(Robert Thomas)*

115

A newly-introduced English Electric diesel *D6853* passes Briton Ferry in 1963 as *7249* runs through light engine, 1963 *(John Davies)*

A container train, headed for Swansea Freightliner terminal at Swansea, passes Jersey Marine behind 47012. 26 October 1977 *(Robert Thomas)*

Engineering works being undertaken at Briton Ferry in the mid-1970s. Three class 37s *(37189, 37234, 37143)* are seen in the yard, one on ballast wagons and two on the *down* strip coil train while two other locos occupy the main lines *(37236 and 47250)*. 21 November 1976 *(Robert Thomas)*

A timber train from Briton Ferry to Chirk leaves the goods yard behind a Colas Rail class 57 loco in 2013.
*(Stuart Warr)*

### Container traffic

A major development during the 1980s was the growth of intermodal containerisation and the volume of rail-borne container traffic. *Freightliner* terminals were opened to transfer boxed freight from rail to road at depots such as Danygraig in Swansea. Significant amounts of this container traffic passed through Briton Ferry and, for a time, *freightliner* trains ran five days a week to west Wales. The lack of investment at the rail terminus at Waterford and the growth of the Ro-Ro road service via Rosslare meant this rail-borne traffic to Fishguard no longer became profitable. Trains were discontinued after an unsuccessful move to develop Fishguard as a container port for Ireland. The growth of road competition led to the demise of the Swansea depot.

The decline in the British fishing industry, with increased competition from other countries such as Spain, resulted in the run-down of Milford Haven as a base for trawlers and the consequent disappearance of rail borne fish traffic. The last fish train left Milford on 29 June 1981. Milk traffic was lost to road

A class 47 diesel, *47076*, heads a Trostre to Margam train of empty strip coil wagons past Briton Ferry East on 26 April 1976 *(Robert Thomas)*

An *up* Swansea to Willesden mail train passes Briton Ferry East station behind *67001*, 5 February 2001 *(Stuart Warr)*

competition later in the 1980s and the cattle trains from Fishguard no longer run.

The decision by British Railways to withdraw from the sundries and wagon-load traffic in 1972 had a drastic effect on freight traffic to and from west Wales. The loss of rail borne traffic generated in Briton Ferry was augmented by the closure in 1978 of the Albion steelworks, for so long the major employer in the town. To add to the economic and social gloom, the Thatcher Government of the 1980s presided over the run-down of the coal and steel industries in south Wales which cut off further sources of rail-borne traffic and added to the air of contraction.

The marshalling yards at Llandeilo Junction, Swansea Eastern Depot, Felin Fran and most of Margam and Briton Ferry became superfluous to requirements. The main freight traffic passing through Briton Ferry now consists of coal trains to Aberthaw Power Station, the remaining oil trains from Milford Haven, the Margam to Trostre strip-coil shipments and the log trains from Briton Ferry to the Kronospan wood panel factory at Chirk, a facility whose development was aided by the Welsh Government.

## Conclusion

Today there are five private freight companies operating on Britain's railways: Colas Rail, Deutsche Bahn Cargo, Freightliner, GB Railfreight and Stobart Rail. A sixth is in public ownership: Direct Rail Services which was previously run by British Nuclear Fuels and the Nuclear Decommissioning Authority. It has since diversified into other freight operations and provides haulage for passenger services. Its freight operations include the Tesco Express trains, run in conjunction with Stobart Rail.

This chapter has portrayed the rise and decline of both the passenger and freight services originating from, arriving at, or passing through Briton Ferry. Whilst there seems to be little to cheer at present in this tale of fading glory, the position of Briton Ferry's railways is one of optimism, possibility and progress from today's low baseline. Things will never be as they were, nor could they be, but possibilities exist which are ripe for exploitation today. With intelligence, imagination and boldness these possibilities can be exploited. What the possibilities are, and how they can be seized, form the subject of Chapter Fourteen.

**Notes for Chapter Six**

1.  More on Val Berni in Chapter Eight on his work at Cwrt Sart and Landore sheds.
2.  Philip Adams: *Briton Ferry 1814–2014: A Most Industrious Town Briton Ferry and its People, 1814-2014*

Chapter Seven

# Locomotives and Sheds

*The locos are black. The coal is black. The tracks are black. The night is black. So what am I going to do with colour?*

O. Winston Link

This Chapter accounts for the origins and the role of Cwrt Sart locomotive depot in the railway system of west Wales, particularly Cwrt Sart. The reasons for its location by the GWR, its construction and layout, and its functions over its lifetime are described. Many of the locomotives based at the depot will be featured. The staffing, duties and working lives of those who drove and maintained these locomotives will be traced in Chapter Seven. Rail staff that lived or worked nearby in the town of Briton Ferry will be featured in Chapter Eleven.

The South Wales Mineral Railway had its own sheds, one near its junction with the GWR to the north of Shelone Road bridge and another at the top of the Briton Ferry incline. The former operated from 1877 until 1910 to provide locomotives to service the lines to the south of the incline. The shed at the top of the incline provided motive power for the line forward to Glyncorrwg. The locos used were small saddle tanks. Several were purchased from the GWR and returned to that company when the SWMR was taken over by them. The SWMR/Glyncorrwg Coal Company's workshops were on Shelone Road, sited opposite the present Briton Ferry station.

## The RSBR

Danygraig was the location for the RSBR's main motive power depot. Until the 1920s it had an additional shed at Aberavon Town

## Why Cwrt Sart?

In Norman times, Cwrt Sart, to the north of Briton Ferry and to the south of Neath, was known as the 'Assart'[1] because forestry there had been cleared, or *assarted* for agricultural use. Monastic communities, particularly the Cistercians, assarted land. The Cis-tercians of Neath Abbey did just this for Cwrt Sart to become an agricultural grange, or court, before the dissolution of the monasteries. Centuries later, Cwrt Sart Colliery was sunk on the assarted land, although the GWR secured a prohibition order to stop the working of that part of the colliery's seam which ran under its locomotive sheds. The colliery land continued as a farm until the 1950s when Neath Council bought it to build a school and houses[2] on the land.

Therefore, a hundred and forty years ago, Cwrt Sart was chosen as the strategic location for a loco-motive depot and district headquarters to serve the south Wales line. This followed an Act of Parliament in 1857 which gave consent for it to be built on sev-enteen acres of boggy land near Cwrt Sart Farm. Work on the depot started a year after work on the Severn tunnel began, but the locomotive depot had been operating for over ten years before the tunnel opened. As the depot was roughly equidistant between both Gloucester and Milford Haven, and the tunnel from south Gloucestershire to Milford, its location continued to be well-chosen, before and after the tunnel's opening.

The official title for the new shed was the angli-cised Neath (Court Sart). Cwrt Sart is an area of Briton Ferry, so it is legitimate to include the shed in a history of Briton Ferry's railways, although its workforce came from areas around both Neath and Briton Ferry.

## The locomotive sheds: construction, layout and activities

### Construction

The building replaced an original structure which the Vale of Neath Railway had built in 1862 to the south of Neath station. The first mention of the new

A view of Cwrt Sart area in the 1930s showing the location of the locomotive shed with an *up* main line train to London in the foreground *(R. Evans)*

shed was in an amendment to an Act of Parliament in 1857 to allow the building of the floating dock at Neath, which also gave consent for an engine shed to be built. It was designed by Joseph Armstrong, with the contract for its construction given to Joseph Rees, a local Neath building firm, at a cost of £25,000.

The builders' first job was to construct a system to drain water from the bog, fed by the Melin brook, on which it was to be built. Work on this and the shed's foundations was started in February 1874. The drainage system removed the water into the river Neath and into two specially created reservoirs, which later became popular for fishermen. The surface was raised to prevent future flooding by filling with hard-core, made up of copper slag from local tips. During the drainage work, the remains of reindeer antlers and bones dated to the last ice age, and several old oak trees, were found in the bog. These relics are now at the National Museum of Wales in Cardiff. Railway construction such as this therefore helped to maintain the interest in geological mapping which had been instigated by earlier canal surveyors.

> 'it is pleasing to note with what rapidity Mr J.C. Rees, the contractor, is carrying out the extensive works in connection with these buildings; the more so as we understand that upon their completion will commence the building of the new railway station at Neath, a boon to the town so long and ardently looked for. The new sheds are now rearing their proportions to the sight of the traveller who cannot but be gratified by their appearance over the old unsightly boggy

the marsh upon which they are being erected. Upon the completion of these sheds we understand that the existing ones will be cleared away to make way for the new station.'[3]

The shed, of approximately 2,000 ft by 4,000 ft was constructed in dressed stone with insets for windows and was floored with brick. The roof of the twin roundhouse structure was supported by eighteen cast iron columns attached to steel bracing girders. It had two turntables under one pitched roof, in and out roads from the coaling stage serving each, and a long road in between. Crossovers were installed between the tracks accessing the roundhouses to create greater flexibility.

*Layout and access*

It was situated in a 'V' between the RSBR line to Swansea Docks and the GWR main line to Neath. A through siding, laid in 1883 to carry materials for the construction of the Neath Harbour Railway, was largely unused. The original access to the shed was by means of a lengthy road that ran parallel to the main lines from Neath Number One signal box at Melyncryddan crossing, half a mile to the north. Later access from the main line was closer, from the Engine Shed box on the east side of the line.[4] Road access to the shed was by means of an unmetalled track which crossed the main line at Farm Road. The shed at Cwrt Sart was the second multiple turntable depot on the GWR following Stafford Road shed in Wolverhampton. Its roundhouses had accommodation for about forty locomotives, with part of Round-

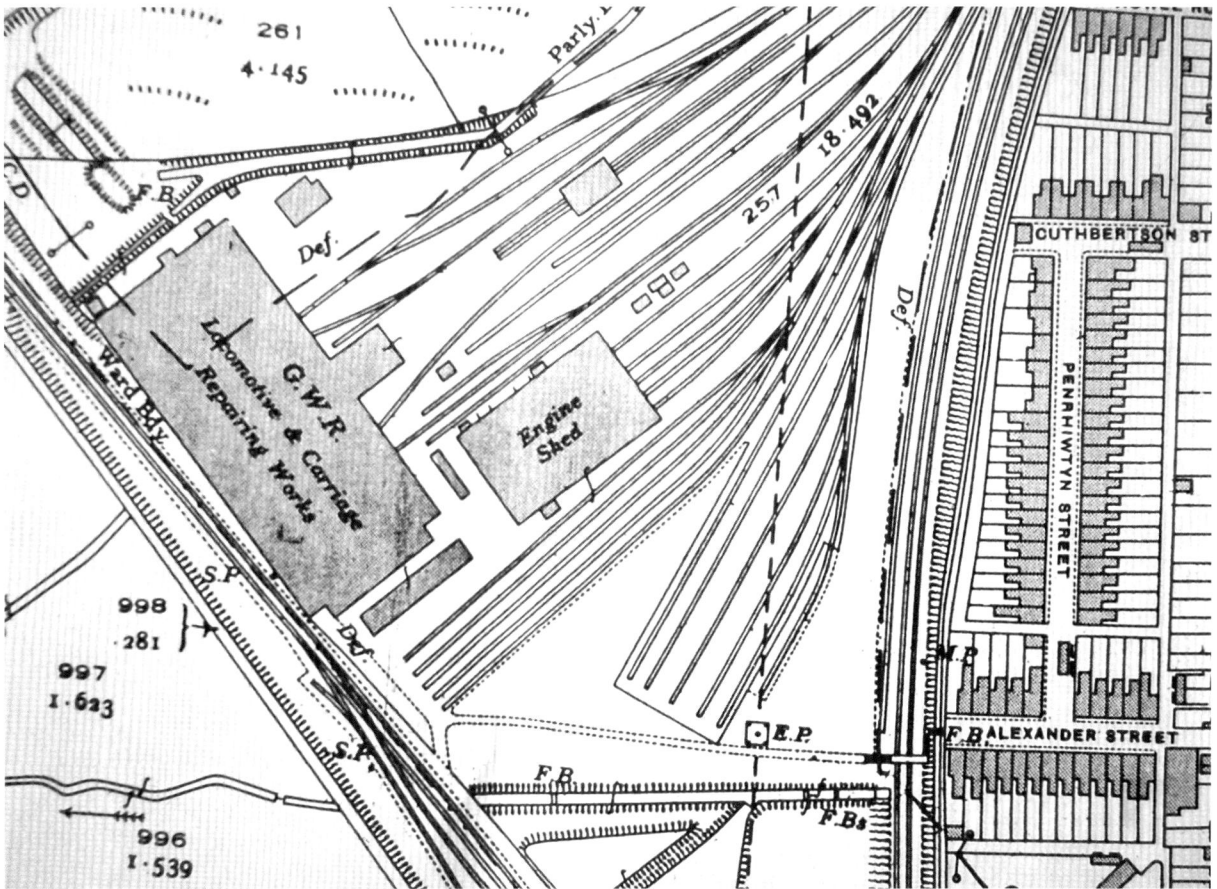

Extract from Ordnance Survey map for 1901 showing location and layout of Cwrt Sart shed.
The *Engine Shed* label on the map should in fact be *Carriage Repair Works*. The *Locomotive & Carriage Repairing Works* should be *Engine Shed*.

house No 2 used as a workshop which could repair three locomotives at a time. The shed had in and out roads from the coaling stage serving each road in between.

The coaling stage, enlarged in 1921, was serviced by an elevated line that delivered full coal wagons for emptying into the locos' coal bunkers under-neath. Engines could be coaled on both sides of the stage. It was crowned by a large water tank which held 90,000 gallons of water, supplied from the Neath Canal. In hot summers shed staff used the tank as their own swimming pool to cool off.

A de-coking line lay to the east of the coaling stage. There were sidings to accommodate locomo-

A 92xxx 2-10-0 on an oil train bound for Llandarcy on the *down* 'flying loop'. The 'spur' on the left was built in 1961 to connect the District line to the shed (*Martin Davies*)

121

Pannier tank No 9675 passes Cwrt Sart shed on a van train to Metal Box, 16 April 1965 (Robert Thomas)

6944 Fledborough Hall passes Cwrt Sart shed on the Swansea District line on an *up* freight, August 1964 (Martin Davies)

Grange 6878 Longford Grange, named after a local residence, is seen (minus nameplates) entering the first roundhouse, as Godfrey Carr and David Evans look on. August 1964 (Martin Davies)

A view inside one of the roundhouses in the early 1950s showing a selection of pannier tanks, nearest of which is Dean 'open cab' *850* class No *1996* built in 1891.
*(Neath Antiquarians)*

An 'Armstrong' outside frame 0-6-0 No *381* stands alongside the original (pre-1921) coaling stage
*(Gerald Williams)*

tives between their duties and to house locomotives in storage. These locos awaited overhaul at Caerphilly or Swindon works, each with a sack over its chimney to prevent rain erosion. Later, the siding was used to hold condemned locomotives, awaiting disposal to local scrapyards.

*Activities in the shed*

Cwrt Sart, rather than Swansea, became the parent depot for the GWR in south-west Wales when Neath was a major 'engine changing' post for the London to west Wales services. It had already become the district headquarters for the GWR after it had absorbed several local railways in the 1860s, well

0-6-0 pannier tank No *9792*, recently outshopped at Caerphilly Works, acts as coaling stage pilot in June 1961. After withdrawal she was sold to the NCB and worked for a number of years at Maerdy colliery.
*(Martin Davies)*

Ex-LMS 2-8-0 No 48436 stands on the western side of the 1921-built coaling stage in 1964 (*Jeff Jones*)

*Stella* class 2-4-0s, based at Cwrt Sart, were the mainstay of West Wales services from Neath in the late 19th century. Here is one at work near Goring in the 1930s. *(Great Western Trust)*

before the locomotive running shed, locomotive and wagon repair shops were opened.

### The locomotives

Few locomotives were assigned to Cwrt Sart sheds permanently, so the choice of locomotives to operate from the depot changed from time to time, either when the duties of the shed changed, or when locomotives came to the end of their useful lives, or when better designs became available to replace existing classes of locomotives.

### Early passenger engines

The depot's locomotives had important main-line functions in the late nineteenth and early twentieth century because engines were changed at Neath on Paddington to west Wales services. Incoming Swindon-based *Barnum* class 2-4-0 locomotives required servicing before their return journey, with two *Stellas* based at Neath for the onward part of the workings. The most common types on the west Wales services onwards from Neath in the 1880s and 90s were the 806 *Armstrong* and 2201 *Dean* class 2-4-0. Despite locomotives from the shed operating such glamorous main line duties, in January 1902, Cwrt Sart was the home of just thirty-eight locomotives, although the figure would almost double in later

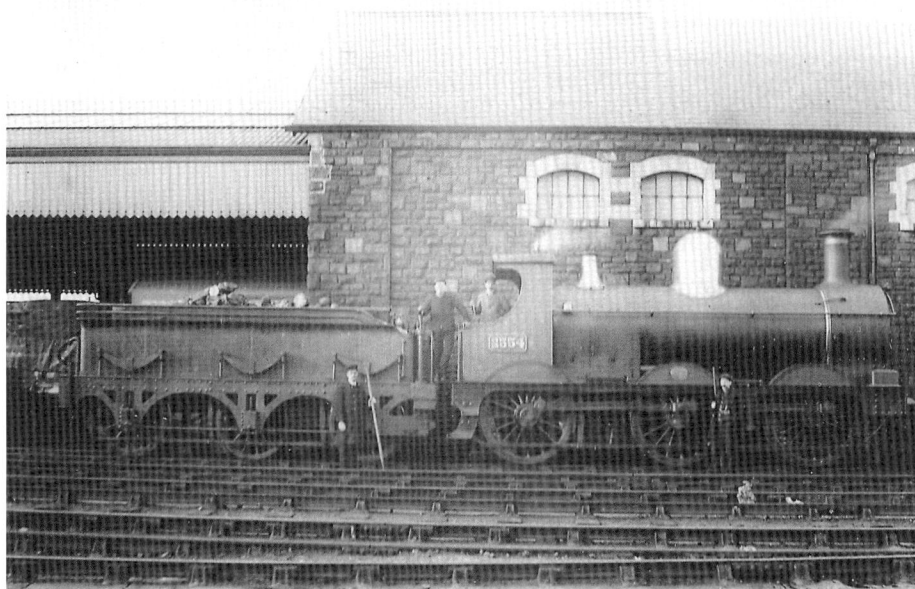

A number of 'Dean' goods 0-6-0s were based at Cwrt Sart in the late 19th century for freight work *(Neath Antiquarians)*

2-8-0 No *2818* on shed in April 1961. Once used on the 'Jellicoe specials' of World War 1, she is now preserved at 'Steam' museum in Swindon. *(Martin Davies)*

years. Apart from the 2-4-0s, eight *Dean* Goods 0-6-0s, and an *Aberdare* 2-6-0 for freight work, several pannier or saddle tanks for local goods, passenger and shunting duties were based here. A pair of 0-4-2 tanks, and several steam-powered rail-motors for local for passenger duties, completed the roster.

A further major operational change on the Paddington to west Wales services took place in 1903, when the introduction of larger *Atbara* class 4-4-0s engines became available to work through from Paddington to Cardiff. This change was complimented by the opening of a new, faster, route via Badminton, and the construction of water troughs at Chipping Sodbury and Goring.

As a result Cwrt Sart lost its place as a change-over point for express passenger trains, but it became more important for freight, becoming primarily a 'freight shed'. The depot would now provide the motive power for the many goods trains originating or terminating in the area as well as local passenger trains, although it did not again have an allocation of express passenger locomotives until 1961.

### The change to heavy freight

In 1921 Cwrt Sart's locomotive allocation still included SWMR loco No 1, RSBR No 29, a steam rail-motor and fifty-five other GWR designed locos of various classes. Later in the 1920s, six *ROD*[5] 2-8-0s, and several members of the *28xx* class, were allocated to Cwrt Sart. This type of loco had been used during the First World War on the *Jellicoe specials*, the procession of long trains that snaked away with coal from the south Wales valleys to provide fuel for the British naval fleets off northern Scotland. Cwrt Sart *28xx* locomotives took the Grangemouth-bound trains up the Vale of Neath line to Pontypool Road. The class were similarly involved in moving naval coal supplies from the district during the Second World War. Afterwards they were dispensed with at Cwrt Sart, for the principal 'heavy freight' loco to become the *42xx* class 2-8-0 tank. Only one *Hall* class loco was allocated to Cwrt Sart during the inter-war years: it was *4934*'s home between October 1932 and January 1934 until 1937 when *5972 Olton Hall* came there as a new engine. No further *Halls* were based there until 1960, when *Olton Hall* returned with other classmates.

### The 'maids of all work'

Fifty-seven engines were based at the shed in 1950[6] but the number had increased to sixty-five locomotives by 1953, with twenty of these stationed at the Neath and Brecon sub-depot and five at Glyn Neath. There were two WD[7] 2-8-0s for long distance freight, fifteen *42xx* 2-8-0 tanks for middle-distance freight, and three *Prairie* tanks for passenger trains to Pontypool Road, Treherbert, and Swansea. Thirty-four *57xx* and eight *94xx* 0-6-0 pannier tanks were based here to be on local freight, local passenger, shunting, and banking duties. One *16xx* lightweight 0-6-0 pannier was used on the lines servicing local works which had very tight curves.

### The age of the Halls and Castles

*42xx No 4252* on the decoking pit alongside the 1921-built coaling stage
*(Alun Hutchinson)*

Allocated to Cwrt Sart for many years, Prairie tank *No 8104* is stored outside the shed in 1961. *(Martin Davies)*

In 1960 five *Halls*, previously used normally for passenger work, were allocated for freight duties to and from the new 'hump' marshalling yard at Margam. This allocation followed the dieselisation of west of England services and the closure of Landore steam depot in Swansea. One of the allocation was No 5972 *Olton Hall*, whose remarkable story is told in Chapter Seven.

The closure of Landore to steam traction had a beneficial impact on Cwrt Sart depot for the period from June 1961 to 1962.[8] Great excitement was engendered amongst Briton Ferry and Neath rail enthusiasts when twelve of Landore's *Castles* were transferred to work the four overnight duties to Paddington. One of these was *5051 Earl Bathurst*

which, like *Olton Hall*, was also fortunate to escape. It was due for scrapping at Woodham's[9] yard at Barry Docks from where it was purchased for preservation and restoration to main line condition at Didcot Railway Centre. It has since seen use on main line steam specials such as the GWR's 150-year Anniversary in 1985. That September it was 'on show' in the station yard at Neath for a while, before taking part in Landore Open Day and hauling a return *steam special* from Swansea to Carmarthen. It was the first *Castle* seen in the area for twenty years.

Other *Castles* on Neath's roster were: *4090 Dorchester Castle*, which worked the last up South Wales Pullman in September 1961, *4093 Dunster Castle*, which worked the penultimate 'Pullman', *Kilgerran*

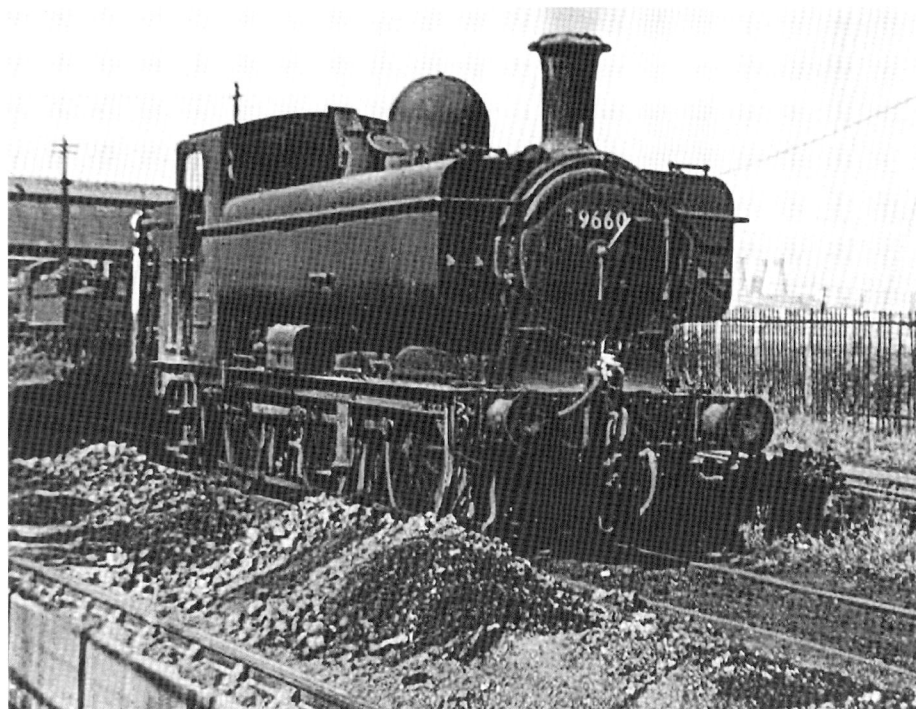

9660 is pictured on shed in 1964. She had been transferred to Neath upon the closure of Tondu shed *(Martin Davies)*

A clutch of Hawksworth pannier tanks were based at Neath for heavier shunting and trip work. No 9446 shunts the coaling stage in its role as shed pilot in 1964. *(Martin Davies)*

*Castle*, *Abergavenny Castle*, *Llanstephan Castle*, *Earl of Devon*, *Wellington*, *Monmouth Castle*, *Tiverton Castle*, *Earl of Shaftesbury* and *Beaufort*. These were joined in 1962 by *Earl of Ducie*, fresh from Swindon works, and selected two years' later as one of the *Castles* to haul the special train from Paddington to Plymouth to commemorate *City of Truro*'s record-breaking run of 1904. It was scrapped at Cohen's, Morriston, in 1964.

The full Cwrt Sart locomotive allocations for June 1921 will be found in Appendix Seven.

### Landore's steam legacy

The closure of Landore shed required the facility to transfer *Castles* to and from High Street station, Swansea. To do so, a new connection was made between Cwrt Sart shed and the *up* 'Flying Loop' on the Swansea District line. The coal stacking sidings at sheds were removed to allow this, enabling locos to run *light engine* from the shed, using the District line and the Morriston branch, to reach the terminus at Swansea.

Hall class 4-6-0 No 6918 *Sandon Hall* at Cwrt Sart in 1964. This is one of the locos transferred to that shed upon the closure of Landore shed in June 1961 *(Martin Davies)*

*5051 Earl Bathurst*, one of the *Castles* transferred to Cwrt Sart in that year, is being prepared to work *The Pembroke Coast Express* to London in September 1961 *(Colour Rail)*

*5051* was one of the locos put into temporary storage when the *Hymek* diesels were introduced. Seen here outside the shed on 16 April 1962. *(Alun Hutchinson)*

Another *Castle* put into temporary storage was *4090 Dorchester Castle*, which worked the last ever steam-hauled 'Pullman' from Swansea to London in September 1961. *(Alun Hutchinson)*

Landore had a reputation for the first-class turn-out of its express locos, with sparkling Brunswick green paintwork, burnished brass and copper-capped chimneys with 'trademark' white buffers. Cleaning staff at Cwrt Sart were determined to match this and the tradition continued when the locos were based at Cwrt Sart. During summer Sundays in 1961 visiting enthusiasts had a memorable experience to see rows of Collett's stylish locomotives lined up alongside the coaling stage, gleaming in the sun.

*Silver buffers*

Silver buffers, silver buffers,
You can see them from afar,
Silver buffers, silver buffers,
They were Landore's calling card.

In the top link, up to London,
Ex-works Castle, a mean machine,
Burnished copper, shining brasswork,
Lined out, gleaming Brunswick green.

It might be Bathurst or Dynevor,
Dunster or Montgomery,
Fairey Battle or Defiant,
Everyone a sight to see.

Some had old single funnels,
Some rebuilt with double blasts,
But all were truly Swindon-crafted,
Machines really made to last

Pembroke Coast, South Wales Pullman,

Were top jobs for Landore men,
Double home was the roster,
To the land of old Big Ben

Seven tons of prime Welsh steam coal,
Shovelled hard into the grate,
Just enough to last the journey,
Right on time, rarely late

The work was hard, it was dirty,
Fraught with danger some might say
But worth it all for the teamwork,
A job well done most every day.,

Old Roy White, that great shed master
Solved a problem with some jest,
Paint silver buffers on your engine
To pick it out from the rest

This saved time for a Landore driver,
Ready for the run back home
Many Castles 'round Old Oak's tables,
But he picked out his very own.

Silver buffers, silver buffers,
You can see them from afar,
Silver buffers, silver buffers
They were Landore's calling card.

*Martin Davies*

*Visitors from afar*

During the time that *Castles* worked the London trains, it was common to see engines from Old Oak

130

'The Spur' built in 1961 to allow locomotives running light engine from Swansea to access Cwrt Sart shed is shown in this study of 2-8-0 2876 with brake van. (John Davies)

The other recipient of Landore's Castles upon its closure was Llanelli. One of its number, 5077 Fairey Battle visits Cwrt Sart shed in September 1961 (Colour Rail)

'Visitors' to Cwrt Sart. Mogul No 6384 from Severn Tunnel Junction in September 1961 (5043, now preserved, can be seen in the distance) (Martin Davies)

A pair of Castles sparkling in the sunshine – 4090 Dorchester Castle and 4099 Kilgerran Castle (Norman Jones)

*7013 Bristol Castle* from Worcester Shed in August 1964. This loco had changed identities with *4082 Windsor Castle* in 1952 in order to have the 'appropriately' named loco available to haul King George VI's funeral train in 1952. (The 'real' *Windsor Castle* was under overhaul in Swindon Works at the time.) *(Martin Davies)*

Common, Cardiff Canton, and Bristol. Freight locomotives came from Severn Tunnel, St Philips Marsh, Tyseley, Worcester and Gloucester and later from depots in other regions.

In the last few years of the depot's life it was common for 9F 2-10-0s, ex-LMS 8F 2-8-0s from various Midland Region sheds to visit for servicing. Other more 'exotic' locomotives like *Jubilees*, *Royal Scots*, *Britannias*, and even a *Clan*, were noted over this period. *Patriot*, *45515 Caernarvon*, received attention in the workshops before returning to its home area, but the only known occasion for an ex-LNER loco to visit was also in 1961 when 2-6-0 *61894* was serviced at Cwrt Sart after working a freight into Margam.

*Modified Hall 7929 Wyke Hall* eases out of the shed before heading to pick up an oil train from Llandarcy to the Midlands. *(Martin Davies)*

'Southern' locos only visited the area en route to scrapyards in Morriston. One such loco, an *S15* 4-6-0 developed a 'hot box' and had to be taken to Cwrt Sart for attention. It is seen here being marshalled by *3687*.

Crosti boilered *9F 92021*, another foreign visitor to Cwrt Sart shed, on the decoking road, August 1964 *(Jeff Jones)*

From 1963 onwards, more and more freight services were turned over to diesel traction. As a result, other steam sheds such as Duffryn Yard, Swansea East Dock, and Tondu were closed and the remaining locos transferred to the parent depot at Cwrt Sart.

*A short reprieve*

The steam passenger activity was short-lived: *Castles* were gradually taken out of service with the introduction of *Hymek* diesels on the west Wales to London expresses in 1962. It was a sad sight that April to witness a clutch of recently cleaned *Castles* stored out-of-service. However, the 'teething trouble' experienced by the diesels, and the demands of the more intense summer service, meant that several Castles, such as *Earl Bathurst* and *Dorchester Castle*, were reprieved to steam again a few months later. Never-

In 1964 *Britannias* had become rare 'birds' in the area. However, Midland region based *70030 William Wordsworth* visited Cwrt Sart after hauling a 'special' into the area. The loco is seen passing Briton Ferry en route to the shed to be serviced. *(Jeff Beer)*

theless, by the summer of 1962 just six *Castles*, including *Earl of Ducie*, remained at Cwrt Sart. Some had been transferred to Llanelli to work steam-hauled services west of Swansea until September.

Others, like *Dorchester Castle*, were sent further afield to the likes of Shrewsbury, with the result that *Beaufort* was the last *Castle* officially allocated to Cwrt Sart. Rebuilt with a double chimney just eighteen months earlier, it was withdrawn in December. Yet *Castles* from Worcester and Gloucester continued to visit Cwrt Sart shed into 1965 on freight runs to Margam, and on the steel billet trains from the Albion Steelworks at Briton Ferry. from Worcester *Castles* such as *Bristol Castle*, *Earl of Eldon*, and *Sudeley Castle* continued to visit Cwrt Sart shed into 1964 on freight runs to Margam, and on the steel billet trains from the Albion Steelworks at Briton Ferry. In fact the last four *Castles* operative on the Western Region, then based at Gloucester shed, including *Clun Castle*, were regularly serviced at Neath.

Therefore, from 1964, Cwrt Sart's allocation was again based around the haulage of freight trains. It had a fleet of *Halls*, *Granges*, *28xx* 2-8-0s, and standard *9F* 2-10-0s including the famous *92220 Evening Star*, the last steam loco built at Swindon Works. This loco was often used on the block oil trains from BP Llandarcy oil refinery to Rowley Regis in the Midlands, still adorned with its specially-permitted brunswick green livery and copper-capped chimney. The 2-10-0s were well liked by engine men from Cwrt Sart shed being good steaming locos and easy to operate. The late Doug Rice, a footplateman at the shed in the 1960s, and in later life a staunch regular

driver-member of the Gwili Railway in west Wales, was one who drove *Evening Star* from the shed.

Robert Davies was a close friend of Doug Rice and worked with him on the Gwili Railway.

> He was a cleaner and fireman at Neath (N and B) shed, and later a fireman at Duffryn Yard. I shared the footplate with him for many years on the Gwili. Great times! I fondly remember our relationship was as close as you could get to working on the 'real railway'; Not a lot of conversation, everything done on 'a nod and a wink '. We knew each other's way of working, there was no need to speak!

*Unsolicited cleaning*

During regular sorties to Neath shed local enthusiasts took an interest in the external condition of the locos stored outside. They took it upon themselves clean the accessible parts of the locos to prevent deterioration of paintwork during prolonged exposure to the elements. This was especially the case when *Castles* were in temporary storage. One of their number, Tony 'Wilbur' Griffiths went a step further and set about adorning the cab handrail of a pannier tank with silver paint. Loco 9446, was stored awaiting transfer to Caerphilly Works for overhaul. On its return after overhaul, it was fully repainted in black, but its cab handrails which were still silver. Clearly, the painters at Caerphilly appreciated Tony's elegant, decorative intervention!

*Closure*

Cwrt Sart shed closed to steam in June 1965. For a year or so, the depot remained open to diesel traction but on the 17 April, 1966 came total closure. All footplate staff were transferred to Neath General Station where they signed on each day. Then there were 27 drivers and 22 firemen (now called second men). Several people retired at the end of steam working or were transferred to Margam or Landore diesel depots.

The workshop staff, too, including fitters such as Gerald Williams, were transferred to Landore or Margam unless they were of retirement age. Ten went to Margam in April 1964, travelling each day from Neath by a specially provided bus service and six were transferred to Landore in May of that year. A solitary member of the workshop staff was retained to operate the stationary boiler at the Carriage and Wagon Works. It closed in 1968 and the shed was demolished in 1969.

When the sheds closed, it was more than the closure of a visible building. Where lots worked together, in the type of social structure described above, the closure had a psycho-social impact, too. It was not just the individual breadwinner who was

The shed in the course of demolition
*(Gerald Williams)*

at risk of losing lost their job; others were affected by the breaking of the invisible bonds that tied together those that worked alongside one another. The bonds, too, within the community of railway workers' families were at risk, but the Retired Rail Staff Association was important in ameliorating this effect. Nevertheless, work would no longer pass so easily from one generation to another and closure of the sheds was more than the closure of a tangible building.

The flat, once boggy, site of Cwrt Sart engine sheds (2018) became playing fields for twenty years. *(Martin Davies)*
*(The author's sons, Keith and Peter davies played football there in the early 1990s)*

**Notes for Chapter Seven**

1. According to Richard Muir's *Landscape Encyclopaedia* (2004), the word is northern French where *essarter* means to 'remove or grub out woodland'
2. Llansawel Crescent
3. *Cambrian*, 24 September 1875
4. It was shifted to the west side in 1928.
5. *ROD* means the Railway Operating Division of the Royal Engineers, formed in 1915 to operate the railways in several theatres of war. It requisitioned locomotives and crews from Britain's rail companies.
6. They are listed in Appendix Seven
7. Heavy freight 'Austerity' locos introduced in 1943 for the War Department (WD)
8. Appendix Seven lists the seventy-four engines based here in June 1961
9. Woodham's held many locos with the original intention of scrapping, but instead sold them for preservation

Chapter Eight

# Staffing

*Heaven helps those who help themselves.*

Samuel Smiles, 1859

## Introduction

Whereas the previous chapter outlined the physical characteristics of Cwrt Sart depot and its locomotives, the current chapter examines the shed's purpose and its operations in more detail by explaining how staff were managed to fulfil its purpose. The shed existed to provide locomotive power as needed for the various freight, passenger and breakdown duties involved. As the parent depot for managing ten separate locomotive depots and sub-sheds between Port Talbot and Fishguard, Cwrt Sart also housed the Divisional Superintendent's Office.

The performance of the locomotives provided for service depended on the management of those who drove and maintained them. Effective management required an organisation structure in which duties were clearly defined and discharged. The performance of such duties required careful selection, training and development of staff by transfer, through mutual improvement classes and by good supervision. These features require the creation of a culture which was supported by good working conditions, terms of employment and social relations.

In this chapter, therefore, the work and duties performed at the depot and the working lives of those who worked there will be traced, sometimes with accounts from the staff themselves. The chapter closes with the effects of the depot's closure on its staff and the local community.

## Organisation and management of the shed

### The Shedmaster

The day-to-day control of the depot overall was the responsibility of the Shedmaster. He was accountable for providing the motive power for the needs of the operating department.

The required engines had to be ready, in good order and repair, to work all trains to the booked times. In the case of special trains on the main line, a notice of three hours was considered sufficient to allow any arrangements to be made. For short trips however, twenty to thirty minutes only was allowed.

Emlyn Davies was the most well-known shedmaster at Cwrt Sart because he played rugby for Wales. He started his working life as an office boy at the Port Talbot Steelworks. After joining Duffryn Yard shed he rose through the ranks as a fireman during the second World War, then locomotive driver, panel foreman and assistant shedmaster before becoming shedmaster at Cwrt Sart in 1961. This was a busy time for the depot because Landore shed had closed and half of its locos and staff were transferred to Neath, which became involved in the rostering of expresses to London. In subsequent years he managed the integration of staff from other local depots such as Swansea East Dock as they were closed.

Davies played for Cwmavon, Cymmer and Glyncorrwg before joining Aberavon whom he captained in the 1949/50 season. He represented British Railway XVs and had won the first of his two caps against the touring Australians at Cardiff Arms Park on 20 December 1947.

Emlyn was well liked and respected by his staff and remained in post until the shed closed in 1965. He was welcoming to genuine railway enthusiasts who behaved safely when they visited the shed during his tenure.

> A lovely man, he always smoked a pipe.
> My father worked with him at Duffryn
> Yard and he thought the world of him.
> (Hugh James)

As local lines closed or lost their passenger services. Emlyn supported his staff in the special

Emlyn Davies had ensured that loco No *3621* and its sister *3693* were specially prepared to work the last passenger services over the Neath and Brecon. The loco is pictured here with a group of staff at the start of the final day of services, 13 October 1961. Staff standing are (from left to right): Stores Clerk, Tom Jones; Bill Saunders; Timekeeper, Ken Webb; Stores Issuer, Sam Lewis; Chief Clerk, Brian Davies; Passed Cleaner, Brian Dyke and Chargeman Cleaner, Powell. On the running plate: Fitter, Raymond Lloyd; in the cab: Fireman, David O'Shea and Driver, Brian Lewis. *(Norman Jones)*

Administration staff in the 1950s.
On the extreme right is chief clerk Sidney Bentley who worked at the depot until its closure in 1965.

preparation of locos for the final trains to run on these lines, ensuring that there was always a fitting send-off.

Following the closure of Neath sheds Emlyn was able to use his invaluable experience in the new role of area manager.

*Organisation*

The organisation chart (Organisation chart showing the staffing at Cwrt Sart page 141) shows the grades of shed staff and the delegation of authority within the shed. The staff responsible to the shedmaster were grouped into five categories whose duties and lines of promotion will now be reviewed.

- Locomotive Running, under the control of a Shift Foreman
- Administrative Staff, under the control of the Chief Clerk
- Sub-shed Foreman
- Mechanical Foreman
- Boilersmiths

*Locomotive running duties*

There were twenty-five operational duties at the Shed, organised into five 'links' for footplate staff. Each duty comprised a fireman and a driver who worked various shifts.[1] About fifty pairs of footplate

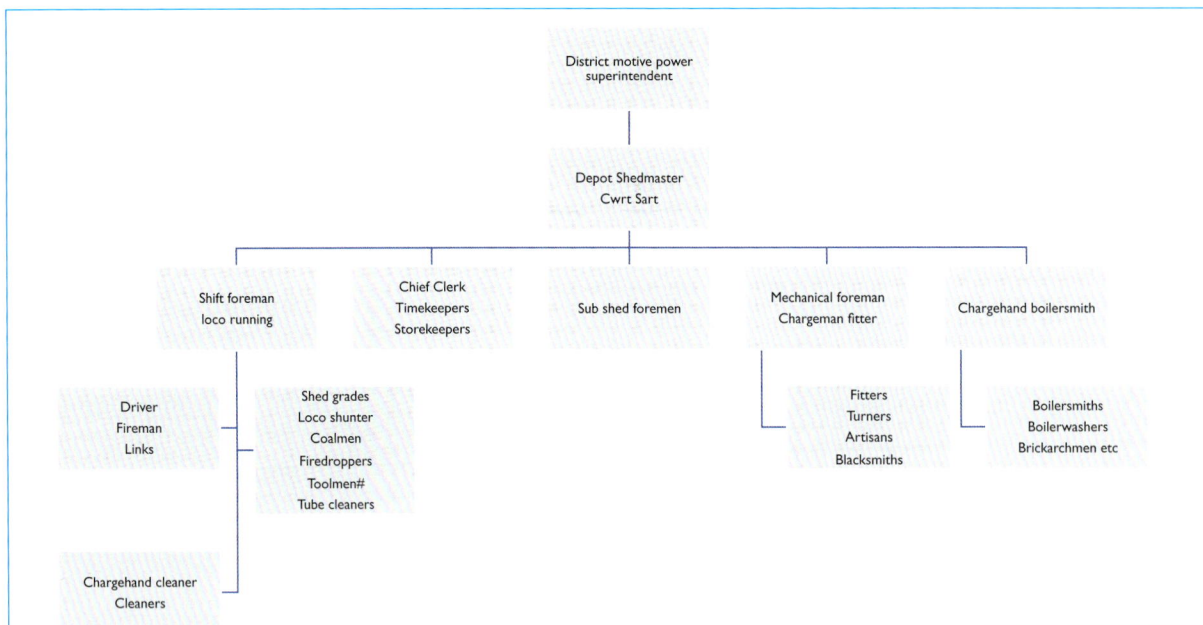

Organisation chart showing the staffing at Cwrt Sart *(Gerald Williams)*

| Link | Duties |
|------|--------|
| 1 | Passenger link with duties to Pontypool, Aberdare and Treherbert |
| 2 | Goods |
| 3 | Goods |
| 4 | Yard pilot work |
| 5 | All movements around the shed |

The five links

staff carried out these duties around the clock, a total of 100 men. Briton Ferry-born Phil Bannister[2], who worked at the depot in the 1950s and 1960s, recorded many aspects of his daily routine and other staff who worked there.

*Chargehand cleaner*

A chargehand cleaner was responsible for his complement of cleaners.

*Shift Foreman*

The Shift Foreman was responsible for loco shunters, coalmen, fire-droppers, and tube cleaners.

*Administration: The Chief Clerk*

The Chief Clerk was responsible for scheduling the preparatory operations of the locomotives in the sheds. With the support of clerks, timekeepers and storekeepers he was accountable for the extremely important *working engine* list which included a seven-day working schedule to manage each type of duty e.g. express passenger, local passenger, express

goods etc. This was supplemented by a *daily* list covering twelve hours which included any special workings along with a *supplementary* list which detailed cancellations, changes to starting times or other alterations. The clerical staff also dealt with important operating and maintenance correspondence such as engine failures, casualties, drivers' daily returns and tickets, mileage, coal and water consumption, engine repairs and stores

*Sub-shed Foremen*

These were responsible for all the work carried out at the sub-sheds of Neath (N and B) and Glyn Neath.

*Mechanical Foreman*

> 'The fitting staff are responsible for all running repairs being dealt with satisfactorily and to time. The foreman should endeavour to get everything done as expeditiously as possible to alleviate friction among the staff and facilitate the departure of engines at their booked times.'[3]

Gerald Williams,[4] a steam fitter at Cwrt Sart from 1960 until 1965 provided much of the information about the work carried on at the shed. His daily routine included a range of skilled work such as attending to worn side and connecting rods, adjusting brake rodding, lifting out wheels and axles, changing springs, and repairing ashpan wear. The amount of pipework on a steam locomotive meant that the specialist skills of a coppersmith was needed to keep each loco running efficiently.

Repairs to the coupling rods of a *Britannia* class loco at Cwrt Sart, 1960s *(Gerald Williams)*

The Carriage and Wagon Works staff of 1948 *(Gerald Williams)*

*Chargehand Boilersmith*

This role entailed supervision of staff working on locomotive boilers on such tasks as re-tubing, replacement of stays, wash-outs and work on super-heaters. Brick arch men, who worked inside the loco-motives' fireboxes, were also responsible to the chargehand boilersmith.

*The Shed Breakdown Crew*

The breakdown crew of eight had an inspector in overall charge, with a breakdown foreman to super-vise a crane driver, a burner, a first aid man, a tool man/cook and fitters like Gerald Williams who were drawn from a pool of seven people. The breakdown gang's equipment consisted of one 45-ton steam crane, one tool coach, one sleeping and dining coach, and a guard's van, hauled usually by a pannier tank.

The crew's duties involved the re-railing of loco-motives, wagons and coaches. The crane would only be used in the case of a very bad derailment or when a major piece of equipment such as a bridge, needed to be moved. In the latter situations, up to four extra staff would be needed. Their duties would be setting up hard wood blocks to level out the crane and lock it to the track. Examples of incidents involving the breakdown crew are detailed in Chapter Seven. The breakdown crew from Cwrt Sart covered the whole of south-west Wales from Port Talbot to Fishguard.

*Carriage and Wagon Works*

Any paintwork that needed touching up was carried out by staff from the carriage and wagon repair shops. The works had a staff of about twenty people to repair goods wagons and passenger coaches.

*The canteen staff*

Railway work was vital to the war effort in the Sec-ond World War and rail staff, including drivers and firemen, worked long hours in demanding condi-tions. Good catering facilities were essential to sus-tain operations so they were provided at Cwrt Sart shed from 1939. The canteen continued in use after the war and became an important part of the social life of the shed. Jack Murdock was responsible as manager for ten canteen staff in 1946.

**Recruitment, training and development of staff**

A job on the *Western* was regarded as a privileged position in the working community and footplate-men, especially drivers, were highly respected in local communities such as Briton Ferry. The respect was hard-earned. The GWR, like other railway com-panies, was keen to ensure that staff were given opportunities both to improve their ability to perform their assigned duties and to enhance their promotion prospects. The company therefore insis-ted upon a rigorous selection procedure even for temporary staff. Promotion was by written appli-cation and not automatic. Therefore, an application for a fireman's job and above involved a visit to Head-quarters at Swindon for interview and pre-employ-ment medical.

On appointment the company therefore provided welfare and educational facilities.

The accepted path for promotion was from *cleaner* to *passed cleaner* to *fireman* to *passed fireman* to *locomotive driver*. A *passed cleaner* was someone who had gained sufficient training to deputise for a fireman when required. Similarly, a *passed fireman* was someone who was regarded as proficient enough to act as a driver when required and was in line for

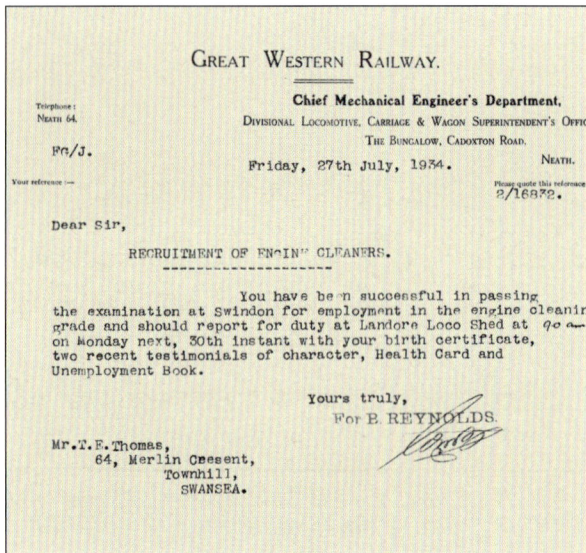

Acceptance letter for the post of cleaner at Landore shed for T E Thomas, 1934 *(Gerald Williams)*

promotion to a driver when a vacancy occurred.

The generally accepted principle of promotion was by 'seniority plus ability'. However employment in the rail workforce entailed much individual mobility with promotion frequently dependent on moving to another part of the country to find a suitable vacancy elsewhere in the GWR. Thus, a cleaner from Cwrt Sart might have to move to Old Oak Common in London to take up a position as a fireman, or for a fireman like David Leonard to move to Cardiff, Bristol or Plymouth to fill a vacancy for a driver. Transfers from the shed were to places far and wide: to Glynneath, Dowlais, Newton Abbot, Tyseley, Swindon, Exeter, Old Oak Common, Neyland, Pontypool Road and Goodwick to name just a few.

The approach taken to promotion differed from other railways: on France's railways, for example, someone could become a full-time main line driver at the tender age of twenty-seven.

Demotion was also a possibility in disciplinary cases. Albert Edward Joseph Jasper Alder was a GWR shunter at Briton Ferry in 1911. The first remarkable incident in his railway career had occurred at Lydney in 1900 where the then foreman 're-labelled a wagon to Whitecroft resulting in six bags of nails being wrongly delivered'. Two years' later at Cwmbran he was 'severely reprimanded for damaging a cask of whisky which resulted in a heavy claim'. No further mishaps were reported until 1910 when Alder, now a shunter at Newport's Dock Street, 'seriously neglected his duty, causing two wagons to be derailed'. His subsequent transfer to Briton Ferry appears to have been successful. So, too, was that of Thomas W J Backshell. The former porter was suspended from his signalling duties at Garnant for negligence resulting in damage to crossing gates. More seriously, he allowed an incomplete train to pass his box without warning the following train. Backshell's career at Briton Ferry was uneventful and he left for Ferryside in 1912.

*Pay rates*

The table below shows pay rates for various jobs at the end of the nineteenth century.

The basic earnings figures in the table show that wage rates were not generous, and men rarely received increases unless they changed to a higher rate job, usually in another, and often far-off, location. The wage rates provide an indication of the industrial relations climate which existed on the railways of south Wales during the early twentieth century. This matter will be enlarged on further in Chapter Thirteen.

Edward Hall moved from Cwrt Sart to Chester as a fireman to gain promotion. William Maddocks was more fortunate. He started as a lad packer in 1883,

| Year | Job | Rate per day | 2016 weekly equivalent[5] | Name |
|------|-----|-------------|-------------------------|------|
| 1883 | Turner | 5 shillings | £139.48 | George Oswald Gibbs |
| 1899 | Turner | 6 shillings | £176.88 | Charles Edward Gibbs |
| 1889 | Cleaner | 2 shillings 3 pence | £66.33 | David Evans |
| 1890 | Shed man | 3 shillings | £88.44 | Henry Enoch |
| 1891 | Fitter | 5 shillings 6 pence | £160.32 | Thomas Fairhurst |
| 1891 | Fitter's labourer | 3 shillings | £87.45 | George Garraway |
| 1893 | Boilersmith | 2 shillings 6 pence | £73.70 | William Alexander Forsyth |
| 1894 | Shed boy | 3 shillings | £89.46 | Edward Hall |
| 1898 | Cleaner | 2 shillings 3 pence | £67.09 | George Gittins |
| 1900 | Foreman | 65 shillings (per week) | £592.17 | C Hedges |
| 1902 | Lad porter | 10 shillings (per week) | £281.98 | Owen John Emmanuel |
| 1908 | Shunter | 30 shillings (per week) | £338.38 | Owen John Emmanuel |

Pay rates for various jobs at the end of the nineteenth century becoming a packer two years' later, then a switch-man at Neath after a further four years, before bec-oming a signalman at Neath and Port Talbot yards in the early 1890s.

Thomas S Attwood was a lad porter at Treharris in 1904, earning fourteen shillings a week. His earn-ings rose to twenty-four shillings a week when he became a shunter at Merthyr in 1907; by moving to Briton Ferry two years' later he increased his pay to twenty-seven shillings.

Edward Stephen Restiaux started as a stores clerk at Swindon and subsequently moved to Shrewsbury, Llanelli, Swansea and Briton Ferry. At retirement in 1920 as a GWR accountant his salary was seventy shillings a week.

*Mutual Improvement Classes*

Free and compulsory state education did not come to Britain until 1890. Prior to that, education, to some extent, was a case of *Heaven helps those who help themselves*, where people might learn to read in chapels or, sometimes, in schools provided by employers. Self-help was what Scottish author Samuel Smiles had advocated in 1859. He called for new attitudes to promote thrift and believed that poverty was largely due to irresponsible habits. Smiles also called for rail nationalisation, so it is instructive to consider the education and training of rail workers during the lifetime of Cwrt Sart loco-motive depot. Self-help alone could not train the staff needed to operate and maintain railway loco-motives and signalling, so one may ask how much railway education and training was due to the efforts of individuals and how much was down to the employer or to the state? Was the learning involved just job training or did it extend to a wider, further education?

An engine shed like Cwrt Sart could not have operated so successfully over such a long period without a system to support the individual skills and abilities that have been described. One important ele-ment of the system for the personnel development of shed staff was the mutual improvement class. It is unsurprising that Mutual Improvement Classes were held at most engine sheds for staff to gain enhanced training. At Cwrt Sart classes were held in the Dis-trict Superintendent's Office building on a Sunday morning. The instructors were senior footplatemen who volunteered their time. Such was the cama-raderie in the depot they were not paid for their activities. Men were proud to pass on their skill and knowledge to another generation. Those attending learned the workings of steam locomotives and took tests, based on the 'rules of the road'. This learning

The building behind the *Class 37* diesel is the original District Superintendent's office. This was later moved to Cadoxton Road, Neath, and then to High Street, Swansea.
*(Gerald Williams)*

was job training and not further education. It was as much for the benefit of the employer as the employee.

David Wooderson was a war evacuee from Kent sent to live with a family in Whitland in west Wales. He described the process of mutual improvement:

> Walford, the son of the house and I, got on well. He was studying to become what was usually called a 'passed fireman' but locally as a 'passenger fireman', in other words a fireman passed to act as a driver when a vacancy occurred…. Not only did he have to know a lot about locomotives, fault diagnosis and so on, but also about emergency single-line working and the like. He would get me to read out questions from a practice book and check the answers. Needless to say, I found this far more interesting than most of what I was supposed to be learning at school. Just as sailors had to 'Box the Compass', naming thirty-two points in order, so he had to 'go around the wheel', meaning eight portions of each crank, say where the other crank would be and what each valve would be doing in forward, mid and back gear. I can still do it.

After the examinations to test their proficiency footplatemen were awarded Certificates of Merit, such as the one below awarded to Mr B Thomas in 1932. Mutual improvement classes were well-attended and became a part of the social network within the locomotive depot and created a means for staff to meet outside their working hours. Social excursions were often organised for those attending the classes to destinations such as Windsor in 1932 and to Twickenham in 1950 for a rugby match.

Mutual improvement was largely for job training, rather than for general, further education, although it is likely that some railwaymen availed themselves of the evening class facilities at Neath Mechanics Institute and the Public Libraries at Briton Ferry and Skewen for that purpose. Others' self-help was obtained through the WEA and Central Labour College, for example Ivor Owen Thomas MP.

*First Aid training*

The nature of railway work meant that accidents sometimes occurred. It has long been a legal requirement for employers to provide first aid at work; thus, it was vital that sufficient volunteer staff were trained in first aid to assist in the event of an accident, before specialist medical staff arrived on the scene. To this end first aid courses were held in the depot by the St John's Ambulance Association on a regular basis, usually on a Sunday afternoon. Participants were expected to sit examinations to test their proficiency and were awarded certificates when successful.

**Individuals and some recollections**

Some of the cleaners, firemen and drivers from the sheds have passed on some interesting experiences from their working lives. To avoid forgetting them, these are reported below. Other events have been gathered from employee records.

*James Adams[6] – fatherhood first*

Jim Adams started work as a fourteen-year-old cleaner at Cwrt Sart shed a rate of one shilling per week in 1884. His career in the shed lasted ten years, ending at the time of his marriage and the birth of his first child, John Charles Adams. By then he was a fireman earning a weekly wage of four shillings and three pence. This was a considerable increase within ten years on his starting wage of one shilling. Although promotion was necessary to achieve this enhanced wage, it is worth comparing the earnings progression of a rail worker with that of an agricultural labourer during this period. The wages of the agricultural labourer barely increased whereas the earnings of railwaymen, although starting from an unfavourable level, could be enhanced through time and promotion.

Adams clearly saw some financial advantage, and perhaps some glamour, in rail work, but he had not, it seems, fully assessed the compatibility of the irregular shifts required as a fireman with his duties as a new father. More than once he was admonished for

| Agricultural labourer | Year | Railwayman |
|---|---|---|
| 13/7½ | 1884 | 1/0 |
| 13/6 | 1890 | 3/9 |
| 13/9 | 1894 | 4/3 |

Earnings progression of a rail worker and agricultural labourer

not turning up for scheduled duties during his wife's pregnancy.

Although he moved to Briton Ferry after his marriage, very convenient to work at Cwrt Sart sheds, it soon became evident that the skills he had learned on the railway were very transferable. As a result, he took up a position as a stationary engine driver at nearby Gwalia tinworks. It involved shift work, but not the irregular shift work required as a fireman at the sheds. During this time 'Gentleman Jim' Adams lost two of his younger volunteer brothers in the Boer and First World Wars. Thomas was a cleaner at Cwrt Sart shed before he left and died defending Ladysmith.

*Phil Bannister: Cwrt Sart shed's poet laureate*

Phil Bannister's evocative description of the tasks involved in a *cheminot*'s life whilst working at the sheds was composed after a working life of many years performing the tasks he described:

> Have you ever worked on the railway like the GWR or British Rail?
> Well I have, so here is some detail.
> The place I started was at Neath Loco Shed
> Where engines came to life brought back from the dead,
> I had to learn all the jobs so that sometime later,
> I would be skilled enough to be put on the roster,
> First learning to clean out the tubes,
> With a long steel rod, you poked, and with a steam lance you blew
> Inside the firebox you had to squeeze because it was very tight,
> And, in order to see, you had a carbon lamp light,
> Boiler washing was another job where you had to wash out all the muck,
> With a hosepipe when now and then you used steam to blow, not suck,
> Two other jobs you did outside which were not all honey,
> Were jobs where you could really earn a bit more money,

One other was fire-dropping, with long bars and long handled shovels
Those were the tools you require,
Because it was with these that you cleaned out the fire,
Fireboxes full, you can bet, on every engine you just sweat,
No, that's not it all my man, there's the smokebox and ashpan,
The engine is then moved down under the coal stage,
To be coaled, and here again you earned your wage,
Shovelling coal whether it be from iron or wooden wagon,
You shovelled into drams to feed the hungry dragon,
Tons you had to shovel galore, tip half in the bunker and half on the floor,
One top job, the lighter up, he goes around with a paraffin lit on a shovel,
Shovels coal in the box, the lamp lights oily waste and faggots to make water bubbles,
Has to keep quite a number in check, so they're ready to go out on time,
So that all the engines can run up and down the railway line,
And so, all these jobs came to pass,
Where are the loco sheds? Well, they're now covered with grass,
I know, for I was there!

*P G Bannister (Neath, Cwrt Sart, shedman)*

*Cyril Davies – retro street wear?*

Cyril Davies was quite a remarkable railwayman who hailed from the Forest of Dean/Newport and initially worked as a goods driver at Cwrt Sart depot. He and his wife, Win, lived in Poplars Avenue – a desirable address but one sometimes afflicted with a little petit bourgeois snobbery. Cyril was not the only railway worker in Poplars Avenue: Arthur Harris at number eight was also an engine driver and Alfred L Williams at number twenty-two was a senior railway surveyor. Cyril was accustomed to go to and from work in his driver's uniform – an innocuous jacket over a navy work suit and an enviable soft peaked cap (which today might pass for retro street wear). Their next-door neighbour was Miss Brooks, deputy head and maths teacher at the Neath Girls' Grammar School. Her mother, Mrs Brooks, felt that workers

Castle 4-6-0 *Earl of Eldon* on the ash pit at Cwrt Sart *(Martin Davies)*

143

wearing the uniforms of their trades somehow lowered the tone of the treeless avenue. As a result, she had what was meant to be a coercive word with Win Davies, asking her to ask her husband not to wear working clothes to and from work. Whether she also approached Mrs Harris and Mrs Williams in like manner is not known. What we do know is that Win Davies was always a loyal Ferry girl: her reply is not known but her husband continued, unintimidated, to wear his working clothes both to and from work.

*Dai Ealey – 'something of a character'*

Sometimes, drivers tried to catch some extra sleep and pretend they hadn't been called for work. Dai Ealey, something of a character, was on call-duty one week.

> On the first night, the driver came in late saying he hadn't been called. This happened again on the next night. On the third night, when he came in late, the foreman asked him if he had noticed anything strange when he left the house. When he replied No, the foreman held out his hand and showed him two nuts. Dai had taken a spanner with him and undid the front gate and put it down on the driver's garden. He then brought in the nuts to prove that he had called him.

Although David had only had four firing turns in his capacity as 'passed cleaner' he applied for a vacancy as a fireman at Reading. Before doing so, he had to undergo a medical examination at Swindon Works.

> The only thing I remember about the examination was being given different strands of wool that had to be sorted into separate groups of the same colour, i.e. red, green and blue. This was to see if you suffered from colour blindness.

On 1 May 1944, seventeen-year-old David Ealey went off to work as a fireman at Reading shed.

*Ken Harris – a pint and a preacher*

Ken Harris was a fireman at Cwrt Sart from 1960 to 1967 during the last days of steam, before joining the nearby Metal Box can-making plant.[7]

Ken progressed from being a cleaner to firing locomotives as part of the Pilot link, a group of workings involving pannier tank locomotives which carried out shunting activities in and around Neath. His first job as a 'passed fireman' was on the Metal Box pilot with driver Emrys Evans. This involved making up a train in Neath station yard for the Metal Box factory, via Briton Ferry and the Canalside branch, and shunting the gasworks siding. Ken often worked on the Briton Ferry dock pilot with driver Walter Woolford, a lay preacher. He prepared sermons at quiet times between shunting duties, whereas other drivers would pop to the Cross Keys Hotel for a pint.

Another of Ken's duties was firing for Len Shiner on the Briton Ferry station yard pilot. This involved shunting the yard and taking trains to the Albion steelworks, as well as shunting Taylor's Foundry sidings. The weekend would bring some variety to Ken's work schedule:

> He prepared sermons at quiet times in between shunting. Other drivers on this turn would pop to the Cross Keys hotel for a pint. We would be involved in shunting turns during the week but, on a Saturday, would take the 11.00 am train to Treherbert. This involved a few hours wait at Treherbert, time for a pint or two of 'frothy liquid'. We would return on the afternoon train which arrived at Neath about tea time.

A night turn to Pontypool Road also provided an opportunity to enjoy some refreshment.

> This involved a water stop at Hirwaun where the guard would fill up the tank while the driver and fireman popped for a pint. We'd soon sweat it off.

Later, Ken was involved in longer distance work, involving trips to Severn Tunnel Junction and beyond.

> The longest turns I worked on were the Rowley Regis oil trains, usually hauled by a *Hall* or *28xx*, changing crews at Gloucester. I usually shared this job with Arthur Barton, one of the top link drivers.

Ken worked on the *Castles* during the brief period when they were based at Neath, firing them on their light engine sorties to and from High Street station via the District line. When other depots would be short-staffed and men from Cwrt Sart would provide cover. In this way Ken also worked at Neath and Brecon, Glyn Neath, Duffryn Yard, Danygraig and Tondu sheds. He worked with several other drivers as he moved through the ranks, such as Eric

Parry James at work at Duffryn Yard with his apprentice fitter and a fitter's mate 1962 *(Hugh James)*

*Hugh James (grandfather of Hugh Newton James, father of (Hugh) Parry James)*

Hugh James was the head of a railway dynasty, each generation of which bore the forename Hugh. He was born in Swindon in 1866 and worked in Swindon Works drawing office during the regimes of Dean and Churchward before taking up the post of Assistant Superintendent at Cwrt Sart shed in the 1920s. The superintendent's office had oversight of all rail operations in south-west Wales with the motive power depot and carriage and wagon workshops being one of the biggest employers in Neath.

Although his son Parry was born in Swindon his other children were born and raised in Neath. He enjoyed a long career at Neath and upon retirement moved to live in the station house in Winchcombe but returned to Neath where he died the age of eighty-seven. He encouraged his son Parry to undertake a railway career and nurtured an interest in railways in his grandson, Hugh, who often accompanied him on railway journeys when he was a young boy.

*Hugh Parry James*

For convenience, Hugh Parry James was known to all by his second name. He, too, was born in Swindon in 1898. Parry's father hoped that his son would follow him into the drawing office. Parry, however, preferred to be close to steam locos and opted to train as

Edmonds of Meadow Road, Glen Tremayne (Shelone Road, Briton Ferry), Dick Evans, (Dick Aberdare,) and Jack Titus of Old Road. Nevertheless, there were other drivers at Cwrt Sart with whom he never worked.[8]

Less arduous tasks were assigned to drivers with health restrictions in the form of pilot duties. Penrose Williams, who had hearing problems was carriage shed pilot, Len Shiner, who had a leg problem worked at Briton Ferry station yard, and Ivor Knight, who was engine shed pilot.

A presentation made to Parry James by his colleagues when he left Duffryn Yard shed *(Hugh James)*

The lifesize *Pendennis Castle* at Didcot Railway Centre (*Martin Davies*)

a fitter in the works, serving his apprenticeship during the First World War when railway work was a reserve occupation. In 1919 he was part of a team working in 'A' shop on the construction of Class 47xx 2-8-0s but afterwards his family transferred to Wales when his father became Administration Manager at Cwrt Sart depot.

After his family had found a convenient home in Rockingham Terrace, Briton Ferry, opposite the station Parry began work as a fitter at Duffryn Yard shed in Port Talbot. He then became the Acting Mechanical Foreman until its closure when a presentation was made by his colleagues to commemorate his long service at the depot. Instead of transferring to the new diesel depot at Margam, he chose to move to Cwrt Sart where he could continue to work on steam locomotives. Staying there until its closure in 1965 and his retirement.

In 1966 he was awarded a Long Service Certificate by Gerald Fiennes the General Manager of the Western Region, in recognition of his fifty-two years of continuous railway employment.[9] In his retirement Parry continued to enjoy railway travel and often accompanied his son on heritage railway trips, before his death in 1978.

*John James' royal send-off*

John James was one of Cwrt Sart's best-known drivers and not a member of the James dynasty. Yet, when he died, a large gathering of a thousand railwaymen from all parts of south Wales attended his impressive funeral at Llantwit Cemetery. Twenty-five changes of bearers were made 'with over a hundred helping to convey their dead comrade to his last resting place'. James had been frequently in charge of the GWR's royal train at Windsor.[10]

*Lewis Davies crafting* Caerphilly Castle

Harold Jenkins of Ruskin Street, a footplateman from Cwrt Sart shed, was a friend of Lewis Davies[11] of nearby Glan-y-mor Street. Davies, a master plumber, was also a skilled engineer who made scale models in his spare time. Davies obligingly built a replica of *Caerphilly Castle* to be used as a training aid for the mutual improvement classes at Cwrt Sart. The powers-that-be were so impressed by the quality of his workmanship that the model was exhibited at the 1924 Empire Exhibition at Wembley. Thus, it took its place alongside one of its life-size sisters *Pendennis Castle*. The latter undertook trials on the LNER and

Lewis Davies, who crafted a working model of 'Caerphily Castle' for use by the Mutual Improvement class, seen with his family at Glan-y-mor Street about 1928. (Houses on the west sid of the street were not built yet) *(Gail Jones)*

showed itself as being more efficient than the famous Flying Scotsman with which it was later exhibited.

### Western Driver

He was a driver for the Western,
Had a good job on the line
Paddington to Swansea,
He'd get there right on time

Had a good mate by his side,
Shovelling coal by the ton,
But the Western driver,
Knows his work is never done

It's not a job but a vocation,
Took twenty years of sweat and toil,
From cleaning tanks and boilers,
To firing boxes and topping up oil.

Now he's a main man for the Western,
In the top link for Landore,
A dream job for a working man,
Now, who could ask for more?

*Martin Davies* (adapted from *Wichita Lineman* by Jimmy Webb)

### David Leonard

David Leonard of Glyncorrwg first worked as a cleaner at Duffryn Yard, but he had to move to Stafford Road in Wolverhampton to secure a fireman's post.

Eventually he returned to a driving position at Glyncorrwg, via a spell at Hereford. The ability to 'up sticks' of course depended on a person's individual circumstances; often a young fireman would have family commitments that prevented him from moving. This explains why it often took fifteen to twenty years for someone to qualify as a steam locomotive driver in Britain. It also explains the age range and career span in many British locomotive depots of which the forty-five-year career of driver Bert Tremayne is an example.

### George H Payne

George Payne started his working life in 1904 as a cleaner at Taunton, moving to Neath two years later as a shunter. He returned to Taunton some seven years later to gain experience and promotion to footplate staff. Following thirty years' experience on the footplate, he was commended for his vigilance in August, 1943 when he was able to bring his train to a halt when a small child ran onto the line some thirty yards in front of his train at Roebuck Crossing. Had he not done so, a fatality would have been the probable outcome, whereas his vigilance restricted the incident to slight injuries.

### Ivor Owen Thomas MP

Thomas, of Regent Street, was imprisoned as a political conscientious objector during World War One. Soon afterwards the twenty-three-year-old joined the GWR to work as a cleaner. After two years his trade union activities and the mutual improvement classes in the shed led him to the National Labour College in London. Thereafter he worked at the NUR Head Office until 1945 when he left the railway, having won the Wrekin parliamentary seat for Labour. He represented that constituency until 1955, after which he continued his career with the NUR and British Rail.

### Bert Tremayne

Elvert Granard (Bert) Tremayne started his railway career as a twenty-year old 'call-out boy' at Falmouth in September, 1913. He joined Truro shed as an engine cleaner and then, to secure a position as a fireman, had to move Neath in June, 1914. Seventeen years later he was made up to a driver. His fireman, Ernie Tomlins, had started railway life as a cleaner at Burry Port and worked with Bert for many years before Tremayne retired from Cwrt Sart depot in 1958 as one of the longest-serving footplate staff on the GWR/Western Region.

Bert Tremayne (right) with his fireman, Ernie Tomlins and guard Charles Dernier alongside a *Dean Goods* 0-6-0 at Cwrt Sart shed in the 1930s *(Gerald Williams)*

*Glen Tremayne*

Grenard, better known as Glen, was born in 1924 in Briton Ferry and lived on Shelone Road from where he followed his father, Bert, into railway service. Like his Cornish father, he was promoted through the ranks of cleaner, passed fireman and passed driver at Barry and Oxford where he finally became became an engine driver. After his return to Neath he often worked on the depot's passenger turns to Treherbert, Porthcawl and Pontypool Road. He was demanding of the locomotives he drove, considering 7008 Swansea Castle, for example, a 'weak engine' because of its lack of a double chimney. Yet he was proud to drive what he called 'Churchward's thoroughbreds'——his 28xx and 42xx classes—their sheer power and reliability. Perhaps his favourite loco on the Cwrt Sart turns was a Collett-designed 'Prairie' tank 8104, which was usually kept in spotless condition. He was still a master of the job when he drove diesel-hydraulics and diesel-electrics, especially liking Class 37s, but he was always best-known as a steam man.

*Gerald Williams*

Like many others Gerald came from a railway family, his father and grandfather both being employed in the service. His grandfather had worked for the GWR at Neyland and came to live in the Penrhiwtyn area of Neath, following promotion, close to his workplace at Cwrt Sart. Gerald's father trained as a fitter there and, just like his father lived within walking distance of his work. Gerald inevitably became

interested in railways and was determined to follow in the footsteps of his forebears.

However, his father had experienced some of the down sides of railway work, such as the unsocial hours, and hoped that Gerald could secure a job in one of the local factories where the working hours and financial rewards were better. Gerald actually started work at the Metal Spinning works in Melyncrythan, but his tenure proved to be short because of his yearning for a life on the railways. A year or so later he joined Cwrt Sart depot to apply his skills to the repair and maintenance of a growing fleet of steam locomotives. Cwrt Sart was becoming one of the most important sheds in south Wales, setting a record in 1962 of 'turning around' a hundred locos in twenty-four hours. Gerald Williams spent five years as a fitter at the shed until it closed in 1965, when he was transferred to Landore depot.

Gerald enjoyed the social side of employment and became engaged in the activities of his local staff association, working tirelessly for his colleagues. Throughout his life the history and activities of Cwrt Sart depot have been a major interest, being a leading member of the Neath Retired Railwaymen's Association.

*David Williams, 'eight and a half stone of dynamite!'*

David Williams[12] was short in stature, but a great character who could hold his own with anyone he worked with. Two of his uncles were locomotive drivers who encouraged him to join the railway. Fifteen-year-old David began his career at Cwrt Sart shed in 1942 before transferring to Reading and Newport. He took boxing lessons while working at Newport and was well able to look after himself. He returned to become a fireman on the Neath and Brecon Railway before leaving the job, citing the unsocial hours as the prime reason. Martin Davies interviewed Williams in 2010 to discover what working life was like on the GWR in the 1940s:

> John Griffiths was my mother's brother
> and Will Speed was married to one of my
> mother's sisters. Will had come down from
> Wednesbury near Wolverhampton to
> work as a fireman. It was their idea for me
> to become a cleaner at Neath loco. I
> started there just after my fifteenth
> birthday, having worked before that in
> the Metalclad, Gasworks Road, Neath,
> where they made shell and bomb casings.
> I remember my first day as a cleaner, being
> introduced to Tom Miller and Dai Cook,
> the two foremen, and to some of the other
> cleaners. The smell of smoke, soot,

burning sulphurous ashes, and steam from the engines was overpowering. Inside the shed it was very dark. The cleaners were all about the same age and I was paired up with Colin Shoney who showed me how to make up oilies from cotton rag waste with a mixture of paraffin and oil. I think we had about six *oilies* each and we used to rub these over the engines and under the motions to get the grime and dirt off them and then finish off with dry waste. The motions under the engine had to be really clean or you would soon have the driver on your back if he had any mess on his overalls. Colin and I became great friends.[13]

All new recruits to the footplate staff were expected to undergo an 'initiation ritual'. David was subjected to a practice known as 'greasing', details of which are best not repeated here! From time to time interesting events added variety to the daily routine. David and Colin were involved in cleaning a small tank loco that was going to be used in a film called 'The Man from Morocco', starring Anton Walbrook. It was the story of the Vichy French, building a railway through the Sahara Desert, but was filmed at the sand dunes in Margam and released in 1945. David picks up the story:

> After we cleaned it I said to Colin 'let's write our names on the dome in chalk and we will be in the film for everyone to see our names. *This engine was cleaned by Colin Shoney and David Williams.*' However, Tom Miller, their foreman, spotted it and made them clean it off.

David's work as cleaner on the night shift involved clearing the inside of the locomotive's firebox, not a task he relished. This was the worst job of all.

> After squeezing through the firebox door, you had to clear any ashes on the brick arch and lift a few fire bars to get rid of any clinker.… It was always hot and choking and I had to put a damp cloth around my nose to breathe. Sometimes I also put some paper, oily waste, sticks of wood that had been nailed together called faggots and coal so that the engine could be lit up.

Night shifts also involved calling drivers and firemen to start work early in the morning.

We had to knock on their doors or throw stones at a bedroom window and shout out. On duty at 1.30 or maybe three o'clock. We used to have old bone shakers of bicycles which had paraffin oil lamps with big bullseye glass lenses in them. They were no good for lighting up the road, but someone could see you coming.

Naturally they were expected to go out whatever the weather.

> One night it was chucking it down, so we went home to Helen's Road and spent a few hours listening to the radio, playing cards and drinking cocoa. When we went back to the shed, we were dripping water everywhere, but the foreman took pity on us and said we could finish early. We hadn't called anyone!

*Val Berni's rise through the ranks*

Val Berni started work at Cwrt Sart in the same year as David Williams, but his promotion came more quickly. Such was the shortage of skilled manpower on the GWR in wartime that one could apply for a transfer to a higher grade and achieve promotion relatively quickly if you were capable and prepared to move. At the age of seventeen Val was thrown in at the deep end

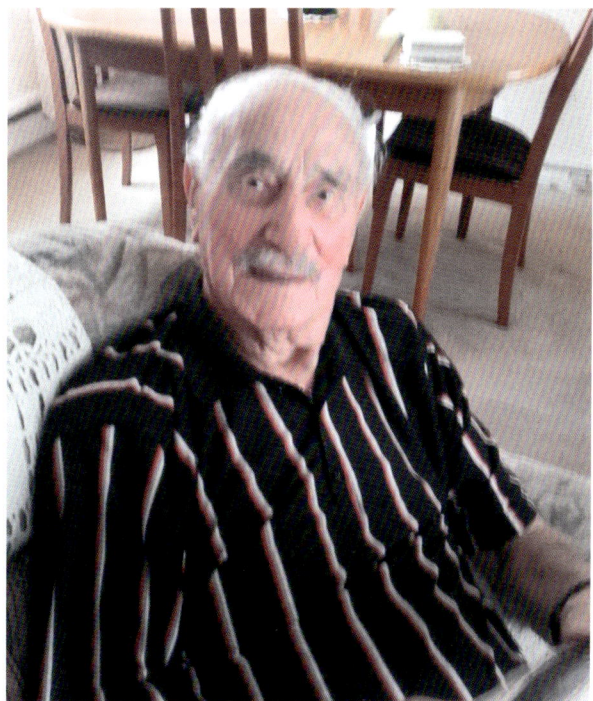

Val Berni in 2017

149

I started work as a cleaner at Neath shed in June, 1942, but I was able to secure a post as a fireman at Old Oak Common on November 16th the same year. Although I had a few firing turns at Neath I was now working at the biggest shed on the Western. It had four turntables with a huge coaling stage.

Val gained invaluable experience while based in London, which served him in good stead in his later career.

I started off on the shunting pilot but later went up to Smithfield on the condensing panniers which involved passing through the underground system via Baker Street. These trips soon developed your firing skills as you had to make sure you didn't fire the engine while you were in the tunnels. This was hard, as the locos used inferior coal and they needed more fuel than was needed on the locos I worked on at Neath.

Work was made easier if you had good company on the footplate. On the Smithfield trips Val worked with a driver named Bill Kate – a real character who was easily mistaken for Mo Marriot, the actor who worked with Will Hay.

He used to say to me: I saw a man who asked me: *Is this Algate East? No*, he replied, *it's All get out!*

Progression to main line working soon followed:

I worked on the Oxford link and then on the next link up – the goods link worked by a *47xx* or a *28xx*. We used to work on a train to south Wales nicknamed *The Long Tom* because it was 100 wagons long. You had a job to see the guard! This was a train of empty coal wagons for such collieries in south Wales as the Garth in Maesteg which supplied good steam coal for Old Oak shed.

Promotion to main line passenger work came quickly from a quite unexpected source.

A chap came up to me one day who said: *How's it looking to do me a favour? Will you swap links with me?* He was finding the firing too hard on the expresses to Swansea and Plymouth and wanted to move to an easier link. Val, then twenty years of age,

Val Berni preparing 2841 at Cwrt Sart shed in 1963
*(Gerald Williams)*

jumped at this opportunity because the pay was much better on these trips.

We had high mileage money then. For every fifteen miles we were paid an hour's pay. Swansea was twelve hours and Plymouth was fourteen-and-a-half. We had two and a half pence per hour from the time we booked on till the time we booked off…. This worked out at 6/8d for the Swansea, and 7/10d for the Plymouth jobs

Working long distances often called for improvisation when it came to sleeping arrangements.

We used to work *The Cornish Riviera*, 10.30 off Paddington with a *King*, or the 12.15 am newspaper train to Plymouth. These would be 'double home turns'. Our newspaper train would get to North Road about 5.15 am, then back down to Laira shed to book off. My lodgings were in Plympton but often you couldn't get into bed until 12.00 as Exeter men who worked an earlier shift were still sleeping! The bed was still warm when you got there. In the summer I used to sleep on the grass at Plymouth Hoe and wash using a shovel or bucket! We were young then!

Another firing turn to Plymouth saw Val involved in the 1948 locomotive exchanges when express locos from each of the *Big Four* railway companies were assessed for use on other regions and as a way of assessing the best features of each in order to design BR standard locomotives.

> I was a spare fireman on the footplate of *Mallard* when it was used on the Plymouth line. I wasn't really needed but I stayed on the footplate in case I was. I fired from Coghill Junction to Taunton to relieve the main fireman.

On his trips to Swansea from Paddington, usually working a *Castle*-hauled parcels train, Val ensured he could fit in visits to his family in Creswell Road, Neath. Often his arrival would be in the middle of the night; in the darkness he would sometimes accidentally hit the gas mantle, the standard lighting for most houses at the time. His mother noticing the damaged mantle the next day, would proclaim in Welsh: *I see that bugger's home.*

Such home visits were often made possible by arranging a 'swap' with some returning Llanelli men at Cardiff, who would take Val's train forward to Swansea. Another reason Val liked working on the Swansea turns was that it gave him a chance to visit his fiancée who also lived in Neath.

His rapid rise became a talking point for some of his former colleagues at Cwrt Sart:

> Some of the men I was cleaning with at Neath couldn't believe how far I'd been promoted in such a short time.

Val enjoyed the time he spent in London, despite the hardship of war time working and the austere living conditions of his lodgings. He was able to able to enjoy life in his spare time. He managed to play rugby for Mill Hill and watch Tottenham play football when he was off duty.

Berni transferred from Old Oak to Cwrt Sart in 1949 because he and his fiancé had made preparations for their wedding to take place in Neath that year. (They were to be happily married for sixty-three years). Now an experienced fireman, Val worked on goods and passenger turns such as the trains to Treherbert, Swansea and Pontypool Road, often firing prairie tanks like *4169*, *5102* or *8104*. He became a driver in 1960 on duties such as the Briton Ferry Dock pilot, the Metal Box workings and the Melyn shunting turns, including the Eaglesbush and Galv works which had no locos of their own.

> We were on the pay roll and got six shillings and threepence every Friday when we were on that job.

Val nevertheless continued to drive on the main line in the passenger and goods links working on an even more extensive portfolio of locomotives such as *94xx*, *56xx*, *42xx* 2-8-0 tanks and, in the early 1960s, *28xx* 2-8-0s, *9F* 2-10-0s, *Halls* and *Granges*.

> A typical working would be the Bristol vacuum from Neath – a train of box vans conveying a variety of machinery and components. It came from west Wales with a Carmarthen crew, arriving in Neath about 11.15 pm. It usually had a *Hall* or sometimes a *Grange* on the front. We worked it to Canton where we were relieved by Bristol men to return on another freight from Bristol to Neath where Carmarthen men would take over.

Other memorable workings were trips to Fishguard Harbour as relief on the Boat trains, working on excursions to Tenby and Pembroke Dock in the summer months, taking locos to Caerphilly Works and trips over Crymlyn Viaduct to Pontypool Road.

Val continued work at Cwrt Sart on both steam and diesel shunting locomotives until the depot closed in 1965. He, along with his colleagues, signed on at the diesel stabling point at Neath station before a transfer to Landore on his forty-second birthday. From Landore, he drove various classes of diesel before becoming an HST driver in October 1976, a post he held until his retirement in 1989 when senior hand at the depot.

Although the work of a footplateman was hard and the hours were long, there were other benefits. Chief among the advantages of railway employment was the issue to staff of free travel passes. These enabled railway men and women to travel far and wide both within Britain and abroad. Val Berni and his wife took full advantage of these opportunities.

> We were in Benidorm in 1950, at a time when package holidays abroad were unknown. On another occasion I travelled to join my wife and family in Majorca, from Neath to Paddington, then from Victoria to the Folkestone ferry for Calais. A rail trip to Paris allowed me to get a connection to Barcelona, where I caught another ferry to Palma. All free!

*Nicknames in the shed*

| Job | Name | Nickname |
|---|---|---|
| Foreman | Fred Hughes | Bungalow |
| Driver | William Griffiths | Billy Spanner |
| Driver | Glyn O'Neill | Peggy Neil |
| Driver | Glyn Jones | Doctor Jones |
| Driver | Ivor Knight | Robin Redbreast |
| Driver | William Hughes | Bill the Beak |
| Driver | William Mills | Billy Bible |
| Driver | William Davies | Billy Leadfeet |
| Driver | Cyril Davies | Cod's Eye |
| Driver | Bill Davies | Professor |
| Driver | William Anderson | Willy the whip |
| Boiler washer | Sam Lewis | Sam Blow |
| Brick arch man | William Harris | Billy brick arch |
| Tube man | George Smith | The western horse |
| Shedman | Phil Bannister | The colt |
| Waterman | Dai Richards | Dai the waterman |
| Fitter's mate | Dick Richards | Dixie's dog |
| Fitter | Albert Williams | Tiger |
| Fitter | Roy Anthony | Antonio |
| Shedman | Jack Jones | Jack the pigs |
| Shedman | Jack Griffith | Jack the block |
| Boilersmith | Will Smith | Willy Hell |

Nicknames in the shed

In many walks of life people are more often known by their nicknames than their real names. Cwrt Sart shed had its share of interesting nicknames[14] such as *Dai Long 'Un* who was a tall driver.

## Social activities

The well-developed network of social contact between those who worked at Cwrt Sart shed is exemplified by the organisation of day trips for members of the Mutual Improvement Classes. Sufficient personnel worked at the shed to allow for the formation of various sports teams. A Neath Loco Rugby Team who played against teams from other depots in the south west Wales area for several years.

There were also football, cricket, tennis and darts teams.

As well as participating in sporting activities, trips were regularly organised to see rugby and football matches.

## Railway families

A common feature of employment on the railways was that work often passed from one generation to another so that families might have three or four generations of railway men. The James family were such

Neath Loco Rugby team who played in a railway competition in Carmarthen Park in 1948

a case, but there were many others. Fitter Gerald Williams followed his father into railway service at Cwrt Sart shed and was the third generation of his family to 'work on the line' since his grandfather had started work at Neyland at the start of the twentieth century before moving to Neath.

Gerald's father trained as a fitter there and, just like his father lived within walking distance of his work. Gerald inevitably became interested in railways and was determined to follow in the footsteps of his forebears.

NEATH MOTIVE POWER SHOPMEN

**Party to Edinburgh**

Rugby Football Match
**Wales v. Scotland**
at Murrayfield,
Saturday, 7th Feb., 1953

President - - - C. W FRENCH

R. A. CAMERON   *Hon. Secretary*
A. J. DAVIES,   *Hon. Treasurer*
Committee: H. Sharp,
           A. Williams,
           A. Evans,
           H. Davies,
           T Hughes.

Poster for a trip to the Scotland v Wales rugby international on 7 February 1953

Driver David Williams with fireman Graham Cook alongside *City of Truro* at Swansea High Street station in 1957 *(Malcolm Williams)*

'City of Truro' at Swansea High Street station in 1957 *(Malcolm Williams)*

Group of railwaymen from Cwrt Sart shed at Neath Station before their trip to an England v Wales rugby international, early 1950s *(Gerald Williams)*

David's son, Malcolm Williams at the controls of *6024 King Edward 1* as it runs into High Street Station prior to working the 1994 special 'The Cotswold Explorer' to Didcot *(Martin Davies)*

GWR Rovers AFC, 1914 *(Gerald Williams)*

However, his father had experienced some of the down sides of railway work, such as the unsocial hours, and hoped that Gerald could secure a job in one of the local factories where the working hours and financial rewards were better. Gerald actually started work at the Metal Spinning works in Melyn-crythan, but his tenure proved to short because of his yearning for a life on the railways. A year or so later he joined Cwrt Sart depot to apply his skills to the repair and maintenance of a growing fleet of steam locomotives. Cwrt Sart was becoming one of the most important sheds in south Wales, setting a

record in 1962 of 'turning around' a hundred locos in twenty-four hours. Williams spent five years as a fitter at the shed until it closed in 1965, when he was transferred to Landore depot.

Gerald enjoyed the social side of employment and became engaged in the activities of his local staff association, working tirelessly for his colleagues. Throughout his life the history and activities of Cwrt Sart depot have been a major interest, being a leading member of the Neath Retired Railwaymen's Association.

David Williams, Dai Long 'Un, who joined the

Mutual Improvement class alongside locomotive Bulldog loco *Terrible* before their 'outing' to Windsor 1922 *(Gerald Williams)*

1962 fitting staff, Gerald Williams is fifth from the left *(Gerald Williams)*

GWR before the First World War, passed through the ranks and became a driver at Cwrt Sart before both his sons, Malcolm and David, followed him as footplatemen there until its closure. One of Dai's career highlights was driving the famous City of Truro down the Vale of Neath and onwards to Swansea when it visited the area in 1957. It travelled in tandem with 4358 on an SLS special.

They transferring to Landore diesel depot to complete their careers as HST drivers from Swansea to Paddington. Malcolm was selected to drive a steam locomotive once again in 1994 to be on the footplate of *King Edward I* on a special Sunday departure from Swansea to Didcot via Gloucester. A very spirited climb of Sapperton bank was one of the highlights of the day, thanks in no small measure to Malcolm and his fireman.

## Closure and its effects

Cwrt Sart remained open after June 1965, when the depot's steam locos had been disposed of, as the temporary base for diesel locomotives such as 08s, class 37s and class 95s. After final closure on 17 April, 1966, all twenty-seven drivers and twenty-two firemen booked on to work at Neath goods depot and all diesel locos used were transferred to Margam or Landore. The site of the shed was eventually cleared to be used for playing field.

The workshop staff were also transferred to Landore or Margam unless they were of retirement age. Ten workshop staff went to Margam in April 1964, travelling each day from Neath by a specially provided bus service. Six were transferred to Landore in May. A solitary member of the workshop staff was retained to operate the stationary boiler at the Carriage and Wagon Works which closed in 1968, the year before the shed was demolished.

### Notes for Chapter Eight

1. *Neath Enginemen*, p.41
2. Peter Bannister, son of the late Phil Bannister (born 1920), has provided the authors with information from his father's working life at Cwrt Sart shed.
3. *Neath Enginemen*, p.173
4. A leading member of the Neath Railway Historical Society and the Neath Retired Railway Workers
5. *www.bankofengland.co.uk/monetarypolicy-inflation*: accessed 6 December 2017
6. He was the grandfather of co-author Philip Adams.
7. He talked to Martin Davies at length in 2004.
8. Arthur Evans, Bill David, Arthur Clements, Bill Giles (father and son), Tommy Scaplehorn, Mervyn Rees (Muff), Bill Gorman, Alec Stephens, Vincent Davies, Tommy Mills, Val Berni (Briton Ferry Lodge), Bill Mills, Ken Parker, Reg Smith John Weekes, Cliff Evans, Graham Crooks and Emrys Jones.
9. Fiennes later gained fame for his book 'How I Tried to Run a Railway'.
10. *The Cambrian*, 10 May 1907. *Evening Express* 6 May 1907.
11. Martin Davies' great-uncle in the back row of the photo of the Mutual Improvement Class
12. He was born in 1927 and grew up in Melyncryddan, Neath
13. David Williams: 'My Memories of the Great Western Railway'
14. Phil Bannister provided this information.

Chapter Nine

# A Rail Enthusiast's Tale

*When books are pow'rless to beguile*
*And papers only stir my bile,*
*For solace and relief I flee*
*To Bradshaw or the ABC*
*And find the best of recreations*
*In studying the names of stations*

C L Graves

George Simenon's 1938 novel, *The Man Who Watched the Trains Go By*, said little about either railways or trains. Twenty years after its publication the co-author of this book, Martin Davies, had become a youth who watched the trains go by. He was not one to watch them go by passively, however. Like many others of his generation, he actively sought them out, both individually at first and subsequently with fellow watchers. This chapter relates how his and fellow enthusiasts' activities became more sophisticated and widespread. Eventually, this interest took another direction, to result in the creation of local railway preservation societies.

Martin (Bowen) Davies was born in Briton Ferry and became seriously interested in railways when he was about ten years old, in the last years of junior school, but his curiosity began much earlier:

> I can trace back this fascination to 1951 when, at the ripe age of three years, I travelled by train with my parents, Keith and Eunice Davies, to visit the Festival of Britain exhibition in Battersea Park, London. Some of my earliest memories are of that journey and the many steam locomotives lined up outside a huge factory, which I found out later to be Swindon Works, the birthplace of Great Western locomotives. This created a spark, to be rekindled later when I seriously took up an interest in steam locomotives and railways. Like many others of my generation I had been bitten by the railway bug and took up the hobby of train-spotting.

At that time, he was living in Baglan, near the railway. Following his grandfather Tom's death in 1957, his father took over the family plumbing business, necessitating a move to Church Street, Briton Ferry. It was conveniently near the railway. As he was in his 'scholarship year' at Baglan Junior School, also stone's throw away from the railway line, it was decided that Martin stay there until the Eleven Plus exam. For two years he travelled between Briton Ferry and school in Baglan during which time his interest in railways crystallised. After a hasty lunch he would sprint with friends such as Godfrey Carr to the Evans Bevan's field to catch sight of the most recent, factory-fresh, *Castle* on the *down South Wales Pullman* with Landore's logo, its silver-painted buffers. This spurred him to write the poem *Silver Buffers*.[1]

Another lunchtime highlight was the passing of *The Worcester*, the nickname given to the freight train conveying components from the Metal Box factory in Neath to its sister plant in the west Midlands city. It was unusual train because it consisted of one or two fully-fitted[2] box wagons and a brake van, with the ensemble being hauled by a 4-6-0 from Worcester shed. This would usually be a *Hall*, such as *Coney* or *Wolf*, or a *Grange* like *Hurst* or *Stowe*. Even a high mileage *Castle* would sometimes be used and, thus, rare engines, such as *Bath Abbey*, *Viscount Horne* or *Dudley Castle*, all early candidates for withdrawal, were seen on this train in 1958/9.

Two of Martin's friends at Baglan, Godfrey Carr and Alan Thomas, were already railway fans. On a sunny day, following an afternoon of spelling tests, sums or arts and crafts at school, Martin would walk home to save his bus fare and buy ice cream or liquorice from Stones ice cream parlour in Bethel Street, once a GWR Temperance bar.

This allowed me to see the regular, late afternoon trains, as the road to Baglan ran parallel to the Swansea to Cardiff railway line. *The Pembroke Coast Express*, usually passed Baglan about 16.10 and was always hauled by a resplendent Castle class locomotive from Landore shed such as *Earl Bathurst*, *Defiant*, *Kilgerran Castle* or *Cadbury Castle*.[3] I reached Briton Ferry about 16.30, after dawdling home to spend the next hour, either on the railway embankment in Rockingham Terrace or alongside Briton Ferry Dock's lines. I'd wait at a disused crane near the goods shed for the next important train of the day to flash by: the *South Wales Pullman*, in the charge of some of Landore's best Castles, maybe *Dunster Castle* or *Fairey Battle*. Its rake of eight chocolate-and-cream Pullman coaches included second-class coaches, such as *Car 54*, and first-class diners such as *Zena*.

Then it was home for tea and television. After catching up with the latest adventures of *The Lone Ranger* or *Champion the Wonder Horse*, it was time to get on his *Palm Beach Tourist* bicycle to meet the gang. This comprised both the *Baglan Boys* (Geoff Carr, Alan Thomas, Jeff (Chick) Jones, Jeff Beer and Terry Thomas) and the *Ferry Boys* (Martin, Alun Hutchinson of Brynhyfryd Road, Hugh James of Rockingham Terrace and Anthony (Wilbur) Griffiths of Hunter Street. Wilbur, a larger than life character, was a well-known 'railway troubadour' who worked

tirelessly as a volunteer to make his mark the Swansea Vale, Gwili and Teifi Valley Railways. The group was joined in 1963 by the *Sandfields* group of enthusiasts, including Phil Gallagher, Brian Thomas, Clive Criddle, Derek *(Steptoe)* Williams, Chris Thomas, James Bradley, Thomas Egan *(Fagin)*, Ramsay Powell, Phil Everley and Jeffrey Needle *(Pin)*.

We'd spend the evenings watching the regular procession of trains on the main line and on the former RSBR lines. Briton Ferry was a busy station and there was much local traffic to and from Aberafan and Swansea.

The group[4] were little more than 'train-spotters', a situation that evidently changed during the rail preservation era.

As keen railway enthusiasts, we spent hours watching the train movements from several favourite haunts in and around Briton Ferry. In the evenings the first notable regular working was the *up* milk, the 15.50 Whitland-to-Kensington milk train. It was a constant source of interest, as it would often be hauled by a *Castle* or *County* class locomotive which would not normally have found its way to south Wales, from outposts such as Penzance, Plymouth or Wolverhampton, fresh from overhaul at Swindon works.

This was followed by the *Fish* and the *Cattle*, other afternoon trains from west

One of Landore's finest, *7028 Cadbury Castle* waits for the signals at Briton Ferry East in 1959 at the head of a *down* parcels train *(Martin Davies)*

Wales. The Milford Haven to Weymouth fish would be hauled by a Neyland loco such as *County of Bucks*, *Stafford*, *Monmouth* or *Worcester*. No sooner would the *Fish* have passed than the express goods from Fishguard to Paddington would follow, taking livestock to the London markets from Ireland. This would be headed by one of Goodwick's quartet of *Halls* such as *Abberley* or *Knowsley*. Like the *Counties* mentioned above they rarely worked further east than Cardiff. The odour from these trains would linger long after they had passed!

Most of the evening express passenger trains were to Swansea, usually pulled by the new *Britannia* class locomotives based at Cardiff. They could be identified from a distance by the characteristic American-sounding chime whistle. These locos bore the names of former GWR engines, but their nameplates were carried on the smoke deflectors rather than above the running plate. These named trains, like the *Capitals United Express* and *The Red Dragon* left Paddington in the afternoon, had additional interest simply because of their imposing names, when they passed through Briton Ferry at 20.15 and 21.15 respectively.

Consequently we considered the locos on other trains less interesting,[5] even though as a child I was so delighted to take the namelsss train to Aberafan Seaside with my family in the summertime days.

In the lighter evenings of summer, we often stayed out late to see the mail trains pass at 21.30 and 22.00, after which we called for chips at Lily White's or Minnie's fish shops. Our main line observations would be interrupted twice a day, by the passing of a two-foot four-inch gauge train hauled by the diminutive loco named *The Doll* (known locally as *The Dolly Puffer*). It pulled a couple of ladles of molten slag from the iron works to the tip at Baglan Bay until this traffic ceased with the closure and demolition of the iron works' blast furnaces which I witnessed from the Warren Hill in 1959.

**Pump House days**

From 1963 onwards, the group spent more time, especially in the summer months, at the *Pump House*, Baglan. It was a pumping station, near a road/rail crossing to Pine Tree garage, which drained the

The *up* 3.50 *Whitland* to Kensington milk train, which passed Briton Ferry about 6.00 pm, leaves Felin Fran behind Swindon's *1021 County of Montgomery* after an engine change *(Michael Hale)*

'The Pump House Boys' at Baglan in 1963. From left to right back row: Alun Hutchinson, David Evans, Anthony 'Wilbur' Griffiths, Phil Gallagher, Martin Davies, Ramsey Powell. Front row: Godfrey Carr, Jeff Jones, Brian Thomas, Derek Williams (Steptoe), Chris Thomas, 'Ollie Beak' *(Jeff Beer)*

marshy land next to the railway. It was the ideal spot for photographing the slowly-disappearing steam railway scene. Our simple *Kodak Instamatic* cameras yielded some reasonable photographs on sunny days.

Between our lineside observations, we played football or cricket in a large field alongside the railway. Alan Thomas, who lived nearby in Swan Street, would bring his transistor radio along to catch up on the hits of the day. At the height of the *British Beat Boom* when the country was gripped with *Beatlemania*, we also enjoyed listening to the *Kinks*, the *Rolling Stones*, *The Who*, *Them* and, of course, *the Animals' House of the Rising Sun'*. On such hot days, the nearby shop supplied us with a welcome supply of cooling orange *Jubblies* or blackcurrant-flavoured *Ice Poles*.

**Stopper to Swansea**

Although there was plenty to interest us in the local area, as our group got older and had access to more pocket money, we often ventured further afield in pursuit of steam locomotives. Initially this resulted

*Britannia*, 70020 *Mercury* heads an afternoon Paddington to West Wales express at Neath in 1960 *(Norman Jones)*

The South Wales Pullman climbing Neath bank behind 5065 Newport Castle in 1957 (Colour Rail)

in local trips, which were nevertheless major adventures for twelve-year olds, from Briton Ferry to Swansea (High Street) on the 14.30 Cardiff to Swansea stopping train. At the booking office on street level, Norman Jones issued our tickets before we climbed the steps to the overbridge to inhale the sweet smell of steam which had lingered in the air and permeated the cracks between the wooden floorboards. If only we could have bottled that smell! This was a most interesting local train because it was the return working of the morning Swansea to Manchester train, and therefore usually involved a named locomotive such as *5016 Montgomery Castle*, or *5955 Garth Hall* of Landore.

Most of the twenty-minute journey would be spent in the corridor, hanging out of the window, soaking up sooty smells of steam and eyeing the landscape while looking out for locomotives. Shortly after Briton Ferry, Cwrt Sart shed came into view on the left, where we hoped to see a *foreign* loco at the coaling stage.

Then the Metal Box factory and the sidings at Melyncrythan were passed. Followed by Neath's three-platformed station, bearing the proud suffix *General*, was reached. Originally built to broad-gauge standards, the gap between platforms allowed the construction of a middle road in standard gauge days. The centre road was used to facilitate loco movements between platforms when

5016 Montgomery Castle heads the midday parcels train to Swansea at Briton Ferry East in 1959 (Martin Davies)

*5091 Cleeve Abbey* waits to be serviced at the turntable behind High Street station 1960 (*Kidderminster Railway Museum*)

trains from Pontypool to Swansea needed to reverse and for temporary carriage storage. The station's bay platform was used by Treherbert trains. Alongside the station the substantial goods yard and depot employed large numbers of people, both in the yard itself and to cover administrative work. My uncle Tom worked there as a clerk after leaving school, but today the yard is the site of a car park.

After Neath station our train crossed over the former Neath and Swansea railway's Riverside station where sometimes an LMS Ivatt *Mickey Mouse* 2-6-0 from Brecon could be seen. As our line curved on a steeply-graded embankment to the summit at Lonlas, it looked down on the Grammar Schools and Neath Technical College.[6] The one-in-eighty ascent to Skewen required heavy freight and passenger trains of more than thirteen coaches to be assisted, usually by *94xx* pannier tanks. Near Skewen station, the well-known *Ritz* dance hall could be seen, a favourite haunt for music fans in the mid-1960s where many were first exposed to the wonderful soul music of Otis Redding's *Respect* and Wilson Pickett's *In the Midnight Hour*.

At Skewen, substantial sidings were used to house wagons from the Main Colliery and, in the 1960s, general freight. Lonlas sidings, near to the British Road Services rail/road transfer depot, stored summer excursion and Royal train stock during the winter months. The junction here, which was removed in the 1960s, enabled trains on the Swansea District line

to have access to the main line.[7] Finally, Lonlas Arches, built by Brunel to protect the main line from landslips, were the last features on the ascent before the line descended through Llansamlet.

As late as 1960, the lower Swansea Valley was still a cauldron of heavy industry. Atmospheric pollution remained rife due to the number of steel, engineering and chemical works in production. The Swansea Vale Smelting Works, Landore Steelworks and the Yorkshire Copper Works were typical of these industries and the surrounding landscape was littered with derelict buildings and huge waste tips, a legacy of the once dominant copper industry. This lunar-like landscape with its smoke-belching chimneys often led observers to compare the Landore area to Dante's *Inferno*.

Our train slowed near Landore to cross the Tawe valley viaduct, from which could be glimpsed the Hafod and Morfa Copperworks below. Famous for supplying copper plate to the Royal Navy, the works had also provided copper fireboxes for famous steam locos *King George V* and *Royal Scot*. In contrast, the Yorkshire Copper Works manufactured copper tubing and fittings for use by plumbers. The ex-GWR Morriston branch, with its low-level station, the Swansea canal and the main Swansea to Brecon road, as parallel transport arteries, could also be seen from the viaduct.

Landore (High Level) station was a substantial structure, with wide and lengthy platforms, a legacy of its former

A long serving member of Landore's stud of *Castles*, *5077 Fairey Battle*, one of the group renamed after famous World War 2 aircraft *(K Jones)*

role as Swansea's principal station before the opening of the loop lines to connect with High Street for the latter to become Swansea's main stop.

As our train skirted Landore shed a few spotless *Castles* would be parked outside, waiting to take their turns on the prestigious afternoon expresses to Paddington. As the train eased down the bank into High Street the elevated Landore Loop West was passed on the right. This took trains on to the one-in-sixty gradient of Cockett bank to west Wales. On the left, shortly afterwards were the busy Maliphant carriage sidings where panniers mingled with *Castles* as empty stock was marshalled. Maliphant is now the site of the *Bi-modal* depot, where Hitachi high speed trains are serviced. The final hive of activity before our train pulled into the terminus was the substantial goods yard at Hafod.

The variety of motive power to be found at High Street made it an interesting place to spend an afternoon. All west Wales expresses to and from London reversed here, requiring locomotives to be changed. Thus, alongside the Landore and Old Oak *Castles* and Cardiff *Britannias*, *Halls* from

Goodwick and Carmarthen, *Granges* from Llanelli, *Manors* and *Moguls* from Carmarthen and *Counties* from Neyland could be seen.

Locos on the Paddington runs were serviced at Landore, but those on shorter trips to Cardiff or west Wales could be turned and watered at the turntable behind High Street station. A panoramic view of the operation could be gained by looking through the window of the gents' toilet on Platform One!

An added attraction of the station was the chance of being invited into the cab of a loco like *Defiant* or *Fairey Battle* to ride to the end of the platform as it reversed its coaching stock from the platform. After a three or four-hour session, we would catch a late afternoon train back to Briton Ferry.

**Go east young men!**

When older, our parents allowed us to travel further afield. A day at Cardiff General provided opportunities to see locos which rarely worked to Swansea, such as the inter-regional cross-country trains which terminated at Cardiff. These brought *Counties* from Shrewsbury,

Another of the aircraft series of *Castles 5075 Wellington* at Cardiff General in 1962 *(Robert Reed)*

Swindon and Bristol, and *Castles* such as *The Gloucestershire Regiment 28th 61st*, from Gloucester whose unique nameplate was always a talking point. On a visit in the summer of 1962 another Castle, *5075 Wellington*, hitherto a rare sight in these parts, but then based at Cwrt Sart, was observed at the head of a London-based express.

As well as being a very busy passenger centre, Cardiff witnessed the movement of substantial quantities of freight through the central roads of the station. Coal, iron ore, steel, engineering products, and chemicals were the major cargoes, but banana trains from Barry Docks would often throw up unusual locos such as ex-LMS *Jubilees* and *Crabs*. Many of the suburban services were still steam-hauled, although three-car diesel sets had been introduced in 1958. A succession of *56xx* and *41xx* tanks from valley sheds like Treherbert, Merthyr and Radyr passed, hauling rakes of six or more non-corridor coaches. A trip to Cardiff's Canton depot was obligatory, necessitating a twenty-minute walk from the station. Access was over a long footbridge that crossed all the running lines. It was a favourite haunt for photographers as it offered unparalleled views in both directions. Patience was often the order of the day if one wished

to go around the shed, to make sure the foreman was out of sight before descending the steps into the shed yard.

We managed to make it casually on several occasions and Godfrey Carr visited the shed *officially*.

> My father had been able to get an official permit which allowed us to be taken on a conducted tour of the shed without worrying about trying to avoid the prying eyes of the shed foreman. One of the highlights of the visit was being allowed to take the regulator on *6905 Claughton Hall*, a long time Landore and, later, Cwrt Sart locomotive.

**Caerphilly**

Trips to Cardiff were often combined with trips within easy travelling distance of Cardiff such as Barry, Newport or Caerphilly Works, with the weather dictating whether we stayed on Cardiff station or travelled further afield. For most people, Caerphilly is known for its cheese and its Norman castle. For us it was the place after which the pioneering Castle class loco was named, and

Cardiff Canton shed with *Britannia Pacific 70022 Tornado* on shed in 1960 *(Colour Rail)*

Caerphilly's Works' attraction was that it had been the GWR's main workshop in south Wales. It fascinated our group because it offered a chance to see locos from throughout south Wales undergoing overhaul. The town was reached by a valley train bound for Senghenydd[8] and the walk from the station to the works was usually quite unchallenging. On one such trip, however, the heavens opened and the relentless rain during the walk did not ease until we reached our destination.

Godfrey was determined to make the mission despite the weather because it was his first trip.

> We eventually decided we had waited long enough at Caerphilly station for the rain to stop and set out for the works. After trudging through the streets in the pouring rain we entered the main site where we were delighted to note about twenty-five locos in various stages of repair. Our hopes were dashed when we were met by the booming voice of the foreman: *Where do you think you are going?* was his welcoming line. Despite our appeal, it became clear that we were face to face with a *job's worth* who told us to leave immediately.[9] Godfrey's disappoint-

ment was obvious: The only loco recorded inside was a stationary boiler from an ex-Rhymney Railway tank, no 37! The rain was still bucketing down so we returned to the station soaked to the skin and travelled home shivering all the way. It took us hours to dry out. A fruitless afternoon all round.

## Bristol

Bristol was a most important locomotive exchange centre for the Western Region because it received inter-regional services as well as the usual services to London, the west of England and south Wales. Therefore, it was a favourite destination for the summer months. Jeff Beer and Jeff Jones were older than the rest of the group and Martin Davies' parents were content for him as a twelve-year-old to accompany them for the day.

A trip to Bristol in those days was akin to an exotic foreign holiday in later life. Long-distance inter-regional services required changes of locos at Bristol, for example on a journey from Bradford to Paignton, Leeds to Weston-Super-Mare, Glasgow to Penzance and Portsmouth to Cardiff. Some 400 passenger trains came to Temple Meads station on a summer Saturday. Jubilees such as *Bengal*, *Galatea* and *Kempenfelt*, and *Patriots* such as *Lady Godiva* and *Royal Pioneer Corps* were stationed at Barrow

Road[10] to work services to the Midlands and the North. *B1* 4-6-0s were often used on the 8.05 am Newquay to Newcastle or the 7.06 Sunderland to Bristol. BR standard locos frequently came from Salisbury or Weymouth, mainly bearing discarded *King Arthur* class names.

> My records for 9 July 1960 listed 170 locos of which fifty were newly seen. A day spent at Bristol was incomplete without a visit to at least one of the three loco sheds at Bath Road, St Philip's Marsh and Barrow Road. Although it was difficult to get around Bath Road, the Western's principal passenger shed for Bristol, we

were compensated by the fact that the shed yard was clearly visible from Temple Meads station.

## Much binding at the Marsh

St Philip's Marsh was quite different. This shed was reached by walking alongside the Bristol avoiding line and staff there were welcoming. It was principally a freight depot, the second largest on the Western Region with two 24-road turntables. They housed an assortment of *28xx* 2-8-0s, 2-6-0s, *Halls*, *Granges*, ex-LMS *8F*s and *Austerity* 2-8-0s. A few *47xx* 2-8-0s were used for the fast, overnight goods trains to London. Pannier tanks of various types were in evidence, *56xx*

*Jubilee 45675 Hardy* heads a West–North express the summer of 1964 at Bristol Temple Meads in 1964 *(Martin Davies)*

165

A line up of *Castles* at St Philips Marsh in 1962 – *4079 Pendennis Castle, 5085 Evesham Abbey* and *5040 Stokesay Castle (Alan Hutchinson)*

A mixed line up at Bristol Barrow Road shed in 1964 with *Standard 5* No *73003* prominent *(Jeff Beer)*

0-6-2 tanks and a couple of *1365* saddle tanks, operating on the restricted lines at Bristol dock. On Saturday 9 July 1960 twenty locos were on shed.

When Bath Road closed in 1961, its *Castles*, *Counties* and *82xxx* tanks were transferred to 'the Marsh' so that one Saturday in August 1961 seventy-one locos were seen at St Philip's Marsh, including six *Castles*, two *Counties*, five *Granges*, sixteen *Halls* and *Modified Halls*, seven pannier tanks, seven *Moguls*, one *47xx*, two *38xx*, four *56xx*, two *52xx*, five *8Fs*, one *82xxx*, one *Mickey Mouse* 2-6-0, one *2251* 0-6-0, one *1365* saddle tank and one *51xx* tank.

Barrow Road shed was harder to access because a wall had to be climbed to gain entry. During the long trek to the wall one could savour the taste of hops from the nearby brewery. The wall was no serious deterrent and, once over it, we were able to see the depot's modern coaling tower and what we really went to see: the *Jubilees* and *Patriots*, *Jinties*, *4F* 0-6-0s, *Black Five* and *Standard Five* 4-6-0s, a couple of Pugs – *51217* and the now-preserved *51218*, which operated around the docks.

Small prairie tank No *4558* waits for the signals outside Tenby station on an afternoon stopping train to Whitland in July 1961. Kiln Park caravan site can be seen in the background. *(Martin Davies)*

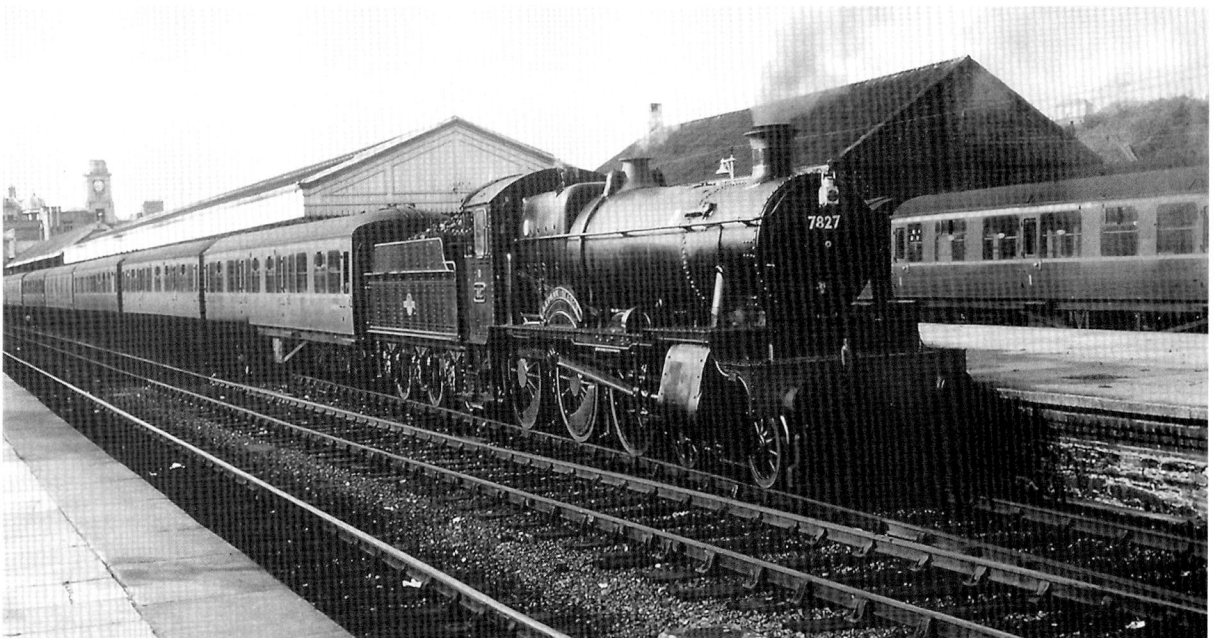

*7827 Lydham Manor*, now preserved on the Paignton and Dartmouth Railway, waits to leave Aberystwyth station in 1960 with a train for Whitchurch *(Colour Rail)*

### Well it's all right, we're going to the end of the line: Summer holidays

My parents ensured that we spent our family holidays in the Tenby area because of our family links with west Wales. Consequently, we often stayed at Kiln Park, a camping site which for me was conveniently separated from the beach by the Whitland to Pembroke Dock railway embankment. This was an ideal situation for me because the branch line offered the chance to see locos which were rare in the Neath area, particularly Churchward's small *45xx* class Prairie tanks. They soon became amongst my favourite locomotives, being the mainstay of the branch from their introduction in the 1920s until the end of steam in 1963. They easily handled the four or five-coach trains which ran on the line; blessed with smart acceleration they soon galloped up the embankment from Tenby station.[11] The more heavily loaded trains, often through-portions of Paddington expresses, brought their larger cousins

*Black 5* 4-6-0 No *45277* at Shrewsbury station in 1964. Coaching stock for a departure over to Swansea can be seen in the central Wales bay platform. *(Jeff Beer)*

such as *4106, 4122, 4132* and *8107* to Tenby, but the highlight of the day was the *Pembroke Coast Express*, whose six chocolate and cream coaches would be hauled by a *Mogul* or *Manor*.[12]

The summer Saturday Birmingham to Pembroke Dock train was a long one which was often in the charge of Carmarthen's *Kingsthorpe* or *Stanley Hall*. The train decanted hundreds of holiday makers from the west Midlands to make their way to the hotels and guest houses of Tenby and Saundersfoot. Other visitors arrived on the Shrewsbury to Pembroke Dock train, hauled from Llandovery by a *22xx* 0-6-0.[13] This class of engine could also be seen on the daily freight, or as pilot for a double-headed eighteen-coach troop train bound for Penally.

When the weather was poor my father would drive us to places like Cardigan, Aberayron, Neyland and Aberystwyth where I spent some time at stations or visiting the sheds. At Aberystwyth one spotted *Manors* like *Barcote* or *Bradley* which rarely came to south Wales. If fortunate, the trip might coincide with the arrival of the Cambrian Coast Express, whose locomotive would be presented to Landore standards. Alongside

the main terminus, the charming Vale of Rheidol Railway has its separate station where one can see the diminutive 2-6-2 tanks, *Llewellyn* resplendent in main line Brunswick green, chugging in with its payload of visitors returning from Devil's Bridge.

In 1962 my father's decision for the family to holiday further afield resulted in a week's touring of mid and north Wales in a Volkswagen Dormobile, providing me with further opportunities to visit railway installations at Wrexham, Llandudno Junction, Holyhead, Bangor, and Colwyn Bay and to get a flavour of the LMS railway scene.

## Railroving

One way to visit railways in other parts of the country was by purchasing a *Railrover* or a *Holiday Runabout* ticket. The Railrover allowed travel for a period on any railway line in the country, so it was ideal for steam enthusiasts. However, for a fourteen-year-old it was too expensive, so the cheaper option, the *Holiday Runabout* ticket was chosen. Although not as versatile, it allowed one to travel each day for a week to a specific destination. This was ideal both for families who couldn't afford the luxury of a week's holiday away, and for railway enthusiasts who could select a major railway hub and travel on from there by separate ticket.

Alan Hutchinson:

As a group we had talked about choosing a suitable destination in the form a big railway centre from which we could travel to other places easily. Jeff Beer and Jeff Jones were working, so we would have to travel in the summer during their holidays. The rest of us, Alan, Martin and me, were still in school but would be able to save up the 17/6d needed to buy the railrover ticket. We decided that the north-west was a good area to visit as there were lots of steam sheds there, we travelled each day over the Central Wales line.

To optimise the use of our time, we travelled on the earliest train possible, the 6.25 am Swansea to York *Mail*. It meant a very early start, but the first train from Briton Ferry was not until 6.26 am. To catch it, Martin's father stepped into the breach and drove us to Swansea Victoria station in his van. The journey to Shrewsbury took four hours, arriving at 10-30 am. However, the long duration of the trip was compensated by

the experience of travelling some of the most spectacular countryside in Wales. Highlights of the morning journey were the sunrise around the shores of Swansea Bay, the spirited climb to Sugarloaf summit, and the crossing, of Cynghordy and Knucklas viaducts, both engineering marvels. The straight along the main line between Craven Arms and Shrewsbury enabled the Fowler 2-6-4 tank loco *42388* to show a turn of speed up to 80 miles per hour and enabled our group to forget how long we had been travelling. We spent a very fruitful day at Shrewsbury, one of the busiest interchange stations in the country, where Western trains met Midland trains.

Locomotives were changed here on the London to Birkenhead trains: an Old Oak *King* would give way to a Shrewsbury *County* such as *County of Hereford* or *County of Radnor* for the onward journey to Merseyside. A Newton Abbot *Castle* like *The South Wales Borderers*, engaged on a Penzance to Glasgow express, would be swapped for a *Jubilee* or a *Royal Scot* for the next leg of its journey to Carlisle.

One of the highlights was the arrival of the Cambrian Coast Express from Aberystwyth, with *Barcote* or *Foxcote*

A busy scene at Carmarthen station in August 1962. *2298* heads an up Aberystwyth train *7821 Ditcheat Manor* waits in the centre road for its next duty, while *5027 Farleigh Castle* rest at Platform 2 having brought in a West Wales express from Swansea. Meanwhile another *22xx* lingers in the Llandilo bay *(Colour Rail)*

Britannia Pacific No 70022 *Tornado* is seen again at Crewe station in 1967 on a *down* express from Scotland. It is now shorn of its nameplates (*Jeff Beer*)

*Manor* at its head, before reversing to shed past the massive Shrewsbury signal box. Meanwhile, the train would go forward to London with a *King* or *Castle*. Many other passenger services ran to Hereford, Cardiff, Crewe, Chester, Liverpool, Manchester, Wrexham, Stafford, Wellington, Bewdley and central Wales. A procession of freight trains brought a range of 0-6-0 pannier tanks, 2-6-0s, 2-6-2 tanks, 2-8-0s, and *Halls* and *Granges*. Added interest came from the running-in turns from Crewe Works, where a red *Duchess* or a *Royal Scot* effortlessly hauled its charge of two or three coaches.

Shrewsbury motive power depot was about three-quarters of a mile south of the station. It was commonly referred to by railwaymen as *Salop*, no doubt in association with the official name of the county until 1980 and its eponymous locomotive *County of Salop*. The shed was an amalgam of two separate ex-LMS and ex-GWR sheds which boasted an eclectic collection of both companies' locomotives. Most important, it was very welcoming to visitors. Examples of all ex-GWR passenger 4-6-0s could be seen; it was one of the few sheds where *Manors* rubbed shoulders with *Kings*. There was a significant array of standard-class locomotives such as *Class 5* 4-6-0s and 2-6-4 tanks, as well as a sizable collection of ex-LMS locos, notably *Stanier 8F*s, and *Black 5* 4-6-0s.

The last train back to Swansea (Victoria) from Shrewsbury left at 5.45 pm to reach its destination at 10.03 pm. Jeff Beer wanted to stock up on cigarettes for this long return journey, but the eighteen-year old smoker got into trouble at the station before we left. He popped into the station buffet to buy his twenty Embassy, to be taken aback when the attendant refused to serve him. Jeff's quick temper turned the air blue, but not from cigarette smoke. He failed to buy any and so had to remain fagless for the return trip.

After a full day, the group were quite happy to collapse in our compartment for the 115-mile journey to Swansea, content to play cards, or listen to Radio Luxemburg on Alan's radio, tuning in to up the hits of the summer. Bobby Darin's *Things*, Pat Boone's *Speedy Gonzales* and the Shadows *Guitar Tango* filled the air. Card games were interrupted by the station calls at the likes of Llandrindod and Llandovery, to observe trains travelling north. A significant number of freights, in the hands of *8F*s were witnessed, while passenger trains were hauled by *Black Fives*, like *45145*, or *Standard Fives*, like *73096*, or maybe a 2-6-4 tank, like *42388* or *42385*, based at Swansea East Dock. Some services were worked by *Standard 4* tanks made redundant by the electrification of the London–Shoeburyness line

The Shedmaster checks that everything is in order as we gaze upon 2-6-0 No *7306* on another Sunday sojourn to Cwrt Sart *(Martin Davies)*

Danygraig shed with one of the unique Avonside 0-4-0 dock tanks, *No. 1104* in 1959. This loco was dismantled at Wards *(Magic Photos)*

and brought in to replace the older Fowler machines. *80072*[14] was one of the first. Our train arrived on time at Swansea, just after 10.00 pm, giving us ten minutes to sprint to High Street to catch the last train that stopped at Briton Ferry.

Six hours at Shrewsbury was time enough to pay a return visit to Oswestry and Wrexham. Oswestry was interesting as the headquarters of the former Cambrian Railways. Its shed supplied *Manors* and *43xx* Moguls for the Cambrian main line from Whitchurch to Aberystwyth and *Mickey Mouse*

2-6-0s for the branch lines around Oswestry.

The nearby former Cambrian Railways' workshops were memorable for three reasons: housing the last *Dukedog*, 9017, under overhaul whilst awaiting its move to the Bluebell Railway for preservation; the two ex-Welshpool and Llanfair narrow gauge locos which were in storage and Shrewsbury's *Carn Brea Castle* which was also being repaired.

A push-and-pull shuttle worked by *5422* from Gobowen was the means of reaching Oswestry. Alan Thomas knew the Wrexham area and guided us to Croes Newydd shed, which serviced the Ruabon to Barmouth route and the industries in the vicinity.

Jeff Beer stands alongside his favourite loco, *4093 Dunster Castle*, at Cwrt Sart shed, one sunny Sunday in the summer of 1961 *(Martin Davies)*

A highlight of the return journey from Wrexham was Telford's Pontcysyllte aqueduct, rising high above the Dee valley, as we crossed the equally impressive Chirk viaduct, with plenty of time for our 5.45 pm departure from Shrewsbury to Swansea.

The third day of the visit resulted in taking a train to Llandeilo and thence the picturesque Vale of Towy branch to Carmarthen. This was worked almost exclusively by panniers like *7439*, which trundled their two-coach trains past the magnificent hilltop castles of Dynevor and Dryslwyn. At Abergwili Junction the line was joined by the line from Aberystwyth for the run into Carmarthen.[15] Carmarthen station was a hive of activity as the focus of services to west Wales. Here all trains between Swansea and west Wales were supplied with fresh motive power from the town's substantial shed and workshops. A visit was paid to them before heading west to Whitland, then famous for its milk trains, before finally heading home.

Later that week the group travelled on from Shrewsbury to Crewe, whose station was one of the busiest on the Midland region and a real magnet for rail fans. Although not able to visit the famous work-shops the group spent productive time at Crewe's North and South sheds to see scores of ex-LMS locos in their own backyard. Most classes were represented with *Duchesses*, *Royal Scots*, *Jubilees*, *Patriots*, *Black 5s*, *3Fs*, *4Fs* and *Jinties* on show, many being ex-works. The visit also revealed the presence of *Duke of Gloucester*, regarded as something of a white elephant due to its indifferent performance in everyday service. The following year Tony Griffiths, who missed out on the 1962 trip, was able to undertake a similar itinerary, being joined that year by Alun Hutchinson.

The school-leavers in the group could afford trips further afield. Alan Thomas, Jeff Jones and Jeff Beer used a *Weekly Rover* ticket to travel to Scotland in 1964, visiting as many depots as possible on their way. This enabled them to visit areas on the Midland, North Eastern and Scottish regions which still had significant numbers of steam locos in use. Jeff Jones recorded the visit as:

A great trip with a fine selection of engines of all classes. It was our first trip to Scotland. We slept on trains and in station waiting rooms. Preston station had a waiting room with a big warm fire, much appreciated at the time.

Ex Cardiff Railway 0-4-0 No *1338* at Swansea East Dock shed on 18 April 1962 *(Alun Hutchinson)*

Assorted withdrawn locomotives at Swansea East Dock en route to scrapyards in Morriston in August 1964 0-6-0 pannier No *7408* and *4088 Dartmouth Castle* are prominent *(Martin Davies)*

Another opportunity to visit Scotland came a few years later when the trio joined a trip from Baglan to the 1967 Wales v Scotland rugby international.

We went by train with the rugby boys from Baglan but didn't go to the match. Instead, we saw it as a chance to see the last remaining steam locos in use north of the border. Travelling on the day of the game, we left Port Talbot at 7.00 am and stayed in the guard's van so that we could look out of the window on the journey. The trip was diesel-hauled by a class *47* for the first stage of the journey as far as Hereford. There we were lucky to have *Black Five 45226* take over which went like a 'bat out of hell' all the way to the Scottish border. Most of the remaining *Britannias* had been concentrated at Carlisle, including ex-Western Region locos like *Tornado* and *Flying Dutchman*. However, it was the unfamiliar *Robin Hood* that took us over the Waverley route before it closed shortly afterwards. *Robin Hood* was in such a run-down state that it struggled with its twelve-coach train and a pilot loco needed to be attached at Hawick. This, a Class 2 diesel *D5025*, was of a type never seen in south Wales and made little difference. It was useless! Eventually a *B1*, *61073*, took over and got us safely to Edinburgh by 1.00 pm, just enough time for the rugby boys to get to Murrayfield for the 2.30 pm kick-off! We spent the afternoon in the Edinburgh sheds in and around Waverley station where the remaining A3s like *Flying*

*Scotsman* and A4s like *Union of South Africa* still worked the east coast trains northwards. After food, we headed home for Wales at 11.00 pm, with a train full of 'well-oiled' Baglan rugby boys to arrive shattered on Sunday morning, after a trip which was well worth it.

**Sunday sorties to Cwrt Sart Shed[16]**

The group therefore travelled extensively in its quest for steam, but on many Sunday mornings the pilgrimages were more modest in extent, often taking the group to Cwrt Sart shed from Maentilo Junction. Of course, there was no such junction: it was simply the label with which Martin's friends branded his home, *Maentilio*.

On arrival at the shed the foreman and staff were very accommodating and, sensing our enthusiasm, were happy to allow us to wander freely between the locos providing we 'used our heads'. Common sense was the order of the day, and it paid off because the visits became even more interesting after the closure of Landore shed in June 1961 when half of its express locomotives were transferred to Cwrt Sart.

We could now expect to find lines of gleaming *Castles* and *Halls* resting in the shed between their regular weekday duties. They were a sight for sore eyes, especially *Dunster Castle*, Jeff Beer's favourite. I captured Jeff, on my Kodak Brownie, standing alongside his favourite loco. After his death in 2002, I presented his wife, Joyce, with a framed copy of the photograph.

**To Swansea and beyond**

Another enjoyable cycling trip on a Sunday morning was to the steam depots of Swansea, via the Jersey Marine coastal route.

*Danygraig*

The first port of call was Danygraig shed and workshops, built in 1895 as the motive power headquarters of the RSBR. For many years it served as the locomotive depot for Swansea docks' locos, a unique collection of short-wheelbase tanks, previously belonging to Swansea Harbour Trust. The Trust needed narrow wheelbase tanks to access the many curves of the dock rail network. The GWR supplemented Danygraig's locomotive allocation with six of its own specially-designed dock tanks, *1101-6*, some small pannier tanks which serviced Tir John power station and the Port Tennant wagon works, and some heavy 2-8-0 tanks which operated at the Jersey Marine Hump Yard.

The adjacent RSBR workshops were equipped for heavy repairs not possible at running sheds like Landore. Thus, *Castles* such as *Abergavenny Castle* or *Halls* like *Sandon Hall* were often to be seen in the lifting shop. Later the shed became a mere storage point for locomotives being transferred between depots in south-west Wales.

*Swansea East Dock*

The former GWR shed was a short excursion from Danygraig. It was built to house the tank locos which hauled freight trains short and medium-distance to, from and within Swansea Docks. Its complement of shunting locomotives included some small ex-Swansea Harbour Trust 0-4-0 tanks to operate at street level around the streets within the docks. These lines even connected with Mumbles Railway.

Some workings were in the hands of ex-Powlesland and Mason tank *1151* and ex-Cardiff Railway *1338* until they were withdrawn in 1963, *1151* succumbed to the cutters torch, but *1338* was preserved and is used by the Great Western Society at Didcot Centre.

Other locomotives based here consisted of *57xx* for shunting, *84xx* pannier tanks and *56xx* 0-6-2 tanks for short-trip freights to destinations like Margam. The *42xx* 2-8-0 and *72xx* class 2-8-2 tanks took the longer distance freights to Llanelli, Cardiff and Severn Tunnel. Hugh James worked at East Dock for a while as roster clerk, a position which enabled him to add some unexpected spice to locomotive workings by removing its usual *56xx* tank and assigning a *Fowler* Class 4 *42388*, to the Swansea-Porthcawl run!

The shed closed in 1963 to be used as a distribution point for many withdrawn locomotives destined for Birds and Cohens scrapyards in Morriston. Often,

Assorted withdrawn locomotives at Swansea East Dock en route to scrapyards in Morriston in August 1964 ex-SR 2-6-4 tank No *31915 (Martin Davies)*

Another eclectic group with an ex-GWR *Hall*, 56xx 0-6-2 tank, *52xx* 2-8-0 tank and 2 ex-SR *N* class 2-6-0s *(Phil Gallagher)*

Steam braked pannier tank No 6778 is prominent in this view of Upper Bank Shed from 1961 *(Martin Davies)*

they arrived in batches of four, the first being in steam and pulling the other three. On arrival at the shed, its fire was dropped and the loco joined the fate of the others. Locos from diverse origins were evident:

- Southern *West Country* Pacifics, Class *N* and *U* 2-6-0s and *QI* 0-6-0s.
- Midland *Black 5*s, *8F*s *Jubilees* and a *Royal Scot*
- Great Western (such as 5054 *Earl of Ducie*, 4088 *Dartmouth Castle*), *Halls* and *Granges*.

## Upper Bank

This shed was reached by cycling along the eastern side of the Tawe valley through Foxhole. It housed the locos working on their Swansea (St Thomas) to Brynamman services of the former Swansea Vale Railway. The Midland Railway extended the shed to service both an original Brynamman line via Llansamlet and a newer route through Clydach in conjunction with Gurnos depot. Long after passenger workings had ceased the Western Region introduced steam-braked *67xx* pannier tanks, suitable for loose-coupled coal traffic in the Swansea valley. From the 1980s the line was the base of the Swansea Vale Railway Society whose volunteers operated steam-hauled trains until the society was forced to vacate the site for housing. The track was saved for use by the Gwili Railway to build its 2017 extension to Abergwili.

## Landore and Paxton Street

The cycle route to Landore crossed the Tawe swing bridge, into the bustling Wind and Castle Streets, the site of the real *Swansea Castle*, but then a centre of banking and commerce. The group's expedition continued along the main shopping zone in the centre of Swansea. At High Street, it was customary to call into the station where there was usually some activity to note before advancing through Hafod to Landore shed. On Sundays, amongst the sixty or so assorted tank and tender locos, would be about twenty *Castles*. Visiting engines from Cardiff, Bristol, Swindon, Old Oak, Carmarthen and Neyland would usually be evident.

Although Paxton Street shed had closed in 1959, it was still worth a visit for the chance of glimpsing some ex-LMS *Black 5*s off the Central Wales line.

Sometimes the group would cycle even further afield. A forty-mile safari to Tondu and back in the early 1960s involved a struggle up Kenfig Hill for Martin Davies.

> The gradient was severe enough for me without the slow puncture which required frequent stops to re-inflate the tyre.

Tony Griffiths had a similar experience during an even more adventurous seventy-mile cycling trip to Radyr in Cardiff. At Stormy Down he freewheeled down to Pyle station to get a train back to Briton Ferry. Having no money for his train fare, he was trusted by the porter to pay the ticket collector at his home station the next day. A sign of the times!

An ex-works *Grange* 6853 *Morehampton Grange* outside Swindon works on the occasion of the Society's trip one Sunday in 1961 *(Martin Davies)*

A society trip to London in 1961 included a visit to Old Oak Common shed, where *5084 Reading Abbey* was photographed *(Martin Davies)*

*West Glamorgan Railway Society*

During my school bus journey to Neath Grammar School I first encountered Tony Griffith, Alun Hutchinson and co-author Philip Adams. The school's location alongside the London-Swansea rail line provided further opportunities of illicit activities for me during rail-side observation at Gaspers Corner. This spot facilitated both smoking a Woodbine and a chance to see the morning Treherbert–Swansea also gasping its ascent of the bank.

When the 10.30 Swansea-Paddington passed in the opposite direction, the contrast was unmistakeable. The London train was splendidly turned out, whilst the likes of *6677*, which had not been painted for at least twelve years, still sported *GWR* on its side tanks. Then the *Castle*, hauling the *Pullman* which followed *6677* at lunchtime, was as resplendent as the 10.30.

I became a member of the Neath and Swansea Railway Enthusiasts' Society (later renamed the West Glamorgan Railway Society) along with several school friends. The society held its meetings in a scout hut in Neath, where we were treated to regular talks, slide shows and quizzes. Set up by John and Michael Davies, Robert Thomas and Hugh James, it attracted other keen enthusiasts such as Alun Hutchinson, Godfrey Carr, Edward Porter, Alun Matthias and Robert Davies.

Membership afforded the opportunity to travel by train to visit far-off railways such as the Somerset and Dorset, and to visit depots in London, Birmingham, Bristol, Gloucester and Worcester. These were well-organised, official, trips with guaranteed shed visits and parental approval. Swindon Works was always viewed as a visit which offered mystery and excitement, making early morning Sunday trips from Neath station one of the more memorable visits. The adventure was enhanced should an unusual loco such as Penzance's *Harlech Castle* be hauling us there. Godfrey Carr took part in such a trip to Swindon in 1961:

We caught a train at Neath hauled by *5062 Earl of Shaftesbury*, at that time a Cwrt Sart engine. As it was Sunday, the Severn Tunnel was closed for engineering works and we were diverted through Gloucester. This meant a trip through the Golden Valley and a climb up the famous Sapperton Bank, handled easily by *5062*. At Stroud we were heartened to see an old veteran of the Porthcawl trains, ex-Landore's *4106*, now on more menial banking duties.

Swindon works at that time employed some 20,000 people. Access was through a subway under the main lines. There we were met by the depressing sight of lines of withdrawn locos parked outside the works, but our spirits were soon lifted by the more acceptable sight of rows of ex-works *Castles*, *Halls*, *Counties*, *Granges* and *Manors*, linked together, with or without their tenders. These were routinely overhauled every few years, depending on their recorded mileage, to be turned out with an expertly lined finish of Brunswick green paintwork. The works was a hive of activity and a tour revealed scores of engines in various stages of reconstruction. This was a period when many of the *Castles* and *Counties* were given performance-enhancing double chimneys and more efficient superheating. It was always uplifting to see a Castle that some months before had been covered in soot and confined to freight work, to reappear as a sleek machine ready for the South Wales Pullman once again.

The trips made to London, Bristol, Birmingham and Worcester provided added excitement because these were places which would not be visited with families. The London trips involved calling at Old Oak Common, Nine Elms, Stewart's Lane, Willesden and Kings Cross to give the group a first encounter of motive power such as *West Country*, *Merchant Navy*, *Duchess*, *Royal Scot* and Gresley's *A3* and *A4* classes. On one such visit Alun Hutchinson saw *Flying Scotsman* at King's Cross. These depots were on a much grander scale than those in south Wales, so Old Oak Common, the largest running shed on the Western Region, seemed a 'cathedral of steam' to their young eyes, with its four turntables and hundreds of locos. Those not seen in west Wales, such as the *condensing panniers*, *47xx* 2-8-0s, *61xx* tanks and *Kings* were a notable attraction.

> On yet another sojourn to Tyseley, Wolverhampton, and Stourbridge Junction, we encountered regional differences in culture. At Stourbridge Town station we decided to get lunch from a nearby *Chippy*. When we ordered rissole and chips, the locals who overheard this order burst into fits of laughter. To them rissoles were an unknown delicacy, or did the word have a hidden meaning? It was very strange because Mary Berry, Jamie Oliver and Delia Smith all offer rissole recipes! The locals were used to *saveloys* with their chips!

## The numberplate

The group were always interested in collecting memorabilia with railway connections. At first this included less expensive items such as tickets, luggage labels, railway maps, old photographs and those that the group itself had taken. This progressed to include larger and bulkier pieces such as shed plates or even the number-plates which were systematically removed as the condemned locos visited works for scrapping. These were stored and offered for sale to the public and, in 1964, Jeffrey Needle acquired a number-plate, previously carried by locomotive *1629* from Swindon Works.

This turned out to be a most intriguing artefact whose origins required some forensic research. Its most obvious source was from a Hawksworth pannier built in 1950, but it could not have come from there as the loco bearing the same number was still in service. The plate was made of brass, and not cast iron, convincing evidence that it had originally been attached to a Dean 0-6-0 tank built at the end of the nineteenth century.

> Jeff had bought the plate for £5 but was prepared to sell it to me for £1.50! The deal was done, but Jeff lived miles away in Sandfields and had no means of getting the 28 lbs object to me. The only way I could move it to Briton Ferry was by bike, so I cycled the few miles to collect it, thinking that I could put it in my bike's saddle bag or even carry it under one arm. I tried that for a while but soon realised it was futile, so the only solution was to place the plate on my saddle and push the bike home. The three miles seemed more like thirty. I eventually got home to polish, paint and display it in my father's workshop where it remained for many years, often being used as ballast for weight training. It last saw the light of day in an exhibition on *The Last Days of Steam* at the Gwyn Hall, Neath in 2004.

The brass number plate from ex G.W.R. Dean pannier tank No 1629 (Martin Davies)

The Neath and Swansea Railway Enthusiasts Society

# RAILWAY REVIEW

VOL. 1
---
No. 5

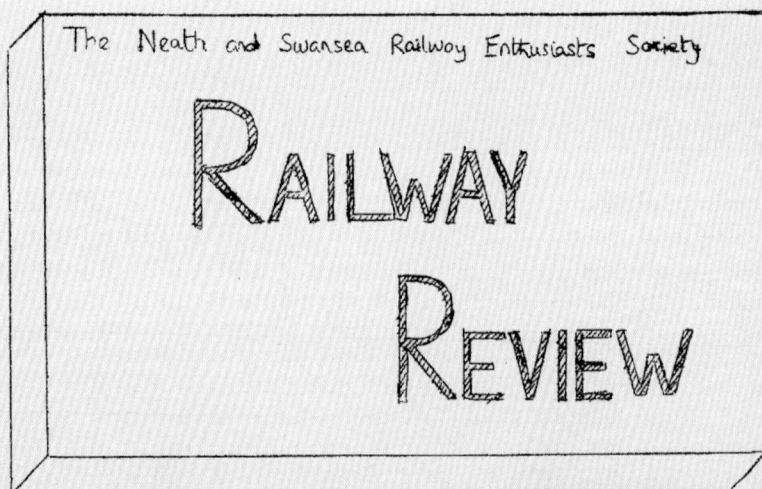

SEPTEMBER
1961

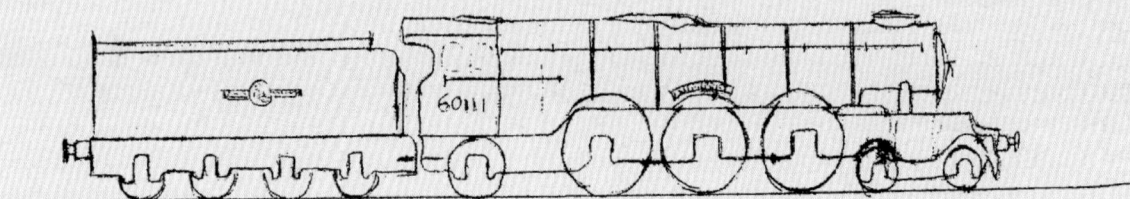

Hon.Editor:    Robert Thomas,             Editorial Board:  J.B.Davies,
               16, Llewelyn Avenue,       M.J.Davies, L.C.Turner.
               Neath.

---

### THE NEATH and SWANSEA RAILWAY ENTHUSIASTS SOCIETY

Hon.Chairman:  John Davies.    Hon.Treasurer: Alun Mathias.
        Hon.Secretary:  Michael Davies.
                        23, St John's Terrace,
                        Skewen, Neath.

Hon. Artist: Hugh James.

---

### Forthcoming Events

Saturday, 14th October

        Circular tour, embracing Cardiff, Newport, New
Tredegar, Bargoed, Dowlais, Pontsticill, Talyllyn Junction, Brecon,
and Neath Riverside. Depart Neath 8-48a.m., for 11-15a.m. from Newport,
changing at Aberbargoed for the New Tredegar branch, then taking the 3-20
ex-Newport from Aberbargoed to Brecon, over a really beatiful line after
Dowlais. Change at Brecon into the 6-20p.m. to Neath, arrive 7-52p.m.

Saturday/Sunday, 28th/29th October

        This two day trip is only a proposal,
and will only take place if there are to be at least 10 participants.
Any members wishing to do this trip mustgive their names in by 15th
September. The trip will be to London, up on thev6 -45a.m. from Neath
on the Saturday, with an afternoon trip from London Fenchurch Street
to Shoeburyness, and back via Tilbury. This is to be the last day of steam
passenger operation on the L.T.&S. line. The overnight stay will be £1
per head, including breakfast. The Sunday itinerary would include visits
to the following locosheds, permits permitting: Old Oak Common, Southall,
Neasden, King's Cross, Finsbury Park, Bricklayer's Arms and Nine Elms.
Return from Paddington on the 5-55p.m. train to Neath.

        It is understood that the Carmarthen to Llandilo branch may not have
long to live, and it is proposed to run a trip to visit this branch
before the end of the year; details will be given well in advance.
                Page  One

Cover of the September 1961 edition of *Railway Review*, the magazine produced for members of the Neath and Swansea
Railway Enthusiasts Society *(Hugh James)*

The last passenger train from Cardigan to Whitland was hauled by double headed prairies *4557* and *4569*. The crew of *4557* watch as the water tanks of *4569* are replenished at Crymmych Arms. *4569*'s fireman shares some time with a lady passenger. September 1962 *(Martin Davies)*

A pair of resplendent pannier tanks, *3621* and *3693*, await departure from Neath (Riverside) station with the specially chartered last passenger train from Neath to Brecon 13th October 1962 *(Martin Davies)*

A special train headed by 0-6-0 pannier tank *6435* at Porthcawl shortly before the end of passenger services on the branch in 1963 *(Robert Thomas)*

## Line Closures and Last Days

From 1962, as diesels took over from steam and the Beeching Axe fell on local branch lines, it seemed that things would become less interesting. This turned out to be unfounded because of the group's new-found mission to record as many images as possible of local branch lines before steam locomotives and the lines disappeared completely. Members of the group bought basic cameras for the purpose, as no-one in the group could afford the more expensive 35 mm models. The Kodak Brownie and Instamatic were mainly used because the large size of the negatives enabled reasonably good photos to be taken on a sunny day. Many survived to be reproduced in this book.

The first of the branches to face the axe in south-west Wales was the Whitland to Cardigan branch, closing to passengers on Saturday 8 September 1962. This was the first and only time Martin Davies ever

*6838 Goodmoor Grange* pulls into Neath with the last regular steam hauled passenger train from to Cardiff, the Swansea to Brockenhurst train on 5 September 1964 *(Martin Davies)*

The same train departs from Cardiff as members of the group look on. From left to right – Phil Gallagher, Clive Criddle, Martin Davies, Alan Thomas, Godfrey Carr *(Uniquephotos)*

travelled on the Cardi Bach, as the branch train was nicknamed. It was so poignant as the last train from Cardigan, the 17.45 mail, made its way sedately along the branch. It consisted of four coaches, instead of the usual two, and was double-headed by two small prairies, 4557 and 4569, which took much longer than usual to reach Whitland. With four carriages, the formation was longer than many of the station platforms. Accordingly, it was necessary to stop at the platform then draw forward and stop again in order to ensure all passengers could safely join or leave the train.[17]

A similar funereal excursion took place the following month for the last passenger train on the former Neath and Brecon Railway, a line which was destined not to celebrate its centenary as a through passenger route. It was the first of the local lines to lose its passenger services, closed a year short in 1962, with the last train from Neath to Brecon and return on the 15 October of that year. Such was the

One of the last remaining duties of the solitary 0-6-2 tank, *6614* of Cwrt Sart was acting as station pilot at Swansea High Street station in early 1965 *(Martin Davies)*

One of Neath's last pannier tanks, *3654* on a Metal Box train at Briton Ferry yard in April 1965 *(Jeff Jones)*

demand for seats on the farewell passage that an additional special last train was organised. It was double-headed by two resplendent panniers, *3621* and *3693*, which had been specially cleaned, painted and serviced at Cwrt Sart shed to be in tip-top mechanical condition.

The train was greeted by crowds at all the stations along the route. At Brecon there were so many people anxious to catch the final train to Neath that a relief train had to be provided. Godfrey Carr's experience was better than anybody's; he had made his privileged farewell trip a year earlier, travelling on the footplate of pannier tank *3741* for most of the return journey between Brecon and Neath, thanks to his uncle's friendship with a driver at Neath and Brecon shed.

> I'll never forget that journey, particularly the climb up to the Bwlch as the pannier barked its way up the one-in-fifty bank and the panoramic views of Crai Reservoir below. Near Crai a sheep had wandered onto the track. Before the driver had time to bring the train to a halt the unfortunate animal was struck down. No doubt there were a few more lamb dinners eaten in Crai over the next few days.

Such incidents were a matter of course on a rural line such as the Neath and Brecon. The driver and fireman had to tread carefully when they had visitors on board. At Cadoxton Halt the two guest travellers needed to alight from the loco and take their places *on the cushions* for the run into Neath Riverside, to escape the attention of the Stationmaster.

Alun Hutchinson's tribute to the line resulted in a much less comfortable experience. In December 1962, on a freezing cold winter's day when Breconshire was carpeted with snow and all other passenger services from Brecon were withdrawn, he nevertheless succeeded in travelling on the Moat Lane, Hereford, Newport and Merthyr branches from Brecon.

The very same month, the last trains between Treherbert and Neath ran along the former RSBR.[18] The following year Porthcawl lost its passenger service as the branch from Pyle was closed. West Glamorgan Railway Society and the Monmouthshire Railway Society ran a special train, utilising pannier tank *6435* and some auto coaches.[19]

The last train to Porthcawl ran on 7 September 1963 hauled by *6419* and the return journey behind *6434*. Excursions continued to run to Porthcawl to the very end: on the August Bank Holiday *Standard Class 4 80133* of Cwrt Sart shed hauled a special from Abergwynfi to the seaside resort.

*6859 Yiewsley Grange* worked the special train from Swansea to Fishguard to mark the end of steam working in West Wales. It waits to depart from Swansea in September 1965
*(Colour Rail)*

*6859 Yiewsley Grange* returns to Swansea late that Sunday afternoon with the return special from Fishguard
*(Martin Davies)*

1964 saw further local passenger services withdrawn from Neath to Pontypool Road, the last passenger train from Neath being hauled by pannier tank *4639*. Tony Griffiths caught it without realising that he would reach Pontypool Road after the last train to Neath had departed. Indicative of the growing popularity of the motor car, his much-needed lift home was kindly provided by a colleague's father in his new *Jaguar*.

The same day, the Central Wales line from Swansea (Victoria) to Pontardulais was closed, with the last train, the 18-25 Swansea–York train being hauled by ex-LMS *Black 5 45406*. The line north from Pontardulais was saved from closure, with future through trains comprising diesel multiple units running from High Street Station, Swansea, to Llanelli, where they reversed to reach Pontardulais. Freight traffic, which had always been buoyant on the line, was transferred to the south Wales main line and onward via the North and West (Marches) line.

Godfrey Carr succeeded in traversing the Carmarthen to Aberystwyth line under steam before the northern part of the line was prematurely closed due to flooding. Ironically that section of line near Strata Florida had been awarded with a blue plaque for the Western Regions 'best kept section of track.'

September 1964 was another milestone which witnessed the demise of steam-hauled passenger trains from Swansea to Cardiff. That summer just two trains remained with steam haulage, the 09.20 Swansea to Brockenhurst and the return 08.48 New Milton to Swansea. The morning train was regularly worked by one of Llanelli's *Granges*, with *Goodmoor* being regular, but the return working involved a variety of motive power: *Halls*, *Granges*, *Manors*, *Castles*[21] and even a *9F* 2-10-0, *Evening Star* was an appropriate choice of motive power.

Prior to that, on 11 July, a *Castle* passed through Briton Ferry on a regular passenger train for the last time. *Swansea Castle* was used and a contingent of group members, who could not possibly have wished to miss this historic event, caught the last steam-hauled Brockenhurst train from Neath to Cardiff. The last *up* train that day from Neath to Cardiff was worked by *6838 Goodmoor Grange*. The last down train that day was worked by *6936 Breccles Hall*.

183

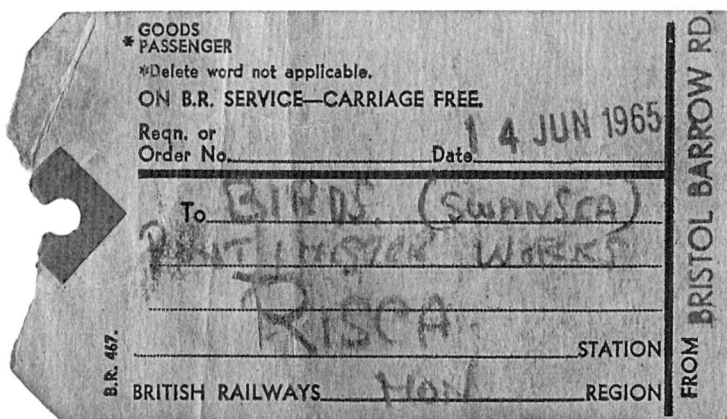

Ticket attached to *4992* en route to Bird's scrapyard, June 1965 *(Jeff Beer)*

Pannier tanks at Llanelli on the special, September 25th 1965 *(Martin Davies)*

*7811 Dunley Manor late of Cardiff East Dock, is seen at Bird's yard, Morriston awaiting the cutter's torch 1965 (Martin Davies)*

Having waved farewell to the last-ever regular steam-hauled passenger train, our trek continued to Cardiff East Dock shed, then Newport, to visit Ebbw Junction and Pill and finally Aberbeeg shed to see these important outposts of the remaining *42xx* and *52xx* tanks still actively employed on the Western valley lines. These examples rarely ventured as far west as Briton Ferry.

Godfrey Carr was pleased to see the last of the class *5233* on this visit because iron ore trains from Newport Docks to Ebbw Vale steelworks were now mainly in the hands of the powerful *9F* 2-10-0s. It was quite a sight to see one of these monsters pounding up the gradient at Aberbeeg shed with a heavily laden train being banked at the rear by a *52xx* tank.

## 1965: The End of an Era

1965 was really a turning point for railways in Briton Ferry and district because that year steam was eliminated as a form of traction in south Wales as services were dieselised. This meant the group needed to go further afield to see steam locos in everyday use. In the holiday periods further trips were planned to Cardiff, Newport, Barry and in the summer to Bristol and Gloucester. Cwrt Sart shed had only a few steam locomotives on its books at the start of the year, *57xx* pannier tanks and a 0-6-2 tank retained for station pilot duties at Swansea High Street.

The panniers were employed on the trains to the Metal Box, pilot duties at Felin Fran and Swansea, a weekly engineer's train to Tondu[22] and banking duties at Margam.

Cwrt Sart shed closed in June 1965 and most of its locos were sent to Wards, Giants Grave, for scrapping. A few escaped: *3654* to Llanelli and *4612* to Cardiff. *3654* lasted into 1966 for steam-heating coaches at Swansea High Street. *4612* went to Woodhams, Barry but can now be seen on the Bodmin and Wenford Railway.

A trip to Bristol would often take in a sortie to the sedate Green Park station and shed in Bath to survey the activity on the Somerset and Dorset line. Trains for Bath left from the platforms housed in Brunel's original trainshed and took the ex-LMS route through Fishponds, hauled by *82xxx* class 2-6-2 tanks. By 1965 the unique Somerset and Dorset *7Fs* had been replaced on the Bournemouth workings by *8Fs* and *9F* 2-10-0s, including *Evening Star* which had been based at Cwrt Sart for a while. *Standard Class 4* 4-6-0s, 2-6-0s and 2-6-4 tanks had superseded the older LMS 0-6-0 and 4-4-0 locos. There was not a diesel in sight and services over the much-loved Mendip Alps line remained steam-hauled to the end.

An early train to Bristol enabled the group to call at Severn Tunnel Junction. By the summer of 1965 this was one of the remaining outposts of steam in south Wales. The depot's 2-6-2 tanks were still being used as tunnel pilots and on the car ferry trains to Pilning. The 5,249-foot Severn-Wye road crossing from Aust to Chepstow would open the following September. Making this early foray also meant that an excursion to Gloucester could be squeezed into the day's activities to see some of the thirty or forty steam locos still operating around Gloucester. One of the last quartet of Castles based there worked a stopping train to Cardiff daily. *Clun Castle* was still operative but *Hereford* and *Ince* were stored out of use at the shed.

The curtain came down on steam in south Wales

The last *Castle* in service, *7029 Clun Castle*, was based at Gloucester. It is seen passing through Gloucester station in June 1965 *(Jeff Jones)*

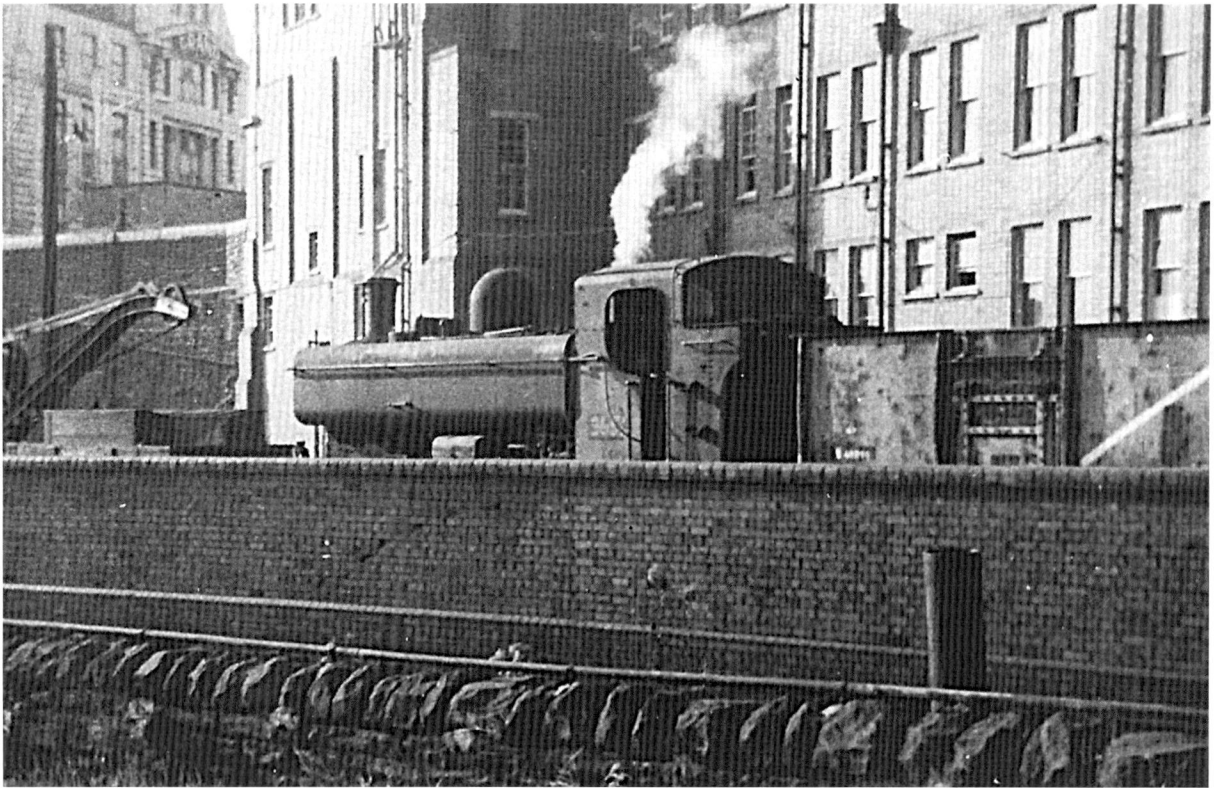

Following the demise of steam on regular services in South West Wales two pannier tanks, *3654* and *9609* were retained to provide steam heating facilities for Swansea High Street station. They were parked near the disused turntable behind the station. In this view *3654* can be seen with the Grand Hotel in the background, November 1965.

Cashmore's yard, Newport with *6909 Frewin Hall (Jeff Jones)*

in December 1965 with Severn Tunnel depot's closure following Llanelli and Cardiff's a few months earlier. To mark the end of steam in west Wales a special rail-tour was organised over the weekend of 25 and 26 September. The first day's itinerary involved visits to mineral lines north of Llanelli and Burry Port, hauled by pannier tanks *3654* and *9609*. At Llanelli station two *16xx* light panniers took over for the more restricted lines near Burry Port. The following day, *6859 Yiewsley Grange* headed the west Wales rail-tour to its destination at Fishguard Harbour and its return to Swansea. *6859* was chosen as it had been specially prepared, along with its sister *6815*, to provide steam-heating for the Royal Train at Cardiff in early August.

### South Wales' graveyards of steam locos

After this, our interest in steam in south Wales was confined to visits to scrapyards. Regular visits to our local scrapyard in Briton Ferry were supplemented by jaunts further west to Morriston and Bynea.

Eastbound expeditions were undertaken to the most famous graveyard of steam, Woodham Brothers at Barry, to Cashmores and Buttigieg at Newport Docks and to Birds at Risca. Cashmore's yard featured the *Mountain of Metal* where the dismembered parts of scores of locos were piled up. While Woodham Brothers' virtuous reputation was earned for its delay in scrapping locos to enable them to be sold, Cashmore's was notorious both for the sheer numbers of locomotives cut up and the speed at which they were put to the torch: over a thousand steam locos were despatched in a decade, with arrivals every few days.

There were several 'harvest years'… it was not long before there were larger catches: Western passenger types such as *Kings*, *Castles* (including *4037*, the last rebuilt *Star*) and *Counties*…. Cashmore's yard mopped up most of the *Halls*, *Modified Halls*, *Granges*, and types of a lower status that were withdrawn en masse at the end of Western Region steam in December 1965. Later culls would include … *Britannias*, *70017 Arrow* and *Polar Star*.

Although Risca was further afield, being to the north of Newport and inaccessible by train. it did not deter the group from visiting. Phil Gallagher recalls a typical visit there in 1965.

> We caught the train to Newport and because the valley lines had lost their passenger services a few years earlier we needed to travel onwards by bus. That day there must have been about eleven or

*Earl of Ducie* awaits the cutter's torch at Bird's scrapyard, 1964 *(Jeff Jones)*

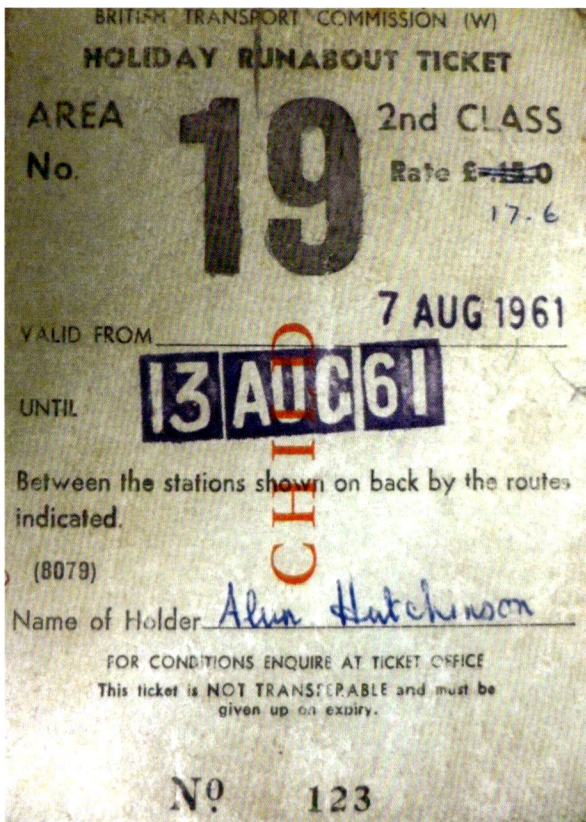

Holiday Runabout ticket for use on the Central Wales line between 7 and 13 August 1961 issued to Alun Hutchinson (*Alun Hutchinson*)

Unlimited travel was allowed over the area covered by the map (*Alun Hutchinson*)

twelve of us travelling together. When we climbed on board the bus the conductor's first question was: *And what football team do you play for?*

Tickets were attached to condemned locos to indicate their identity and destination.

Our interest in railways then started to wane as our attentions turned to other pursuits, notably football, rugby, music, motor cycling, and of course the opposite sex. Within a few years employment or university beckoned and some of our group, myself included, moved to other parts of the country. I took up my first teaching appointment in Tottenham in 1970 and for a

Godfrey Carr and Alan Thomas are pictured at Woodham's scrapyard alongside *5051* in 1964 *(Martin Davies)*

few years lost touch with some of our group. However, I returned to Briton Ferry in 1975 when my father passed away and soon became reacquainted with old friends. Our interest in railways was rekindled in the mid-1970s when steam returned to the main line after a three-year ban, a period which is dealt with in the next chapter.

### Notes for Chapter Nine

1. *Silver Buffers* by Martin Davies is in full in Chapter Seven
2. A freight which was vacuum-fitted throughout
3. *Cadbury Castle* was the only one of its class to be scrapped at Briton Ferry (1964)
4. Alan Thomas, Jeff Jones, Jeff Beer, Terry Thomas, Alun Hutchinson, Anthony Griffiths, Hugh James, Phil Gallagher, Brian Thomas and Clive Criddle
5. Such as the locals to Porthcawl, Treherbert and Margam steelworks, the freights to London, Cardiff, Swansea Docks, Llandarcy, Pontypool Road and Llanelli
6. Later Neath-Port Talbot College where Martin Davies later spent much of his working life
7. Restoration of this junction could play a significant part in plans for a revitalised Swansea Bay rail system.
8. The scene of Britain's worst ever mining disaster in 1913 when some 419 miners lost their lives.
9. Tony Griffiths, Alun Hutchinson, Alan Thomas and I had previously been able to visit uninterrupted
10. The ex-LMS shed
11. From 1958 the regulars from Whitland shed were 4557, 4558, 4569, 5520, 5549 and 5550 and 5560
12. Such as *Baydon*, *Ramsbury*, *Lechlade* or *Longworth Manor*
13. Such as 2220 or 2283
14. Now preserved on the Llangollen Railway
15. The section from Abergwili north has been restored by the Gwili Railway since closure in 1973
16. A fuller discussion of the locomotives and workings from Neath shed are dealt with in Chapter Six
17. R. Parker, *The Railways of Pembrokeshire*, p.215
18. An account of the last day is recorded in Chapter 4
19. 6435 is now preserved on the Bodmin and Wenford Railway in Cornwall
20. 13 June 1964
21. *Ramsbury Manor* and *Blenheim* are examples
22. which ran until 9 June when hauled by 4612

Chapter Ten

# Scrapping and Preservation

This chapter outlines the huge changes that took place in the 1960s on the railways of west Wales. The ending of local passenger and goods services, line and station closures, and the scrapping of locos were the principal events that characterised the decade. Finally, however, it reveals how some of the young local *observers* of railways became the *preservers* of some celebrated former Cwrt Sart locomotives and, sometimes, whole railway lines. These groups of erstwhile observers not only preserved locomotives they later, commissioned them to run on special services on the main lines. The Chapter concludes by assessing their legacy.

In the meantime, elsewhere on the world's railways things were often quite different. In October 1964, in time for the Tokyo Olympic Games, the Tokaido Shinkansen ran for the first from Tokyo to Osaka at speeds up to 137 mph. With sixteen-car trains running, it became the world's busiest high-speed line. France had also considered a TGV in the 1960s to connect the main cities across France on high-speed and conventional lines. The French government approved funding in 1976 for the first line from Paris to Lyon. The TGV was 'the train that saved French Railways'. By 2000 Shinkansens had carried their billionth passenger. France's TGV emulated this three years later. Elsewhere the future was much more optimistic than in Britain.

## The ending of local passenger and goods services – the last trains

The contrast with Britain could hardly have been greater during the 1960s and 1970s. Britain's railways had a great history, but an indecisive and uncertain future in which the local scene reflected the national picture.

In the early 1960s several local railways served by Cwrt Sart shed lost their passenger services when the Government decided to reduce British Railways' operating deficit. In 1962 passenger services were withdrawn from Neath (Riverside) to Brecon.

*4639 of Aberdare being prepared to run the last passenger train from Neath to Pontypool Road on Saturday 15 June 1964 (Gerald Williams)*

Hugh James captured the scene at Cwrt Sart depot as 4169 is prepared for its use on the last train to Treherbert.
*(from a water-colour painting by Hugh James)*

Closures were sometimes commemorated by the running of special, chartered trains along the routes to be axed.

A special last train was chartered on Saturday 5 October, hauled by two of Neath's best panniers. Locomotives *3621* and *3693* were specially cleaned and painted for the occasion. Jim Jones, a driver at Neath & Brecon shed, whose family ran the Dock Hotel in Briton Ferry, was sent to collect loco *3621* from the shed on the morning of the final run. His near neighbour, Martin Davies, travelled on the last train to Brecon and on the final train from Neath to Treherbert.

The locomotive on that occasion was *4169*, which had been a regular performer on the line since it came to Neath in the early 1950s. It, too, was specially prepared for these workings.

The Beeching Report had also recommended the cessation of passenger services to Pontypool Road. Indeed, on 13 June 1964, this proved to be the case when the last services were run. This was the precursor to the closure of the line from Glyn Neath to Pontypool Road later that year. Today this route, including its famous and spectacular Crumlin Viaduct, is known as much for the location for the film *Arabesque* starring Sophia Loren and Gregory Peck

as for its viaduct. Of course the locomotive for the last train from Neath to Pontypool Road, the 9.10 pm, was a pannier tank, *4639* of Aberdare, which was turned out to a high standard by the staff at Cwrt Sart depot.

## Line and station closures

Often, as was the case in the closure of the line from Glyn Neath to Pontypool Road, the ending of either passenger or goods services was accompanied both by line and station closures. The locos that had been used on such routes were afterward's either transferred for use at other depots or immediately consigned to the scrapyard. Thus, locos were concentrated in fewer and fewer depots, and as this progressed some depots were closed.

### Depot closures and locomotive transfers

As more freight services became subject to diesel traction, motive power depots in west Wales were closed to steam traction and the remaining locos transferred to Cwrt Sart. Thus, the shed acquired engines from Duffryn Yard (nicknamed by some Cwrt Sart enginemen as *Suffering Yard* when they

Neath Shed Yard with a brace of *Modified Halls*, *6991 Acton Burnell Hall* minus nameplate is featured. Sunday 27 September 1964 *(Alun Hutchinson)*

51218 at Barrow Road shed in 1962. This loco was later based at Neath for operating at Swansea Dock when East Dock shed closed in 1964. *(Alun Hutchinson)*

*80133* has arrived at Neath Station with a train from Pontypool Road, late 1963. *(John Hodge)*

Evening Star at Cwrt Sart shed in 1964 *(Martin Davies)*

Line up of active pannier tanks on the decoking line at Cwrt Sart shed, with *9780* prominent. October 1964 *(Martin Davies)*

*9716* and a clutch of other condemned pannier tanks outside Cwrt Sart shed following its closure in June 1965. They were despatched to Ward's. *(Jeff Beer)*

worked there), Swansea East Dock and Tondu. Among these locos were the remaining 0-4-0 tanks still used on the sharply curved lines between Swansea East Dock and the South Dock. There were two locos of LMS origin, *41535* and *51218*, which had been drafted in to replace the redundant Swansea Harbour tanks. The latter, replacement, locomotive, which is now preserved on the Keighley and Worth Valley Railway in Yorkshire, was a major problem as it kept breaking down. This was a consequence of it developing 'hot box' problems when running light engine to and from Swansea Docks. Consequently, the mighty British Rail (Western Region) had to hire a locomotive from Ward's scrapyard at Giants Grave to replace the replacement![1]

Another newcomer to Neath shed in 1963 was a

The special train at Neath Riverside behind *4612* and *9675* (*Alun Hutchinson*)

BR standard class 2-6-4 tank no *80133*, the only member of its class to be so allocated. It was employed on the Vale of Neath and Porthcawl services in tandem with Neath's prairie tanks.

There were still sixty plus locos at Neath in mid-1964, but by the end of the year most of its tender engines had been withdrawn or transferred. In October 1964 one of the last tender locos based at Neath, *Evening Star*, was rostered to take one of four special trains from each region from Swansea to Swindon works.

As there were few cleaners remaining at Neath by 1964, it was left to a group of volunteer railway enthusiasts to groom *Evening Star* ready for its special train. 1961's tally of seventy-four locomotives had reduced to sixty, with just nine tender engines remaining. By early 1965 Neath's allocation was made up totally of tank locomotives, the majority being pannier tanks.

### Cwrt Sart shed's swansong

In April 1965, two of Cwrt Sart's best pannier tanks, *4612* and *9675*, were specially cleaned and adorned with silver paint on their buffers, immaculate chimney tops and smokebox doors, to work a special, chartered train. The driving force behind this event

*6116* at the head of *Y Glyn Crwydryn* during its water stop at Hirwaun, 24 April 1965. (*Jeff Beer*)

were the West Glamorgan and Monmouthshire Railway Societies. They collaborated to organise a farewell tour of all the railways in the Swansea area that had lost their passenger services. The train, named *Y Glyn Crwydyn* was hauled from Cardiff by an immaculate 2-6-2 tank *6116*. It handed over to two pannier tanks *4612* and *9675* at Neath Riverside. From Neath, the train travelled to Coelbren, where it reversed to take the ex-Midland line down the

Swansea valley to St Thomas. It then followed the former RSBR tracks to Dinefwr Junction and then looped west along the Swansea District line to Felin Fran. Having been a passenger on the train Martin Davies can vouch for the fact that the two locos touched a speed of sixty mph on the level near Llandarcy. From Felin Fran the special followed the ex-GWR Morriston branch to gain the main line at Hafod Junction. This was a swansong for Cwrt Sart shed before it closed to steam on 13 June 1965.

Of the shed's last ten locos three, including *4612*, were transferred to Cardiff, the remainder being dispatched to Ward's, at Giant's Grave, Briton Ferry, for scrapping. *4612* survived into preservation simply because it was bought from Barry scrapyard as a source of spares for the Keighley and Worth Valley Railway. It was resold and totally restored to operating condition at the Flour Mill workshops, Forest of Dean, for service on the Bodmin and Wenford Railway in Cornwall.

### Scrapping of steam locos

Many steam locomotives were neither transferred to work at other depots nor were they immediately scrapped. Such was the speed with which dieselisation was enforced that railway works such as Swindon, which had traditionally scrapped life-expired locomotives, found that they could no longer cope with the large number of condemned locomotives. After withdrawal from running depots throughout the country they were earmarked for scrapping at yards near the steelworks and ship-breaking yards of Sheffield, Scotland, Teeside, Tyneside and south Wales. Indeed, the volume of locos to be dealt with resulted in some remaining in storage for long periods to await their downfall. But not all: a small number were quickly purchased from storage yards by preservation societies. From their ranks many survived, often being purchased to avoid their intended fate.

### Scrapping in Briton Ferry

Thomas W Ward Ltd established its shipbreaking yard on the River Neath at Giant's Grave in 1906. Over the years it dismantled hundreds of vessels, passenger liners and both merchant ships and warships, including submarines. From 1959 until 1966, when British Railways implemented its plan to

0-4-2 tank *1401* which starred in the film *Titfield Thunderbolt* was dismantled at Briton Ferry in 1959
*(From a watercolour painting by Martin Davies)*

replace all steam engines as quickly as possible, it also dismantled steam locomotives. Such was the speed with which dieselisation was enforced that railway works such as Swindon, which had traditionally scrapped life-expired locomotives, found that they could no longer cope with the large number of condemned locomotives.

Ward's took delivery of its first consignment of steam locos in 1959, the year which also saw the demolition of the Briton Ferry Iron Works. A branch line around Briton Ferry's Iron Works led to Ward's shipbreaking yard at Giant's Grave: a constant source of scrap steel for the nearby steelworks.

From the top of the nearby Warren Hill viewers saw the blast furnaces being reduced to rubble in clouds of dust. After demolition, the iron works sidings were used to store the withdrawn locomo-

tives and the scrap arising from the ironworks and locomotives' demolition.

A branch line curved past Briton Ferry's Iron Works to follow the river bank to the Wern Works and then Ward's shipbreaking yard at Giant's Grave. The latter was a constant source of scrap steel for the steelworks. From the mid-1960s, Ward's had a second source of scrap arising from the dismantling of steam locomotives as they were phased out by British Railways, about one hundred and sixty locos were cut up at Giant's Grave, all of which were small tank locomotives because longer wheelbase tender locomotives could not traverse the sharp bends. Some larger locos including a few *42xx* 2-8-0 tanks were nevertheless dismantled on sidings near the iron works. Among the smaller victims was locomotive *1401*, a small 0-4-2 tank used in the Ealing

An aerial view of Ward's scrapyard, Briton Ferry 1965 *(Gerald Williams)*

An 0-6-2 tank from Abercynon awaits the cutter's torch at Ward's, 1965 *(Jeff Jones)*

A pair of condemned 84xx pannier tanks, *8471* and *8403*, late of Bristol Barrow Road stored at Briton ferry dock awaiting disposal to Wards, 1965 *(Jeff Jones)*

A small number of ex-Southern Region tanks were dismantled at Wards, among them was *30107* seen at Giant's Grave in 1964 *(Phil Gallagher)*

A line up of condemned locos at the Albion Steelworks bound for destruction at Slag Reduction *(Martin Davies)*

A general view of Ward's yard in 1965 with a line up of *94xx* and *57xx* 0-6-0 pannier tanks *(Gerald Williams collection)*

comedy film *The Titfield Thunderbolt*, featuring John Gregson, Hugh Griffith and Sid James. The film was shown to new arrivals at their Christmas party at Neath Boys Grammar School in 1959.

Briton Ferry's metals industries were complicit overall in the scrapping of no fewer than 184 steam locomotives. Barlborough Metals and Slag Reduction Ltd each scrapped just a single machine, but Steel Supply at Neath Abbey wharf broke up twenty-two, and the oxy-acetylene torches of T W Ward at Giant's Grave dismembered no fewer than 160 in the late 1960s and early 1970s.

The curvature of the branch line to Giant's Grave was so severe that only small tank locos could be moved to the scrapyard there. A compelling story attaches to this fact. Swindon Works sold two large locos to Ward's in 1962, *King* class 4-6-0 locos *6023* and *6024*, despite the fact the movement of this type of loco was officially forbidden west of Cardiff. When the mistake was realised, the engines were resold to Woodhams at Barry Docks, with the result that they survived for preservation. Ironic indeed that *6024* should pay a visit to the down loop line at Briton Ferry, a mere half-mile from its intended graveyard, when it ran light engine to Swansea to pick up a Swansea to London steam special in 1997.[2] A list of the 159 locos dismantled by Ward's is shown in Appendix Eight.

Steel Supply stored larger tank and tender engines at Briton Ferry dock prior to scrapping, the most notable of which was *7028 Cadbury Castle* of Landore the picture shows this locomotive awaiting its fate near the Albion steelworks in 1964. Evidence of its earlier presence there remained in the form of its double chimney, which lay cast aside on waste ground for quite some time, obviously being too heavy to be removed by collectors. However, many

*6661* passes Briton Ferry en route to Wards with its cab numberplates still attached 1965 *(Jeff Jones)*

*7028 Cadbury Castle* was the only one of its class to be dismantled at Briton Ferry. It awaits its fate in 1964. *(Martin Davies)*

of the number-plates still attached to these locomotives found good homes. Page 201 shows the scene following the discovery of such a smokebox plate by a group of local enthusiasts. More unusual was the case of 0-6-2 tank *6661* which arrived at Briton Ferry en route to Ward's with both of its brass cab side plates still attached. A well-known custodian of heritage items ensured that these were preserved for posterity.

*6024 King Edward I* stops at Briton Ferry East as it makes its way light engine to Swansea to work an excursion to Paddington, 1997. Hugh James stands alongside the loco. *(Martin Davies)*

The group pictured after the discovery by Jeff Jones of the front numberplate from *4233*. Pictured are: (back row) Clive Criddle (holding the 'Stones latest EP), Martin Davies with numberplate, Terry Thomas. Front row: Alun Hutchinson, Jeff Beer and Godfrey Carr *(Jeff Jones)*

Briton Ferry woods and Shelone provide the backdrop for two pannier tanks awaiting scrapping at Ward's, 1965 *(Jeff Jones)*

Blue Pullman cars awaiting disposal at Briton Ferry *(Robert Thomas)*

Southern stock awaiting disposal *(Robert Thomas)*

In the 1970s and 1980s, Ward's began dismantling coaching stock, and diesel and electric multiple units as well as brake vans. When the *Blue Pullman* units were superseded by the HSTs they, too, were cut up by Ward's.

### Preservation – the Cwrt Sart survivors

Not all the resident locomotives of Cwrt Sart suffered the indignity of the scrapyard and the final ignominy of meltdown in the open-hearth furnace or the oxygen converter. Some survived, after a temporary visit to the scrapyard, for the most extraordinary of reasons, and took on entirely new roles. Indeed, today, we would surely refer to one such transformation as 'identity theft'. That transformation concerned *Olton Hall*, a mixed-purpose locomotive tastefully painted in GWR's Brunswick green livery, which was allocated to Cwrt Sart in the early 1960s.

At the end of 1963 it was scheduled for scrapping and 110 tonnes of locomotive and tender were sent to Woodham's yard in Barry for that purpose. Fortunately, the yard was so busy that *Olton Hall*'s rendition was delayed. In the interim, a group of steam enthusiasts from Wakefield purchased the delightful locomotive for preservation and then sold it to the West Coast Railway Company at Carnforth.

The identity theft followed. In 2001, J K Rowling's book *Harry Potter and the Philosopher's Stone* was to be filmed, and a locomotive, to be known as *Hogwarts Castle* was required to haul the *Hogwarts Express* from platform 9 ¾ at King's Cross. *Olton Hall*

was the chosen locomotive whose Brunswick green livery was transformed into the maroon livery of *Hogwarts Castle*. In its new identity, the film brought the locomotive worldwide fame amongst children and adults alike. Warner Bros studios even made a fibreglass replica for display in its studios at Orlando, Florida. The loco is now on display at the film company's Harry Potter exhibition in London. One just wonders whether *Hogwarts Castle*, or the real *Olton Hall*, will ever again steam through Briton Ferry?

*Hogwarts Castle* was fictitious but *Drysllwyn Castle* was not. It was the original name carried by another of Cwrt Sart's engines to survive the cutter's torch. Built in 1937 as 4-6-0 *5051 Drysllwyn Castle*,

*Olton Hall* in Harry Potter guise *(Railway Magazine)*

it was renamed Earl Bathurst some months later following objections from aristocratic members of the GWR board. They disliked their names being carried by a batch of ancient 4-4-0s used on the Cambrian routes in mid-Wales, preferring their names to be carried by the grander express locos instead. Earl Bathurst spent its entire working life in south Wales. Allocated to Landore when new, where it remained until it was transferred to Cwrt Sart in 1961. Two years later it reached Llanelli, not many miles from the real medieval Drysllwyn Castle in the Towi Valley, from where it was withdrawn and disposed of to Woodham's, Barry.

Purchased from the scrapyard in 1970 by the Great Western Society, it was restored to main line running order bearing its original *Castle* name within the decade. In 1985 it returned to the area to be on show at Neath before working a steam special from Swansea.[3]

Another happy story on the non-scrapping of steam locos at Briton Ferry concerns the second rebuild and steaming of locomotive *2857*.[4] This was certainly not such a celebrity as *Hogwarts Castle* or *Earl Bathurst* but a fund to preserve this former Cwrt Sart locomotive was, nevertheless, launched by a group of Severn Valley Railway members. In 1971, when the price of such a condemned *28xx* was just £3,500, *2857* was selected as being in the best all-round condition of the fourteen of the class remaining in Woodham's Barry scrapyard. The fifty-odd year-old freight locomotive was hardly a glamorous attraction in the appeal for donations and a further problem was that its price was rising faster than funds were being raised. For a long time, it looked as though the bid to purchase would fail, but the fund-raising eventually succeeded in meeting its target and the loco was moved by rail to the Severn Valley Railway four years later. That was a happy

*5051 Earl Bathurst* at Swansea station before heading the *St David's Day* special to Paddington, 1 March 2007
*(Martin Davies)*

2857 preparing for service at the Severn Valley Railway, 2015 (*Philip Adams*)

ending, but an even happier story came some years later, and, in all places, at Briton Ferry. By now the locomotive's condition had naturally deteriorated and a new cylinder block was urgently needed. A replacement would have to be made from new, and at great expense even providing the original engineering drawings were available. 2857's prospects for returning to service therefore looked very bleak indeed, but Briton Ferry unexpectedly came to the rescue.

During the demolition of the town's Albion Steelworks, a spare cylinder block, which was itself destined for melting down, was fortuitously discovered under a pile of coke. The astute demolition workers identified and retrieved it for re-use. The 2857 preservation group were delighted with the salvaged block, saying: 'When one considers the quantity of scrap that arrives at a steel works, the survival of any heavy castings for very long is surprising, but to find the exact castings we needed was utterly incredible.' 2857 would soon be able to steam along the Severn Valley Railway once again!

The story of 2857 does not quite end there. Bewdley Brewery, from the town of that name in the Severn Valley, decided that it was apt to name its strongest beer after the powerful locomotive which was stationed there after its overhaul in 2011. The beer, pale straw in colour and brewed with First Gold, Celeia and Worcestershire Fuggles hops, is still going. So, too, is 2857 which celebrated its 100th birthday in 2018.

2857 beer (*Philip Adams*)

The spare cylinder block for 2857 (*2857 Society*)

*6695 climbing Castle Hill on the West Somerset Railway in 2003 (Martin Davies)*

Other Cwrt Sart locos were rescued and preserved. *2818* was a 'twin' from the same class as *2857*, but thirteen years' older. This heavy freight locomotive, however, has a claim to fame that its younger sibling cannot share because the latter was not built until the war was nearly over. Although principally used for coal and steel traffic between Llanelli and Severn Tunnel Junction, *2818*'s ability to haul heavy and lengthy coal trains resulted in it being used to operate the 'Jellicoe Special'[5] trains from Pontypool Road to Grangemouth. The Royal Navy's Grand Fleet favoured south Wales steam coal for its Scapa Flow fleet – based in Scotland's Orkneys. The likes of *2818* played their part in the arduous journey to get the coal there. *2818* is now preserved at the *Steam* museum in Swindon.

*5239* was another Cwrt Sart survivor. A steadfast workhorse, it dutifully performed short-haul coal trips from pit to port after its introduction to service in 1923. After thirteen years of rusting away in Barry scrapyard the eighty-two tonne locomotive, now renamed *Goliath* was reincarnated for a new working life at the Dartmouth Steam Railway (formerly the Paignton and Kingswear Railway). Other known Cwrt Sart survivors include 0-6-2 tank *6695*, the pannier tank, *4612*, and 2-8-0 No *3814*.

*5239 at work on the Dartmouth Steam Railway (Martin Davies)*

*6695* was once known for slogging its way up the Afan valley, until the RSBR line closed in 1962. Restored for use on the Swanage Railway in Dorset, it has subsequently worked on a more appropriate ex-GWR environment, pitting its wits against the gradients of the Quantock Hills in West Somerset. *4612* was transferred to Cardiff East Dock when Cwrt Sart closed in 1965 and ended up in the *Graveyard of Steam* at Woodhams, Barry. Originally purchased as a source of spares by the Keighley and Worth Valley for its own working pannier, *5775*, it was resold to the Bodmin and Wenford Railway where it now is fully operative after restoration at the Flour Mill, Forest of Dean.

*9642* is another locomotive with local connections that still lives. After spending most of its life in the west country, it was consigned to Hayes scrapyard in Bridgend. For a time, it was used by them as a shunting locomotive until it was bought by two businessmen, the Jones brothers, for overhaul at NCB workshops, Maesteg, to run special trains. After a few years work a group of enthusiasts from Briton Ferry and Baglan helped restore it to working order. They were occasionally joined by Godfrey Carr's father, George, who lent his boiler-making skills to the renovation. Group members travelled back and forth to Maesteg on weekends and on summer evenings to undertake the work.

> I spent many happy hours stripping the paintwork on the loco down to the bare metal on the loco, as we got down to the original coat of paint with the GWR initials showing through. (Martin Davies)

The loco was later bought by a group of enthusiasts from the Swansea Vale Railway who intended using it on their line in Llansamlet. After a preliminary rebuild at the BP refinery it moved to Swansea and thence found regular work on the Dean Forest

9642 after restoration at NCB Maesteg *(John Wiltshire)*

9642 at the Dean Forest Railway *(Martin Davies)*

Railway for some ten years. It is now based on the recently extended Gloucester and Warwickshire Railway.

## Main line steam specials and a rekindling of enthusiasm

In Chapter Nine Martin Davies explained how his rail group's interest waned temporarily as its attention turned to other pursuits, or as employment or university beckoned. The group were unable to resist the enticement of steam heritage railways as they sprung up throughout Britain in the early 1980s, however. As steam excursions on the main lines became very popular, the group, who had moved to other parts of the country, became re-acquainted and interest in railways was rekindled despite raising young families.

Initially the group organised a series of railway talks and slide at the Puddlers Arms, Briton Ferry, which attracted friends old and new. So successful were the talks that professional railwaymen like Doug Rice and Dai Brooks, a Port Talbot signalman were attracted to the talks as well as lapsed train-spotters and members of the public. Among the lapsed train-spotters were proficient photographers like Dai Brooks and Dai Goldstraw who gave some notable presentations. Wynne Morgan and Joe Cox were other regular attendees. For good measure, Goldstraw and Hugh James, both talented artists, captured the railway scene in their work, with one of Hugh's most celebrated paintings proudly displayed in the public bar for many years.

It was hardly surprising that the group, which had been so involved in preservation activities, soon became interested in the testing of preserved locomotives on main lines. A pioneering run was made by *King George V* in 1971 whose success led to the operation on the main line of other steam locos such as *Clan Line* and *Princess Elizabeth*. The group's interest was revitalised, too, by visits to re-opening heritage railways such as the Severn Valley, with

whom the group had a very fortunate connection. Godfrey Carr's uncle Roger, was a pioneering member who first worked as a volunteer guard before becoming a director of the railway for some forty years.

*The Western Envoy*

The enlarging *Puddlers' Boys* group's activities soon involved travel on main line steam specials and trips to lines such as the Dart Valley, the Bluebell Railway and Didcot Rail Centre.

*Pendennis Castle* had been purchased for preservation directly from British Railways to run successfully on main line specials from its base in Carnforth. However, by 1976, because of route availability problems in north-west England its owners found it difficult to operate it. Consequently, they controversially decided to sell the locomotive to an Australian company, Hamersley Iron, to operate as a tourist attraction on their 240-mile iron-ore line. A farewell special was hastily arranged before the iconic loco was shipped down under.

4079's headed its farewell special, 'The Western Envoy' on 29th May 1977 before being shipped to Australia, where it stayed until it was repatriated in 2000. It is seen outside Didcot Railway Centre shortly after its return from 'down under' *(Martin Davies)*

The group travelled on its last run, as the *Great Western Envoy*, from Birmingham to Didcot in May 1977. The locomotive put on a solid performance that day, handling the gradients with ease, a fitting tribute to a fine locomotive which was shipped to Sydney from Avonmouth three days later. In 2000 however, *Pendennis Castle* was repatriated by the Great Western Society and is now undergoing a main line overhaul with every prospect of steaming on British lines once again.

*The Blowout*

Travelling in search of steam was sometimes hazardous.

> A group of seven from the Puddlers' Arms arranged to travel on a steam special between Newport and Chester. It involved two locomotives *35028 Clan Line* and *6201 Princess Elizabeth*, but it also involved two cars: Martin Davies took four in his Ford Escort while I travelled with Hugh James in his Jaguar.
>
> We had agreed to meet up at Newport. En route, I suddenly noticed a blue car resting in a hedge, whose number plate I recognised as Martin's. Our friends were severely shaken up following a tyre blowout which had caused it to veer into the path of an oncoming car. To miss the oncoming vehicle, he steered into the hedge. It was simply the three sizeable souls in the back seat that prevented the car from tipping down the bank beyond the hedge. The police kindly escorted the five occupants to Bridgend station to get to Newport in time for the steam special. Martin was so shaken up that he re-started smoking, having only recently given up. He must have smoked about forty fags on that steam special. (Tony Griffiths)

*Mystery Trips*

Other rail-related pursuits during the late 1970s included travelling on the popular *Mystery Trips*, an inexpensive day out. In the summer months the special trains usually visited seaside resorts such as Weston-super-Mare, Paignton or Weymouth, whereas at other times of the year they would go to a city destination such as London. A friend who worked on the railways sometimes tipped us off as to the destination. This enabled the group to plan cheap outings to various football grounds like Brentford or Birmingham. Saturday afternoon away games in places like The Hawthorns in West Bromwich allowed us to see stars like Jeff Astle and Asa Hartford when the Albion were playing at home.

*Return of the 'Prodigal'*

Several of these trips included group members' children, as they became old enough to appreciate the venues attractive for children of their age, whilst railway preservation continued to attract the adults. Godfrey Carr is a good example: a boilermaker by trade, he helped in the early restoration of the former Port Talbot Railway 0-6-0 saddle tank on the Severn Valley Railway. Similarly, Tony Griffiths lent his engineering skills to the Great Western Society at Didcot, the fledgling Swansea Vale Railway in Llansamlet, and then the Gwili and Teifi Valley Railways.

Steam returned to west Wales in 1985 as part of the Great Western Railway's centenary celebrations, with *Earl Bathurst* returning for the first time since 1963 to take place in an open day at Landore shed, its home from 1937 to 1961. It journeyed to Swansea with *6960 Raveningham Hall*. It called at Neath sta-

*6960 Raveningham Hall* at Neath 1985 *(Martin Davies)*

tion en route as a result of Hugh James and friends' powers of persuasion to raise funds for charity. Cwrt Sart's last shedmaster, now District Manager at Margam, devised a rota of former Cwrt Sart drivers and firemen for footplate duties.

That weekend *Raveningham Hall* was used on a shuttle service between Swansea and Carmarthen while *Earl Bathurst* was the chief attraction at the special Landore open day and became the haulage for the last train of the weekend.

It was a wonderful weekend and generated great interest among local people. We were fortunate for the first time in twenty years to take photographs of steam locomotives in the local area. The icing on the cake was the chance to travel behind *5051* on Sunday's final train where its spirited run included a memorable assault on Cockett bank.

*King George V* climbs the bank out of Swansea at the head of a steam special to Carmarthen in 1987 (*Martin Davies*)

*A* King *conquers Carmarthen*

The success of this weekend led to a similar event two years later. The 1987 workings were notable for the use of *6000 King George V*, the first time a locomotive of this class had ever worked west of Cardiff. *6000* had made the news in 1927 as the most powerful steam locomotive in Britain. It had successfully represented the GWR in the USA when it operated on the Baltimore and Ohio Railroad. The brass bell presented by the American railway company still adorned its buffer beam in 1985.

Track renewal and bridge strengthening since the 1960s made it possible for the route west of Cardiff to accommodate the *King*'s 22-tonne axle loading. Hugh James invited Godfrey Carr and Martin Davies to join him on the momentous test run of the loco between Swansea and Carmarthen. Neither thought they would ever see a *King* at Swansea, let alone ride in the cab on one to Carmarthen, as it shared its duties with *7029 Clun Castle*, the last of its class to run in regular service.

*Narberth's slippery slope*

The Swansea to Carmarthen line was an ideal route to run regular steam shuttles and the trains were well patronised. The chance to travel on and photograph the trains lifted the spirits but it was to be a few years before steam returned to the Swansea area. In 1993 a series of 'return to steam' specials were run west of Carmarthen, but some were dismayed by the

*80079 at Tenby station (Martin Davies)*

205

choice of locomotives. Rather than using an ex-GWR loco, an ex-LMS *Black 5* and a Standard *Class 4* tank was used on the basis that the locos had to be pathed along the former LMS Central Wales line from Shrewsbury to Llanelli. Some steam, whatever its origin, was better than none.

Nevertheless, this was likely the first occasion locos of these classes had been used in west Wales to the destinations of Milford Haven, Fishguard and Pembroke Dock. The group[6] travelled on Sunday 30 May to Pembroke Dock, but standard tank *80079*, recently outshopped by the Severn Valley Railway, was from a class alien to the line.

After Swansea, the loco was turned on the triangle at Carmarthen and the seven-car train made good time to Whitland where it veered on to the Pembroke Dock branch. Shortly afterwards intermittent rain impacted on further progress by making the line very greasy on the steep section between Narbeth and Cold Blow summit, after Narberth station and tunnel. The remedial work in progress to repair the roof of the tunnel added to this problem by demanding a speed restriction of fifteen mph. Consequently, the loco could not get sufficient power to haul its train up the bank. Climbing at a snail's pace, it lost its grip on the wet track and slipped seriously. Even making full use of the sanders the loco was still unable to shift its load. With the line to Pembroke Dock blocked, the crew had to call for assistance in the form of a diesel locomotive.

The closest diesel available was sixty miles away at Margam depot. Fearing for further delays, the closest available motive power, *44767 George Stephenson*, the *Black Five* resting in Carmarthen station, was summoned from its slumbers to rescue the static steam special from Narberth bank. Eventually, after much patience, *George Stephenson* pushed it up the bank. Arriving in Tenby a few hours late, the train was terminated there instead of Pembroke Dock. The bank out of Tenby station is also formidable, but with the additional power of George Stephenson on the front and the standard tank behind, the train easily ascended Cold Blow summit. Passengers, disappointed that they had not reached Pembroke Dock, had another chance to do so that autumn when another special was run successfully, but this time using twin tanks *80079* and *80080*.

*The Reign of* King Edward I

*King Edward I* visited Swansea for the first time, newly restored, on 20 May 1994 on a special from Gloucester. Two days later the group travelled behind it on its return trip from Swansea to Didcot via Gloucester. Its crew included Malcolm Williams, a former Cwrt Sart driver, then working at Landore, whose work on the footplate resulted in a memorable climb of Sapperton Bank. The following year *6024* returned to Swansea to head a St David's Day special to Paddington.

*5029 Nunney Castle* at the head of a return excursion to Bristol at Fishguard Harbour in 2011 *(Martin Davies)*

*60163 Tornado passes Briton Ferry on a special to Swansea in 2016 (Martin Davies)*

*A4 'No 9' passes Briton Ferry on its return from Carmarthen, 2016 (Stuart Warr)*

It visited Briton Ferry and Swansea again in 1997 to haul a special to Paddington and reached Fishguard to commemorate the 200th anniversary of the aborted French landing there. Since then the loco has been a regular visitor to Carmarthen, Pembroke Dock and Fishguard in south-west Wales.

Earl Bathurst paid a return visit in August 2006, to commemorate the centenary of the opening of Fishguard Harbour. Its last trip through Briton Ferry was in 2007 when it took a St David's Day special to Paddington from Swansea. Other notable preserved steam locomotives to pass through Briton Ferry include *5029 Nunney Castle, 7325, 60009 Union of South Africa, Blue Peter, Britannia, Oliver Cromwell, Duke of Gloucester, Black 5s 44871* and *45407* and *60163 Tornado*. Briton Ferry has also witnessed many

*City of Truro* at Taunton, May 2004

*71000* at Fishguard Harbour, 2009 *(Martin Davies)*

excursions employing diesel power, including heritage traction, over the last twenty years.

*Go West Old Boys*

In the 1990s and 2000s the group ventured further afield to experience long-distance steam travel. Most steam specials to west Wales and the west of England started the steam leg of their journey at Temple Meads, Bristol, where the group boarded trains hauled by *6024* or *5029* to Carmarthen, Pembroke Dock and elsewhere. In 2004, *City of Truro* ran to Kingswear and back to commemorate the centenary of its record-breaking trip down Wellington bank. It was not allowed to match its 102 mph speed record on the return journey on that memorable day which proved to be one of her swansong trips on the main line.

*Fighting for survival*

On 3 May 2003, a swansong of another kind was in prospect for the Swansea City football supporters in the group. They had booked a trip to Devon before realising that Swansea City would be fighting for its survival in the Football League at the Vetch Field that very day. Godfrey Carr, a Cardiff City supporter, was not bothered in the least, but Alan Thomas and Martin Davies were loyal *Swans* fans who never missed a home game. The only group member to see the match was Alun Hutchinson whilst the others were travelling on the first outing by a double-headed *Castle* over the Devon banks since the 1960s.

Fortunately, Alan Thomas brought his radio along, as he had done on steam trips in the sixties, and we were able to follow the game as we enjoyed the memorable journey behind *Earl Bathurst* and *Nunney Castle*. The locos made mince-meat of Dainton and Hemerdon banks that day. The *Swans* also made mincemeat of Hull with the final score, Swansea 4 Hull 2. Alun Hutchinson relayed the score from the Vetch Field at regular intervals and each time the Swans scored the Swansea fans in the group punched the air. A Plymouth pub was the venue to celebrate both the impressive performance of Swansea City to secure Football League status and that of the two *Castles*.

The group made further memorable trips behind *5051*, notably *The Torbay Express* from Bristol to Kingswear in 2003, its commemorative run to Fishguard in 2006, and its final steaming from Swansea to Paddington on St David's Day, 2007. Excursions to Fishguard and Milford Haven using an improved *Duke of Gloucester*, and pioneering runs to Pembroke Dock by *King Edward I*, *Oliver Cromwell* and *Nunney Castle* were further worthwhile experiences.

*Overview – observers and preservers*

Martin Davies' interest in railways continues to this day. Since 2002, he has organised the Open Meetings of the Swansea Vale Railway Society in Pontardawe and gives slide presentations on railways and related topics to local groups when not pursuing other interests like walking, music, art, and watching *The Swans*. Since the 1980s, Godfrey, Phil, Tony have also been regular members of the Swansea Vale Railway and have regularly attended its meetings.

Godfrey Carr, a lifelong Cardiff City supporter, has been a long-serving member of the Severn Valley Railway and helped raise funds for the restoration of ex-Port Talbot Railway 0-6-0 loco *813*. He travelled on many of the main line steam excursions mentioned above.

Tony Griffiths was a founder member of the Railway Club of Wales and was heavily involved in its activities until its demise a few years ago. He was also a long-time volunteer on the Gwili Railway and lat-

Alan Thomas and Godfrey Carr seen outside Swindon
Works on a visit with Martin Davies in 2003 *(Martin Davies)*

terly the nearby Teifi Valley Railway, working on the
footplate and other aspects of the railway's operations.

Phil Gallagher, IT specialist, former competitive
runner and DIY expert, is a regular SVR meeting
attendee who travelled on most of the main excursions.

Alun Hutchinson, a former systems analyst,
marathon runner, talented cricketer and lifelong
*Swans* supporter is a keen rail traveller who is close
to his ambition of travelling on every piece of railway
track in Britain.

Jeff Jones has developed a great interest in diesel
traction and is an active member of the Swansea-
based bus museum. There he has spent much of his
spare time restoring and operating a London Transport *Routemaster*, which is often seen at transport
rallies up and down the country.

Hugh James's lifetime interest in railways and his
art work has sometimes to take a back seat to his hectic schedule as local councillor, but he is still a tireless promoter of steam specials in South West Wales.

Alan Thomas was another season ticket holder
at the Liberty Stadium until his early death a few
years ago, who retained a lifelong interest in railways
and travelled in the group on many of the specials.

Jeff Beer, who died in 2002, was an avid supporter of Baglan Rugby Club who retained his interest in railways all his life.

Yes, I was a *train spotter*, a pastime regarded by
many as an enjoyable but frivolous indulgence. Yet
it had a clear end product and that was the education
it provided in terms of heightened awareness of people and places. This derived from many visits to distant places and some wonderful friendships.

My self-description of *rail enthusiast* however,
also implies that I understand the significance of railways' historic contribution to social and economic
activity. I have no hesitation in advocating the future
contribution railways can make to the prosperity of
south Wales and elsewhere. They have a particularly
important part to play if the public is to maintain the
levels of mobility that we have come to enjoy in the
past forty or fifty years, and to do so in a sustainable,
responsible way.

(Martin Davies)

This chapter outlined the huge changes that took
place in the 1960s on the railways of west Wales as
observed through the eyes of teenage rail enthusiasts
in the Neath-Port Talbot area. The ending of local
passenger and goods services, line and station closures, the scrapping of locos, and the preservation
of some, were the principal events that characterised
the decade in this and many other areas.

The fact that the group lived in such an area
where it could monitor the arrival, disposal and
preservation of, at first, steam locos and rolling stock
meant that accurate historical records of these activities could be made by group members in both visual
and tabular form.

The activities of such individuals and groups,
initially trainspotting, led to their participation in
the rail preservation movement, the establishment of
a heritage railway network and a source of pressure
in support of railways generally. The effects of these
activities are threefold: the groups' legacy is to
enable future generations to understand the part that
railways have played in Britain's social and economic
history. More importantly they also indicate the
potential of railways within an integrated transport
future. In addition, preservation activities, which are
mainly voluntary, are recognised for their enormous
current contribution to tourism and community
development, no more so than in Wales.

(Philip Adams)

**Notes for Chapter Ten**

1. *R.O.F. 7 No 6*, for a few months.
2. *King Edward II* has passed through Briton Ferry on several
   occasions hauling steam specials to and from West Wales.
3. See also Chapter 11 'A Rail Enthusiast's Tale'
4. *2857.org*; accessed 5 April 2017

5. Admiral of the Fleet John Jellicoe commanded the British
   Grand Fleet at the Battle of Jutland, 1916
6. Comprising Alun Hutchinson, Godfrey Carr, Phil
   Gallagher and Martin Davies

Chapter Eleven

# The Townspeople

*People's backyards are much more interesting than their front gardens, and houses that back onto railways are public benefactors.*

(John Betjeman)

This Chapter examines the impact that railways had on the people of Briton Ferry and the influence that the people had on the town's public and industrial railways, particularly during the twentieth century. It details the demography of the rail staff of 1911, having covered occupational aspects of those who worked in, or from, Cwrt Sart locomotive depot in Chapter Eight. Finally, this chapter recollects some experiences of the townsfolk who did not work on the railways but lived near, used, and often loved them.

## The railwaymen of 1911

With a railway history of almost 170 years, readers will no doubt ask why the year of 1911 was chosen for a study of rail workers. It was the last year for which full census figures are available, but there are other reasons for choosing that year. Firstly, the decade immediately before World War One was, perhaps, the one during which railways were at their zenith: in west Wales the Swansea District line was about to open, with Briton Ferry becoming a key junction. 1911 also provided a major point for change in the industrial relations on Britain's railways in the form of the first national rail strike, before the insidious advent of the lorry, bus and the motor car in the inter-war years.

That a cohort of more than 200 rail workers of various occupations lived in a town like Briton Ferry in 1911 is hardly surprising, given the high level of activity in such towns at the time. Many of the railway workings were industrial, serving the metals industries in and around the town's river and dock. Quite a few railwaymen were employed by the ship-breaking, ironmaking, steelmaking, tinplate and copper smelting industries themselves, and not by the railway companies. Nevertheless, the large number of rail workers, paled in comparison with the

tally of resident steel and tin workers.

The metal industries had seen an influx of migrant workers to the new works in west Glamorgan, particularly after the railway had reached west Wales in the second half of the nineteenth century. The railways, too, had their own influx, both of construction workers and, afterwards, of those running the networks. The GWR and the SWMR experienced their build-ups of manpower over the second half of the century, whereas the needs of the RSBR had to be filled more quickly in the 1890s. A feature of the rail expansion and migration to Briton Ferry was the need for around ten per cent of the rail workers to seek board and lodge with local families because of incomplete housing provision. Many of these migrants were from west Wales or west of England railway families, or had other rail connections, often transfers initiated by the GWR itself, whilst others were opportunistic and unskilled itinerants – the 'railway navvies'.

Industrial companies operating in Briton Ferry, including railway companies, built houses for their workers, mainly through local building contractors. Several houses in Charles Street, Rockingham and Morgan Terrace, for example, were built for the RSBR[1]. Such was the demand for housing, it was reported that the RSBR company had gone ahead to build twelve houses in Hunter Street without submitting plans to the Local Board.[2] The company's growth attracted many to the town, whether to build, operate or maintain its new lines, some just boarding until their work was complete. Arthur Steel, Manager of the SWMR even sat on the Local Board.

A glance at today's street map between the A474 road and the rail line north of the present Briton Ferry station reveals much about the effect the rail routes had upon the town's settlement pattern. From Alexander Street to the eponymous Short Street, each cul-de-sac street becomes shorter, to follow the path of the rail line until the A474 reaches Station Road, where access to the RSBR's Cwrt Sart station was afforded. Then, one sees that the orientation of horseshoe-shaped Morgan Terrace was chosen to overlook the RSBR. Further along the A474, Farm Road follows as the next turning on the left, to give access to the GWR running sheds.  Clearly, while Betjeman's assertion that houses' gardens might back onto railways applied to London, it certainly did not apply to Briton Ferry. Here houses faced the railways, or were built at right angles to the lines. Except for the houses in Railway Terrace and Hunter Street, whose backs faced the RSBR[3] because of the rival GWR's insistence that it must follow that route, in Briton Ferry the general pattern was that houses admiringly faced the railways.

Despite the substantial complement of rail workers, there were streets in the town which had none.

Horse-shoe shaped Morgan's Terrace house many railway workers and was adjacent to the RSBR station, Cwrt Sart Station (*Philip Adams*)

Villiers Street, once a principal commercial street in Briton Ferry, is an interesting example. This was the work locale for a phalanx of drapers, fish merchants, banks, boot repairers, grocers and restauranteurs. The street even boasted a tin worker's household, but not a single rail employee, despite its contiguity with the main railway lines through the town. To find a rail employee you would have to turn left at the bottom of that street at the Royal Dock Hotel into Charles Street. There, opposite Briton Ferry station, you would likely encounter Mr and Mrs Rowe who were running the GWR temperance bar.

The settlements near St Mary's Church at Warren Hill and George's Row, which had housed metalworkers for over seventy years, were not the addresses of railway men. It was the same story at Giant's Grave, the other early Briton Ferry settlement, where streets such as Owen's, Cemetery and Victoria Rows and St John's Terrace accommodated shipbreakers,

river pilots and some metalworkers. Not until the ship-breaking yard operated its own rail locomotive was there a railway person from the hamlet of Giant's Grave itself.

Some streets, such as Glanymor and Ruskin, were still in the course of construction and were shorter in length than today. This simply meant that one was less likely to find railway men living there, but some did. Elsewhere, streets such Park Street,[4] on the western side of the lines, whose lengths were also curtailed by the proximity of the railway, nevertheless housed a small number of rail staff. Most of the longer streets in the town, some of which were built in part by the railway companies, accommodated railway staff. This pattern sometimes took the form of clusters, with the Cwrt Sart area having the most noteworthy assemblage, with over forty rail staff in the streets around Morgan Terrace and Pantyrheol.

This was to be expected in Cwrt Sart, given the area's proximity to the locomotive running sheds and workshops, but other significant clusters, of a half dozen or more workers, were found in Lowther, Thomas, Hunter and Regent Street East. Middleton Street and Ynysymaerdy Road  had similar patterns of resident rail staff, too. It was not unusual to find fathers and sons, or brothers, from these addresses, working together on the GWR and the RSB, but sometimes within the metals industry. Their work on the railways was of several types:

- motive power operations staff, such as drivers, fireman and guards
- other operational staff such as shunters, signalmen and track maintenance
- workshop maintenance activities such as engine fitters and wagon repair staff
- administrative support such as clerks, ticket office and even (temperance) bar workers

Briton Ferry railway staff's occupations were recorded in the 1911 census return, in trade union and GWR employment records. Within the rail-based occupations *engine driver* was the most common, followed by *track maintenance* and *engine maintenance* in the locomotive sheds. It is possible that the number of drivers is over-represented in these figures, and fireman and cleaner under-represented, because self-reporting of *engine driver* was a flattering generic description to cover all three jobs. *Shunting* and *signalling* also provided plenty of railway employment, as did some supporting work, such as dock operations and wagon maintenance. Specialised occupations such as *railway policeman* and *safety valve inspector* were represented, but were

211

less numerous. Whilst more than seventy percent of the town's rail staff was employed by the two main rail companies, the GWR and RSBR, the industrial railways' complement was also substantial, accounting for well over twenty per cent.

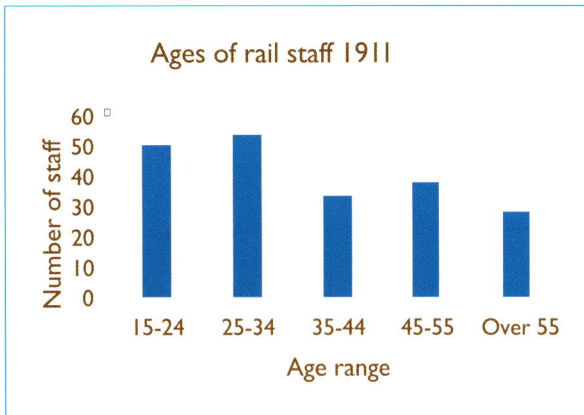

## Ages of rail staff 1911

Ages of Briton Ferry Railway Staff in 1911

The youngest staff, aged fifteen years, were Willie Evans, an apprentice fitter, Gladstone Thomas, an engine cleaner, and Cyril Charles Cox, an RSBR messenger. The eldest footplateman was sixty-six-year-old fireman John Halliday, with William Tissington still working as a steelworks engine fitter at sixty-eight-years of age. Overall, staff were quite young. Over a half of the 203 staff whose ages are known were less than thirty-four years of age, and fewer than a third had passed their forty-fifth birthday. It was from these younger age groups that many men from less essential rail occupations were later conscripted for the war.

The chart *Briton Ferry railworkers jobs 1911* (see below) groups the 206[6] workers into broad occupational classifications. A large proportion of these lived in Briton Ferry. Several reasons can be given for the particular spread of rail occupations in the table: the fact that the docks were an integral part of the rail system, the existence of the west Wales area's rail headquarters at Cwrt Sart sheds, and the inclusion of unusual occupations such as temperance coffee bar staff.

The table *Where Briton Ferry railworkers were employed* (see page 215) lists the seventy percent (144

Daniel Jenkins, mechanical supervisor at Glyncorrwg Workshops, maternal great-grandfather of Philip Adams

| Occupational class | Number | Percentage of total | Notes |
|---|---|---|---|
| Engine driver | 35 | 18 | Some firemen may have been reported as 'driver' |
| Track maintenance | 27 | 14 | Platelayers, strikers, packers, and inspectors |
| Engine maintenance | 20 | 10 | Includes turning, moulding and apprentices |
| Shunter | 19 | 9 | |
| Signalling | 19 | 9 | Includes lamp men |
| Clerks, stores, parcels and booking | 16 | 8 | Includes checkers and messengers |
| Engine firing and cleaning | 12 | 6 | It is possible that several engine cleaners recorded their occupation as 'fireman' or 'driver' |
| Dock operators | 11 | 5 | Includes weighing and discharging wagons, dock gate operation |
| Wagon maintenance | 11 | 5 | Includes wagon building, painting and examination |
| Porters | 11 | 5 | Includes carriers and carters |
| Managerial and administrative | 9 | 4 | Includes railway police, and temperance staff |
| Stationmasters | 4 | 3 | Includes an inspector |
| Unspecified | 3 | 2 | |
| Labourer | 3 | 2 | |
| TOTAL | 206 | 100 | |

Briton Ferry rail workers' jobs in 1911

| Employer/location | Employer known | Percentage | Notes |
|---|---|---|---|
| Great Western Railway | 77 | 53 | Includes GWR staff engaged in Briton Ferry Dock operations |
| Rhondda and Swansea Bay Railway | 25 | 17 | |
| Steelworks | 18 | 12 | Briton Ferry and Albion steelworks |
| Tinworks | 7 | 8 | Vernon, Villiers, Baglan Bay, Wern, Gwalia and Whitford tinworks |
| Briton Ferry Ironworks | 6 | 4 | |
| Glyncorrwg Colliery/SWMR | 6 | 4 | Glyncorrwg Colliery and ex-SWMR staff |
| Port Talbot Railway | 2 | 2 | |
| Shipbreaking and Contractor | 2 | 2 | T W Ward, Giant's Grave |
| Copperworks | 1 | 1 | Cape and Red Jacket works |
| TOTAL | 144 | 100 | |

Where Briton Ferry rail workers were employed in 1911

Dr E. V. Pegge, well known Briton Ferry medic

of 204) of the known rail workers' employers listed in Appendix Five.

Daniel Jenkins of Barn Cottages, Shelone Road,[8] worked at the nearby Glyncorrwg Colliery Company's locomotive shed and foundry. When the SWMR ceased operating in 1910, Daniel, who was mechanical foreman at the Shelone Road sheds, had reached fifty-seven years of age and had raised eight children, four boys and four girls. All the boys followed their father and became mechanical engineers in various industries. A newspaper reported that he and his wife, Ann, were celebrating their sixtieth wedding anniversary in 1935, adding that four of his children had also celebrated their silver weddings.

Edward Pegge was from a medical family. He was a near neighbour of Jenkins, living nearby on Shelone Road, at the Elms. Pegge and Dr James Symes, as the town's general medical practitioners,

sometimes had the unpleasant task of attending to persons who had been killed or injured in the area's rail accidents. However, Pegge also had another, more interesting, connection with the railway. As a rugby player of some prowess for Neath, London Welsh and Wales, with heavy medical duties as well, it was difficult for him to meet all the demands upon his time. This came to a head during the 1887 season when he missed the departure of Neath RFC's train for the team's tour to the west of England. Undeterred, in order not to miss the kick-off of the first match, he simply chartered a special train from Briton Ferry to arrive at the match in time.

**The impact of the First World War**

Three years on from 1911 there were 643,000 railmen in Britain. By the end of the war 184,000 railway men had joined up and 18,957 of them had lost their lives fighting in the armed forces. The rail workers of Briton Ferry had decisions to make about the war. Some attested and volunteered at the outset in 1914 and 1915, some were conscripted from 1916, some wore War Service badges to work in their reserved occupation whilst others objected to war, conscription, or both, and were imprisoned as a result.

The depletion of the labour force led to an increase in the volume of work for those who remained, which meant longer hours, greater responsibilities and a struggle to keep up with the cost of living. For example, by June 1917, the London and North-Western Railway had 12,000 fewer workers than 1914 while carrying an additional million tons of goods a year.

*Briton Ferry casualties*

Approximately twenty Briton Ferry railway men went to war and seven were killed. They either

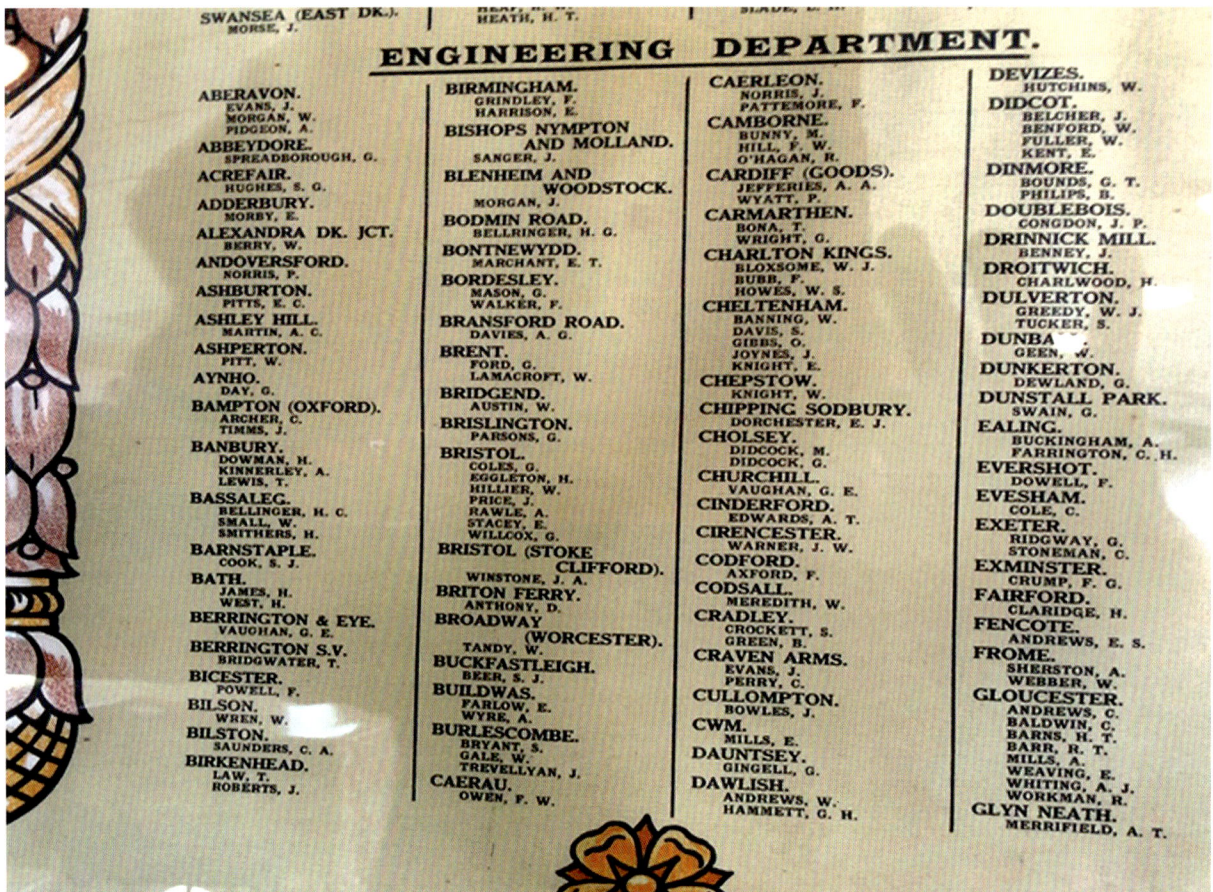

G.W.R First World War Roll of Honour showing fatalities in the Engineering Department *(Didcot Railway Centre)*

worked on the GWR, RSBR, Neath and Brecon Railway or the North Central Wagon Company. Little is known of three of them.[10] R H Palmer, a signalman in Briton Ferry's passenger department died from appendicitis. A clerk from the same department, WD Jones, was killed as was D Anthony, a ballast loader in the passenger department.

*A volunteer*

The first to die was John Edward Baker, originally from Kent, he served seven years with the Royal West Kent Regiment in India before the war and then moved to Victoria Row, Giants Grave, to work as a carriage cleaner with the GWR. As a reservist, he was immediately recalled to military service in August 1914, but was killed in the battle of La Bassée in October and became Briton Ferry's oldest military casualty at forty-two years of age.

*The railway conscripts who died*

*Victor Emanuel*, of 8 Regent Street East, attended the Neath County School and became a clerk at Neath Railway Station. He was sent overseas as part of a draft for the 2nd Battalion South Wales Borderers and was twenty-six when killed at the battle of Langemark on 16 August,1916. His battalion chaplain wrote to his parents to say that he fell when the line was advancing under heavy fire. 'Wounded at first he was sub-conscious but not in great pain and he passed away about an hour later and a cross will be erected on the spot where his comrades buried him'.

*William Basil Lyn Pudner* of Mansel Street was a porter on Neath station. He served in the 6th Battalion South Wales Borderers, a pioneer battalion tasked with the heavy digging and carrying work that trench warfare and infantry duties called for. He was killed on 19 July 1917, aged twenty-six, while out with a working party.

*William Charles Weller James* of 4, Pant Yr Heol was a third-generation GWR employee. He was the fourth, and last, of the railway men from Briton Ferry to be killed doing military service in the war. He worked as a clerk on Maesteg station and joined the 16th (Cardiff City) Battalion Welsh Regiment in 1916. During the Third Battle of Ypres, near Langemark, on 27 August,1917, he lost his life.

There was, however, another 'railway man of 1911' who was killed in the war. *Cyril Cox* of Morgan Terrace had left his job as a GWR messenger to work in a tinplate works by the time of his enlistment in 1915. Cox served in the Hawke Battalion of the

214

RNVR. He was due for leave during the week of 25 August 1918, but exchanged his leave period with a fellow sailor to enable him to attend Neath's Autumn Fair. By changing his leave dates, the twenty-two-year-old naval rating had chosen to be on duty the day he was killed.

## Workers of national importance

Despite the pleadings of the anti-war movement, led at first by Keir Hardie, many rail workers, who could have claimed their work was of national importance and remained in their jobs, made their way to recruiting stations to join the volunteer army. Others, who sported war service badges, opposed conscription, but remained silent. By September 1914 railway managers had to ask the government to rule that no rail worker could enlist without the permission of his employer. Nevertheless, the GWR dismissed employees who refused to attest.

By 1917 the demands on the railways were becoming increasingly onerous, especially with the 'combing out' of previously exempt staff for conscription. The remaining staff, especially on the footplate, worked longer and longer hours with poor remuneration. This was a situation that was to come to a head with a National Rail Strike in 1919.

## The opponents

*Garnet Waters* and *William Davies* did not stay silent whilst continuing to work in their 'badged' occupations. They strongly opposed conscription, if not the war itself, by distributing anti-conscription literature. Both were sentenced to imprisonment with hard labour, because of their stance against the Military Service Acts. Their case had serious consequences, as will be described below.

Another Briton Ferry railway man who strongly opposed the war, but escaped incarceration, was *Cecil Waters*, a signalman and politically-active ILP member. Ivor Owen Thomas was another: he was known throughout south Wales for his fight for Civil Liberties during the war and joined the GWR soon afterwards, having experienced the vicissitudes of the Military Tribunal system and Carmarthen prison. Through the NUR and Labour Party's further education system he progressed to become MP for the Wrekin.

## Davies and Waters' case[11]

Waters was a steelworks locomotive driver,[12] an Independent Labour Party (ILP) member and Chair of Briton Ferry No Conscription Fellowship (NCF).

A fellow member of both organisations, William Davies, a GWR shunter, also opposed war and conscription through the NCF. They were sentenced by Neath Magistrates to a month's imprisonment with hard labour for distributing a leaflet against recruiting in Briton Ferry.

They alleged that the Military Service Act was being used to prejudice workers in labour disputes. This was 'a question on which the whole interests of the working people are concerned and a matter on which we had the clearest and most definite pledges from Ministers when the Bill was passing through Parliament.'[13] Waters was reinstated following imprisonment, but Davies was not offered re-employment. His treatment caused burning indignation in south Wales and his case became conflated with actions that were taking place elsewhere in the country.

The case was an unwelcome addition to other industrial relations matters; many NUR branches consistently called on the union's executive for concessions from the railway companies because of increases in food prices. By 1916 calls for an end to the 'industrial truce' agreed with the government grew, along with demands for strike action. Finally, the government called a meeting at the Board of Trade to lecture the NUR about the need to prevent industrial stoppages 'even for one hour' as it would impede the war effort. The future NUR general secretary, J H Thomas, shot back by asking Ministers: 'If the position be so serious the rail companies should be called in so that they should be told of their responsibilities.' The meeting had its effect and war bonuses were increased in September 1916, but the battle to improve the conditions of rail workers continued, as will be reported further in Chapter Ten.

## Women rail workers

Two of the most significant changes to come about due to the impact of the war were the acceptance of women into NUR membership and the introduction of national collective bargaining. At the start of the twentieth century, many within the trade union movement opposed the 'dilution' of the workforce through the employment of women, not least because the lower pay women usually received undercut the wages of male workers. In 1914 there were just three female porters. In the Spring of 1915 the restriction on women was lifted and they could work as carriage cleaners or clerks. The 1915 NUR annual general meeting voted to allow women to become members for the first time and, after conscription was introduced in 1916, as porters and ticket collectors, but ASLEF saw to it that they could

Mabel James a female railworker in World War Two, picture at Briton Ferry station (*Briton Ferry Photographic and Internet Technology Group*)

not become shunters or engine cleaners. By the end of the war 35,000 women were in 'male' grades out of a total female rail labour force of 100,000, but five years' later the figure was a mere 200. 'Cruelly, women were largely written out of most railway histories'.[14]

Briton Ferry's railways employed townspeople like Mabel James during the Second World War to cover for conscripted rail workers. After the war female employment in the industry reverted to normal. Today's position was outlined in 2015 by Claire Perry MP, Parliamentary Under-Secretary of State for Transport, in a speech to support the new *Women in Rail* group.

The group had been recently created to improve diversity in UK rail. Both she and the group were clear that much still needed to be done:

> We might have started the war with 13,000 women working in rail, but by its end there were 70,000. It's not news to anyone in this room that the rail sector is not hiring or promoting sufficient

numbers of women. We make up 51% of the population, 7% of the national workforce but only 15% of the rail workforce. Out of the 87,000 people working in rail, only 13,492 are women, almost exactly the number of women who were working in rail in August 1914, at the dawn of the First World War. We can't make precise comparisons between then and now, but it is significant that in absolute terms the number of women working in rail is no greater than it was a hundred years ago.

Perry continued to say how wrong it is that only 19% of women in rail are in managerial roles and that women make up only 4% of rail engineers and that only 0.6% of women have progressed to director or executive level. At least we can look forward to a future in which, for customers, the face of the railway is as likely to be female as it is male.

A significant feature of early and mid-twentieth century work was that of large centres of employment. This arrangement often enabled work to pass from one generation to another where families had several generations in the same centre of employment. Career advancement in the rail industry differed from other large employers because rail work required greater mobility of place than in the factory, or primary metal manufacturing. Nevertheless, the existence of 'family employment', as covered in Chapter Six and Appendix Five, still held good and several 'railway families' were identifiable.

People in places like Briton Ferry who were employed in the same industry not only worked together, but often worked and spent leisure time together. This helped to create social structures which afforded what we today call 'psycho-social support'. In difficult times the families, organisations and societies involved helped one another. With the shrinkage of the railways and the loss of other mass-employment industries in the final quarter of the twentieth century, the diminution of 'railway families' and their equivalent in other employment has caused this hidden support to be lost, often with some unwelcome consequences.

**Experiences from the townsfolk: the sounds of Briton Ferry's Past**

For some reason, it was not the sounds of the hooters from the various works that attracted the attention of some of the townsfolk of Briton Ferry, but the locomotive whistles.

> 'a little while back Ebbw Vale, or some such district, was pilloried as the noisiest place in south Wales; but it seems to have a formidable competitor, if we may judge from the wail subjoined by a Briton Ferry victim: "From Swansea to London is there a single town where so much noise is allowed? One engine can be heard nearly two miles away. Some people about a mile away seek peace in back rooms at night". Three fourths of it (the noise) could be done away with – much mellower whistles could be used.'[15]

That was one point of view, perhaps that of a shift worker who could not sleep after a busy night shift. Shift workers needed their sleep more than most:

Caroline Jackson reminds us of the importance of shift work on the railway:

> I was so proud of my uncle, Len Griffiths, who was a tapper on the railway. He lived

at 62 Neath Road. I remember as a little girl, around 1950 or so, getting up when it was dark for him to go on shift. I had a saucer of weak tea with sugar while he had his special enamel box filled by my auntie Lil. Then we snuggled back under the eiderdown while he went out into the night. I thought he kept our trains safe. He was so proud of the railway.

Penny Gower was a Librarian in Briton Ferry. She perceived the clatters of the railways as pleasant sounds, not as noise, suggesting that the ambience they provided was quite acceptable in such an industrial town.

> The grunting and chugging of steam rollers, the rattle and chuff of steam trains, the bump and shudder of trucks shunted in sidings. The splash of the water tank in Rockingham Terrace. The piercing sound of guard's whistles and the rumble of porters' trolleys along station platforms. The trundling of the 'Dolly' train over the level crossing at Dock Street.[16]

Writer and broadcaster, Mavis Nicholson, did not seem to mind, either:

> At the bottom of our street was Rockingham Terrace. We could see the trains pass from our front door... Then the older children went to school. One or two would be crying and their mother scolding them. There was quiet after the last had hurried past, and I then waited for the trains to go through the station at the bottom of the street. The ones which didn't stop were the goods trains. Fewer and farther between were the passenger trains which hissed to a stop and then hissed to a trundling start.[17]

And when Carol Hutchins heard the sounds of the trains it was a cause for excitement:

> I still live by the railway line where they used to shunt coal and iron ore back and fore to the works and harbour that were around the docks at the time, now all gone. When I was young sometimes I would hear the train coming which had steam engines. I would run up the lane and always missed a ride on the gates of

the level crossing in Church Street, but would run up the steps of the footbridge which went over the track to be in the steam from the engine below, but ended up with black, sooty spots over me.

On the Swansea to London line by the power house there was a signal box and you could see the men changing the signals. There was also a big tank of water that was used for the steam engines; some would stop and fill up. The drivers were very proud of their engines so when they stopped they cleaned the brass on the outside of the engine and whatever they could reach. In front of the power house there was a siding where the coal wagons parked for the coal men to fill their sacks and load onto their lorries. The coalmen had a wagon each; one was Abraham the coal.'[18]

Hugh James, pictured alongside *60163 Tornado* at Carmarthen station, 2017 *(Hugh James)*

Hugh Newton James of Briton Ferry, a recent Mayor of Neath-Port Talbot, was the third generation of his family to work on the railways and the third to be christened Hugh. He followed his father into railway service in the early 1960s when he became rostering and timing clerk at Swansea East Dock shed until he joined the commercial department at Neath goods depot. As was the case with many others, his next appointment took him away from south Wales to Paddington station. There, from 1965 to 1968, he was editorial assistant for the Western Region on the

in-house journal *Rail News*, using his artistic talents and flair for public relations to the full. This period coincided with the end of steam working on the former Great Western lines. Hugh worked behind the scenes to secure *Castle* haulage for the last scheduled passenger working from Paddington. This train to Banbury workings in November 1965 would normally be rostered for a *Grange* but Hugh used his persuasive skills to ensure that the last remaining *Castle*, *7029 Clun Castle* was used.

He left the railway for other public relations posts in London until a return to south Wales became possible, first as Publicity Officer for the Welsh Hospital Board, then Alcoa UK's Public Affairs Manager, at Waunarlwydd. His career changes in no way hampered his great interest in railways: indeed, his PR connections enabled him to play a large part in the movement to bring steam back to the main line. He worked closely with Neil Spinks, the BR Public Relations Officer to organise the Return to Steam in south Wales in 1985-1987. Without his tireless efforts behind the scenes, there is no doubt that south and west Wales would not have witnessed so many steam specials over the last thirty years.

His effusive, nostalgic description of the steam era he knew so well, came about not only from his employment on the railway but also because his home faced the railway at Rockingham Terrace.

It became anathema to take pride in the history and fine traditions of the old railway companies … in 1962 the named trains such as the *Red Dragon*, *Capitals United Express* and the *Pembroke Coast Express* were consigned to history.[19] … I for one will never forget the sight of the *up South Wales Pullman* express passing my home in Briton Ferry, hauled by a gleaming *5077 Fairey Battle* of Landore shed.

## Rail families intermarry: the Coxes and Hutchinsons

In an industrial community which employed many rail workers, it was unsurprising when members of one rail family married into another. The Coxes and Hutchinsons were a typical example, as Margery Lewis (née Hutchinson) reports:

*The Coxes*

My maternal great-grandfather, was George Cox of Gloucestershire. His initial employment was as a chairmaker, but like many of his contemporaries he realised that the rapidly growing railway industry provided a more secure source of employment than chairmaker. He started work for the GWR and came to the Neath area in the 1850s. By 1871 he had gained promotion from porter to become a 'railway inspector' in the carriage department, a post he held for some thirty years.

His son George was born at Neath in 1865 and followed his father into railway employment. He first lived in Aberavon to work as a railway guard on the RSBR, after which he lived Morgan's Terrace, Briton Ferry. This was very convenient for work, as his house was only a stone's throw away from Cwrt Sart station.

George's son, Alfred, survived the First World War to follow his family into railway service, initially as a cleaner but later as a fitter in Cwrt Sart shed. Alun Hutchinson, his nephew, often saw him in the workshops during his visits to the shed in the early 1960s. Alf retired a few years prior to the closure of the shed 1965 but he lived well into his nineties.

*The Hutchinsons*

Edward Hutchinson married Rosalind Cox, sister of George and Alfred (parents of John, Majorie, Alun and the late Audrey). He was an engine driver in the Albion Steelworks until his retirement, but his first job was in Neath Registry Office. At the time, the salary of a civil servant was significantly less than the wage earned by manual workers in the Albion Steelworks and Eddie soon realised he would be financially better off working in the steelworks, where he also had friends. He was initially employed as a shunter but followed the traditional route of promotion on industrial railways he became a locomotive driver. He talked fondly of working on the steam engines, especially *Albion No 1* and *Herbert Eccles*. However, in latter days he welcomed the comfort of the cab of the diesel locomotive he operated until his retirement from ill-health in the mid-1960s.

Allan Colwill was a train-spotter: *A very popular hobby (in the days when boys had hobbies!)*

My father started work at fourteen firing on the line locally, but I'm not sure where he was based, but I can remember riding on the footplate of a train in the Briton Ferry sidings. Fairly soon afterwards he was transferred to Didcot and worked there for a period, possibly towards the end of the war.

Typically, we'd gather at the bottom of Shelone Road, sitting on the wall as we waited eagerly for trains to rush by, hoping to catch the number off the engine. These were the days when an *Ian Allan* train spotting book was the bible that allowed you to record the event by underlining the engine number. I once managed to fall off the wall onto the grassy bank below and broke my arm. A favourite was something we called *The Milk Train*, it came through around 6.00 pm every evening on the freight route which came via the old swing bridge, rather than the main line through Neath. I recall a train called the *Evening Star* which was another favourite. In the 1960s, Cwrt Sart still had railway sheds, for repairing and storing trains. We would walk there, from somewhere behind the Giant's Grave flats, crossing railway lines in the process. On arrival at the sheds we would ask permission from the foreman to walk around, and then had the freedom to roam. It sounds way out of keeping with today's health and safety environment.

The trains running through the centre of Briton Ferry were a common sound at home day or night. The railway noise seemed to dominate the town. I can remember going to the beach at Aberafan by train, and walking from the station to the beach. When Briton Ferry station closed my father bought a quantity of flagstones from the platforms and used them to lay a garden path. The stones are there in Jack-y-Du Road to this day. I seem to remember Wards had their own trains, with green coloured saddle tanks and Metal Box had its own private sidings for bringing steel on site.

Lloyd Griffiths was yet another train spotter, same place, but almost a generation later:

We spent many an illegal hour roaming the sidings beneath Brynhyfryd bridge in the mid-1980s. We used to go to Margam Railway sheds with our fathers and we would then get a lift back to the sidings in a freight train (it would never happen now!) where our fathers would meet us. Great days!

Dorothy James (née Barnett) was something of a rarity in that she was a female trainspotter:

Trainspotting; rather casual, but beguiling. You just went down to the bridge at the bottom of Brynhyfryd Hill, sat on the wall, or climbed over it onto the embankment and waited. You saw the trains and underlined them in the Ian Allan book.[20] *Namers* were the interesting ones – the *Castles* and the *Counties* and the *Halls*. Double-headers were exciting, as was the occasional grass fire caused by engine sparks. The night mail (special treat, parental escort required) was *Pacific* class and had the distinctive *Wild West* hoot.

The Aberafan Beach train will be a happy memory for most Briton Ferry children of the 1950s. Two or so non-corridor coaches and two possible trains a day there and two back. Whole street loads of us disgorged from the train in summer evenings, pink, peeling, damp and sandy.

At the bottom of Villiers Street, on a single track, the *Doll* (how did it get its name?) carried molten slag. You could stand on the bridge and feel the great wave of heat rise up. There were rail underpasses which regularly flooded. *Commit no nuisance* said a notice on one, sternly but vaguely. And allotments on the Llansawel side, rented from the railway. The *Incline*-ghost of the mineral line and popular walk. I have a vague memory that the hill on one side was still smouldering.

In retrospect, I'm struck by the informality and familiarity of our interaction with a potentially dangerous environment, untroubled by health and safety concerns or opportunities for litigation – my father borrowing the porter's trolley to wheel my going-to-university trunk down the hill to the station; my trips to Neath to sit at the station waiting room – big coal fire

regularly topped-up, and do my homework there, just for fun and the mild buzz of comings and goings around me; relations living near the line coming out to wave you off. Shunting: the most comforting sound to hear in nights of worrying about the Bomb. Reassurance that normal life was going on.

The Bridge: my mother remembered the days when you were rowed across the river from Giant's Grave. It was exciting and a favourite walk before it opened for traffic. I remember the train journey to Swansea through a desolate, dying industrial landscape of grey mud and iridescent pools. But the trains themselves began to be less exciting, no longer arriving at the station with a thrilling hiss of steam and pounding of pistons, they merely sidled in and slid along the platform.

Giant's Grave was a specialist community centred around Ward's and complicated by the Pill and redundant canals. There was a mountain of scrap hovered over by a crane and dwarfing the two houses below. Anybody brought up in Giant's Grave would have tales to tell-including smuggling, but that would be another book. Both my grandfathers worked in the Brass Stores. Much of a ship's fittings could be bought locally, and many a house, (including ours) would have shipping companies' logos on their crockery and cutlery. I still have a chest of drawers with *Second Lieutenant* written on its back.

Many of the ships broken up were naval vessels, but the one they all remembered was the White Star Liner *Canopic*, scrapped 1925. Long after the glory days a new ship was still an event. In Glanymor Street, the cry would go up: 'There's a ship coming in to Ward's' and we'd all troop upstairs to watch the tugs bringing it in.

There was no such elation with the withdrawn railway engines that came to be broken up. They crept in as forlorn flotillas, surreptitiously and anonymously, with their brass number plates and other limbs already subducted, denuding their dignity, in sad contrast with the fanfares that awaited the arrival of the, still, fully-fitted ships.

## Travellers

Malcolm Hill was a civil engineer and noteworthy local historian:

> My chapel in Briton Ferry was Bethel Chapel. The RSBR line was inches from the back of the Chapel. When a train passed the preacher stopped speaking. The Sunday school had an annual outing to Jersey Marine,[21] using the RSBR line across the swing bridge over the River Neath. The station was, of course at the end of Bethel Street.[22]

As a child he found out that sobriety and piety were not always characteristic of all RSBR passengers:

> On occasion the passengers themselves could be noisy. One unexpected and rowdy fracas arose when a train load of 'drinkers' arrived from Aberafan Seaside in a bad state. Their arrival had got so out-of-hand that people from the churches and chapels met them at the station holding crosses and wearing robes, with the chapel ministers and deacons in their Sunday best. My mother told me to keep away.

At other times, more harmonious sounds could be heard aboard the train. Nigel Gower lived in Shelone Terrace, which faced all three of Briton Ferry's rail lines. He recalls:

> Catching the Briton Ferry train to Aberafan beach during the balmy days of summer that we experienced in the 1950s with the likes of 'Trevor' Thomas and Dickie Griffiths whilst plagiarising Johnny Duncan's version of *Last Train to San Fernando ... Last train to Aberafan ... if you miss this one you'll never get another one....* Also sticking one's head out of the carriage window and inevitably catching a fleck of ash in the eye from the smoke of the engine.

Bronwen Williams'[23] life was touched by the RSBR, in a more fundamental way. Born in Treherbert in 1896, her father, Gwilym, had worked hard as a miner. As a 'self-made' man he built up a successful hardware business in the town and his family lived in some comfort, so much so that the family were able to employ a maid. His daughter,

Bronwen Bowen (née Williams) with her granddaughter Andrea, Wern Bank, Briton Ferry 1954 *(Martin Davies)*

showing much promise in music was sent to a boarding school in Kent. However, the sudden death of her mother changed her life dramatically. Her father remarried, taking his former maid as his new wife. Unfortunately, she was not prepared to be responsible for bringing up her step-children. The result was that his children were 'farmed out' to relatives. Bronwen was sent to live with her mother's relatives in Baglan, travelling by the RSBR to Briton Ferry to her mother's family who were very welcoming, but not very well off. Times were hard and Bronwen was forced to find work as a pianist in the Assembly Rooms public house. The RSBR, of course, ran behind the pub on an embankment. It was at the Assembly Rooms that Bronwen met her future husband, Tom Bowen, who worked in the Vernon Tinplate works alongside which ran the RSBR line. Bronwen and Tom went on to raise four daughters in the harsh years of the depression. The family couldn't afford holidays when they were growing up, so Mary, Evelyn, Ivy and Eunice were sent by train from Briton Ferry East during the school holidays to stay with their aunt and uncle at Trealaw.

Eunice, the third of the children, lived in Briton Ferry throughout her life, apart from a short period in the 1930s when she took up a post in London. Her father, a tinplate worker, was out of work at the time and the family desperately needed another breadwinner. Having left Neath Road School at the age of fifteen, Eunice realised that there were few job opportunities in depression-ridden Briton Ferry. So it was that she was among the first people to have travelled from the new station in Rockingham Terrace after it opened in July 1936.

Eunice Davies (née Bowen) taken in 1965 at Gower's Buildings, Church Street *(Martin Davies)*

She would often reminisce about her time in London. It was the first time she had travelled by train alone and the longest journey she had made in her life up to then. The exciting prospect of starting a new life and career, and the knowledge that she was helping her family by working ,was tempered by the sadness of leaving home and the uncertainty of working 'in service' in Dulwich. The GWR played a 'bit part' in the next stage of her life. After regular correspondence with Eunice by letter, her mother, Bronwen, decided to visit her in London some months later.

Upon seeing her mother appearing, Eunice was so overcome with homesickness that she decided to return home there and then. Upon returning she was fortunate to take up a post as housemaid with Mrs Thomas, *Dantwyn*, Neath Road. It was while working there that she met my father Keith.

(Martin Davies)

Ira Llewelyn travelled from Rockingham Terrace station.

I went to the army in 1946, was posted to Bodmin and later to Crookham in Hampshire, the biggest depot in the

Ira Llewelyn 2017 *(Ira Llewelyn)*

country. To go home for the weekend on a forty-eight-hour pass, I used to travel from Crookham to Reading by an Aldershot Traction Company bus. I caught the 01.05 am from Paddington to board the 2.40 am at Reading to reach Briton Ferry at 6.30 am, the only London train that stopped at Briton Ferry. Going back to Reading I'd catch the Royal Mail which left Neath at 9.20 pm and see them sorting the mail during the journey. It would get me to Reading by five-to-two in the morning. I was exhausted

Allan Williams of Porthcawl used the station when he lived in the Harp Hotel with his parents, before his marriage and move to west Africa to teach. The first part of the newly-weds' journey was by train from Briton Ferry.

We were going to Cape Coast, Ghana, for my first job. All the wedding presents had been packed into an old wardrobe which I must admit was massive. I borrowed a trailer and took it to Briton Ferry railway station. There it was weighed and the pointer went off the scale. 'Hmm,' said the station master, 'don't know what to say

about this. Where is it going?' 'Ghana,' I replied. 'Oh, where's that. Isn't it near Glasgow?' At Cape Coast, it was unloaded from a freighter and brought ashore by canoe, reminiscent of the old 'Hawaii Five-O' clip. Some thirty percent of the cargo went overboard. Luckily our wardrobe did not.

*Glyn Williams*

Glyn Williams' regular bus journeys in the 1950s from his Briton Ferry home to Neath Grammar School were in a South Wales double-decker. The grandstand view of the main railway line from his seat upstairs coincided with the passing of a London express, inevitably hauled by a Castle, often Old Oak Common's *Isambard Kingdom Brunel*. Glyn was impressed by the loco's unusual nameplate whenever it sped past. The resonance of its name led him to find out more of the person behind the name. For Glyn researching the life and works of Brunel has become a lifetime interest and he is now recognised as one of the leading local experts on the 'Little Giant', giving fascinating presentations to various groups throughout Neath-Port Talbot.

**Notes for Chapter Eleven**

1. *Cambrian*, 23 March 1890
2. *Glamorgan Gazette*, 2 November 1894
3. See Chapter Two
4. Later Herne Street
5. Ynysymaerdy Road was built for Briton Ferry Co-operative Society by Messrs Gower Bros for £1162 (*South Wales Daily News*, 13 September 1897).
6. Listed in Appendix Two
7. Some GWR staff records were available but not those of the other rail companies.
8. He was the maternal great-grandfather of co-author Philip Adams.
9. They are listed in 'Ferry Boys at the Front Records' and elsewhere in 'Neath and Briton Ferry in the First World War' (Jon Skidmore, 2018)
10. Reported in *GWR Great War Book* on 30 September 1918; 31 October 1918 and 31 May 1919.

11. The case is covered in more detail in *Not in Our Name: War dissent in a Welsh Town:* Philip Adams (2014)
12. He drove *The Doll* (see Chapter Five)
13. J H Thomas MP
14. Wolmar
15. *Evening Express*, 9 February 1895
16. Penny Gower in 'Briton Ferry: a much-loved community', (2014)
17. Mavis Nicholson, p25
18. 'The Railway': Carol Hutchings
19. Hugh James in 'The Red Dragon … and other old friends'
20. *ABC of British Railways' Locomotive* book
21. Using Briton Ferry Road station
22. Formerly Charles Street
23. Maternal grandmother of co-author Martin Davies

# Chapter Twelve

# Accidents, Incidents and Preventions

*I was in a terrible accident yesterday and worked some hours among the dying and the dead.*

(Charles Dickens, after the Staplehurst crash, 9 June 1865)

## Introduction

From their inception, railways have experienced accidents and incidents of various origins and consequences. This chapter examines the factors that shaped them locally and their effect on the public and railway staff. Briton Ferry has, thankfully, never experienced a disaster of the magnitude of those on the south Wales to London line at Southall or Ladbroke Grove, but the area has been far from fatality, or injury-free.

Background factors such as the government's attitude to regulation, the rail companies' stance on competition, innovation and investment in safety technology have been, and still are, of direct importance in shaping the railways' accident performance. The organisation and culture of the rail companies, too, in terms of rules,systems of work and abilities of staff, in facing the operational demands upon them, in both war and peacetime, have also played important roles in safety.

This chapter selects incidents experienced over the last 170 years which indicate the changing safety performance of local railways as far as these activities and conditions are concerned: equipment failure; shunting of rolling stock; crowded platforms; level crossings; trespass and vandalism; public behaviour; collision and derailment, and engineering work. It concludes by reviewing the risks that have been all but eliminated for rail staff and travelling public and those that remain.

## Equipment failures

The High Speed Train from Swansea to Paddington which thundered through Briton Ferry on 19 September 1997 never delivered all its passengers to their destinations. The train, which could operate at 200 km an hour, had left Swansea with a defective auto-

matic warning system (AWS). This led to its passing a signal at danger and colliding with an accelerating freight train. Seven deaths and 139 injuries to its passengers was the result. Manslaughter charges against Driver Harrison of Swansea were dropped when the enquiry into the crash revealed that drivers had problems in sighting the signal at Southall due to its poor location, resulting in it being passed at danger. This was an engineering failure to locate signalling equipment properly, not driver error.

The disaster on the Paddington main line at Ladbroke Grove two years later resulted in another thirty-one deaths and 258 injured. Yet none of Briton Ferry's railways has experienced a fatality-free existence. Deaths, personal injuries and many damage accidents have occurred over the years. The victims have been both rail staff and the public, sometimes when boarding trains, sometimes on the rail infrastructure. Some of the incidents were brutal and tragic, and some, in retrospect, quite avoidable.

No fatalities were involved, but a collision at Briton Ferry in December 1898 bore some similarities to the Ladbroke Grove crash in October,1999. In the Briton Ferry case, two goods trains collided on the junction of the RSBR between Cwrt Sart station and the Neath river bridge.

It appears that a train was standing on the junction and another on an off-siding, both waiting to go in the direction of Swansea, when the signal was given to one to proceed. The other, mistaking the signal, also started, and when coming to the crossing both collided, the one being derailed with its six wheels and the other being jammed against the derailed one. This incident turned out to be one of material damage only, but there were some common underlying factors the Ladbroke Grove crash the common one being the difficulty for drivers in sighting badly positioned signals.

One of the earliest reports of equipment failures

was a wire rope failure on the SWMR's Briton Ferry incline in 1872. Four trucks loaded with coal, perhaps weighing forty tons, were about to be let down the incline when the haulage rope broke. The brakemen fortunately saw their danger and jumped off uninjured. The trucks ran free down the incline and collided with the empty ones being drawn up, smashing them into fragments. The men at the bottom 'flew in all directions' with no bodily injuries on this occasion, but the company's medical officer, D Emanuel Griffiths, was rarely short of work in treating injured SWMR staff.

In September 1893, another smash occurred on the incline. This time, owing to a defect in the drawbar gear of one of the descending wagons, four of the five wagons 'got loose and ran wild at terrific speed'. The signalman at the foot of the incline 'promptly opened the safety points, and thus turned them into the adjoining field, where they were completely smashed up'. The report of the incident referred to the 'signalman's presence of mind' and explained that 'every care is taken to thoroughly examine each wagon before it proceeds down this steep bank'.

On the narrow gauge industrial line, used to remove iron slag from the blast furnaces to a tip at Baglan, an unusual incident occurred in 1896. As it was passing over the bridge near the GWR line it gave way and the 'locomotive and the slag wagons were precipitated to a depth below. GWR staff were making alterations to the bridge at the time the slag train passed over'.

## Shunting work

Exposure of rail staff to hazards during shunting operations has, thankfully, become a diminishing concern. Today there are fewer wagons which are universally equipped for automatic coupling and have no need of antiquated methods of work such as the use of the shunting pole.

Such was the intensity of the freight movements around Briton Ferry dock that a tank locomotive known as 'the dock pilot' was permanently based there for shunting purposes at the shunters' cabin alongside Port Wallaroo level crossing. (This was the first loco that co-author Martin Davies was likely to encounter after leaving his home in Church Street.) The locomotive was attached to a 'match truck', a small wagon on which the shunters would travel from one part of the siding to another. It was equipped to carry the shunter's 'poles'. The pole allowed the shunter to hook and unhook the coupling chains of the wagons without the need to step between the wagons, a practice which had led to many fatal accidents in the past.

For most of the nineteenth century, being a shunter had been the most dangerous and unpleasant job because the job of coupling and uncoupling meant creeping under the buffers of wagons and handling heavy iron chains ... sometimes the engine drew the wagons too far apart and the couplings would not reach or pushed the wagons against the shunter.... On a wet day there was the added danger

SWMR accident on Briton Ferry incline *(Simmonds)*

Shunter's wagon (Match Truck) as used at Briton Ferry, seen at Didcot Railway Centre (*Martin Davies*)

that when wearing a mackintosh ... could be caught by the wheel and pull him to death. This dangerous way of working was considered as inevitable until an imaginative goods guard used a length of gas pipe to avoid having to stoop to uncouple – he had invented the shunting pole. To encourage men to use a pole companies offered prizes to those most efficient at using them.... A dextrous shunter could couple and uncouple twenty trucks in exactly two minutes.[1]

Shunting was a very skilful job and it was fascinating to watch a shunter at work. He had to liaise closely with the footplate crew when sorting the order in which wagons were marshalled to form trains. Wagons were often propelled into sidings by gravity, so it was important that the driver made sure the loco pushed the uncoupled wagons hard enough to roll into the appropriate siding.

When freight traffic was in its heyday, the risk of injury from shunting operations was high. for several reasons. The volume of freight traffic to be shunted was great, as was the risk of crushing or trapping by, or between, wagons. Shunters and guards had often to cross the track to the opposite side of a wagon to apply the brake because wagons had brakes and brake levers on one side only. It was not possible to keep all the levers or destination labels in a train facing the same way, so staff were at risk of being knocked down and crushed. Coupling and uncoupling manually also ran the risk of tripping or crushing, especially due to poor sighting in the dark.

Shunters were encouraged to detach loose coupled wagons quite rapidly. 'Fly shunting', which was frequently used at Briton Ferry yard, entailed even greater risk. This required the shunting pole to be placed on the couplings of the wagon to be detached before the loco driver would move. After it had

moved the shunter would indicate to the driver to pull the wagons and then slow at the point where the shunter could detach the loosened couplings with the pole, allowing the wagon, or rake of wagons, to remain free as soon as the driver speeded up again.

In 1912, wagon inspector Francis Edward Adams of Park Street, Briton Ferry submitted a patent[2] to solve the problem of the single brake.

> In either side brakes are locked on or off by a rack extending from an arm on the brake shaft and engaging a fixed bracket and main hand levers, at diagonally opposite corners, are connected by the mechanism shown in the drawings.

No doubt the patent arose from the rule requiring the provision of a brake lever on either side of a wagon which was introduced in 1911 which gave companies twenty years leeway to fit to their rolling stock.

A case of high-speed shunting was reported at Pontypool Road[3] where a train of twenty-seven wagons, with three each for Cardiff, Swansea and Whitland, two each for Pontypool, Llanelli, Neath and Neath Abbey and one each for Aberdare, Aberbeeg, Bridgend, Briton Ferry, Carmarthen, Cefn, Ebbw Vale, Haverfordwest, Newport and Pontypool (Town), were sorted and dispatched within thirty minutes. Unsurprisingly, a hundred shunters were killed at work each year well into the twentieth century. Modern, automatic coupling is much safer.

Sometimes the risk of being struck whilst shunting was amplified by unusual circumstances, for example where the injured person was aware of an impending hazard but was unable to move in time, or in one case mentioned below, move at all. William

Foundation stone from the Rhondda Tunnel, the longest single bore tunnel in South Wales *(Afan Argoed Mining Museum)*

Williams, a Neath river pilot, was killed during shunting operations when he failed to move in time to avoid a van which was being shunted on the Briton Ferry dock siding and was run over.

Shunting incidents sometimes involved experienced rail staff and George Haines, a goods guard from Landore was an example. In 1917, he was killed shunting at Baglan sidings. W. Sayer, foreman shunter, told the coroner at Briton Ferry that, after setting a train of wagons, he missed the guard and, after going back over the sidings, he found the mangled body of the deceased over the railway. Eleven wagons had passed over his body.[4]

Two months later another shunting fatality occurred in which the deceased was unable to move in the face of an oncoming train. This time the victim was an experienced traffic inspector. Fifty-four-year old Edward Killick of Old Road, Neath, was struck by a light engine and van whilst supervising shunting operations at East Box, Melincryddan. The coro-

The RSBR swing bridge over the River Neath shortly after construction with the swing section open for river traffic, 1900's *(Robert Thomas)*

The Tower Hotel (originally Jersey Marine Hotel) adjacent to Briton Ferry Road railway station 2018 *(Martin Davies)*

ner said it was probable that Killick had caught his foot in catch points and was unable to extricate himself to escape from the oncoming goods engine. Both legs had to be amputated, but Killick, who had spent the whole of his working life with the GWR, did not survive the incident. All six of his brothers had worked with the GWR with 370 years' service between them. His death was the family's last link with the company.

It was little wonder that the townspeople took an interest in railway safety. Philemon Williams lived at two railway-facing streets Rockingham Terrace and Gower Street, from where he could observe all train movements. His interest led to him building a model steam locomotive which is said to have included an improved version of the GWR's *automatic train control*.[5]

**Unsafe procedures – crowded platforms**

One of the most tragic accidents on the area's railways occurred at the GWR's Briton Ferry Road Railway station, Jersey Marine, at Easter 1871. A party of excursionists had, in the early part of the day, visited the burrows and the Jersey Marine Hotel. Sisters, Mary Jane and Isabella Hill, aged twenty-three and thirteen respectively, died after falling under a train at the station. After the arrival of the train, but before it had stopped, a rush was made for the carriages. The sisters were literally forced between the carriages and the platform, the younger sister, it is supposed, falling between the buffers, drawing the other sister with her.

Approximately 1600–1700 passengers had been conveyed by train to the station that Good Friday to enjoy a day at the seaside. The 'excursionists' were due to be taken home by the special train at 8.11 pm, and regular passengers who were due to travel on the 8.23 regular train, both leaving from the down platform. The 8.11 train comprised a locomotive and ten coaches, manned by four guards and a travelling inspector. Seven GWR police and porters were at intervals on the platform to assist passengers to get on the train and to prevent crushing.

The formal investigation report into the accident concluded that 'passengers were noisy and pushing so violently that GWR staff were pushed against carriages and had difficulty in getting the doors open.... The elder sister was holding her younger sister's hand, apparently with the object of catching hold of the carriage door before the train came to a stand. The guard (in carriage six) saw a girl fall between carriages five and six and felt the front wheel of the sixth carriage lift as if it was going over something.'

Astonishingly, before the inquest result, a newspaper claimed that

> 'Not the slightest blame is attached to the officials of the railway, the accident having occurred entirely through the too prevalent practice of struggling for places.'

Yet the rail company knew the approximate number of passengers who would be returning on the train in question, based on the number of arrivals earlier in the day. Adequate rail staff were present who failed to anticipate events and take adequate measures – a contrast with the crowd controls in place today to direct fans at international rugby matches to their trains at Cardiff Central. Following a scathing Board of Trade investigation under Lieutenant-Colonel Rich, the attitudes of the press changed dramatically from support for the railway company to criticism and support for passenger safety:

> (There is) ... no prospect of any warning conveyed by an inspecting officer of the Board of Trade attracting attention, but it is, nevertheless, a melancholy satisfaction sometimes to refer to their reports on accidents and to imagine the improvements that might be effected if railway companies could be compelled to adopt precautions for the safety of their passengers.

The gist of Rich's report was that the station was big enough for normal use but was too small for the volume of excursion passengers using it on the fateful Good Friday. For future excursions, he recommended that crowds should not be admitted to the station until the train in question had come to a standstill. The admission of passengers to the platform is evocative of the uncontrolled admission of football fans prior to the disaster at Hillsborough Football ground in 1989.

In the 1870s, the passengers, or the guards on the platform, had the opportunity to manually open and close the train doors individually and manually. It is worth considering passenger behaviour today with that of the 1870s. Today external carriage doors cannot be opened by passengers until train staff have enabled them to be openable. The current reluctance of rail unions to permit drivers alone, in the absence of a second competent member of staff, to be responsible for opening and closing doors in all circumstances is understandable when passenger behaviour can be so unpredictable. Self-evacuation of passengers in emergencies can also be problematic. Some would say that the situation at Briton Ferry Road in 1871 resembles that at many commuter platforms today.

*Rail staff*

Accidents sometimes also befell rail staff at stations. One Saturday evening in 1905, on a return excursion from Bristol, guard Charles Mills of Landore slipped and fell between the platform and his train at Briton Ferry. He was dragged the length of the platform and received terrible injuries to both legs. Fortunately he survived and became a signalman, but William George Williams, a RSBR lamp-man of Whitegates Lodge, Briton Ferry, did not survive, after being struck on the forehead by the 7.40 passenger train from Swansea. The prominent deacon of Jerusalem Baptist Church left a widow.

**Unsafe level crossings**

Where the public or rail staff interface closely with the track itself, there is a likelihood of mishap. This was the situation for many years. This remains a possibility at level crossings and where trespass opportunities or rights of way across the lines exist. Level crossings of various kinds have been in widespread use since the early days of the railways. Current policy is to reduce risk by replacing crossings with bridges or underpasses for use by pedestrians and vehicles where it is reasonably practicable to do so. 'Reasonably practicable' is a modern legal term, but arguments as to what actually is reasonably practicable have taken place since those early days.

As early as 1873 the subject of dangerous level crossings at Briton Ferry had been raised. The GWR line runs through the centre of the town, and persons have to cross over the level crossings and thus considerable delay, inconvenience, and danger are experienced. The inhabitants have complained, and besought the railway company until they are tired, to have a bridge erected over the said crossings, but doubtless the recent narrow escape may induce the company to do something.

By 1882 the matter had become the subject of a Board of Trade enquiry into Villiers and Regent Street level crossings. The Briton Ferry Local Board had made several applications to the GWR for footbridges over these crossings. After a thorough investigation, it was decided that a bridge must be placed over the Villiers Street crossing for the use of foot passengers, and that gates must be worked from the signal box (which is newly erected), which are to close the line when vehicles are passing, similar to those at Llanelli. The foot bridge is to cover two lines, viz, the main and the line that runs close to it on the town side of the docks. The crossing near Bethesda Chapel is to be the same as it is now, and also the Regent Street crossing, which was shown by Mr Lloyd as a private one, and that the railway company claim their right over it by closing it for foot passengers every Good Friday.'

A few years later the Local Board were informed by the GWR that its directors had authorised two subways. The Church Street subway was to have a

Villiers Street subway 2012 *(Martin Davies)*

heading of eight feet and that at Regent Street of thirteen feet. The Local Board were against the subways and continued to petition for footbridges.

The response from the GWR, whether reluctantly conceded or not, was admirable. The company's plan for subways bettered the improvements proposed by the Local Board, whose idea was simply to isolate the public from danger by giving control of the gates to rail staff. By providing subways, the Company avoided the need for human intervention to operate crossing gates. Thus, unintentional contact between the public and trains at these crossing points was eliminated. Where subways were been installed the hazards remained, as at Pantyrheol.

There, safely in crossing the lines was again brought into focus in 1892 when a 'little girl called Cosker attempted to cross the GWR line at Pantyrheol when she was knocked down by the 12.55 passenger train and instantly killed.' In the same year an express train 'dashed into a donkey and cart which were being driven by a boy over the level crossing at Baglan near Briton Ferry'. The donkey was killed, the shafts of the cart cut away, but the boy was uninjured. He was discovered crying over the unfortunate state of his steed. Even the provision of a footbridge was not failsafe if it was not used, as the Neath Coroner was to later point out when considering the death of Mrs Andrews. Her case followed that of Harry Hennatt, an elderly gentleman from Ynysymaerdy, who was killed by a shunting engine at the GWR level crossing, despite the fact that the railway company had built a footbridge due to the large amount of traffic.

In 1905, sixty-seven-year-old Mrs Ann Andrews of Giants Grave was crossing the GWR line at Morris's accommodation crossing, Melincryddan, when the express train, due at Neath at 12.10 pm knocked her down and killed her. She had been to Neath market with her grandson and was returning to Giant's Grave. A gateman called Philip Peters shouted words of warning to her as she was about to cross. Her grandson was just a little in front of her and 'he escaped being killed by inches only'. She was knocked down by the engine which caught her in the neck.

At the enquiry held by Mr Howell Cuthbertson, Coroner, the GWR were represented by Mr Dalton, Chief Inspector and Mr Martin, stationmaster, Neath. The relatives of the deceased were represented by Mr Jeffreys, solicitor. The coroner said no one was to blame:

> Some people went about as if they were in
> dreamland and did not use their eyes.
> When about to cross a line he always

looked both ways to see nothing was coming. As to a bridge, well, people would not use it. Take, for example, the bridge which the company had constructed at Port Talbot. It was not used by the public who continued to cross the line as they did before. Of course, the jury could make the recommendation if they liked.

The jury returned a verdict of accidental death, adding a rider that gates be automatically locked from the box on the approach of trains. In this case a subway would have virtually eliminated the risk of being struck by a train. That the risk did not justify the costs of providing one was a decision made by the GWR, no doubt in the absence of the level of pressure the Briton Ferry Local Board had earlier applied.

Deaths from such rail accidents were reported more sympathetically if the victims were well-known in the area, as can be seen in a comparison of two reports on accidents involving Bates and Williams:

> In 1915 Edward Bates, a Neath labourer, of no fixed abode, who was admitted to Swansea Hospital on 13 October suffering from injuries to the head, the result of being knocked down on the GWR line at Briton Ferry, succumbed to his injuries on Tuesday morning.

Compare this terse report about Bates, a person unknown in the locality, with the report on well-known 'Captain Williams', and a former railway employee, too.

> In July 1919 'quite a gloom was cast over the locality' when William C Williams, known as 'Captain Williams', and by the children as 'Uncle Bill' was knocked down by a passenger train on the RSBR line, dying from the effects. The deceased was a deacon of about thirty years standing of Jerusalem Baptist Chapel. He had also worked on the railway for a period of twenty-four years. The last rites were performed at the funeral by his pastor – the Rev Rees Powell, assisted by Revs Thomas Hughes and J Gwynne Thomas. A very unique scene was experienced at the grave side, when the brother of the deceased sung a verse of a well-known hymn.

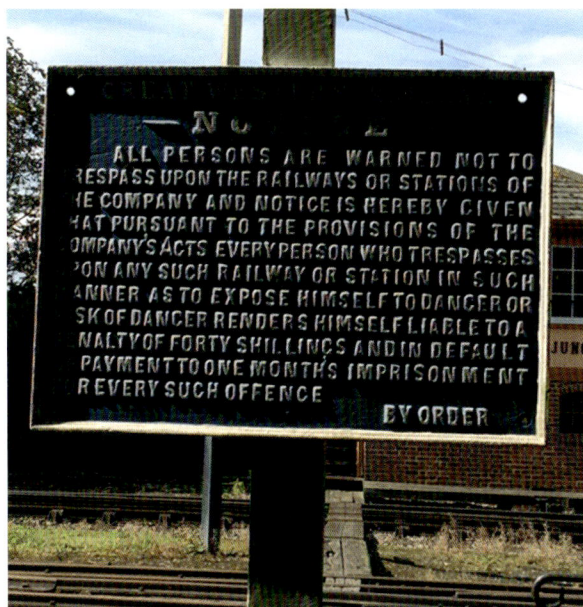

Prohibition Sign *(Didcot Railway Centre)*

**Trespass and vandalism**

Trespass on the lines and vandalism have always been problematic for our railways.

> The new rail routes often provided a tempting alternative to established public thoroughfares. Their average gradients were usually gentler than on the roads and their courses straighter and shorter, too.[6]

**12-11 Trespass prohibition**

What may surprise readers is that acts of trespass have not only been committed by members of the public but they have been perpetrated by railway staff, too. Sometimes it was custom and practice for rail staff to trespass.

There are, of course, public rights of way, paths on which the public have a legally protected right to pass and re-pass. In 1902, it was made public that there is no legal right of way under what is known as 'the dark bridges' in Briton Ferry and the railway company, having leased the land leading thereto, had a perfect right to barricade the same; and 'it is through the generosity of the company that the inhabitants are permitted to pass that way, which is a great boon to a large number of workmen.' The alternative to affording the use of this subway would, no doubt, have been trespass to cross the rail lines.

In 1878, forty-year-old engine driver Robert Emanuel of Ritson Street was crossing the railway near Briton Ferry when a mineral train knocked him down. 'His two legs were cut off.... He died after two hours' fearful agony'.[7] Four years later seven-year old William Thomas of 23 Regent Street was killed by the *up* mail train on a Tuesday evening when putting buttons on the GWR rail lines.[8] On the nearby ironworks line eleven-year old Edward Cummings was run over with one of his legs being cut off at the thigh,[9] with him in a critical condition. In 1888 a seven-year old girl called Mary Jane Cosker was killed instantly at Pantyrheol by the 12.55 passenger train when crossing the line.[10]

Sometimes it was not clear whether there was intent to upset a train, or simply a case of a loosened object falling from a train,[11] for example at Briton Ferry station a member of GWR staff found an oak pole, four feet six inches long and four and a half inches in diameter, lying across the rails of the up main line shortly after the 7.33 up passenger train had passed. 'It was evidently done on the supposition that the passenger train had not passed.'

At other times it was quite clear:

> 'an attempt was made on Saturday morning to overthrow what is known as the Llanelli Docks and London goods train at a point near the Cwrt Sart Crossing. The driver of the train was nearly thrown off his feet by a sudden jerk. After stopping the train, he went back to ascertain the cause, and found pieces of a heavy permanent way rail chair. The chair had been placed against one of the fixed chairs on the up line, and so strong had been the impact of the engine that both chairs were broken. The police are said to have an important clue, which will probably lead to the arrest of one or more youths'.

Previously, in 1873, a Moses Cole was 'cut to pieces' on the SWMR. He had been working as a surveyor and was returning home when the incident happened. It should be noted that there was no regular passenger train from Glyncorrwg to Neath or Briton Ferry, so it was custom and practice for persons to travel in trucks or the train van. On this occasion, Cole tried to move from one truck to another whilst the train was in motion to get a more comfortable seat. He lost his footing and fell between the couplings, the train passing over him, cutting him to pieces. 'The fragments of his body were collected and conveyed to his late residence ... he leaves a wife and a large family ... and was much respected for his general courtesy and obliging manners.'[12]

Trespass fatalities continued: Joseph Astley was a sixty-year old labourer who lodged in Church Street, Briton Ferry. He was making an unauthorised crossing of the GWR line near Baglan Bay Tinplate works when he failed to heed the shouts of some railwaymen and was killed during the shunting operations.[13] Just before Christmas in the same year a twenty-two-year old, James Morresey, was crossing the line at the GWR station when he was struck by the up London express and killed.[14] He had recently left Ireland to work in a tinplate works.

Suicide by members of the public on the railway infrastructure has been a long-standing matter. Where public access to the track is possible, in densely populated areas especially, substantial steps have been taken in recent years to isolate the public from the trains by means of fencing. This solution is not practicable at the train/passenger interface on platforms, so it is here that possibility of suicide is greatest. Briton Ferry's last rail suicide was sustained by a leap from the station platforms in front of a train at Easter, 2011.

As stated earlier,it was not just the public who were guilty of trespass: James Harris, a GWR employee who was run over and killed by the 9.30 pm goods train from Swansea was trespassing. He was returning to his home at Briton Ferry Road with his nine-year-old grandson from Neath Abbey on a Saturday night.

> 'His watch stopped at 12.23. The little boy, who happily, escaped, is said to have warned his grandfather of the approach of the train. He afterwards informed his grandmother of the occurrence. The body was in a fearfully mangled condition, and conveyed home'.[15]

This was followed by another 'terrible railway accident at Briton Ferry'[16] in 1896 which involved two young railway employees.

> At 6.00 pm on Monday evening, call boy Lewis John Reynolds of Church Street, and engine cleaner Robert Leyshon[17] ... boarding at Lowther Street, Briton Ferry, aged respectively sixteen and seventeen years, went on duty at the engine shed and left at 6.00 am the following morning to go homewards. At 6.30 am two bikers named Bishop, a signalman, and Burnie were proceeding along and, when near the bridge at Cwrt Sart, which crosses the RSBR, one of them stumbled across the body of Leyshon. It was terribly mutilated. A few yards further the mangled remains of Reynolds was found.

It was quite dark at this time, but the identity of the lads was discovered, after considerable difficulty, by means of the lanterns carried by the bikers. The authorities have taken every precaution for the avoidance of such accidents, but it is the old, old story – a short-cut home. It is supposed that the lads, wishing to get home by the quickest cut, went along the line between Cwrt Sart and Briton Ferry. When near the bridge between the two, they were run over by a heavy shunting engine from Port Talbot. At a spot a few yards from the bridge the bodies were found, and cans and food were lying close by. It is somewhat strange that the accident should have occurred at all, because the lads knew that the engine arrived at the crossing between six and half past every day except Sundays. It is suggested, however, that they must have been under the impression that it had either passed or was considerably late. One thing is, however, perfectly clear, that the engine alluded to, and which was driven by William Jones and Henry Lewis, did run over them because blood was found on it. Intimation of the accident was immediately given by Bishop and the bodies were removed to the Grandison Hotel, Penrhiwtyn, where the inquest will be held on Monday morning. Leyshon lived with his brother in Lowther Street, Briton Ferry, whilst Reynolds lived with his parents.

It is debatable whether the provision of a subway or a bridge would have prevented this event because the motivation of the deceased was to get home as quickly as possible after a twelve-hour shift by intentionally using an illegal and dangerous short cut. Whether Bishop and Burnie, who found the bodies, were also taking a short cut is another question.

## Public behaviour

Aggressive behaviour towards rail staff by members of the public is not new. As long ago as 1890, a brutal attack on a signalman in Briton Ferry resulted in a prison sentence for 'obstructing a railway servant in the execution of his duty'.[18] Nor is bad behaviour on board trains new; in 1919 a collier, Edward Daniels of Marsh Street, Aberafan, was charged at Neath with 'behaving in a riotous manner in a railway carriage between Neath and Briton Ferry … the defen-

dant had been drinking and wanted to fight everyone in the compartment. Some women pulled the communication cord and so frightened were they that they got out on to the line'.[19] Daniels was fined the maximum penalty of forty shillings or twenty-eight days in prison.

Public behaviour can be very unpredictable due to unforeseen circumstances. One-hundred-and-forty years ago Edwin Hardy was charged under the Explosives Act for depositing gunpowder at the GWR station in Briton Ferry. It was intended for delivery to the nearby Messrs Lewis' shop, but there was no one there to receive it, so Hardy decided that the best course of action was to leave it at the nearby station.

Mr Herbert S Sutton of Glyn Leiros, Neath, penned a most learned letter to the *Western Mail* about various clauses in the Explosives Act and its correct interpretation in the unusual circumstances of the judgement, castigating the magistrates for a 'grievous miscarriage of justice'.[20] Sutton's point was that Hardy had travelled from afar to deliver the gunpowder and, in order not to let down the shop owner, had informally agreed with a porter to leave the potentially dangerous delivery at the station. One assumes that the gunpowder delivery was for use at a local quarry.

## Collisions and derailments

Collisions arising from poor signalling and communication have fortunately become rarer during the period this book covers. Derailments, too, are also much less frequent an occurrence than they once were. An early and typical derailment incident was reported in 1882, when seventeen wagons were derailed on the GWR line between Briton Ferry and Port Talbot. Five wagons were irreparably damaged causing severe delays whilst recovery work proceeded. The morning mail, which was due at Port Talbot at 3.40 was typical of the extent of the delays to trains.[21]

### A head-on collision

There can have been no other occurrence in railway history where two trains, driven by brothers, crashed head-on. That is exactly what happened on the SWMR in 1902 in Gyfylchi tunnel. Three trains ran daily in each direction through the tunnel but they normally passed each other at Cymmer. On the journey in question the Colliery Company's cashier, Mr J Perret, needed to get to Briton Ferry urgently and requested that the trains should, instead, pass at Tonmawr to save time.[22] However, telephone communication between Tonmawr and Incline Top failed to occur and control over the trains' movements was lost. The trains were, therefore, heading towards each other on a single-track, approaching the one-mile-long Gyfylchi tunnel. The driver of the down train, Rowland Hughes, could see the silhouette of the oncoming train at the tunnel mouth. He tried to stop his train just before it was struck by the other. Rowland Hughes of Ynysymaerdy knew that his elder brother, John, was driving the other engine:

> Death seemed to be staring me in the face. Then the collision took place. I was stunned, but I soon regained consciousness and then I heard my brother's voice calling 'Rowland'. Thank God, he was alive.

About twelve people in total were on the trains. Two passengers were killed and several badly injured.[23] The Hughes brothers nevertheless continued to work on the railways for many more years.

Collisions were not always train-to-train: sometimes they were train-road vehicle. On a fine and clear day, at 3.13 pm on 9 October 1950, driver Lewer was attempting to move an articulated Scammell lorry across the tracks at Cwrt Sart Farm level crossing to collect a bulldozer. He had misjudged the width of the far side gate and stopped with the rear of the 36'3" long lorry on the down line. A Cardiff to Swansea four-coach train, hauled by a 2-6-2 tank locomotive, struck the lorry. The locomotive's bogie wheels derailed, spreading the gauge and resulting in the locomotive becoming completely derailed. This severely damaged the loco before it fell over on its left side at the bottom of an eight-foot embankment. The 204-ton train had also severely damaged the lorry, turning it 180 degrees, and severing the cab from its trailer before depositing it seventy feet from the crossing. The permanent way was wrecked for 90 yards, with the up line becoming fouled. Prompt action enabled an oncoming express to be stopped.

With nine people receiving injuries and all being discharged from hospital within ten days, Colonel D McMullen of the Ministry of Transport was complimentary about the recovery effort in his formal investigation report :

> Ambulances and doctors from Neath arrived on the scene within seven minutes and ambulances from Port Talbot within fourteen minutes, a most commendable performance. Rail staff from the nearby engine shed, many of whom were

qualified in first aid, also rendered considerable assistance. The crossing attracted 160 train and fourteen motor vehicle movements in twenty-four hours, including express Swansea–London train services and motor vehicle trips to the farm and engine sheds canteen. Its gates had catches, but no locks, beyond which were safety bays of 38' on the up side and 28'6" on the down. A whistle board is posted with a telephone provided to contact Cwrt Sart Junction signal box some 530 yards away and a sign which read: Rights of Way Act, 1932. This way is not dedicated to the public.

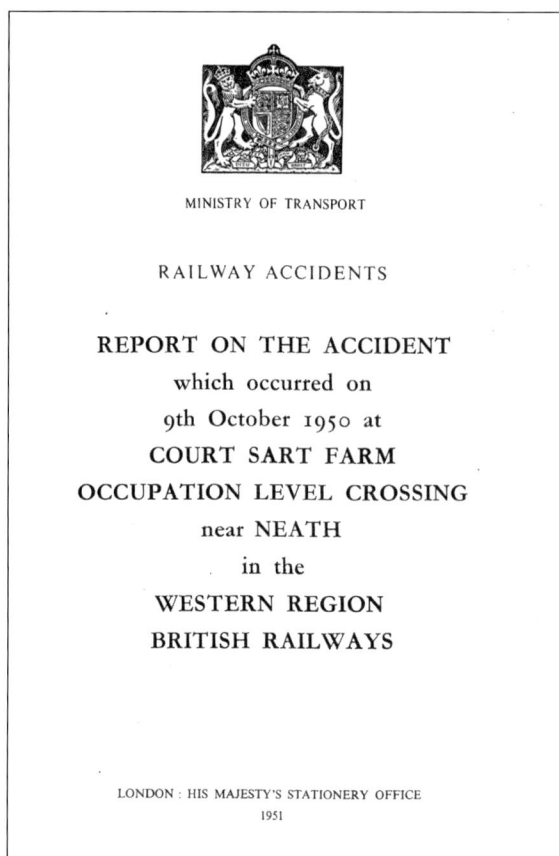

MINISTRY OF TRANSPORT

RAILWAY ACCIDENTS

**REPORT ON THE ACCIDENT**
which occurred on
9th October 1950 at
**COURT SART FARM
OCCUPATION LEVEL CROSSING**
near NEATH
in the
**WESTERN REGION
BRITISH RAILWAYS**

LONDON : HIS MAJESTY'S STATIONERY OFFICE
1951

Accident report

The Report continued:

> This is yet another case of the derailment of a passenger train resulting from its collision with a motor vehicle at an unguarded occupation crossing and it was indeed fortunate that there were no serious injuries. The accident took place in spite of the fact that the crossing is provided with a telephone and the gates are set back to form safety bays. The former was, however, not used because road users (even regular users) were

Farm Road Accident *(Gerald Williams)*

unaware of its existence, and the latter were of insufficient length for the unusually long lorry to stand clear of the lines.

Walter Adams of Penrhiwtyn Street (left), was killed at Farm Road crossing. His colleague Jack Jenkins, was a steam raiser (right) in a further incident *(Gerald Williams)*

The report exonerated Lewer, the driver of the lorry, 'whose only fault was to misjudge the width of a gateway', but not the vehicle's owners who knew that the use of this special lorry required special procedures. McMullen also urged caution about the increasing dangers that might arise if the proposed housing development and school planned for construction at Cwrt Sart Farm went ahead:

> (If it) materializes, and unless very positive action is taken to prevent it, this occupation crossing will soon assume the character of a public crossing, even if the road bridge over the railway is constructed.

Today the crossing is shut off behind a permanent fence.

### Maintenance and engineering

One of the saddest, and most gruesomely reported, deaths of staff during routine rail maintenance was that of forty-nine-year old William Clapp, a ganger who had been a GWR employee for thirty years. 'He was walking his length, as is customary for gangers to do on mornings, when he was knocked down by the *up* passenger train which passes the spot between seven and eight am. The brains were picked up at some distance from the body. The remains were conveyed home in a sack.'[24]

Construction engineering work could be no less hazardous, especially when work was being carried

Overturned locomotive near Farm Road crossing 1950 *(Cliff Morgan collection, Neath Antiquarians)*

out to a tight time-table. In August 1893, David Heale, a labourer, was killed whilst working on the RSBR railway cutting at Briton Ferry. The inquest jury drew attention to the importance of proper and adequate supervision at the top of the cutting while the men were engaged beneath. A year later, as the RSBR directors and other dignitaries were watching the 400-tonne Neath River bridge being swung open from the river bank, Joseph Surr, a riveter's assistant fell from staging on the bridge into the fast-flowing water. Yockney, the RSBR engineer, and Russell, the bridge works foreman, both dived into the river to rescue him. They had to be recovered by boat without Surr's body, which was found two hours later.[25] Even in the familiar surroundings of permanent workplaces, fatalities were not avoided. In the locomotive running depot at Cwrt Sart, forty-seven-year-old wagon repairer James Davies was crushed between the buffers of two carriages, leaving a widow.[26]

*Fires*

There are no known deaths from fires recorded, but fires there were aplenty, especially in the early days when the construction materials selected for some railway buildings were inferior in terms of their fire resistance than later. The first booking office for goods at Briton Ferry station was a wooden structure, discovered to be on fire one morning in 1870. Fortunately, the stationmaster had the assistance of some passing sailors to use the water supplies for the hydraulic engine which works the dock machinery to limit and put the fire out. This raised the demand to the GWR for 'better accommodation in the shape of a new station, waiting rooms etc ... instead of the wooden huts that ... are a disgrace to the place.'

Similarly, in 1894, the wooden GWR signalman's hut at the Villiers street subway was discovered to be on fire. The severe frost had induced the signalman to leave rather more fire in the stove than usual after he had left duty at 6-00 am. Water from the nearby dock was used to extinguish the fire. Of rather more concern was a heather fire at Baglan, caused by a spark from a passing train which was eventually 'prevented from reaching the powder magazine of the artillery'.

**Review and conclusion**

The period covered in this chapter shows overall, if not always constant, progress in risk reduction for both the public and rail workers. This has been achieved by reducing the frequency of people's exposure to the hazards of rail operations. The public has been physically separated as much as possible from their interface with the network and workers' safety is being improved by automation of work systems.

*Railway staff*

With a workplace death toll of more than seven hundred railway 'servants' in the 1870s, it was evident that pressure was needed to reform both the arrogant, management style of the companies, which operated on a pseudo-military command structure,

and the legal concept of 'common employment'. The formation of the ASRS in 1872 provided the first challenge to remove the hazards faced by railwaymen due to the under-staffing and underpay which led to long hours of work and compounded the safety problem.[27] It took some time, but the Railway Employment (Prevention of Accidents) Act of 1900 was a start; the reversal of the Taff Vale decision[28] and its consequences would sustain the move forwards. Today, attitudes are different: today people do not expect, and would not tolerate, the sort of response given by Mr Jones of Neath, the employer of the deceased navvies working on the RSBR tunnel, that *accidents are inevitable*.[29]

During the 1920s and 1930s the toll of rail fatalities decreased to average thirteen a year, far fewer than in the nineteenth century.[30] World War Two and its extraordinary wartime conditions changed all that. It resulted in a continuing rise in fatalities afterwards, amongst both rail-workers and public, with the sixty deaths in 1947, and 209 in 1949. These were attributed mainly to lack of track maintenance and obsolete signalling. It was of little consolation that the roads were more dangerous in wartime, experiencing some 9,000 fatalities annually.

By 1977, the annual figure of employee fatalities was reduced to thirty-six and more recently has run at fewer than ten each year. In the year 2015–16 there were no workforce fatalities, for the first year ever. At the 2017–18 renewal of the Wales and Border franchise the Welsh Government required a safety critical conductor or guard on all train services, including the south Wales Metro.

*The public*

Some *leger de main* was involved in the Board of Trade's statistics to classify many accident causes into categories such as 'want of caution, misconduct, trespass or suicide', thus favouring the notion that accidents were rarely due to rail companies' mismanagement but almost exclusively to their staff or to the public's behaviour.[31] Although there are examples of companies such as the GWR instigating quite advanced safety systems there seems to have been a quite strong 'blame culture' into the early twentieth century. Perhaps 1901 was the nadir for rail safety. Strengthening trade unions and stronger rail safety legislation saw ensured that was the case.

Passenger behaviour was often disregarded as a factor contributing to the 1,171 fatalities. Evidently the Board of Trade wished to encourage passengers to use the railways, or at least, not to discourage them, so some statistics seem to have been 'spun'. The competition between rival companies to get lines built quickly to secure traffic, often over difficult terrain, provided little incentive, or opportunity, to control safety. A railway navvy's life was quite cheap as, and railway construction very labour-intensive: when the Rhondda tunnel on the RSBR collapsed during its final phase of construction there was no way to identity the dead bodies involved in the collapse.[32]

*Today*

The evolution of rail safety saw a shift from prescriptive behaviour-dependent safety, in the railways' early years, towards engineered safety (which took more account of peoples' real behaviour to make things safer) in modern times. This shift was particularly necessary because of the increased train speeds through a heavily populated area. With time, better safety systems have been introduced for controlling the movement of trains and passengers and restricting public access to the rail network. The risk entailed with trains travelling at up to 200 km an hour is quite different from those experienced a hundred years ago. Today there are fewer trains operating on a more streamlined network; a century ago the network was both far more extensive and complex.

Today the likelihood of accidents is reduced because safety systems are more sophisticated and effective. Should a failure occur in these systems, however, the severity of an incident is far greater, as we know too well from the Southall and Ladbroke Grove incidents. In 2016-17 there were fifteen passenger fatalities in derailments or collisions, the first for ten years. There was one workforce fatality, and that was in a road traffic accident. Public fatalities decreased and, of the 309 experienced, 273 were suicides or suspected suicide, and thirty-six were non-suicides. Three level crossing pedestrian fatalities occurred. Over 1,000 level crossings have been closed since 2009.[33] 72% of fatalities are when trespassers are struck by trains and 17% are electrocutions.

Modern railway safety is also about more than personal injuries and damage to physical assets. Railways' safety responsibilities have extended to include the long-term health and environmental effects of their extensive activities. The prolonged consultation on HS2 demonstrates that fact, but the difference between the time of Dickens and today is, perhaps, that these responsibilities are now acknowledged and every attempt is made to discharge them. There have been impressive improvements in rail safety over the last one hundred years or so, but preventable dangerous activities such as trespass, to write graffiti, and cable theft regrettably persist. People still put themselves in harm's way by taking shortcuts, playing on tracks, or picking up objects dropped in error from platforms. That is why this is a key chapter in the book.

## Notes for Chapter Twelve

1. Magg's *Railway Curiosities – the Invention of the Shunting Pole*
2. *Barry Dock News*, 1912, quoted patent 5827/1912
3. Bradley
4. *Herald of Wales and Monmouth Recorder*, 22 September 1917
5. Correspondence with Dr Jeff Davies (Oakham) and John Bowles, 2017
6. Bradley, p.320
7. *Cardiff Times*, 9 February 1878
8. *Cardiff Times*, 27 May 1882
9. *South Wales Daily News*, 26 December 1882
10. *South Wales Daily News*, 30 December,1892
11. *South Wales Daily News*, 18 September 1880
12. *Western Mail*, 27 October 1873
13. *Llais Llafur*, 2 August 1919
14. *Pioneer*, 20 December 1919
15. *South Wales Echo*, 11 August 1890
16. *The Pontypridd Chronicle and Workman's News*, 27 November 1896
17. Leyshon was seventeen and Reynolds sixteen years of age
18. *South Wales Echo*, 10 May 1890
19. *Cambrian Daily Leader*, 18 October 1919
20. *Western Mail*, 14 December 1877
21. *South Wales Daily News*, 26 December 1882
22. The SWMR was authorised for mineral traffic only and was not equipped for the carrying of passengers.
23. *Evening Express*, 18 August 1902
24. *Weekly Mail*, 7 April 1883
25. *Cardiff Times*, 1 September 1894
26. *The Cambrian*, 23 December 1904
27. ASRS figures for one company in the year 1872 listed 1,387 accidents against the company's 73!
28. See Chapter Thirteen
29. 'while expressing his regret for the fatal termination of a useful and necessary precautionary job ... it was one of those 'inevitable though lamentable incidents which are, or appear to be, inseparable from works of that character.'
30. Wolmar, p.265
31. The current ORR definition of 'general public' means 'neither passengers nor workers'.
32. *South Wales Daily News*, 24 January 1889
33. Office of Rail and Road: *Rail safety statistics 2016-17*, released September 2017

Chapter Thirteen

# Ownership

*I want to see a publicly-owned railway, publicly accountable*

(Tony Blair)

## Introduction

Government has played a seminal role in the history of Britain's railways.[1] Its influence on their ownership and control – through rationalisation, nationalisation and privatisation – is the focus of this chapter. Britain's railways originated as private companies in the nineteenth century, but the demands upon them during the First World War resulted in much-needed consolidation in the post-war years. Although this rationalisation helped prepare the private railways for the following war, the effect of the Second World War was to exhaust them yet again. The solution this time was not to rationalise the railways but to completely nationalise them into public ownership.

Even after nationalisation, further rationalisation was deemed to be needed to tailor the rail network to mid-twentieth century demands. It was reduced in size, and steam power dispensed with, in favour of a modernised system that made fewer demands on the public purse. By the end of the twentieth century, a different model of re-privatisation was introduced, and that is the model we have today. It is a controversial model that merits discussion.

Changes in the railways' ownership affected the industry's employee relations and the workforce's working conditions. This chapter highlights significant matters of workforce relations at national and local levels. The examination starts with the iron control that the private rail companies exerted over their employees at the end of the nineteenth century and then considers the consequences in the twentieth century. The chapter then assumes a wider focus, chronicling the history of railway management and ownership, but not the rail services and facilities, which were covered in Chapters Three, Four and Six.

## Industrial relations

At the start of the twentieth century industrial relations within the private rail companies were poor. The worst labour conflict of the nineteenth century had occurred in Scotland in 1890 because the railway company concerned had consistently overworked its staff 'with twenty-five hour shifts not uncommon at holiday times'[2]. Companies such as the GWR fined staff for minor disciplinary offences. The unions' demands for a ten-hour working day and overtime pay attracted sufficient attention for parliament to debate rail workers' long hours. Unions, such as the Amalgamated Society of Railway Servants (ASRS) realised that political will, in addition to industrial action, would be needed to secure their claims.[3] The rail companies' view was that 'trade unionism was not compatible with the military style discipline required to run a railway and was therefore akin to mutiny'.[4]

Nevertheless, at ASLEF's Neath branch dinner of 1890, Mr Church, its Chairman, enunciated that 'in addition to the usual advantages of friendly societies … one of its objectives 'was to relieve suffering arising from illness and accident … permanent disablement through accidents or constitutional disease'. He added that 1200 new members had joined the union in the previous year to boost membership to its current total of 6,500.[5]

It was unsurprising, therefore, that labour disputes began to arise from the legal status of trade unions. It had been thought that trade unions were immune to being sued because they were unincorporated under the law of trusts. This assumption was thrown into question when the Amalgamated Society of Railway Servants (ASRS) struck in protest against the Taff Vale Railway Company's (TVR) treatment of a member who had been refused higher pay, and was punished for his repeated requests by being transferred to a different station. When the TVR subsequently employed replacement staff, the strikers engaged in a sabotage campaign, greasing the rails and uncoupling the carriages. Although the TVR and the union settled, and workers returned to duty, the TVR perversely decided to sue the union for damages. The court ruled in favour of the TVR, but its decision was reversed by the Court of Appeal, then restored on further appeal to the House of Lords.

It became clear to the TUC and its Parliamentary Committee that, if the right to strike was ever to be preserved as an important tool of trade union policy, then the Taff Vale decision must be reversed by Parliament. To do so the unions had to secure greater and more influential representation in Parliament. This was achieved via the newly formed Labour Representation Committee, a mass movement which led ultimately to the creation of the modern Labour Party. The party, in partnership with the Liberal government, secured the passing of the Trade Disputes Act of 1906. The Act overrode the *Taff Vale* ruling and provided the foundation for a law on the right to strike, protecting a union against claims for economic losses, providing a strike was 'in contemplation or furtherance of a trade dispute'.

By 1907 the new-found power of the unions presaged the first-ever national rail strike, which was averted when a conciliation scheme was introduced by the government. At Cwrt Sart engine shed, seventeen of the thirty-six cleaners employed requested a wage increase, 'with six pence a day being demanded in some instances'.[6] But by 1911 the conciliation scheme had secured no improvement in the rail men's terms and conditions: their average weekly wage had stagnated for five years at a weekly twenty-five shillings and nine pence. In current terms this amounted to weekly pay packet of £144. It then dwindled to £140 over the next few years, with spending power eroded by price inflation. Those who are nostalgic about the 'age of steam' should remember that romanticism is usually tempered by economic realism....

## First national rail strike and the Llanelli Riots, 1911

Such straitened circumstances, as exemplified by the Cwrt Sart cleaners, led to the first-ever national rail strike in August 1911. In the years preceding it, membership of rail trade unions in places like Briton Ferry had grown steadily and substantially.[7] The national strike arose from a widespread dissatisfaction with the activities of the so-called 'conciliation boards' that had been set up to negotiate between workers and employers. A series of local disputes had

Llanelli goods yard 1958 (*J Davenport*)

led to unofficial local action before a meeting was convened to coordinate national strike action. The unions issued an ultimatum to the rail employers: either accept direct negotiation with their representatives within twenty-four hours or see labour withdrawn and work cease.

The government did not want the railways to be shut down. The Prime Minister reassured the employers that police and 58,000 troops would be deployed to keep the trains running. Troops were dispatched to thirty-three towns in England and Wales. The Home Secretary, Winston Churchill, suspended the Army Regulation, which obliged local authorities to request troops before any could be sent to their area. Worse, the strike led to the Llanelli Riots, in which six people died in clashes between rail workers and the troops tasked with preventing strikers blockading the line.

> Suddenly, a bullet slams into the throat of a man sitting on the wall, driving him backwards into the garden. Everyone runs, someone shouts, 'That's a bastard shot!' Blood splashes the grass. One of the men cries out, as a bullet glances off his thumb, bringing down the man behind him.
>
> There is more firing. Three men are down. The two most seriously injured are carried into the house and are laid out, bleeding profusely, on the table in the middle room, where they die. The landlady of the house is weeping uncontrollably – some women have fainted. Men are cursing and shouting. Outside on the railway track Major Brownlow Stuart orders the soldiers of the Worcester Regiment, who have fired the shots, to withdraw to the railway station.

These events occurred not in some beleaguered war zone, but in the back garden of a house in the High Street, Llanelli. It was the last time troops on the British mainland fired on workers during an industrial dispute: the first-ever national railway strike was a genuine rank-and-file revolt over unfair pay while directors and shareholders were benefiting from substantial profits. After the shootings, the strikers, their supporters and other local people rose up, fighting with soldiers and police in a protest at the injustice the community had suffered at the hands of the military.[8]

A Royal Commission was set up to examine the failings of the Conciliation Boards, with employers guaranteeing there would be no victimisation. The GWR cynically broke this promise, endorsing personnel records with a 'D' to indicate prominent activists and strike supporters, as used by Special Branch to endorse the records of war resisters in south Wales and elsewhere during the First World War.

After growing rapidly in the 19th century – the so-called *Railway Mania* – the railway system had reached a zenith of activity in the years immediately prior to the First World War. Coal tonnage, exported through the south Wales ports that were reliant on an effective rail network, peaked at fifty-seven mil-

Coal sidings at Swansea Docks
*(Swansea Docks Retired Section)*

lion tons in 1913. The rail workers, whose efforts were critical in this process, felt justifiably aggrieved that wages consistently failed to reflect their true endeavours and their economic importance.

### The impact of the First World War

For the duration of the war and its immediate aftermath, railways were removed from the control of private companies and managed centrally by the government, which dutifully promised to maintain shareholders' dividends. In contrast, ordinary rail workers received scant government solicitude and even less protection. The Taff Vale – as well as other companies – that had sparked the strike ten years earlier were now forcing its drivers to work twenty hours at a stretch. The NUR executive committee noted that while the financial position of shareholders was protected by the government, workers' wages were set at the discretion of the employer; it demanded a similarly guaranteed protection for its members. Derby MP, J H Thomas, first raised this 'most one-sided arrangement' in the House of Commons in 1914. Two years later, with the introduction of military conscription, he would raise the case of two Briton Ferry rail workers, an event dealt with below.

## The second national rail strike

The historical order of industrial relations had been irrevocably changed by the events that preceded the outbreak of the First World War; the future of the railways would now be determined more strategically, because of the demands that the war had made on its infrastructure.

The Government's financial arrangements for compensating private railway companies, combined with the minimal maintenance of the network, meant that by 1918 rail companies faced bankruptcy: it was clear that the railways could not be retained in the private sector. Compounding these problems was the matter of rancorous industrial relations. The struggle to maintain industrial peace with the NUR through the war years now resulted in pent-up pressure that could no longer be ignored. The eight-hour day had become standard for all rail men (in February 1919) but failed to resolve all grievances. Whereas footplate crews had benefited from a significant wage award, it came at the expense of fellow workers. The government's attempt to suppress wages to 1913 levels forced the NUR, with support from the ASLEF footplatemen, to call a strike; this began on 27 September,1919, motivated in large part by workers feeling that their war-time sacrifices had been inappropriately acknowledged and disproportionately rewarded by those in power.

## Nine autumn days[9]

On Saturday, 27 September, Briton Ferry and Skewen NUR branches, Neath NUR branches 1 and 2 and ASLEF members held morning and afternoon meetings in the Glamorgan Hotel, Neath. Ben R Bowen,[10] Chair of Neath NUR 1 and Harry J Corbey of ASLEF, presided to implement the branches' strategy for strike action in pursuit of their demands. Their objectives, whilst gaining public support, included setting up pickets that would successfully prevent blackleg action, at the same time as they ensured strikers' families would receive food and fuel and that perishable goods would continue to be delivered and stranded members would be returned home.[11]

On this busy day union officials arranged with the Chief Constable and the Mayor, John Rowland Jones, to ensure their intentions were unequivocal and clearly understood. Relations between the civic officials and the strikers were cordial and constructive. Consequently, the rail unions were promised the use of the Gwyn Hall at Neath for a public meeting the following day. Action started in earnest at 6.15 that evening when Neath and Skewen branch members marched from Neath to Briton Ferry for a mass meeting due to begin at seven o'clock near the Villiers Hotel.

*Sunday 28 September*

The battle to win over the hearts and minds of the public in support of the unions' case continued.

*Monday 29 September*

Branch officials again met at the Glamorgan Hotel at ten in the morning to review the local situation, with BR Owen presiding. It was particularly important to do so at this juncture because Charles Aldington, the GWR's General Manager had sent a circular to all staff from his Paddington headquarters, calling for volunteers to work. Union representatives reported that isolated cases of strike-breaking were occurring. Member Smith of Briton Ferry reported that foreman platelayer T Evans was at work in Port Talbot. Cecil Watters, a signalman and Port Talbot NUR Branch Secretary, said he would deal with the matter. Unconfirmed reports were made that a member named Sartin was working. William George Griffiths,[12] Briton Ferry's station master, remained at work but only to carry out his usual duties, which would not violate the action in any way. The Unions' general response was to arrange for notices,

Pennyslvania - Formerly The Glamorgan Hotel, Neath
*(OldNeath.co.uk 2015)*

ASLEF logo

announcing a series of public meetings to clarify their case, to be put on cinema screens at Briton Ferry, Neath Palace and the Gnoll Hall, Neath.

*Tuesday 30 September*

The most important item on the agenda of the morning meeting was to ensure that food and fuel supplies were available for strikers' families. In 1919 wartime rationing was still in force and the government announced its determination to withdraw ration cards from strikers and their families. Jones' *Richmond Stores* in Penrhiwtyn, close to Cwrt Sart engine sheds, had refused to give provisions to strikers' wives, but the Co-operative movement stymied government intentions by publicly agreeing to honour in its shops any vouchers issued by the local Strike Committee.

The meeting decided that arrangements be made with George Lansbury, its editor, to ensure that the *Daily Herald* could continue to be delivered to the area during the strike because it supported the Unions' position. Compositors and printers' assistants nationally threatened to strike to stop newspapers altogether unless the railway men were allowed the daily forum of the press to present their case. Sporadic reports continued to be reported of men working: Frank Barton in the Carriage Department[13] and T Webby in Skewen. A wire was received from J H Thomas in support of the branches actions.

*Wednesday 1 October*

At the morning meeting it was clear that support in the area was strong, with several requests for union speakers to attend public meetings. It was resolved that John Rowland Jones[14] and Harry Corbey[15] go to Glynneath and Resolven respectively to present the Unions' case. Arrangements were made to print 5,000 leaflets, *Why the strike?* to be ordered for printing at Stacey's, Neath, with 1,000 copies earmarked for Briton Ferry and Skewen branches. Despite two negative reports, a communique was sent to Port Talbot branches to say that 'we are as solid as adamanite rock'. The first said that a *42xx* loco had worked a

goods train with inspector D. Williams and driver Perkins on the footplate, and the other that blacklegs were handling coal from barges at Briton Ferry.

*Thursday 2 October*

At the morning meeting the Committee noted a joint message from J H Thomas and Prime Minister, Lloyd George, urging the unions to 'go back and negotiate'. The Committee had already shown reasonableness and sympathy in cases of personal difficulty, such as allowing union member Charles Gosney[16] to remain at work on the Neath and Brecon railway. The approach was working. As if in reciprocation, the Chief Constable agreed to relieve member J. Jones from 'special police duty', during the strike. An important message was received from Briton Ferry Town Council which had resolved to give the strikers its full support. Similar messages came from Porthcawl and further afield.

*Friday 3 October*

The morning meeting discussed what strike payments would be made to members, despite noises emanating from London that the government was considering conceding to the unions. Baglan Foundry workers announced their support for the strike by refusing to accept blackleg coal, but Joint Committee members expressed concern at the introduction of naval ratings to the docks area to break the strike.

*Saturday 4 October*

Two disconcerting reports were heard at the morning meeting. The first was that twenty-one men were 'working trains at Briton Ferry'. Member Willie Dowdeswell[17] then reported that an engine shed labourer had been enticed to work by Chief Clerk H James of the Locomotive Department, being promised three days' pay for a single night's work. Any adverse effect that the reports may have had on morale, however, was nullified by wires from Aberdare, Cardiff, Landore and Port Talbot that they were all 'holding firm'.

*Sunday 5 October*

During the day it became evident to union officials that the rumours of a settlement, which they had received wind of on the previous Friday, were true, as wire messages were now confirming. A special joint meeting was held that evening to consider whether pickets should be withdrawn, and work resumed. It was decided that a recommendation to settle would be put before members at a mass meeting the following day in the Gnoll Hall.

*Monday 6 October*

A letter, which had been submitted earlier by Hugh Edwards, MP for Neath 'offering his services in this crisis', received a tart response from Councillor C Gibby who suggested that the 'best services (Edwards) could render would be to retire from the House of Commons'. Instead the Unions thanked Mr Gibbs of Unity House, London, for his information and advice on the conduct of the strike.

The handling of the strike by the rail unions locally was masterly. They were resolute, and their consummate communication skills won both public support and co-operation from the authorities. They made judicious decisions on matters, such as inter-rail union solidarity, and showed that their cause was just and reasonable, to eventually win the day. This was no mean feat considering that NUR president Charlie Cramp, who visited Briton Ferry, had warned the strikers that 'all the powers of hell, the press, platform and perhaps the pulpit' would be used against them, 'but unity and determination would win the day'. After nine days of strike action the government capitulated, agreeing to the standardisation of wages across the railway companies at the current rate and the introduction of a maximum eight-hour day, a settlement exactly in accordance with what the Neath and District joint branches had demanded. The railway men of the District agreed to return to work 'conditionally upon the naval ratings imported into the town being immediately removed.'[19] They were.

**Inter-war rationalisation**

During the First World War, few resources had been invested in the railways and infrastructure and stock had become increasingly run-down. Only essential maintenance work had been carried out on the network, increasing an already substantial backlog of maintenance. Rolling stock had begun to deteriorate, the result of excessive wear and tear rather than war damage. In mainland Europe, damage to the railway systems had been so widespread that, ironically, it gave them an opportunity virtually to re-build their railway systems from scratch, rather than having to patch and mend, or modernise in a piecemeal fashion like Britain.

Nevertheless, during the 1914–18 conflict, the network had operated more efficiently than ever before under unified government control, carrying increased traffic with fewer workers and less rolling stock. Inevitably, such a situation begged questions about the ownership and shape of any peacetime railway. Concurrent with this dilemma, rail was also facing increasing competition from an enlarged road transport network, a development that led to the closure of 1,300 miles of passenger lines which had never been profitable. Peacetime allowed the government to formulate a more holistic approach to transport matters. It created the inaugural Ministry of Transport and 178 independent rail companies were 'grouped' into four main private companies, known as the 'Big Four'. This was a covert manoeuvre – 'disguised nationalisation'[20] rather than 'rationalisation' – because the government now determined rail fares, which were mainly mileage-based. The rail companies were hampered by several events. Their principal problem is that they were regarded as 'common carriers', a status that obliged them to carry goods of any sort to any destination, regardless of cost. Although the rail companies had extensive lorry fleets, they could only be used to take goods to their railheads and they were now in competition with private hauliers, often using army surplus vehicles that ran on subsidised fuel.

Despite all this, the GWR recovered its post-war timetable more quickly than any other rail company. Despite a falling off in passenger numbers between the wars, the GWR was still able to give a return of 7-8% to its shareholders in the 1920s. Its success was partly owed by offering cheap, long distance excursion fares to passengers, a trend that more than compensated for the 8% drop in normal traffic. Other factors, however, militated against the GWR: the ASLEF strike of 1924 and the loss of an already diminishing, coal-carrying traffic following the General Strike in 1926 dealt heavy financial blows.

Nonetheless, with government support, the GWR did invest in the 1930s, both in station refurbishment and safety features such as Automatic Train Control. Timings improved to attract passengers and a GWR publicity machine was created. The Railways (Agreement) Finance Act of 1935 made £27 million available for investment at a guaranteed rate of return for investors to enable new works by the Big Four rail companies. This included providing four tracks on busy routes and more platforms and goods facilities at strategic locations. Briton Ferry benefited from this strategy of rationalising the former RSBR, SWMR and GWR lines, with resultant improvements to the track layout through the town, including the opening of a new station at Rockingham Terrace.

Another European conflict was becoming increasingly likely when the Government passed an Act

Track realignment at Briton Ferry in 1935 with the 1918 (pre-alignment and 1960 (post alignment) layouts shown (G. Cooke)

in 1937 intended to prepare the industry for another huge war effort, belatedly having realised that without the network and its staff in World War I, the result may have been different. Several railway workshops were tasked with designing and building armoured trains, weapons, naval vessels and even submarines and planes well before hostilities broke out in 1939. Spitfires were built at Eastleigh workshops, submarines at Swindon, planes at Derby and Wolverton. Docks such as Swansea were to be turned to military use.

## The Second World War: Keep Calm and carry on

Unlike the situation in the First World War, railways in the Second War provided potential targets for aerial attack. Despite general conscription from 1939, rail workers were classified into a 'reserved occupation' and could only volunteer to serve in the armed forces with permission. 60,000 rail workers got permission, 3,500 of whom were killed. Others qualified in air raid precautions or railway Home Guard units. Women were permitted to work as guards and porters, but not on the footplate. The number of women employed by the rail companies increased from 25,000 to 105,000. The railways again became the mainstay of Britain's internal transport system because they were harder to bomb and easier to repair than other transport modes. Propaganda posters said that 'railway equipment is war equipment'. Indeed, the pre-war investment that had been made in the rail network proved adequate to repair bomb damage. Rapid-repair rail maintenance groups were formed. The availability of wagons to deliver war supplies, as well as normal goods, was speeded up by shortening loading and unloading times. Passenger trains were fewer, infrequent, and often delayed. Travel for pleasure was discouraged in order that 1,300,000 child evacuees could be moved and a thousand special trains per day could carry the labour force directed to work in the munitions factories. However, the railways were so busy during the Second World War that, at the end of hostilities, they were again in a poor state of repair.

## Real nationalisation – as British Railways

There was little appetite amongst the rail companies to resist nationalisation post-war. They received generous terms of compensation but realised that they would be unable to invest in both refurbishments and to stem the losses that were still accruing through the loss of freight and passenger traffic. The government had to intervene again. Unfortunately, the Railway Executive that ran the nationalised British Railways[21] from 1948 were part of an unwieldy British Transport Commission which received too little input from rail managers regarding its operations. Furthermore, the austerity in which these two bodies had to operate led to hostile relations between them. 'The railways lacked a champion … there was no equivalent of Aneurin Bevan, the Health Minister'[22] to lead a progressive, modern, course; but, after 1948, no rail worker was again regarded as a 'servant' of their company.

Nationalisation resulted in mistakes, the biggest of which was to continue with steam traction. Steam locomotives were cheaper to build, but more expensive to operate. Coal supplies were indigenous and in greater abundance than diesel fuel, so it seemed reasonable to continue building steam rather than diesel or electric locomotives. As a result, new steam shunting locos were still being introduced at Briton Ferry after the Second World War whilst the use of comfortable diesel railcars on local services was discontinued.

Other matters were against the railways, too. The British Transport Commission de-nationalised road

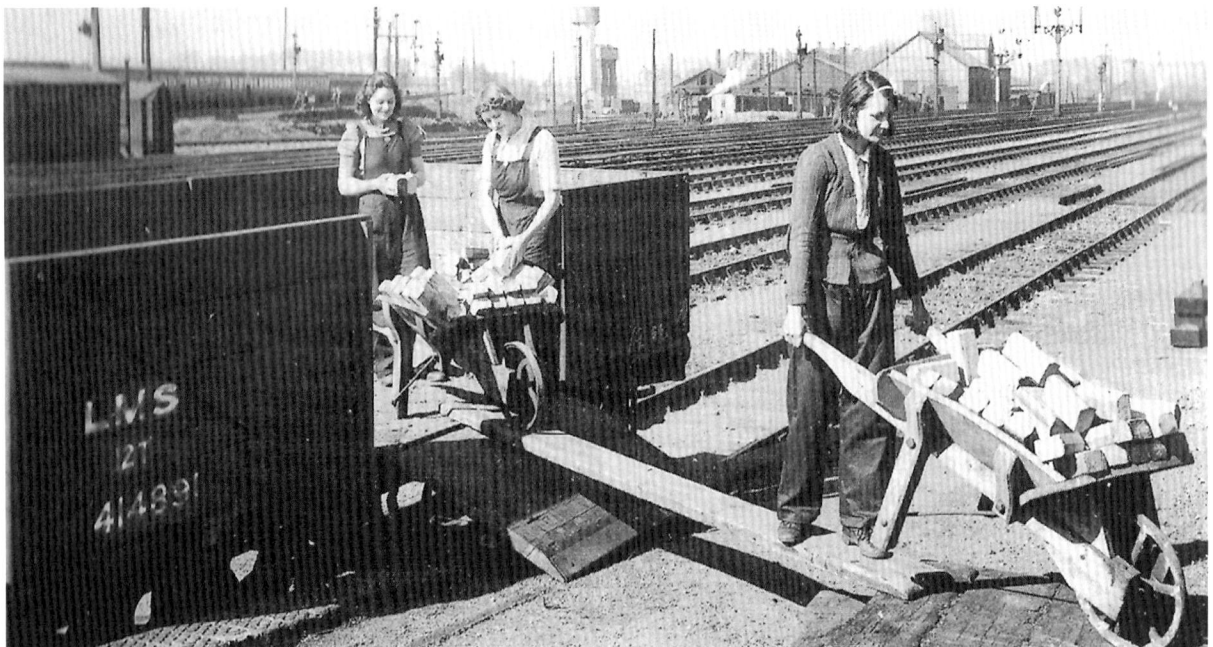

An obviously posed publicity picture of women at work at Reading in April 1944 *(National Railway Museum)*

BR logo

The Beeching Report recommended the withdrawal of local passenger services from Briton Ferry and closure of the station (Network Rail)

haulage in 1953, putting further pressure on any possibility of profitability on rail freight operations. Soon afterwards the motorway building programme was underway. It looked as though the railways would be in no fit state to compete with the car, whose annual rate of growth in ownership between 1948 and 1964 was 10% per annum. Economic recovery and the end of petrol rationing were the main reasons for this. In contrast, railway traffic, although it remained steady during the 1950s, experienced steadily deteriorating economics. Labour costs were rising faster than income, with fares and freight charges repeatedly frozen by the government to try to control inflation. By 1955 income no longer covered operating costs, and things got steadily worse.

The 1955 Modernisation Plan was an attempt to stem losses because the railways' assets were deteriorating quicker than they could be renewed. The promised expenditure was over £1,240 million.[23] The plan was that steam locomotives would be replaced with diesel and electric locomotives, and that traffic levels would increase, to be back in profit by 1962. Instead, losses mounted because the scattergun approach to investment meant that the projects invested in were not always those needed. By 1960 the House of Commons *Select Committee on Nationalised Industries* criticised the plan and advocated a change from British Railways investing its way out of its crisis to a strategy of cutbacks on the network and services. By 1961 losses were running at £300,000 a day.[24] Eventually the British Transport Commission could no longer pay the interest on its loans. The government lost patience and looked for more radical solutions. There were political problems, too. The appointment of a pro-road Minister of Transport, Ernest Marples, who, with a vested interest in getting motorways built, saw the philosophy of *road=investment*, but *rail=subsidy* being accepted when nothing could be further from the truth.

## Beeching's cuts

The outcome was the *Beeching axe*. Dr Beeching's two reports on *The Reshaping of British Railways* and *The Development of the Major Railway Trunk Routes*, which were published in 1963 and 1965 respectively, identified passenger services that should be withdrawn or modified, and the stations and halts earmarked for closure.

The first report pinpointed 2,363 stations and 5,000 miles (8,000 km) of rail line for closure, 55% of stations and 30% of route miles, with its principal objective a reduction in rail subsidies to a level sufficient to keep the network running. The second objective identified a small number of major routes that would benefit from significant investment. The 1963 report also recommended some less well-publicised changes, including a switch to containerisation for rail freight – a proposal that proved shrewd and far-sighted.

Does Beeching really does deserve his reputation as the bogeyman of the railways? In his defence it can be claimed he inherited an uneconomic, deteriorating network that was dysfunctional; line closures significantly preceded his report; the government was minded to make substantially more cuts to assets than Beeching had identified. On the other hand, Beeching is justifiably criticised for failing to recognise the social benefits of having a rail system.

> Beeching has become a handy scapegoat for our frustration at the failings of the transport system and the destruction of 'traditional' branch line England by modern car culture. The real instigators of rail closures were civil servants trying to work out how you adapt a country that was built around the horse and cart and steam train, to accommodate the cars people wanted to drive and the lorries business wanted to use.

247

There are doubts over his figures and, ultimately, the promised savings never materialized, but Beeching did not single-handedly cut the rail lines – successive government ministers did and, with or without his help, they would undoubtedly have cut the network, report or no report. Most people unthinkingly assumed that cars, lorries and buses were the future, and they were right – but only up to a point. Successive governments set the railways an impossible task. On the one hand, they were expected to act commercially, (but on the other they had a social remit) and were not allowed to raise fares in line with inflation.

Protests to save some stations and lines resulted, but the majority were closed as planned, and Dr Beeching's name remains synonymous with the mass closure of railways and the loss of many local services. A handful of axed routes have since reopened or been preserved as Heritage Railways, while others been incorporated into the National Cycle Network, or used for road schemes. Others now are lost to construction, simply reverted to farm land, or remain derelict.

### Barbara Castle's 1968 Transport Act

This Act relieved the railways of the impossible paradox set by Ernest Marples: to stop making losses on *socially* necessary rail services. It did not stop closures altogether, but their pace dwindled to a halt, boosting industry morale and creating an environment more conducive to innovation. The railways no longer had the role of common carrier and decided to use the competitive advantage arising from this to introduce fast inter-city services that would compete with business-people using motorways. An important result was the *InterCity* concept and the *High-Speed Train* (HST). Born in the early 1970s, HST first sped along the south Wales line through Briton Ferry in 1976, but without the railway's common carrier obligation to transport pigeons or such-like consignments.

### The age of the train

From the mid-1970s, with the introduction of HST and the more enlightened chairmanship of Sir Peter Parker, British Rail (BR) moved from difficult times into an era of resurgence for train travel. Parker worked under both Labour and Conservative governments to reorganise BR into business sectors like *InterCity*. He fought off the 1982 Serpell report that reflected Mrs Thatcher's antipathy to rail travel and aimed to decimate the network from 10,370 route miles to 1,630, at the time when BR was said to be at its nadir.[25] Gradually, the wiser philosophy that investment was regarded as a means of reducing costs in the long term was applied. InterCity moved into profit and, by 1990, Britain's railways 'were the most efficient in Europe and the least subsidised … though fares were high compared with those on the continent'.[26] A workforce of 600,000 in 1950 had shrunk – or been slashed, according to one's perspective – to 275,000 by 1979.

The Privatised Railway – First Great Western HST in green livery passing Briton Ferry

## John Major's 1993 Railways Act: privatisation and disintegration

The 1993 Railways Act came into effect in 1997, encouraged by EU legislation[27] that set two main objectives: to separate the operation of railways from their infrastructure; to allow access to rail operators from other countries.[28]

These objectives did not mean that the same organisation was barred from operating both infrastructure and traffic. It was simply an accounting convention: the 'books' of each must be kept separate. Rail privatisation was promoted in the early 1990s in the UK with promises of a better, cheaper service for rail users and reduced taxpayer subsidy. Private rail companies, it was argued, would inject capital and business expertise that would transform the sector's performance, while competition between operators would drive efficiency and innovation.

The Prime Minister, John Major, wanted a regional model for privatisation, where track infrastructure and operations would remain intact, but he made the crucial mistake of allowing a group of ministers and civil servants to separate them. BR was restructured in March 1994 to be fragmented into almost a hundred distinct companies, based on the separation of the management of the rail infrastructure from the operation of trains and the ownership of rolling stock.

The major components of the industry now comprised: *Railtrack*, a private company responsible for railway infrastructure and fourteen major stations (with the rest leased to the train operating companies); three rolling-stock leasing companies; twenty-five main passenger-train operating companies; five operators responsible for freight services and depots; and nineteen geographically-based maintenance suppliers.

> It was a tragedy that, just as BR had entered something of a golden age, with a structure that was robust and commercially-minded, the organisation had to be broken up based on false assumptions.[29]

## Since privatisation

An early consequence of the 1993 Railways Act was the failure of Railtrack and the need for increased safety investment in the network following the Hatfield and Potters Bar crashes in 2000 and 2002. The Railways Act of 2005 saw a major reorganisation of the railways with the abolition of the *Strategic Rail Authority* and an enhanced role for *Network Rail*,

which had replaced Railtrack. The extra investment took total government rail subsidies to £7 billion in 2007–8. Prime Minister Tony Blair had advocated a 'publicly accountable, publicly owned' railway, but this aspiration failed to be put into practice.

A White Paper, *Delivering a Sustainable Railway*, was published in 2007 by the Department for Transport, under a Labour Government. This looked ahead over a thirty-year period but also set out the UK Government's planned funding for the railways in England and Wales for the period 2009–2014. It recognised that improvements had been made since privatisation but still saw the four key tests ahead for the railways as capacity, quality of service, value-for-money and the environment.

In 2010 the Coalition Government,[30] picked up on value-for-money by asking Sir Roy McNulty 'to examine the opportunities and barriers to improving the value-for-money of GB rail for taxpayers, passengers and freight customers'. Implied in its terms of reference were recommendations for the future of rail transport, specifically looking at cost reduction and the franchising system, but not specifically identifying rail closures. The report was published in 2011, seventeen years after privatisation. It concluded that:

> Rail costs needed lowering by some 30%
> to be comparable with other west
> European railway systems' costs.
> Presumably, a 30% reduction in fares for
> passengers would be a consequence.

Nevertheless, McNulty saw three key areas, but not the only ones, which could result in this level of cost reductions.

- Reform of franchising
- Standardisation of rolling stock
- More efficient freight organisation

A government White Paper commented on McNulty's[31] envisaged savings of £2.5 billion being achieved by 2019 through four reform objectives: value for passengers, fiscal deficit reduction, support for economic growth and delivery of environmental goals. This was little different from the 2007 White paper.

By this time subsidies had dropped back to the typical level of £4 billion. Over the privatised period, up to 2011–12, passenger journeys had increased from 735 million to 1.6 billion, freight traffic saw a sixty per cent increase to 21.1 billion tonnes per kilometre per annum. Now 11.5% of all GB freight was being carried by rail. Such positive statistics as these enabled the Department of Transport to say that 'The rail industry is not broken'.

The House of Commons Transport Committee had an alternative view, citing the need for affordability and clarity, particularly of a 'more transparent approach to fares and ticketing'. In general terms, the committee castigated the organisation that has resulted from privatisation, saying:

> The structure of the industry is byzantine. Diagrammatic depictions resemble the cartoons of Heath Robinson. There is suspicion that the labyrinthine, opaque arrangements in the railway industry provide opportunities for money to leak out of the system, some of it in the form of unjustified profits.

The committee identified 'complex bureaucratic interfaces between Network Rail and the Train Operating Companies' and 'a Rail Delivery Group dominated by firms whose interests are profit maximisation'. This is very similar view to that of 'RailfutureWales' who advocate a 'simpler system of ownership and operation directly accountable to the Welsh Government, with track and train managed by a not-for-dividend body appointed by the Government.

Appendix Three shows that only twelve of the thirty-two rail TOCs are owned by UK companies and that includes Northern Ireland's nationalised Railways. The remaining sixty-three per cent are foreign-owned, often by other governments.

The railways remain heavily regulated in terms of fares, timetables, ticketing arrangements and standards of reliability and punctuality. The Government's policy to reduce public subsidy by increasing fares is not proving to be popular.

It is significant that when a new air route is introduced it is the air industry that announces it, but if a new rail service is introduced or a rail line opened or re-opened it is the Department for Transport that trumpets the fact, a difference that suggests de facto nationalisation. Whatever the outward signs might indicate, however, the reality is that Britain stands as the only example of almost complete 'privatisation' in the wake of the EU Directive.

## The case for and against rail privatisation

*For*

It is argued that there are four theoretical benefits that arise from privatisation. They are: increased efficiency through reducing costs and cutting waste,

increased concern for consumer needs; less subsidy from the government and the provision of a market-led service. The Secretary of State for Transport[32] cited the practical evidence of the benefits in a speech to the TOCs to commemorate twenty years of privatisation:

> For most of the time since the Second World War rail traffic has been falling, but since privatisation, journeys have doubled with 4,000 more services a day. The network is roughly the same size as fifteen years ago and there's been growth on lines that not long ago everyone had written off.
>
> Rail freight has grown by 60%.
>
> We now have the safest major railway in Europe.
>
> A recent EU study found that our railways are the most improved in Europe.
>
> Punctuality is at near record levels.

To this the authors would add:

> An efficient National Rail Enquiry Service and improved information systems on platforms, although this may have happened anyway without privatisation.
>
> From the financial years 2005-6 to 2015-16, rail passenger traffic in Wales has increased from twenty million passenger entries and exits to thirty million.

*Against*

1. Rail is a natural monopoly. Therefore, there is little scope for competition because duplication would lead to higher average costs.

2. Franchising requires regulation and gives little scope for competition especially where the duration of contract is felt to be too short.

3. Management through franchising results in lack of organization of the national network, eg complications over tickets which use more than one TOC.[33]

4. It is unclear where overall responsibility for safety lies in a fragmented network.

5. It is not easy to curtail subsidies so less profitable services will be under continuous threat.

6. Fares continually rise with a dystopian/byzantine ticketing and pricing system.[34]

A very practical case against privatisation exists: the ownership and operation since 1996 of the London King's Cross–Edinburgh line, electrified by BR from 1976–1991. The table below shows that none of the private companies operated the line profitably, whereas state ownership of the company did. None of the other theoretical benefits have materialised.

Within a month of the November 2017 announcement, Andrew Adonis, Chair of the National Infrastructure Commission and a former Minister of Transport and HS2 pioneer, resigned, considering the arrangements for the partnership model an 'extraordinary decision' which was 'a nakedly political manoeuvre'. Virgin Trains East Coast claimed that the reason for the long delays in its services was that the track was outside its control and that promised improvements had not been made which lost it the expected increase in passengers. It was Adonis who had set up East Coast, the directly-operated and profitable state-run railway.

## Conclusion

Bowman's research[36] concluded that:

The British rail industry can barely be called privatised in a meaningful sense any longer because of the extensive subsidies provided for infrastructure provision and, from 2014, the official re-designation of Network Rail debt as a public liability. The way such subsidies have been channelled through Network Rail has allowed backers of rail privatisation among the train operators and the political elites to maintain their narratives about the promise and outcomes of privatisation.... Accounting and critical accountants have a role to play in challenging the political narratives about (such) transformation of public utilities.

The TUC and its member rail unions state that four myths are being promulgated about rail privatisation,[37] reflecting Bowman's research. They are: that rail privatisation has created passenger growth, has resulted in new investment and innovation, has resulted in cheaper and better services for passengers and is a better deal for the taxpayer. Its conclusion is that privatisation of our railways has led to a fragmented and dysfunctional system. Wolmar's conclusion is brutal, calling it 'pretend capitalism with the taxpayer picking up the tab.'[38]

| Dates | Franchisee | Ownership | Notes |
|---|---|---|---|
| April 1996 to 2006 | GNER | Private | Terminated by Government for financial reasons |
| 2007 to 2009 | National Express East Coast | Private | Company ended franchise after 18 months stating it would not work |
| 14/11/2009 to 28/2/2015 | East Coast (Directly Operated Railways) | State | East Coast returned £1 billion to HM Treasury over this period |
| 1/3/2015 to (2023) | Inter-city Railways (Stagecoach/Virgin railways) known as known as Virgin Trains East Coast | Private | June 2017. Stagecoach claimed it had 'overpaid' for a £3.3 billion contract to run the eight-year franchise. Most of the premiums due to the Treasury fell at the end of the franchise. The franchise was unworkable because the growth in passenger numbers expressed in the franchise bid had not materialised. |
| 2020– | Partnership model | Private | In November 2017 it was announced that the franchise would be terminated three years early in favour of 'a long-term regional partnership bringing together the operator of track and train under a single leader and unified brand'.[35] |
| 24/6/2018 to 2020 | London North Eastern Railway | State | The Minister of Transport announced to the House of Commons that the contract would be terminated on 24 June 2018 and that London North Eastern Railway would become the *Operator of last resort*. The option of stagecoach continuing until 2020 on a not-for-profit basis, but with a performance-related payment at the end was rejected, but bids for later franchises were not. |

Operators of the East Coast Main Line *(Philip Adams)*

Since privatisation, more than £11 billion of public funds has been 'mis-spent': on debt write-offs, dividend payments to private investors, fragmentation costs (which include the profit margins of complex tiers of contractors and sub-contractors). Higher interest payments were made to keep Network Rail's debts off the government balance sheet.

At the same time, privatisation has failed to deliver on its promises. Genuine private investment makes an insignificant contribution to the railways, representing about one per cent of the total money that goes into the railway annually. Fares are among the highest in Europe, with many services overcrowded and reliant on obsolete rolling stock. In most European countries, apart from Britain, the tracks and other infrastructure are publicly-owned and there is also a publicly-owned train operator that provides the majority of passenger train services.

Rail policy is still driven by the Government. This was implicit in the White Paper of November 2017. The Government's plan is to 'get private and public sectors working more closely together to increase performance and rebuild the railway'. This is to be achieved through partnerships between train franchisees and track operators, as envisaged in such schemes as the 'East Coast Partnership' from 2020, devolving Network Rail and running the partnerships under Route Supervisory Boards, comprising train and track operators and passenger representatives. In Network Rail's Control Period Six, from 2019–2024, £47.9 billion will be invested in rail, of which seventy-two per cent, £34.7 billion, will be government money.[39]

Many people in south west Wales would agree with several, but not all, of the statements in the 2017 White Paper:

> Today, Britain has some of the most congested and intensively used railway lines in Europe. Rising demand is putting significant pressure on the railway infrastructure. That is why the Government is investing record sums to increase capacity, boost reliability and improve journeys. Along with flagship schemes like HS2, Crossrail, and the Great North Rail Project, we are modernising the existing railway fabric, upgrading stations, and introducing new trains and carriages across the country. We recently announced that we expect around £47.9bn to be spent on the railway between 2019 and 2024, of which we're providing up to £34.7bn directly to deliver a more reliable railway. Our

investments will meet demand for more capacity on the network, adding new links, restoring lost capacity and connections, and supporting the Government's Industrial and Housing Strategies. This will include continuing to look at opportunities to restore capacity lost under Beeching and British Rail cuts of the 1960s and 1970s, where this enables new housing or economic development, or eases congestion elsewhere on the transport system, and offers value for money. We will also bring more private sector finance, funding and expertise on board to help provide capacity for the future. We have laid a firm foundation of investment, but challenges remain. Passenger satisfaction compares well with other countries overall, but average figures hide variation and overall satisfaction with train services is low in many areas. Network Rail has delivered a number of large scale investments in a challenging environment, but some major projects like the electrification of the Great Western Main Line have been beset by problems. Overcrowding on the busiest services is an increasing issue. Infrastructure problems and congestion on the network and on stations have affected service reliability.

*Heads you win; tails I lose* was *The Observer's* description of how the franchising system works from the taxpayer's point of view. Wolmar, too, explains how the taxpayer/customer loses out: 'The operators receive money for not running trains whilst, at the same time, allowing their supplier, Network Rail, to provide them with a better service.... Privatisation was always going to be partial and tightly regulated … because (the railways) are such an important part of the infrastructure.... The shape of the future is shrouded in uncertainty.'

In recent times, opinion polls have shown very high levels of support for rail nationalisation, or rail services run on a not-for-profit and democratic basis, instead of the present system of profit-oriented train operating companies. The exact shape of the railways may be uncertain, but their effective, ultimate, ownership will, of necessity, certainly remain in the public sphere in future. Andrew Adonis should, perhaps have added the word 'officially' to his comment about the railways that 'The state must *(officially)* regain its authority as guardian of the public interest. '

In May 2018 the Department for Transport announced that the government-owned London North Eastern Railway would become an Operator of Last Resort. Although the Wales Act, 2017, allowed the Welsh Government, through Transport for Wales, to select the new franchisee, it did not permit an Operator of Last Resort to tender. Thus Keolis Amey, a private consortium, secured the franchise to become Transport for Wales' *Rail Operator and Development Partner* for fifteen years. This was to be a 'not-for-profit' arrangement in which the specification for bidders was less restrictive than in previous franchise tenders, enabling the creation of the South Wales Metro. However, the specification for bidders was not made public.

The ownership only of some key Valley lines passes from Network Rail to Transport for Wales,

indicating that the thrust of the franchise was indeed to establish the South Wales Metro and other main line services from Cardiff. Very little is to be provided specifically for west Wales, except some updated rolling stock, improvements to Carmarthen and Llanelli stations in 2021 and 2025 respectively and a first-class service from Swansea to Manchester in 2024. The new diesel units on the Milford to Manchester service which are due in 2023 will still be two or three cars only, although some are likely to be built at CAF Llanwern.

The subject of Chapter Fourteen is *The Future;* it will cover the opportunities for integrated transport systems in Wales under the ownership pattern of the day: The Wales and Borders Franchise, 2018–2032.

### Notes for Chapter Thirteen

1. Northern Ireland's railways are nationalised in that they are owned by the devolved Northern Ireland Executive. The Executive make a capital grant to Translink to operate rail services and to maintain and develop rail infrastructure and rolling stock.
2. Wolmar, p.199
3. Examples of wage rates from the Neath Division of the GWR at the turn of the twentieth century were given in Chapter Eight
4. Expressed by Wolmar
5. *Cardiff Times*, 12 April 1890
6. *Evening Express* 24 April 1908. Equivalent to £2.75 a day increase in 2017
7. The 1911 list of Briton Ferry rail workers identified fifty trade union members. This represents a minimum density of 25% of the railway population.
8. *www.Llanellirailwaystrike.org.uk* Accessed 9 April 2017
9. The daily notes are based on document SWCC/MNA/PP/33/1 held at the Richard Burton Archives, Swansea University
10. He was a guard who lived at King Street, Neath
11. Crymmych, Fishguard, Severn Tunnel Junction, Bristol, Carmarthen, Cardiff and Pontypool Road were examples of locations cited at meetings.
12. He lived in Osterley Street, Briton Ferry
13. A signalman of Llewelyn Street
14. A signalman of Llewelyn Street
15. An engine driver who lived on Old Road
16. Of New Henry Street, Neath
17. An engineman of Richmond Terrace, Neath
18. J Hugh Edwards was an anti-socialist National Liberal MP who was deposed in the 1922 election by miners' leader William Jenkins by 6,235 votes
19. *Cambria Daily Leader*, 6 October 1919
20. Wolmar, p.178
21. British Railways existed from 1948–1997, but see 'BR' in *Definitions*
22. Wolmar
23. Equivalent to £31.25 billion in 2017
24. Equivalent to £7.5 million in 2017
25. Between 1970 and 1982 revenues had declined from £2,300 to £1,800 and costs increased from £2,500 to £2,700 million (Wikipedia)
26. Wolmar, p.296
27. Directive 91/440/EEC of 29 July,1991: *Development of the Communities' Railways*
28. For example, Arriva Trains (Wales) which are owned by Germany's state railways.
29. Wolmar, p.300
30. The Department of Transport and the Office of Rail Regulation commissioned Sir Roy McNulty
31. 'Reforming our Railways – putting the customer first', (2012)
32. Patrick McLoughlin MP, 9 July 2013. Accessed 28 June 2017 at: *https://www.gov.uk/speeches/20-years-since-rail-privatisation*
33. In May 2018 the rail Delivery Group introduced a consultation into ticketing, admitting that 55 million different fares existed and that only 34% of customers were very confident they had bought the best value ticket for their journey
34. Fare increases to regulated fares, which comprise about half of all tickets, are calculated using the previous July's Retail Price Index (RPI) measure of inflation. The Rail Delivery Group claimed in January 2018 that fares 'account for about 70% of the cost of running our trains'. Others say it is less.
35. *Guardian*, 30 November 2017
36. Andrew Bowman: 'An illusion of success: the consequences of British Rail privatisation' in *Accounting Forum* Vol 39 Issue 1, March 2015 (Elsevier).
37. *http://actionforrail.org/the-four-big-myths-of-uk-rail-privatisation/* Philip Hadley. Accessed 17 June 2017
38. Wolmar, p.311
39. The White Paper makes no mention of such a Route Supervisory Board for the Wales and Borders franchise within which both the appointed franchisee and Network Rail would work under the control of the Welsh Government.
40. *Guardian*, 9 February 2018

Chapter Fourteen
# The Future

*Neither a wise man nor a brave man lies down on the tracks of history to wait for the train of the future to run over him.*

(Dwight D Eisenhower)

This book has related how 170 years of railway history has impacted on the Swansea Bay area with special reference to Briton Ferry and its people and, by implication, similar towns. The present chapter aims to review the contribution the railways made to the development of such towns and how ownership of the railways affected the populace. A more important question is whether railways have a place in meeting the area's economic and social goals and what future policies and projects can therefore be expected.

## Railways' contribution to the economic development of south Wales

In the 1850s and later, when the railways began to arrive, the most important consideration for the public was that more efficient trade and manufacturing was possible than that provided by use of the canals. The railways enabled the transformation from an agricultural to an industrial existence, by making it easier for people to migrate. Migrants used the private railway system to relocate from places such as west Wales to new centres of manufacturing employment in the towns of south Wales. For many, this led to a better standard of living. Over the last fifty years, however, that nineteenth century migration has been somewhat reversed. Much manufacturing work has now disappeared from many south Wales communities with replacement employment being created over a wider geographical area. West Wales has seen much leisure and retirement-based inward migration and increased employment in that sector.

## The consequences of different ownerships

During the second half of the nineteenth century, several separate privately-owned rail companies were introduced to south Wales. By 1914 these had been swallowed up by the biggest of them, the GWR.

However, it was not monopolistic enterprises like the GWR that led to the unitary management of the railway system: it was war. The importance of railways during wartime meant that they had to be managed by the government, but with little of the needed investment being forthcoming. This lack of investment required correction after World War One, so smaller railways were grouped together in 1923 to be operated more economically and to benefit better from investment. This so-called *rationalisation* was effectively *pre-nationalisation*. The GWR made reasonable returns for shareholders between the wars and sought infrastructure improvements. Yet it was the government that determined rail fares and provided grants for the improvements, particularly in the late 1930s. Thus, many of the complex, duplicated and inefficient rail layouts and facilities created by the private companies were improved at this time. In doing so the government was also preparing the railways for an impending second war and the Railway Executive, indeed, took ownership of the entire network for war purposes. After the Second World War, it was something of a fait accompli when nationalisation became official in 1948. The nationalised railways did make wasteful mistakes, such as staying with steam traction under the 1955 modernisation plan, but it recovered well in the 1970's when the government allowed the (nationalised) rail managers to both manage and modernise. Given the growing success of the modernising railways, the political decision to privatise in the 1990s was an unnecessary, knee-jerk, political decision. Several south Wales communities benefitted by regaining their stations, but at the cost of higher fares, complex ticketing, and token services. Behind these lay hidden state subsidy of its private operators, through Network Rail and the Welsh Government.

The railways' trajectory during the twentieth century was, therefore, been that of a national, social asset which was dependent on underlying state support. Overall, the changes of franchisees under private ownership are still providing only illusory economic competition, although some successful initiatives have taken place.

## Passenger transport and the area's future economic and social goals

Whilst many south Wales towns are no longer the industrial towns they once were, they are not completely post-industrial dormitory towns. It is simply that many of their working population work further afield. In Briton Ferry's case, some people work in the Swansea Bay area and others within the wider area between Llanelli and Cardiff. That Swansea Bay area now has its own regional economic development board[1] is a recognition that many leave their 'dormitory' address to perform their daily work within a wider Swansea Bay area. This situation requires a different approach for the transport of passengers for both work and leisure purposes. The development board has recognised that the area requires an integrated transport network and that the train can play an increasing role in it, particularly in east-west movement. The concept which underlies such a network, and needs to be seriously considered, is the combination of several forms of passenger transport. The four 'I's: *information*; *interchange*; *investment* and *imagination*[2] form the basis of such a plan for passenger transport. We stand some way from this at present.

## Future policies and projects: devolution of transport, reform of franchising and Brexit

Although the starting point for this assessment of the future of railways will be at the level of Wales, rather than Great Britain, the Principality's relationship with the British government, too, must be considered here. A major factor which influences the Welsh Government's stance on transport policy is political and economic devolution. The funding for Britain's railways in the 21st century, in terms of value for money, was discussed in Chapter Thirteen. However, it is the methods for determining the *distribution* of funding within Britain that has created recent discontent in the Principality and concern by the House of Commons Transport Committee. Several rail investments in England have suggested to the people of Wales that only the needs of London and the South-east merit heavy rail investment. Whilst many people in Wales were tolerant of HS1, their tolerance does not extend so readily to the money spent on HS2 and Crossrail 1 and 2.

Many in the regions are discontented because they believe that much of that expenditure should have been invested in improving the infrastructure and services in regions away from the south-east. This discontent has implications for the demands of political and economic devolution in Wales and elsewhere, as well as future rail policies and projects in Wales. The creation of the National Infrastructure Commission as an executive of HM Treasury from January 2017, initially suggested that both it and its counterpart, the Welsh National Infrastructure Commission, offered some hope for a more balanced and structured distribution of investment.

We shall now consider the Welsh government's present powers regarding rail projects and examine proposed projects in the greater Cardiff and Swansea Bay regions and the prospective economic and social opportunities they offer. The Railways Act of 2005 gave new powers to the Welsh Assembly in relation to the railways in Wales. As well as becoming a joint signatory with the Department for Transport for the Wales and the Borders Franchise, the Welsh Assembly Government was also empowered to:

- Give financial assistance to any organisation to develop Welsh railways (including Network Rail and Train Operating Companies);
- Publish guidance jointly with the Secretary of State in relation to, and make any proposals for, closures of services or facilities that it funds;
- Fund experimental services for a trial period of up to five years.

In addition, the Transport (Wales) Act 2006 gave the Assembly new responsibilities for preparing a Wales Transport Strategy and a general duty to 'develop policies for the promotion and encouragement of safe, integrated, sustainable, efficient and economic transport facilities and services to, from and within Wales.' through *Transport for Wales*.

The impact of this change became most evident at the end of the Arriva Trains (Wales) franchise in 2018, when Transport for Wales awarded the franchise to Keolis/Amey and incorporated the Cardiff Capital Region Metro into the franchise. Transport for Wales intend to cap Keolis/Amey's profits and to identify the franchise under the Transport for Wales logo.

Management of the Welsh road network is devolved but only the franchising of rail services was fully devolved from 2017, and not rail infrastructure management. The Welsh Government[3] provides £170 million a year to support the Wales and Borders franchise but the provision of rolling stock still remains in the hands of the franchisee. The 2018 rail franchise tender was, nevertheless, called 'the largest ever Welsh Government procurement'. Of the four bidders that applied for the franchise, the incumbent, Arriva Trains (Wales), dropped out in October 2017, despite making a profit of £27.5 million in 2017 and paying £20 million in dividends. They were followed by Abellio in February 2018, after the collapse of its partner, Carillion. Transport for Wales awarded the contract to Keolis Amey (Wales), to run from 14 October,2018 for fifteen years.

Under future franchises TOCs are to become *Operating and Development Partners* who will receive level subsidies during their franchises, unlike the TOCs, whose subsidies declined. This situation exists despite a call from Welsh MPs for further devolution of the rail industry, which the British Government rejected in March,2017. Welsh MPs pointed out that Wales had 6% of GB's rail network but only received 1% of the spending. The government responded by saying that much spending in England benefitted Wales. The DfT also claimed it would continue to liaise closely with the Welsh government on the specification and funding of Network Rail's operations in England and Wales for each 'control period' to ensure that Welsh requirements for increased capacity on the network are reflected.

Therefore, Welsh Ministers do not manage Network Rail in Wales (or the Borders) although the Government of Wales Act, confers powers upon them to develop and fund infrastructure enhancement schemes, new rail passenger services, invest in improving the journey experience for rail users and fund rail freight improvement schemes. The Welsh Government thus works with the Department for Transport and Network Rail to run better railways in Wales by improving the lines to reduce delays and allow more services to run, reopening old lines for passengers, building new stations and improving the accessibility and safety of stations.

Brexit's effect on the future of the railways is not likely to be known for some time, as are Brexit's effects upon devolution. Does Brexit mean that the government are now free to re-nationalise the railways? Following the EU (Notification of Withdrawal) Bill[4], the Government have announced its intention to sponsor a Great Repeal Bill which will entail the passage of much secondary legislation. There are fears that proper parliamentary scrutiny may be lost in the process.[5] This can impact on the future of railways in Wales, because the question whether devolved governments can preserve their existing bills, which have derived from EU legislation and have had many positive local effects, has not yet been ans-

wered. Do the Welsh and Scottish Governments not have a role in this scrutiny? Does the Great Repeal Bill not allow the country to retain the best of the EU-derived law which applies to railways and to repeal the less welcome aspects? Value-for-money considerations will continue to bear heavily on government policy, whatever else happens in terms of Brexit and devolution's impact on future policies and projects for Welsh railways. If these considerations assume that savings can be achieved through better organisation of the railways in Wales, can these be achieved whilst maintaining or enhancing present services?

Previous projects in Wales have been funded and delivered in several ways; by the Department for Transport and Network Rail, or by Welsh Government/European Regional Development Fund (ERDF) and delivered by Network Rail or funded by Welsh Government/ERDF and delivered by Welsh Government. After Brexit, it is unclear what, if anything, might replace the ERDF.

## Future policies: inter-modal transport projects

Between the financial years 2005–6 to 2015–16, rail passenger traffic in Wales increased from twenty million passenger entries and exits to thirty million. The implications of these figures have provoked much thought about the nature of future transport systems within, and to and from, Wales. The proposed transport formats for the future, many of which are yet to be finalised, are not wholly untested, so the advocates for any proposed new systems in Wales have been able to draw from successful and unsuccessful experiences both in Britain and elsewhere.

The most prominent concept underlying the proposals is that of the *inter-modal public transport system*, whereby a combination of several modes, such as train, tram, bus, cycling, walking and park-and-ride, gives the most efficient, economical, healthy and sustainable outcome for the requirements of modern life. It is a concept entirely compatible with the Active Travel (Wales) Act of 2013 *which requires local authorities to continuously improve facilities and routes for walkers and cyclists and to consider their needs at the design stage of new roads*. At the very centre of this 'format for the future' is the introduction of transport interchanges. Their main characteristics are described in Appendix Four.

## Electrification

On 22 March 2017, the first test run took place from London to Swansea of the Hitachi hybrid power train using diesel power into Swansea. Electrification to

Bi-model inter-city express train at Paddington, where it will use the overhead lines *(Martin Davies)*

improve capacity and service provision from London to Cardiff was timed for completion by 2019, and to Swansea by 2023, with 'discrete sections of electrification between Cardiff and Swansea by 2019'.[6] This was a Conservative Manifesto pledge made by Prime Minister Cameron. The Cardiff to Swansea electrification was cancelled in August 2017, as was the Leeds-Manchester and East Midlands electrification.[7] The estimated costs for the Cardiff to Swansea section, which were £213 million in 2013, had risen to £433 million by 2016. The decision and the reasoning underlying it were later examined by the House of Commons Transport Committee which accepted that too ambitious timing had led to unacceptable cost escalation. Nevertheless, Barry equated the £433 million Cardiff to Swansea electrification cost to the approximate cost of just one mile of HS2 line.[8]

The reasons given by the government for the cancellation were: that the cancellation would avoid disruption such as raising existing bridges to give the electric trains' pantographs sufficient clearance and that the cancellation would allow Swansea to get bi-mode/hybrid trains[9] in late 2017, rather than waiting until 2019. These justifications for cancellation were fatuous: such disruption would occur on any

electrification conversion and the hybrids could be run during the proposed conversion anyway. The cancellations engendered further bitterness in Lancashire, Yorkshire and the east Midlands, as well as west Wales, when, only days later, the Government announced backing for Crossrail 2, the £31 billion north-south London rail route.

The DfT justification for substituting the hybrids for electrics in the long-term was that hybrids will deliver over 130 extra seats and fifteen minutes faster journey times between Swansea and London. At the same time this announcement was made, the DfT also announced some unspecific promises of significance for the Swansea Bay area, and its west Wales hinterland, for:

- direct services from Pembroke Dock to London via Carmarthen on hybrid Intercity Express trains
- station improvements in and around Swansea, including looking at the case for additional provision

It is not clear from the above statements which route the hybrid Intercity Express trains would follow east of Llanelli; whether their onwards journey

Hitachi bi-modal train at Briton Ferry, operating on diesel power *(Martin Davies)*

will be a reversal via Swansea High Street station, or direct via the Swansea District Line, including a new stop at a *Morriston Parkway* interchange. Signalling and track improvements between Cockett Tunnel and Baglan had also been planned.[10] What is certain is that the negative decision regarding the future of the Cardiff to Swansea electrification will have a greater adverse impact on the Swansea Bay region than the definite electrification of the Cardiff metro.

On the Cardiff to Swansea electrification, the House of Commons Transport Committee later concluded that...

> As it stands the Department has not yet made the long-term case for bi-mode operation, with a view to conversion to alternative train traction power sources at some point in the future.

The Committee challenged the coherence of the DfT's strategy in using hybrids-as-diesel west of Cardiff, whilst challenging industry to phase out diesel traction by 2040. This implied that hybrids might then be replaced with battery, hydrogen or other traction technologies then in development. The Committee also took a dim view of the way the cancellation decision was handled and recommended that the cancellation itself be cancelled. In its report *Rail infrastructure investment*[11] it said that:

> Rail electrification schemes cancelled in July 2017 be re-categorised as *pending*, and placed

in the Rail Network Enhancements Pipeline for further development and design work. If new battery and hydrogen technology is proven, the Department and Network Rail should make a comparative cost/benefit analysis against any outstanding electrification projects ... (and) learn the lessons of earlier schemes and strive to reduce costs....

The Committee was also concerned about unfair project appraisals, with their negative effects upon places like south Wales:

> Current transport scheme appraisal methods disadvantage regions in need of economic regeneration. This is working against the Government's intention to rebalance the economy. The current appraisal methods, which heavily weight journey time saved, will always favour London. The consequent transport investment increases economic activity and congestion. The appraisal method does not solve congestion but subsidises it. Appraisal methods should instead weigh heavily the regeneration impacts of investment in transport in regions with spare economic capacity.

This exactly described the situation west of Cardiff. Within days of the House of Commons

Transport Committee report being made public, an announcement was made by the Welsh Government. A *Global Centre of Rail Excellence* is to be created, with the former Nant Helen opencast coal site at Onllwyn being the Welsh Government's preferred option. This suggests a new future for the Neath Valley freight line because the £100 million project will regenerate the site, create a development centre for rolling stock testing and maintenance, and practice the application of clean hydrogen and battery-powered rail traction.

*The environment*

Rail is the most emissions-efficient major mode of transport[12] and electric trains powered by renewable energy can offer practically carbon-free journeys and transport. Rail contributes less than 1.5% of Europe's transport sectors emissions even though it has over 8.5% of total market share.[13] The reduction of $CO_2$ and $NO_x$ that is achievable through electric trains is not achievable when diesel-alone is used or diesel-under-the-wires. Hybrids-as-diesel are inferior to electrics in terms of decelerating climate change and global warming. For this reason, the government's appeal to train operators in February 2018, of its vision to decarbonise rail transport by eliminating diesel-only trains by 2040 was disingenuous because many trains west of Cardiff and elsewhere would still be hybrid.

The main benefit for most passengers within the Swansea Bay area, whether electric or hybrid trains are introduced, is not the saving of time. That would certainly be the case for west Wales travellers to destinations outside Wales, but the main benefit for 'Bay' travellers from these developments will be the avoidance of road congestion and atmospheric pollution, with time savings arising as an extra benefit from better public transport connectivity.

Next, we shall review how the concept of transport interchanges within an inter-modal transport system can be, or has been, partly applied in south Wales. We start with the system known as the 'Cardiff capital region metro'.

*Cardiff capital region metro*

This metro will cover ten local authority areas and extend on its southern boundaries from Porthcawl in the south-west to Severn Tunnel Junction in the south-east. Its northern extent will be from Treherbert on the north-western side to Y Fenni (Abergavenny) on the north-east. Jeremy Miles, Labour AM for Neath, says this metro is 'in truth the south-east Wales metro'.[14] He is dead right, as you will,

without doubt, conclude for yourself when you read below where the investment will be.

One of the reasons for developing the metro concerns population growth: Cardiff City's population is expected to grow by 80,000 to 430,000 by 2030 and the wider Cardiff capital region from 1.5 to 1.6 million over the next fifteen years.

The metro will comprise heavy[15] and light rail and bus rapid transport for these reasons:[16]

- Heavy rail because longer trains can deliver more capacity
- Light rail for lighter density routes but with closer station stops
- Bus rapid transport to cater for high and low-density routes at lower capital costs

It will be engineered in two phases; the first requires new stations, line enhancements and improvements to current stations and phase two will involve faster and more frequent and new services and the introduction of bus rapid transit routes.

The target is to provide no less than four services an hour so that passengers can just 'turn up and go', with one smart-card type ticket to cover whatever modes of transport are involved in the journey. The benefits of such a high frequency, integrated and extendable system will not merely be to passengers, but will link communities together and help transform the economy. Its positive social and environmental impact will shape the region's identity.

> As part of its procurement, the Welsh Government is leading on the development of proposals for the creation of a South Wales Metro service, including responsibility for the operation of infrastructure on the Valley Lines. They have been working closely with Network Rail to agree the principles for the proposed transfer of ownership of the Core Valley Lines. Such transfer is supported in principle by the Government, subject to final agreement and recommendation of approval by Network Rail.[17]

From the overall franchise value of £5 billion, £800 million will be spent to provide 148 new trains. CAF of Spain are building seventy-seven at their new factory at Llanwern and Stadler of Switzerland are to build a further seventy-one for introduction in 2022, (thirty-five regional and thirty-six three-car). They will be air-conditioned, wi-fi-enabled, with power and USB sockets and provide step-free access.

The Metro will benefit from a new £100 million depot at Taff's Well to cater for thirty-six metro vehicles, 400 train crew, thirty-five maintenance and fifty-two control centre staff, with completion also due in 2022. Cardiff 's Canton maintenance depot will be updated to support tri-modal rolling stock. Train parks will be established at Rhymney and Treherbert. Arriva's staffing of 2,200 will be increased by 600.

*Public transport systems in the west Glamorgan area*

The second project which has been advocated concerns the public transport systems in the west Glamorgan area around Swansea. Three proposals which merit consideration both individually and collectively are at the discussion stage. They are *Swansea Public Transport Hubs* – Professor Cole's Report; *Swansea Light Rapid Transport System* proposals by RailfutureWales and the *Swansea Bay Metro System* – Professor Barry's report. In this Chapter the previous rail improvement projects, at Gowerton and on the Swan Line, are included to provide background information to these three studies.

*Cole's Proposal One: Swansea Public Transport Hubs*

The first proposal by Professor Stuart Cole of the University of South Wales emerged from consultancy work for the Welsh Government. The Swansea Bay City Region Board were called upon by Wales' Transport Minister to consider Cole's study on potential transport improvements in the area. The study reviewed what needed to be done to move towards a network of transport hubs. The Board regard the Swansea Bay area, in which lie several de-industrialised communities, as 'self-evidently a vibrant region (which) requires an integrated public transport network'. Cole's emphasis on buses, rather than a light rail system, to reduce congestion was because the various population densities of the settlements comprising the Swansea Bay City Region 'may not be sufficient to justify such a system'.

The study highlighted that the four radial routes into Swansea that suffered peak period congestion had no bus priority lanes along them. 'The primary radial road route from the east (east Swansea, Briton Ferry, Neath, Port Talbot) along Fabian Way (A483) and on the Tawe bridge is one of four that suffers from peak period congestion'. Additionally, much car access to the radial routes was via the M4 motorway, which, in turn was causing frequent motorway congestion at points between junctions 42 and 47. The report recommended two principal policy changes: better land use planning to integrate new

developments with transport routes and linked local transport hub and sub-hubs to improve cross-region routes.

Although the report was primarily about increasing the use of (low emission) buses and decreasing east-west car use and traffic congestion, the report made some significant observations about potential improvements to east-west rail travel on the *Swanline*,[18] alluding particularly to the frequency of local services and journey times on the line.

'Train frequency (currently every two hours, requires an increase to every thirty minutes) at Baglan, Skewen and Llansamlet (to) lead to (road) traffic reductions. However, increased park-and-ride capacity will be required if the maximum effect is to be achieved. Baglan is a convenient location to attract traffic from the westbound M4 and land is available adjacent to the station.' However, 'the present journey time of twenty to twenty-five minutes to Swansea station requires to be more competitive with a maximum car journey of fifteen to twenty minutes.' The train also has the advantage of going directly to the city centre.

In advocating improvements to frequency and to journey times and the provision of park-and-ride facilities, Cole has clearly seen the advantages of public transport interchanges along the Swanline to further ameliorate traffic congestion on east-west routes in the Swansea Bay area. He has cited the rail improvements in Gowerton as an example of what can be achieved, even though Gowerton is not yet a full interchange due to insufficient bus connectivity at the station. What his report might also have added was that better frequency of train services, especially where transport interchanges exist, will also benefit secondary roads and streets in towns like Briton Ferry, Neath and Skewen by reducing congestion and possibly the need for expensive car ownership.

A recent report by the Campaign for Better Transport[19] commented on the decline in supported Welsh bus services. This does not necessarily mean that bus services overall have declined. It may simply mean that commercially-operated services are profitable, but likely expensive. The total spending by Welsh Local Authorities on such bus services declined from roughly £26 million in 2010/11 to around £16 million in 2017/18 with Neath-Port Talbot, Cardiff and Wrexham spending nothing during 2016/17 and 2017/18. Despite reporting such figures, the Campaign nevertheless went on to say:

> Wales should develop a National Investment Strategy for Buses and Coaches … initiating pilots to bring together different transport contracts and services … using the Wales and borders rail franchise to integrate buses and trains more effectively, in particular developing stations as transport hubs for the surrounding areas with integrated time-tabling and joint ticketing … in particular the TrawsCymru[20] bus network could be integrated with the rail network and with other bus services.

## Gowerton

We now examine railway improvement at Gowerton and why it was done. Gowerton's example has implications for existing stations on the *Swanline* and may offer similar opportunities for other lines. The line through Gowerton was singled in 1986 as an economy measure and its station became a request stop. In 1998 a mere 5,900 passengers used the station. Five miles of the line was upgraded to double track between Llanelli and Cockett, including the Loughor Viaduct, replacing and strengthening bridges, modernisation of signalling and power equipment to allow for a high-frequency operation. The station at Gowerton was improved by adding a second platform with better access and lighting, a real-time customer information system and an upgraded car park. The improvements have enabled an increase in the frequency of trains to Gowerton station with half-hourly peak weekday services, hourly off-peak weekday services, and additional weekend services.

After the line was redoubled in 2013 and the station modernised 110,000 entries and exits immediately resulted. With an approximately one-hourly service interval in each direction, a total of 167,184

passengers used the station in 2017. The table below shows that over the last five years from an overall increase in journeys of ninety-eight per cent has been realised at Gowerton. No doubt, some of the increase is attributable to passengers preferring the facilities to those at Llanelli, but the figures are impressive nonetheless. The cost of the project was £27m (of which £13m was from the European Regional Development Fund).

## The Swanline

The *Swanline* service from Swansea to Cardiff entailed the construction of five new stations on the existing south Wales main line at Pyle, Baglan, Briton Ferry, Skewen and Llansamlet. It aimed to provide an hourly service from these stations. The service was created in June 1994[21] by British Rail's Regional Railways through a partnership with local government authorities who secured EU development funding for the stations and to own the trains needed to operate the service.

Under the 1997 privatisation, responsibility for *Swanline* services passed from BR to *South Wales and West Railway*, a newly created, franchised train-operating company. In 1999, the company halved the service to two-hourly, citing poor passenger usage. The cut resulted in a 45% reduction in passengers for the next decade. In the meanwhile, the company disposed of the surplus rolling stock elsewhere. Arriva Trains Wales took over the franchise in 2003 with passenger numbers at its nadir. Even with the inferior bi-hourly Monday to Saturday service, by 2013/2014, Arriva's passenger usage exceeded the best performance figures for the hourly service under the previous franchisee by over ten per cent. In the current decade, whereas the number of passenger trips on Arriva Trains (Wales) has increased by 17%, the increase at Briton Ferry has been 27%.[22] The company made profits of £27.5 million in 2017 and paid £20 million in dividends.

The *Swanline* service's two-hourly frequency is still regarded as unattractive to users because of the extremely restricted journey-to-work options for Swansea commuters. As the service takes up valuable space on the busy section of line between Bridgend

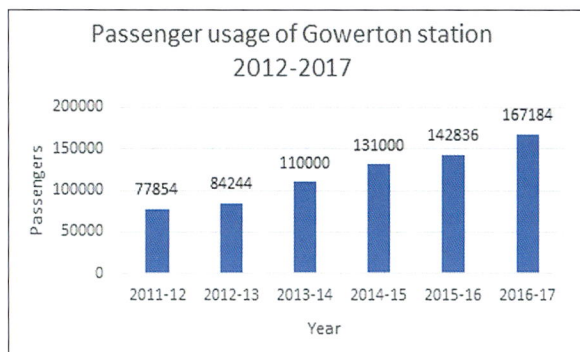

Passenger usage of Gowerton station
*(Philip Adams)*

| Briton Ferry to | Llanelli | Cardiff |
|---|---|---|
| Car | 30 minutes | 50 minutes |
| Train via SWML | 43 minutes | 52 minutes |
| Train via SDL | 20 minutes[27] | |
| | | |

Travel times within the Swansea Bay area: Briton Ferry to Llanelli and Cardiff *(Philip Adams)*

and Cardiff, Swanline services demand a re-think if the two-hourly service between Port Talbot and Swansea is to be improved. An opportunity has been possible since the re-signalling work of 2007. The new turnback facility it made possible at Port Talbot station was intended primarily for turn-backs from the Cardiff direction, but is also capable of use by services from Swansea. It has been proposed that a more useful service could be offered by operating Swanline trains between Swansea and Port Talbot only,[23] or even Port Talbot to Llanelli and Carmarthen using the Swansea District line (SDL).

*Briton Ferry and Baglan*

Briton Ferry is of strategic importance for road traffic in south west Wales because it is the complex crossing-point of the River Neath for road traffic, to and from west Wales and Ireland and to the City of Swansea, by means of its two bridges. These bridges were intended to alleviate road traffic on the former east-west A48 route through Briton Ferry, Neath and Skewen. Each did so, but only temporarily, with the result that increased car ownership and road freight usage has made the old route and the adjacent roads and streets[24] more congested than ever. The congestion and its ill-effects, especially at the ever-lengthening 'peak times' is unpleasant and unnecessary.

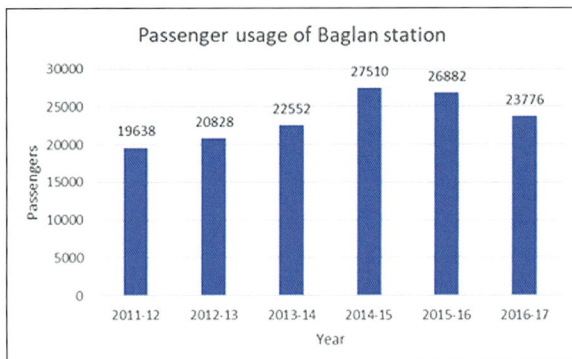

Passenger usage of Baglan station 2012–2017
(Philip Adams)

Passenger entries and exits at Briton Ferry station, 1998–2016[26] (Philip Adams)

Historically, as we have described, Briton Ferry has also been an important railway centre, both for its own industrial needs and because it lay on the east-west route across south Wales. During a thirty-year period of rapid growth of car ownership (1964-1994), Briton Ferry lost its remaining station altogether. Fortunately, much of the railway-owned land around the main routes through the town was retained, enabling a very modest station to be re-instated. Also retained was a tremendous asset, the Swansea District line, the rail equivalent of the M4 motorway through west Glamorgan, both of which afford the by-passing of both Neath and Swansea to reach west Wales faster. West Wales is open to further tourist and business exploitation by greater use of this line.

Briton Ferry and Baglan lie within the County Borough of Neath-Port Talbot. The borough overall saw an increase in rail passengers of 1.1% from 2014 to 2015, but smaller stations such Briton Ferry and Baglan saw increases of 4.25% and 22% respectively. Usage of Briton Ferry station has gradually increased to a figure of 36,900 in 2016/17. Compared with Gowerton's progress, these are still small numbers.

Previous mention was made that, in 1999, the franchisee for the *Swanline* halved the service to two-hourly, citing poor passenger usage and resulting in a further 45% reduction in passenger usage for the next decade. The ORR has stated that data collection methodology has improved since 2004, so how reliable were the figures upon which that decision was made? It is evident that the type of service required for *Swanline* passengers demands a much greater frequency than two-hourly. Had an hourly service been in place after 2003 then the *Swanline* may still have an hourly service and its usage figures shown an even greater increase.

At Briton Ferry and Baglan, unlike Gowerton, the track does not require 'twinning' to improve movements, and the Swansea District line provides an alternative to the south Wales main line for journeys to and from west Wales from Briton Ferry.

The journey-to-work distances are, approximately, twenty miles from Briton Ferry to Llanelli and thirty-five to Cardiff. Journey times by car are thirty and fifty minutes respectively. By train, the journey time to and from Llanelli and Cardiff on direct trains is approximately forty-five and fifty minutes, as shown in the table below. The Llanelli journey time sometimes involves a change at Swansea adding approximately thirty minutes, and the Cardiff journey a change at Neath adding some time, cost and a risk of missing closely-timed connections.

*Cole's proposal*

Professor Cole's report emphasises the use of improved bus services in the area, particularly on four radial roads into Swansea, which themselves require priority lanes to be created for these buses. With this proposal Cole advocates transport interchanges as part of an implied inter-modal transport system. Neither the existence of the Swansea District line, nor Briton Ferry's station, were mentioned as significant in the Cole report, although it does say: 'A suggestion has been made to develop a park and ride on the Swansea District line at Felindre. This is presently not feasible because train frequency is low. It may be feasible for LRT for Swansea in the longer term.' None of this is fundamentally at odds with the two studies which follow. Indeed, Cole's study generally complements the others and some of the specific proposals he quoted were no doubt given as examples for further consideration at later stages in the proposal's implementation cycle.

*RailfutureWales' Proposal: Swansea Light Rapid Transport System*

*Railfuture* is the UK's leading independent organisation campaigning for better rail services for passengers and freight. Its *Wales Development Plan* is a vision of how the rail network can play a more important role in the lives of Welsh people, thereby improving the quality of life for individuals and boosting business and the economy. It is both a longer-term vision and one that contains proposals that can be quickly implemented without great expense. The principles that *Railfuture* advocate for passenger traffic are:

- A service frequency of less than two hours on all routes
- A clock face timetable[28]
- Integration with other transport modes and through ticketing
- A maximum fifteen-minute wait on change of train
- Minimum facilities at stations-covered waiting areas, real-time information, communication to a call centre, staffed interchanges when changing, toilets and refreshments or vending machines available
- On board information regarding connection at forthcoming stops

RailfutureWales[29] specifically refers to the 'Introduction of regular passenger services on the Llanelli/Pontarddulais/Port Talbot goods line', the Swansea District line. The report suggests a new station at Morriston, near junction 45 on the M4.

It also proposes that the Nottingham to Cardiff service via Birmingham should run through to west Wales and that the Heart of Wales line should provide a two-hourly service with extra trains between Ammanford and Swansea. All these provide better connectivity on the conventional rail system.

This report emphasises the development of the conventional rail network within the Swansea Bay area as the core of an inter-modal transport system. It advances the service standards to be achieved by the conventional rail core to make this a success. This includes 'interchanges' to cater for light rail lines *1* and *2*. It implies that adequate bus services should be available at some of the interchanges, but says little about either. The principles underlying the design of the routes for light rail lines *1* and *2* are

Swansea LRT proposals (*RailfutureWales*)

easily justified, although further sites for light rail stations and interchanges 'should be discussed at later project stages'. This report has the merit of looking outside the immediate Swansea Bay area to consider west and mid-Wales conventional rail services into England.

It is implicit in both the Cole and Railfuture-Wales' reports that the Swansea District line can both alleviate some of the present east-west travel problems in the Swansea bay area and encourage wider economic development in west Wales. The (draft) schematic on page 266 shows the conventional rail line by-passing Briton Ferry from the proposed Llandarcy interchange. The *up* Swansea District line actually runs alongside the *Swanline* at Briton Ferry station and joins it a little way beyond. The *down* SDL runs through the station.

The report does not detail the work needed to create either stations or full interchanges at sites on the Swansea District line such as Llandarcy and Morriston. Both require a completely new station whereas Briton Ferry would only need an *up* platform widening. Presumably the report does not use Gowerton as the exemplar to secure improvements in passenger usage because further work is still needed to make Gowerton into a full interchange. Nevertheless, the report is in general agreement with and complements Professor Cole's proposals.

*Barry's Proposal: The Swansea bay Metro System*

Professor Barry of Cardiff University has proposed a scheme which tackles the issue of the *regional periph-erality* of the Swansea Bay region. This means that the region suffers economically because of the time taken to travel to other big centres of population and economic activity within the UK. He makes the point that HS2 will bring all major English cities, save Newcastle, within ninety minutes of London. Unless things change, the journey time from Swansea to London will be twice as much as this, at 180 minutes. The consequence of this poor connectivity is that the opportunities for development and regeneration in the Swansea Bay area will be lost. The economic benefits of a scheme that would cost over £1 billion by 2030 would soon exceed the cost. Some of the supplementary recommendations in his scheme are aspirational and flexible, where the choice of mode would be determined later.

Whilst the schemes presented by Cole and Rail-futureWales are largely limited to considering improvements within the Swansea Bay region, Barry's proposal fits the regional proposals into the national system by considering the Swansea Bay Metro/Swansea Bay City deal along with the Great Western mainline upgrade. He states that two fundamental proposals should form a key part of the regional planning process if the national connectivity benefits are to be achieved: first, the low line speed between Bridgend and Cardiff, which means that the fifty-five km Cardiff to Swansea journey takes fifty-five minutes, requires improvement. The second weakness is the meandering line, between Briton Ferry and Swansea via Neath, which adds to the time taken. He says of this:

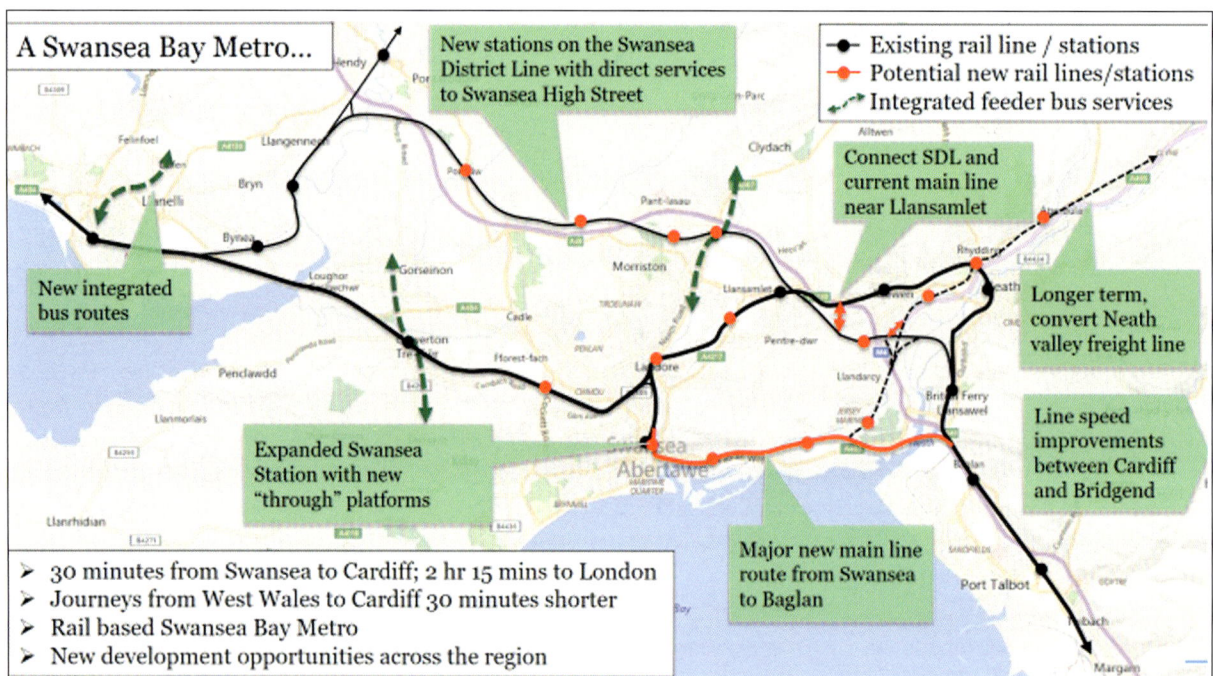

Line improvements for the Swansea Bay Metro *(Barry)*

Let's upgrade and electrify the line from Cardiff to just west of Port Talbot with a focus on more capacity (including the application of moving block signalling) and higher line speeds of up to at least 125 mph. Then, let's build a new section of track that spurs off the current line just west of Port Talbot, heads over the River Neath and approaches Swansea along the coast parallel to Fabian Way. It could then elevate on the approach to and over the River Tawe, to a new station adjacent to the current one near The Strand. This would deliver a more direct route to Swansea about ten kilometres shorter than the current route that meanders via Neath. This could reduce journey times between Cardiff and Swansea (with stops at only Bridgend and Port Talbot) to perhaps thirty minutes. This strategic UK scheme would also allow much of the existing line via Neath and the Swansea District Line to support new stations and more local services.[30]

Further time is then incurred at Swansea High Street for onward journeys to west Wales because it is a terminus, not a through, station. Using the Swansea District line to access west Wales more quickly would address the problem for west Wales passengers, but not for those whose destination is direct to Swansea City centre by train, or direct to Neath. This proposal caused concern in the form of a petition 'to keep Neath on the main line' after the suggestion was made, fearing a 'detrimental effect to the economy and regeneration' of the town.[31]

Barry's scheme to reduce the 'negative abstraction impact of HS2 on south Wales', has merit because he also proposes a connecting scheme within the Swansea Bay region. Here the Metro System's aim is to help grow the economy of the entire Swansea Bay Region by supporting places of present and future employment via a transport network with fast and frequent connected services. This is achievable through four less expensive and more easily achievable projects:

The first is for an integrated system, based on a combination of heavy and light rail and bus.

The second is more do-able, and less expensive: new stations on the Swansea District line (SDL) with direct services to Swansea High Street.

Thirdly, re-connecting the SDL with the current main line at Llansamlet for trains from Swansea in both directions. This 'Lonlas link' was a mile-long connection, in both directions, closed in October 1965 joining the SDL with the Neath-Swansea line between Skewen East junction and Peniel Green tunnel.[32]

Finally, the re-instatement of the Neath Valley freight line and links to the SDL for traffic south between Cardonnel and Danygraig and north from Cardonnel up the Neath valley.[33]

The detrimental effect on Neath's economy looks less threatening, should the third and fourth of the above projects be enabled, for example allowing eastbound passengers from west Wales passengers to favour Neath instead of Swansea.

A more detailed proposal for the Metro system shows seven lines and thirty-one stations. The lines are:

1. Llanelli to Swansea Central via the SDL, Llansamlet and Morfa. This line comprises new and existing tracks.
2. Port Talbot to Llanelli via Neath and SDL. This uses existing lines but requires a reconnection of the SDL with the existing main line at Lonlas Junction, Skewen.
3. Port Talbot to Llanelli via new line across the entrance to the river Neath and Swansea Central.
4. Port Talbot to Swansea Central via Neath and Llansamlet. This already exists.
5. An on-street extension from Swansea Central to Mumbles.
6. A potential extension from Pontarddulais to Ammanford and Heart of Wales Line.
7. A potential inclusion of the existing Neath Valley coal line.

The stations are classified into four groups in *Barry's schematic of the Metro* on page 268:

*Brown oval:* Main stations: at Llanelli, Swansea Central and Port Talbot

*Black dot:* Existing stations at Pontarddulais, Llangennech, Bynea, Gowerton, Llansamlet, Skewen, Neath (referred to as Neath #1) and Baglan.

*Red dot:* Potential new stations: At Pontlliw, M4 *J46*, M4 *J45* park and ride, Llansamlet Interchange, Phoenix Way/Winch Wen, Morfa, Station Road, SA1, Swansea Bay Campus and Briton Ferry. The latter's existing station on the *Swanline* needs either minor platform extension or track re-alignment to serve the up SDL which passes within two or three metres of the up platform.

*Lined red dot:* Expanded network stations: Aberdulais, Neath #2, Neath Abbey, M4J43 at Llandarcy,

265

## A Swansea Bay Metro

*A high quality rapid transit network with fast and frequent services, providing people & employers with mores workplace choices, connecting major developments & public services and enabling place based regeneration to help grow the economy of the entire Swansea Bay Region*

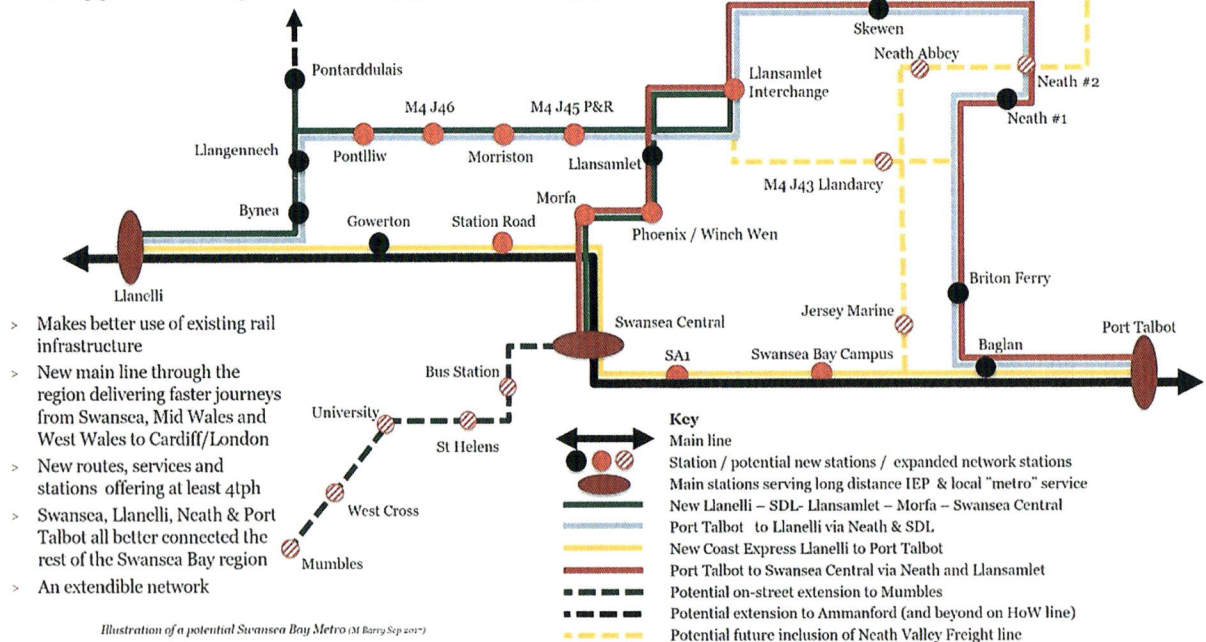

> Makes better use of existing rail infrastructure
> New main line through the region delivering faster journeys from Swansea, Mid Wales and West Wales to Cardiff/London
> New routes, services and stations offering at least 4tph
> Swansea, Llanelli, Neath & Port Talbot all better connected the rest of the Swansea Bay region
> An extendible network

*Illustration of a potential Swansea Bay Metro (M Barry Sep 2017)*

**Key**
Main line
Station / potential new stations / expanded network stations
Main stations serving long distance IEP & local "metro" service
New Llanelli – SDL- Llansamlet – Morfa – Swansea Central
Port Talbot to Llanelli via Neath & SDL
New Coast Express Llanelli to Port Talbot
Port Talbot to Swansea Central via Neath and Llansamlet
Potential on-street extension to Mumbles
Potential extension to Ammanford (and beyond on HoW line)
Potential future inclusion of Neath Valley Freight line

Detailed schematic of metro showing proposed new stations *(Barry)*

Jersey Marine, Swansea bus station, St Helens, University, West Cross, Mumbles.

The potential new stations and expanded network stations (lined red dots) are in three geographic groups:

Barry does not say exactly where the 'new section of track that spurs off the current line just west of Port Talbot' would be built in the 'aspirational' plan. Would it be necessary anyway, with the Swansea District line doing exactly that at Cwrt Sart's flying loop in Briton Ferry? This line splits near Llandarcy to give access both to west Wales and south to Swansea Docks. The tricky and expensive engineering work will be to extend the line from the vicinity of Fabian Way to High Street station. The likely less expensive link between the SDL and existing line at Skewen would enable access to and from Swansea Central without a new rail bridge at the mouth of the River Neath. The downside of using this alternative would be the loss of Swansea Central as a through station.[34]

Briton Ferry's station could, with little modification, again be used by trains on both the *Swanline*, to Neath and Swansea and the *Swansea District* line towards Llanelli and west Wales. This might be the basis for development as a full interchange using the adjacent under-used rail yard for additional operations. Briton Ferry yard could serve as a train park for the Swansea Bay Metro, in similar fashion to

those planned for Rhymney and Treherbert for the Cardiff region metro.

*The Barry's schematic of Line improvements for the Swansea bay metro*[35] on page 270 shows a plan for a 'new coast express line' from Llanelli to Port Talbot. As suggested above, this may not be crucial because the existing and under-used Swansea District line from Briton Ferry, on to Swansea via Jersey Marine, could be used with the main cost involved being the creation of an interchange at Jersey Marine. It would also be used for faster access to Llanelli and to six new or existing stations between Llandarcy and Llanelli.

A summary of Professor Barry's proposal for a Swansea Bay Metro was posted on BBC Wales News website and responses were invited from the public. Responses suggested that people were seeking easy movement between different modes of travel, especially for those who find difficulty in walking any distance, or who are disabled. Many wished to see transport interchange schemes for the area but doubted they would happen on grounds of cost.

*Furnace Old Boy* described the problem:

Has the good professor, or Lee Walters AM, ever caught a train from Llanelli? There is very little parking (so people use Gowerton), no connecting bus service to

| Group One | Group Two | Group Three |
|---|---|---|
| M4 at junction 46 | M4 at Junction 43 (Llandarcy) | Station Road |
| M4 at junction 45 (with park and ride) | Jersey Marine | Morfa |
| Pontlliw | Neath Abbey | Winch Wen |
| Morriston | | |

Potential new stations on expanded network

View northwards showing the *up* Swansea District Line within a few metres of Briton Ferry station platform
*(Philip Adams)*

View southwards showing the *up* Swansea District Line (left) running alongside Briton Ferry station *(Philip Adams)*

the town centre, and if you are disabled, you have to leave the station, cross a level crossing and enter via the other side to change platforms.

Lee Waters, Llanelli AM, articulated the goal: I think what we all want to see is a public transport system that turns up and goes. People will use buses and trains if they're easy and convenient to use.

## Conclusion

When one examines the picture in more detail for Wales, some of the DfT's statements in the 2017 white paper, and subsequently, become less and less convincing as one moves westwards and northwards into the Welsh rail network. For example, Leanne Wood, Plaid Cymru Leader, stated that the party were considering the issue of a rail bond to finance electrification to Swansea – a model which could also be used to create a metro public transport network for the Swansea Bay and Western Valleys Region as well as the reinstatement of the Carmarthen to Aberystwyth line.[36] Nevertheless, the progressive policies shown by the Welsh Government for the Cardiff Capital Region Metro, itself a vindication of devolution, must now act as a template for west and north Wales, perhaps continuing onwards from the Swansea Bay area.

This process of de-industrialisation of large parts of the Swansea Bay region has included the shrinkage of its extensive rail network. As a result, the predominant remnant of the area's once complex railway system is the main west–east south Wales line. The remaining lines, however, may yet serve further important purposes such as the reduction of road congestion from the east of Port Talbot to the west of Pontarddulais and to permit commuters from settlements within the area to be better conveyed within, and in-and-out of, these often too-congested communities. These two factors will assist regeneration.

This cannot be achieved solely by using the main west-east south Wales line to revitalise and extend the Swanline services, an opportunity which has been much impeded by the decision not to extend electrification from Cardiff to Swansea. It can be achieved by a change in transport philosophy. The change required is to use the south Wales main line (conventional rail) route as it is now, or in a developed form, as the heart of an integrated transport network for the Swansea Bay region. Such an integrated transport network (or *inter-modal public transport system*) requires as its core element an inter-

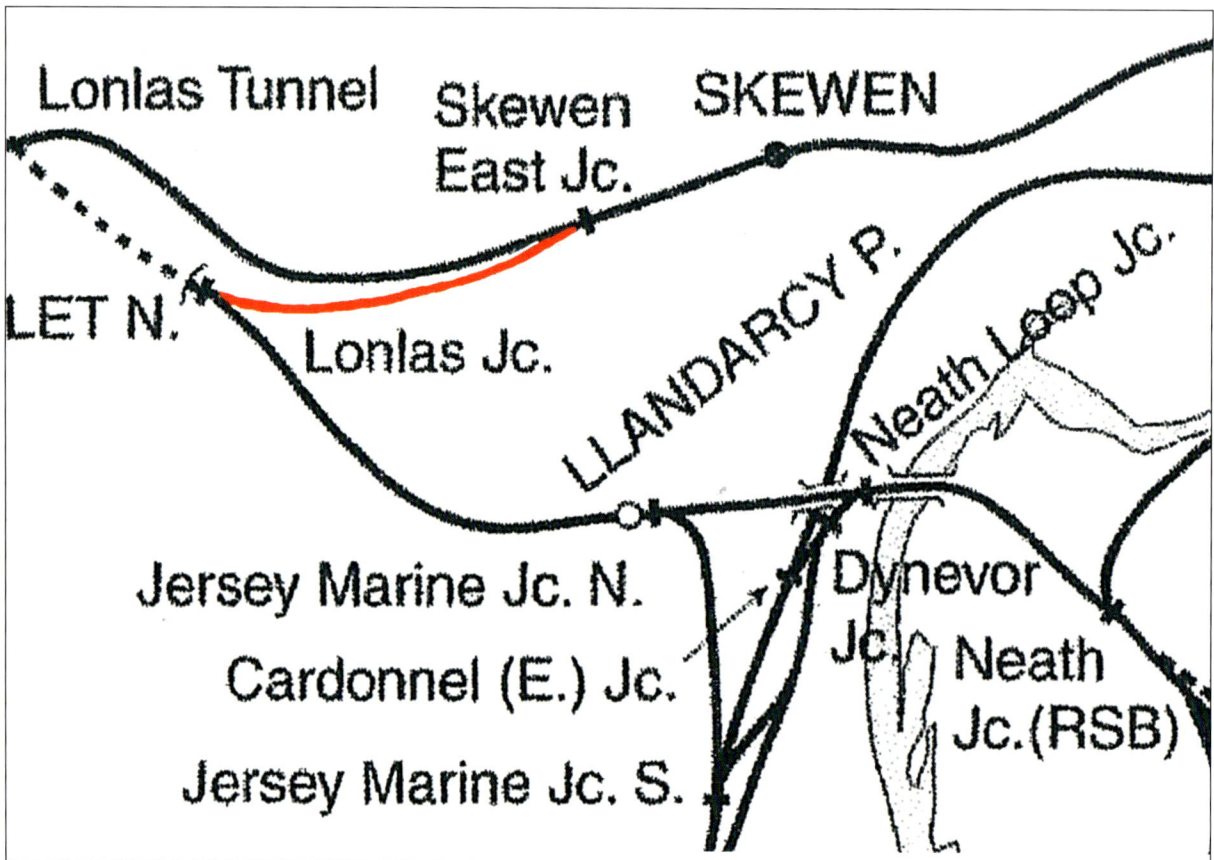

Proposed reinstatement of Lonlas link between Swansea District Line and current South Wales main line  *(Red Dragon)*

change scheme which enables easy movement between heavy rail, light rail and bus modes of travel, especially for those who find difficulty in walking any distance or who are disabled.

The principles for Swansea Bay Region have already been laid out in the plans for the Cardiff Capital Region Metro and in the three studies examined in this Chapter. Each study contains slightly varying suggestions for the siting of new, and improvement of existing, stations into proper interchanges but these variations could be resolved beneficially should approval for a Swansea Bay inter-modal public transport system be arrived at. These studies provide a convincing case for the need to act.

This action calls for: integration of transport modes, through ticketing within and between modes, improved passenger information and a minimum standard of facilities and frequency of transport services at interchanges, following the principles advocated in Appendix Four. It has often been done elsewhere, so why not here? It is time to stop treating our infrastructure assets with contempt and disregarding their future value for us all.

## Epilogue

### Fifty years later: Dai and Llew at the Travellers Rest, Pontnant, a village near Swansea

*Llew:* We were delighted when we heard the news last week about your firm's relocation to Wales, Dai, but we did not expect to be seeing you so soon. We in the village all think it was a brave, but wise move.

*Dai:* Well, this is just a preliminary goodwill visit really, Llew. Our new site is not quite ready but the decision to move from the South-east was an easy one for the Board. It makes more and more sense to set up all our future operations here. We do so much research at our Bay Innovation Centre at SA1 that the decision to move was obvious – and we have found that the people here have the skills and aptitude for our type of work. The transport network here now is so good that it was a bit of a 'no brainer' to move. We didn't know photovoltaic from opto-electronic - but look at us now!

*Llew:* Dai, this one's on me because you were right all along. I was always sceptical when you said that the way we generate energy and transport people and goods would have to change drastically; and that it would be information technology, education and modernised transport that would do it. It has become so evident I must now say that you were dead right, but for along time we were left in the back woods here.

*Dai:* Indeed Llew, you've just got to look across the road at the school roof to see how things started to change.

*Llew:* Yes, Dai, sponsoring the community co-operative to get photovoltaic panels put on the roof of the village school was forward-thinking, but hardly original. Your point is that so few things here are fossil-fuelled now, from that small start. We first attempted to become a sustainable energy village over fifty years ago, even before the government passed the death sentence on new hybrid and diesel cars. It all worked somehow, but you've got to admit that even I thought the decision not to electrify the trains through to Swansea and beyond was a cardinal mistake.

*Dai:* Indeed, but remember, Llew, a half century before that, most of the energy in the area came not from the sky but from the ground in the form of oil or coal. People were naturally saddened when the coal mines and steam trains went because of the loss of jobs in the pits and on the railway, not to mention the loss of community spirit. Not everyone can work in the village these days of course – some travel to work elsewhere in the hospitals, the university and even at the tidal lagoon.

*Llew:* Absolutely Dai, so, how did you get down here from London?

*Dai:* It's easier to explain my trip back Llew: I'll book a walk-on through ticket, with seats allocated for the whole of the journey using my contactless card. The autonomous navette comes at the time I say to take me to the tram stop at Pontnant. It is very reliable and there is no problem at the interchange at Ponty because the connecting services are so frequent and punctual. By taking the train from Ponty Parkway it's much easier because you do not have to worry about parking in Swansea. Since they integrated the buses, trams and trains into a complete transport system around Swansea Bay it's been marvellous. I can get from Paddington to Cardiff in two hours and to Swansea just half an hour later since they electrified and improved rail line all the way to Swansea.

*Dai:* But has the effect of all this been on the village that positive then, Llew?

*Llew:* Well, as a resident, it seems to me that the village is less noisy now but more prosperous; it's free of parked vehicles and congested traffic and children are walking to and from school again. The school run is a thing of the past and the kids are a lot fitter. Walking, and not just to school, became cool after the whole county signed up to *20's Plenty*. You know yourself that childhood obesity was becoming such a big problem that people began to realise how important active travel was; that's what we call it in Wales, you know? People have slowly realised that it's better if they can, to walk, cycle or to use our public transport systems. They are cheap and efficient now, so any private car ownership is the exception rather than the rule these days—and most are electric now.

*Dai:* I agree. We were getting into a crazy situation then: it took us a bit too long to learn that the damage being done to coal miners' health in the pits a hundred years ago was being done again to our children – and right at the school gates. This time it was the pollution from those bloody awful Chelsea tractors that we all loved so much!

*Llew:* So, what do you think, Dai?

*Dai:* When you look back it is obvious the direction in which things were moving – the wrong direction, particularly here. The country had said we'd reduce greenhouse gas emissions by half by 2050. Then, just after we got the car manufacturers telling lies about diesel emissions, we found ourselves introducing hybrid trains west of Cardiff. At the time the government were announcing a ban on future production of diesel and hybrid cars from 2040. How crazy! The policies were contradictory, and objectives were conflicting, so time was running out. We had enough warnings with the summer temperatures. It was only the younger generations, and their determination to change things for the better, that got us out of deep, deep, trouble.

People around here are now almost entirely green. From solar panels at first, the villagers have installed domestic electrical energy storage systems, to take less from the grid and even to supply it at peak times, and they think things like the electric car club and navette bus are the best things since sliced bread.

*Dai:* And on that note, it's my turn to get you a pint, Llew, to celebrate what a progressive move it has been to bring Virtual Energy to west Wales, rather than to lie down on the tracks of history!

**Notes for Chapter Fourteen**

1.  The 'Swansea Bay City Region Board'
2.  Welsh Government study: Cole: 'Swansea public transport hub' (March 2016)
3.  The Railways Act 2005 transferred most of the functions of the Strategic Rail Authority to the Secretary of State for Transport and to make the National Assembly for Wales joint signatory with the Secretary of State to the Wales and Borders franchise for train operating services in Wales.
4.  The EU (Notification of Withdrawal) Act 2017 and the EU Withdrawal Act 2018 provides for repealing the 1972 European Community Act and for Parliamentary approval of the withdrawal agreement being negotiated between HM Government and the European Union.
5.  Institute for Government, March 2017: *Legislating Brexit: The Great Reform Bill and the wider legislative challenge*
6.  Sir Peter Hendy's report to the Secretary of State for Transport on re-planning of Network Rail's investment programme (2015)
7.  DfT Press Release from Chris Grayling, Secretary of State for Transport, 20 July 2017
8.  *Wales online*
9.  Electro-diesel locomotives provide continuous journeys along routes that are only partly electrified without a change of locomotive, extensive running of *diesel under the wires* (using a diesel locomotive where electrified lines are available) or where diesel-only engines are banned. They may be designed or adapted mainly for electric use, mainly for diesel use, or to work well as either electric or diesel.
10. Network Rail Upgrade Plan – Wales 2017/2018
11. Fourth Report of Session 2017–19, 19 June 2018
12. International Union of Railways/CER (2015): *Rail Transport and the Environment, Facts and Figures*
13. Road 70.3%; navigation 15.5% and aviation 5.7%
14. September 2017
15. Or 'conventional' rail
16. The same reasoning applies to the proposed Swansea system
17. 'Connecting people: a strategic vision for rail'. Department for Transport, November 2017
18. The 'Swanline'
19. Campaign for Better Transport: *Buses in Crisis; A report on bus funding across England and Wales 2010–2018*
20. TrawsCymru is the network of medium and long distance express bus routes in Wales, sponsored by the Welsh Government.
21. Passenger figures for the period between 1994 and 1997 are not available.
22. ORR statistic: Increase from 27.6 million passenger journeys (2010–11) to 32.3 (2016–17) for ATW and from 31,748 to 36,872 at Briton Ferry
23. RailfutureWales
24. Those adjacent to the former A48, now the A474
25. 'Rail station usage Wales: Swanline entries and exits': Welsh Government analysis of ORR statistics
26. Sources: ORR and Welsh Government analysis of ORR statistics. No data available for 2003/4.
27. Estimated non-stop timing
28. Where a public transport service is run at consistent intervals i.e. departures take place at the same time or times during the day.
29. On track for the 21st Century: A development plan for the railways of Wales and the Borders' RailfutureCymru/Wales (2016). *Wales Development Plan for Improved Services* (3rd Edition)
30. *Wales Online*, accessed August 2017
31. *Wales Online*, accessed 2 May 2018
32. This is comparable with the 2018 reinstatement of Halton Curve, a line one mile 1,231 yards long which joins the North Wales Coast line to the West Coast main line enabling direct passage between Chester and Liverpool
33. The location of the Centre of Rail Excellence at Onllwyn will see the coal freight line used for access to the rolling stock maintenance and development centre.
34. *http://www.bbc.co.uk/news/uk-wales-south-west-wales-41323109*
35. Draft 3.0 of 6 August 2017
36. BBC Wales 21 October 2017

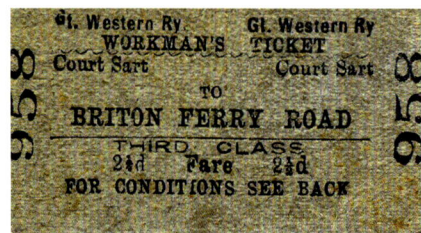

Tom Thomas's GWR workman's ticket from Cwrt Sart to Briton Ferry Road. Tom, of Jac-y-du Road, was a shift rollerman at Elba Steelworks in Jersey Marine. The advantage of the railway was that it enabled him to cross the river to work all his shifts because the river ferry did not operate at night time.

Appendix One

# Abbreviations and definitions

## Abbreviations

| | |
|---|---|
| ASLEF | Associated Society of Locomotive Engineers and Fireman |
| ASRS | Associated Society of Railway Servants |
| ATC | Automatic train control |
| ATOC | Association of Train Operating Companies |
| ATW | Arriva Trains Wales |
| BR | British Railways |
| DfT | Department for Transport |
| GWR | Great Western Railway – see below |
| HST | High speed train |
| ILP | Independent Labour Party |
| LMS | London, Midland and Scottish Railway |
| LNER | London and North-eastern Railway |
| NUR | National Union of Railwaymen |
| ORR | Office of Road and Rail Regulation |
| RDG | Rail Delivery Group |
| RSBR | Rhondda and Swansea Bay Railway |
| PTR | Port Talbot Railway |
| RMT | National Union of Rail, Maritime and Transport Workers |
| SDL | Swansea District Line |
| SR | Southern Railway |
| SRA | Strategic Rail Authority |
| SWR | South Wales Railway |
| SWMR | South Wales Mineral Railway |
| TGV | France's high speed train (**T**rain à **G**rande **V**itesse) |
| TOC | Train operating company |
| TUC | Trades Union Congress |
| VNR | Vale of Neath Railway |

## Definitions and railway lexicon

**ATOC**
See *Rail Delivery Group* and *National Rail*, below.

**Automatic train control**
Is a general description of safety systems to control train speeds. Many different safety systems have used this generic term. The first, used from 1906 by the GWR, was actually an *automatic warning system* whereby the driver still had to control the train. In the 1970 BR introduced a variant called AWS (*automatic warning system*). ATS (*automatic train stop*) was a development in which the train was rigidly stopped. Today, true ATC is replacing ATS; for example, on the Japanese Shinkansen, ATC gives a gradual deceleration. It has many subsequent variants.

**British Railways (BR)**
British Railways existed from 1948 until 1997. It became a statutory corporation in 1962 under the British Railways Board. Its double arrow logo is still used as a generic symbol to denote rail stations and is printed on tickets as part of the Rail Delivery Group's *National Rail* brand.

**Common employment**
A legal concept which was used a defence by employers, and lasted until 1948, that the risk of being injured by the actions of their co-workers were accepted by the 'servants' of the rail company involved, with whom they were in 'common employment.'

**Control period**
A planning and budgetary period for Network Rail's projects

**Crossrail 1**
The high-frequency east-west commuter and passenger service passing through London, Bucks, Berks and Essex to relieve pressure on existing east-west

underground lines. Also known as the *Elizabeth Line*, owned by Transport for London and a franchised operation from 2017.

## Crossrail 2
The north-south commuter/suburban line from Hertfordshire to Surrey via Victoria and King's Cross. This is recommended as a priority project by the National Infrastructure Commission. It will be the fourth major rail project in London since 2000, after the east London line, Thames link and Crossrail 1.

## Franchising
This involves companies making bids for the right to run a train service: e.g Virgin Trains won the right to run cross country and West Coast Intercity services for a period of seven years.

## Gauge
Track gauge is the spacing of the rails on a railway track and is measured between the inner faces of the load-bearing rails. The standard gauge is 4 feet $8\frac{1}{2}$ inches (1,435 mm). Brunel's wide gauge was 7 feet $0\frac{1}{4}$ inch (2140 mm).

## Grouping
The Railways Act of 1921, also known as the 'Grouping Act' was for the purpose of reorganising over 100 pre-war competitive rail companies into a less wasteful, but still private, structure.

## GWR / GWR
GWR was the acronym for the Great Western Railway which existed from 1833–1948.
GWR is a train operating company belonging to First Group whose franchise started in September 2015 and is due to run until April 2020. It was previously called GW Trains and First Great Western.

## Heart of Wales Line
The line from Llanelli to Craven Arms and Shrewsbury. Once called the 'Central Wales line' from Swansea to Shrewsbury via Gowerton and Pontarddulais.

## HS1
High speed 1: the line connecting London to the Channel Tunnel since 2003

## HS2
High speed 2: the Y-configured line proposed in 2009 connecting London, Birmingham, east Midlands, Leeds and Manchester. Phase 1 London to the west Midlands; phase 2a west Midlands to Crewe; phase 2b Crewe to Manchester and west Midlands to Leeds

## High speed train
Also known as an Intercity 125, a diesel-powered passenger train with a service speed of 125 mph (201 kph) launched in 1976 and first used on the western region main lines of British Rail

## Loop
A railway branch line which leaves the main line and rejoins it after a short distance

## Marches Line
The line from Newport to Shrewsbury and Crewe. Sometimes known as the 'North and West' line.

## National Rail
The trading name of the Rail Delivery Group. The group are not an organisation but a brand formed by the train operating companies to promote passenger rail services in Britain.

## Network Rail
The owner and infrastructure manager of most of the rail network in Britain. It is an 'arm's length' public body of the Department of Transport which re-invests its income in railways.

## Pannier tank
A small steam locomotive with an overhanging rectilinear water tank along each side of the boiler

## Passenger
A person on the railway infrastructure who intends to travel, is in the process of travelling, or has travelled. This is regardless of whether they have a valid ticket. This does not include travellers who trespass or who commit, or who attempt to commit suicide. People who are injured in this way are classed as members of the public.

## Prairie tank
A steam locomotive with a 2-6-2 wheel configuration, based on the Whyte notation for classifying steam locomotives

## Rail Delivery Group
Formerly the Association of Train Operating Companies(ATOC). This body represents twenty- three train operating companies and delivers these services:

- National Rail Enquiries
- Manages rail discount cards
- Licenses rail travel agents
- Produces the definitive National Routing Guide which defines the validity of tickets.

### Regulated fares

'Around forty percent of rail fares are "regulated", including season and commuter tickets on most commuter journeys, some off-peak return tickets on long-distance journeys and anytime tickets around major cities. The government uses July RPI measure of inflation to determine the increase in price of these fares.' (National Rail).

### Saddle tank

A small steam locomotive with a water tank that fits over the top and sides of the boiler like a saddle

### Shinkansen

Japanese for 'new trunk line', the network of high-speed lines operated by Japan Railways group of companies. Known colloquially in English as 'bullet trains' because of their speed and shape.

### Strategic Rail Authority

This was a non-departmental public body whose main function was to award and ensure compliance with rail franchises in return for public subsidies. It operated from 2001-2006 until its functions were transferred to the DfT Rail Group.

### Swansea District Line (SDL)

A line created by the GWR in 1912 to speed up services for Fishguard boat passengers by avoiding the bottlenecks and steep gradients around Swansea. The line was subsequently used for freight traffic from west Wales, but is currently under-used.

### The 'six foot'

The distance between the second and third rails on a double track ie the clearance afforded to passing trains.

Appendix Two

# Timeline

| Date | National events | Local events |
|------|-----------------|--------------|
| 1850 | | SWR arrives (broad gauge) |
| 1853 | | SWMR authorised (standard gauge) |
| 1861 | | Briton Ferry Dock opened |
| 1863 | | GWR absorbs VNR and SWR |
| 1872 | | Standard gauge replaces broad gauge in south Wales |
| 1876 | | Cwrt Sart engine shed opened |
| 1894 | | District Superintendent's Office opened at Cwrt Sart shed |
| 1895 | | RSBR opened at Briton Ferry on 14 March |
| 1900–1901 | Taff Vale v ASRS case | |
| 1906 | Trade Disputes Act | GWR took over managing RSBR |
| 1907 | | Port Talbot Railway started operating |
| 1910 | | Briton Ferry Incline closed to traffic |
| 1911 | First national rail strike | |
| 1912 | | Swansea District line opened |
| 1919 | Second national rail strike | |
| 1923 | Rail grouping into GWR | |
| 1933 | | RSBR passenger services put onto GWR lines Closure of Jersey Marine and Cwrt Sart stations |
| 1935 | | Briton Ferry East and Cwrt Sart stations closed |
| 1936 | | Rationalisation of track layout at Briton Ferry. Station opens at Rockingham Terrace |
| 1937 | Railways Act | Briton Ferry (West) station closes |
| 1948 | Rail nationalisation British Railways formed | |
| 1955 | British Rail modernisation plan announced | |
| 1962 | | RSBR closed to passengers. Record turnaround of 100 steam locomotives in 24 hours at Cwrt Sart shed |
| 1963–1965 | Beeching Reports | |
| 1964 | | Briton Ferry station at Rockingham closes |
| 1965 | | Steam traction eliminated throughout South Wales- all depots closed to steam including Cwrt Sart |
| 1968 | Transport Act | |

| | | |
|---|---|---|
| 1969 | | Cwrt Sart engine shed demolished |
| 1976 | | First High Speed Train through Briton Ferry |
| 1982 | Serpell Report | |
| 1993 | Railways Act (Privatisation) | |
| 1994 | Railtrack launched on stock exchange | Swanline stations open at Briton Ferry Baglan etc |
| 1997 | Southall crash | |
| 1999 | Ladbroke Grove disaster | |
| 2001 | | Wales and Borders franchise created from Valley Lines and Wales and West franchises. Operated by National Express |
| 2002 | Railtrack abolished | |
| 2002 | Network Rail formed | |
| 2003 | | Wales and Borders franchise awarded to Arriva Trains (Wales)/Deutsche Bahn |
| 2005 | Railways Act: abolition of Strategic Rail Authority | |
| 2006 | | Transport (Wales) Act |
| 2009 | Directly Operated Railways nationalised | |
| 2011 | McNulty Report | |
| 2013 | | Active Travel (Wales) Act |
| 2015 | Hendy report (Network Rail) | |
| 2015 | Inter-city railways de-nationalised | |
| 2016 | | Professor Cole's study: Swansea Light Rapid Transport System |
| 2017 | Hybrid test train runs | Hybrid test train runs. Cardiff to Swansea electrification cancelled |
| 2017 | | Professor Barry's study: Swansea Bay Metro system |
| 2018 | | Hybrid/bi-modal trains introduced on some Swansea to Paddington services. Wales and Borders franchise awarded to Keolis Amey under Transport for Wales identity |

# Ownership of the railways in the UK

## April 2018

| Company/franchisee | Holder of franchise | Whole/part owned |
|---|---|---|
| Arriva Trains (Wales) | Deutsche Bahn, then KeolisAmey from 14 October 2018 for fifteen years | W |
| C2c rail | Trenitalia | W |
| Caledonian Sleeper | Serco | W |
| Chiltern | Deutsche Bahn | W |
| Cross Country | Deutsche Bahn | W |
| Crossrail | MTR | W |
| East Midlands | Stagecoach | W |
| Eurostar | SNCF (55%), CDPQ (30%), Hermes 10%, NMBS (5%) | P |
| Gatwick Express | Keolis | P |
| Grand Central | Deutsche Bahn | W |
| Greater Anglia | Abellio and Mitsui/East Japan Rail Co | P |
| Great Northern | Keolis and Govia | P |
| Great Western | First Group | W |
| Heathrow Express | First Group | W |
| Hull Trains | First Group | W |
| Island Rail | First Group | W |
| London North Western | Abellio and Mitsui/East Japan Rail Co | P |
| London Overground | Deutsche Bahn for TFL | W |
| Merseyrail | Abellio and Serco | P |
| Northern | Deutsche Bahn | W |
| Northern Ireland Railways | Translink part of NI Government | W |
| Scotrail | Abellio | W |
| South Eastern | Keolis and Govia | P |
| Southern | Keolis and Govia | P |
| South Western | First Group and MTR | P |
| Stobart Rail | Stobart Group | W |
| Thameslink | Keolis and Govia | P |
| Transport for London | MTR | W |
| Transpennine Express | First Group | W |
| Virgin Trains | Virgin and Stagecoach | P |
| Virgin Trains East Coast | Virgin and Stagecoach | P |
| West Midlands Rail | Abellio and Mitsui/East Japan Rail Co | P |

### Owning groups

| Group | Ownership |
|---|---|
| Abellio | Nederlands Spoorwegen |
| Amey | Grupo Ferrovial SA |
| Keolis | France's SNCF (70%) and Quebec Investment Fund (30%) |
| Govia | Go Ahead (65%) Keolis (35%) |
| MTR Corporation | Hong Kong Mass Transit Railway |
| Serco | Serco Group PLC |

*(Philip Adams, 2018)*

# Transport interchanges

*Whether you live in a city or a small town, and whether you drive a car, take the bus or ride a train, at some point in the day, everyone is a pedestrian.*

(Anthony Foxx, US Transportation Secretary)

The core element of an interchange scheme focuses on easy movement between different modes of travel, especially for those who find difficulty in walking any distance or who are disabled. The key elements of interchange scheme are usually promoted by expert transport protagonists by easily-memorable mnemonics. We shall now consider two of these: the 'Five Cs' and the 'Four I's'. They both represent the same idea of an *inter-modal public transport system*.

Railfuture Wales' proposals for the future of Welsh Railways draws on these concepts.[1] So, too, does the work of Professor Cole's study of journeys in the greater urban area of Swansea. In general terms, the organisation has called for integration of transport modes, through ticketing within and between modes, improved passenger information and a minimum standard of facilities at interchanges.

**The 'Five Cs'**

This approach ensures that access to and within the interchange itself is based on five core elements:

> *Connectivity* – to ensure that all the walking routes at the interchange are continuous and afford easy walking (and wheelchair use between the modes).
> *Conviviality* – the interchange design ensures that people can change between modes of travel.
> *Comfort* – allow easy access which is safe and where people feel comfortable when using the facilities.
> *Convenience* – that serves the purpose of being in close proximity to the activity required.
> *Conspicuity* – that the signage and interpretation is clear.

**Information + Interchange + Investment + Imagination = Integration**

This is a related, but somewhat broader, concept for integrated passenger transport. It is based on four elements:

*Information*
Comprehensive, clear and easy to find at main terminals or interchanges and en-route via mobile phones with real time as the ultimate form. Clear and conspicuous directional signage at bus or rail stations also applies because not all travellers have online sources; hard copy timetables are still in high demand.

*Interchange*
The ease of interchange between car /cycle /walking and public transport must be so that it is physically seamless. To be truly so, the convenience of interchangeable and through tickets between different modes also applies.

*Investment*
Minimised journey times to be achieved through investment in more capacity, bus priority schemes, more frequent and faster new trains and buses, investment in stations and bus waiting facilities to improve the passenger comfort and enhance Wales as a tourist friendly destination.

*Imagination*
Imagination – see what the traveller expects; planners try out their ideas and test them to perfection - themselves.

---

1. *On track for the 21st Century: A development plan for the railways of Wales and the Borders:* RailfutureCymru/Wales (2016).

Appendix Five

# Rail workers in Briton Ferry in 1911

| Name | Age | Address | Job | Company |
|---|---|---|---|---|
| Henry Sainsbury | 49 | 36 Lowther Street | Shunter | Tinplate works |
| Ernest William Harrison* | 27 | 43 Lowther Street | Signalman | RSBR |
| Evan Taylor Engineering | 59 | 51 Lowther Street | Moulder | Glyncorrwg |
| David John Rees | 17 | 49 Lowther Street | Loco driver | Steelworks |
| David Harris or Henry | 23 | 49 Lowther Street | Loco driver | Steelworks |
| William John Donovan | 29 | 56 Lowther Street | Loco driver | Tinplate works |
| James Jones | 20 | 11 Sand Lane | Striker/platelayer | GWR |
| Thomas William Martin | 31 | 22 Hunter Street | Loco driver | BF Steelworks |
| William Parry | 52 | 6 Hunter Street | Loco driver | Tin works |
| William Henry Jay* | 41 | 3 Hunter Street | Shunter | RSBR |
| Patrick Noonan* (Boarder) | 22 | 3 Hunter Street | Shunter | GWR |
| Rupert Victor Rapson (Boarder) | 22 | 3 Hunter Street | Railway policeman | GWR |
| John Gilbert* | 49 | 8 Thomas Street | Loco Driver | |
| Daniel Harris* | 48 | 9 Thomas Street | Chief Platelayer | GWR |
| Harry Jones (Boarder) | 23 | 9 Thomas Street | Clerk | GWR |
| Frank Howell (Boarder) | 17 | 9 Thomas Street | Clerk | GWR |
| Willie Evans* | 20 | 18 Thomas Street | Loco driver | |
| Richard Arthur Austin Myerscough | 31 | 27 Thomas Street | Engine fitter | Steelworks |
| David P Hill | 43 | 30 Thomas Street | Loco driver | Tinplate works |
| Edward Francis Gaine* | 39 | 11 Ritson Street | Signalman | RSBR |
| William Morgan | 39 | 51 Ritson Street | Loco driver | Tinplate works |
| Thomas Maddocks | 63 | 15 Railway Terrace | Signalman | GWR |
| James C Mallett | 41 | 33 Railway Terrace | Signalman | GWR |
| William Rowe | 63 | GWR Coffee Tavern, Charles Street | Temperance hotel keeper | GWR |
| Emily Rowe | 53 | GWR Coffee Tavern, Charles Street | Temperance hotel keeper | GWR |
| William Jones (Boarder) | 29 | 16 Charles Street | Signalman | |
| George Henry Lewis | 34 | 18 Charles Street | Carman (contractor) | |
| William Price | 30 | 24 Charles Street | Dock gateman | GWR |
| Charles Frederick Chapman | 32 | 31 Neath Road | Wagon lifter | |
| Thomas Sidney Attwood | 23 | 85 Neath Road | Shunter | GWR |
| Pryce Lewis | 19 | 85 Neath Road | Shunter | |
| Edward George Brooks | 21 | 85 Neath Road | Shunter | |

| | | | | |
|---|---|---|---|---|
| Fred Moss | 66 | 175 Neath Road | Wagon repairer | |
| David John | 62 | 181 Neath Road | Platelayer | Ironworks |
| David Gwilym John* | 19 | 181 Neath Road | Porter | GWR |
| Gwyn Lewis Ray | 29 | 233 Neath Road | Traffic manager | Steelworks |
| William G Williams* | 60 | White Gates Lodge, Neath Road | Lampman | |
| William Meyrick Davies* | 24 | 48 Church Street | Shunter | GWR |
| Owen J Emmanuel* | 23 | 19 Regent Street West | Weigher | GWR |
| Sidney Burgess | 19 | 23 Regent Street West | Loco driver | Ironworks |
| Leyshon Down* | 50 | 27 Regent Street West | Hydraulic engineman | GWR Dock |
| John Reed* | 37 | 62 Regent Street West | Dock gate man | GWR Dock |
| Edward Leavers Down* | 46 | 10 Regent Street East | Hydraulic engineman | GWR Dock |
| Charles Anthony | 50 | 6 Regent Street East | Wagon repairer | |
| Ellis Roberts | 36 | 30 Regent Street East | Loco driver | PTR |
| Thomas Davies* | 25 | 34 Regent Street East | Shunter | GWR |
| William Saer | 21 | 34 Regent Street East | Shunter | GWR |
| William R Langley* | 27 | 34 Regent Street East | Shunter | GWR |
| William Parr | 35 | 11 Regent Street East | Capstan man | GWR Dock |
| John Benjamin Williams | 47 | 15 Regent Street East | Loco driver | Steelworks |
| Thomas Rees | 21 | 47 Regent Street East | Labourer | GWR |
| Martin Bowen | 30 | 90 New Hunter Street | Rail carpenter | GWR |
| William Towell | 40 | 81 New Hunter Street | Engine fitter | |
| Ben Morris* [1] | 31 | 72 New Hunter Street | Signalman | GWR |
| Edward Hamer | 32 | 66 New Hunter Street | Signalman | GWR |
| Gladstone Thomas* | 15 | 64 New Hunter Street | Engine cleaner | Steelworks |
| William Pollard | 42 | 62 New Hunter Street | Engine fitter | Steelworks |
| Morgan Morgan | 49 | 34 New Hunter Street | Loco driver | Steelworks |
| John Griffiths | 60 | 40 New Hunter Street | | |
| Thomas Davies | 34 | 1 Park Terrace | Shunter | Ironworks |
| Francis Edward Adams | 56 | 1 Park Terrace | Wagon examiner | GWR |
| William Thomas Bowen | 30 | Hazeldene, Park Street | Clerk | RSBR |
| TJ Evans | 21 | 41 Victoria Terrace | Rail Traffic checker | |
| Daniel Jenkins Engineering | 58 | 3 Barn Cottages Shelone Road | Workshop foreman | Glyncorrwg |
| William Thomas | 45 | 8 Barn Cottages | Dock gateman | GWR |
| William Davies* | 29 | 32 Shelone Road | Shunter | GWR |
| Thomas Arnold* | 58 | Dock House | Dock Foreman | GWR |
| James Brown | 57 | Dock House | Platelayer | |
| Bertie William Mogford* | 26 | 5 Ynysymaerdy Road | Signalman | RSBR |
| William H Prout | 32 | 9 Ynysymaerdy Road | Engine fitter | Steelworks |
| John Hughes | 42 | 21 Ynysymaerdy Road | Loco driver | |
| Roland Hughes | 39 | 23 Ynysymaerdy Road | Loco driver | SWMR |
| John William Hughes | 37 | 25 Ynysymaerdy Road | Loco driver | SWMR |
| Dan Bromham | 46 | 27 Ynysymaerdy Road | Rail guard | |
| Thomas H Anthony* [2] | 29 | 29 Ynysymaerdy Road | Loco driver | GWR |
| Robert Davies | 43 | 39 Ynysymaerdy Road | Loco driver | Whitford galvanising |
| Trevor Davies* | 18 | 47 Ynysymaerdy Road | Note-taker | RSBR |
| Dennis McCarthy | 38 | 10 Water Street | Loco driver | Ironworks |
| Thomas John Deacon | 23 | 18 Water Street | Striker | GWR |
| William Jarvis | 49 | 19 Water Street | Loco driver | Steelworks |

| | | | | |
|---|---|---|---|---|
| Albert Farrant | 28 | Brynawel 20 Neath Road | Platelayer | |
| Edward Stephen Resteaux | 58 | Mount Pleasant | Railway accountant | GWR |
| Jeremiah Grace* | 40 | 27 Woodland Row | Platelayer | RSBR |
| William Tissington | 68 | Woodbine Cottages | Engine fitter | Steelworks |
| Hendry Morris | 34 | 186 Neath Road | Loco driver | Steelworks |
| John Alfred Thompson | 18 | 198 Neath Road | Platelayer's labourer | |
| Thomas Benjamin | 57 | Oakfield Villas | Carrier | |
| Edwin Roberts | 64 | 242 Neath Road | Traffic manager | |
| John Lewis | 54 | 286 Old Road | Signalman | |
| Thomas B White | 21 | 26 Pantyrheol | Wagon painter | |
| Thomas H Jones | 23 | 26 Pantyrheol | Loco fireman | |
| Thomas Jones | 56 | Honddu Cwrt Sart | Loco safety valve examiner | |
| Thos Chas Davies | 38 | 38 Honddu Cwrt Sart | Engine fitter | |
| John Holloway | 57 | Sidney House Cwrt Sart | Wagon Builder | GWR |
| Thomas Williams | 42 | Sidney House Cwrt Sart | Wagon Builder | GWR |
| Edward Harris | 38 | Preswylfa Cwrt Sart | Railwayman | |
| David Trevor Jeffreys | 53 | Cartref Cwrt Sart | Engine fitter | |
| Fred Lewis | 23 | Cwrt Sart | Booking clerk | RSBR |
| Charles Edwin Gibbs | 48 | Brynawel Cwrt Sart | Engine fitter/turner | GWR |
| John Samuel Church | 50 | Brynawel Cwrt Sart | Accountant | Rail contractor |
| JA Williams | 36 | 1 Farm Road | Loco driver | GWR |
| Benjamin Thomas | 30 | 3 Farm Road | Loco fireman | |
| George Henry Payne | 25 | 3 Farm Road | Loco fireman | GWR |
| Evan Williamson | 29 | 5 Farm Road | Loco fireman | |
| E Thomas Isaac | 34 | 2 Morgans Terrace | Signalman | |
| Wm Thos Jones | 35 | 2 Morgans Terrace | Signalman | |
| Harry Wm Stagg | 35 | 4 Morgans Terrace | Loco driver | GWR |
| Herbert George Lewis | 33 | 6 Morgans Terrace | Engine fitter | |
| George William H Cox | 46 | 7 Morgans Terrace | Railway guard | RSBR |
| Alfred G Cox* | 18 | 7 Morgans Terrace | Engine cleaner | GWR |
| Charles Cyril Cox[3] | 15 | 7 Morgans Terrace | Rail messenger | RSBR |
| Edward A J J Alder | 30 | 16 Morgans Terrace | Shunter | GWR |
| Dennis O'Shea | 28 | 17 Morgans Terrace | Platelayer | RSBR |
| John Andrews | 53 | 17 Morgans Terrace | Engine fitter | |
| Charles Hoare* | 49 | 19 Morgans Terrace | Platelayer | RSBR |
| George Jarrett | 47 | 3 Tucker Street | Permanent way inspector | |
| Benjamin John Howells | 35 | 4 Tucker Street | Signalman | GWR |
| Ephraim Williams | 28 | 4 Short Street | Carting agent | |
| Wm David Griffiths | 51 | 12 Shelone Terrace | Station/dock messenger | GWR |
| Albert Lambert* | 18 | 47 Brynhyfryd Road | Porter | RSBR |
| Frank Lambert* | 29 | 47 Brynhyfryd Road | Packer | RSBR |
| Thomas Fishlock | 58 | 39 Ruskin Street | Platelayer | Copperworks |
| William Williams | 45 | 12 Pill Terrace | Loco driver | Shipbreaking |
| John M John | 42 | 2 Rockingham Terrace | Loco driver | |
| David John | 38 | 2 Rockingham Terrace | Loco Fireman | |
| John Davies | 40 | 14 Rockingham Terrace | Ganger | |
| Thomas James Davies | 17 | 14 Rockingham Terrace | Porter | |
| William H Knight* | 30 | 20 Rockingham Terrace | Shunter | GWR |
| Daniel John | 34 | 58 Rockingham Terrace | Stationmaster | |
| William George Reynish | 29 | 68 Rockingham Terrace | Railway guard | RSBR |
| Henry Harris | 52 | 67 Rockingham Terrace | Packer | GWR |

| | | | | |
|---|---|---|---|---|
| Fred H Howard* | 19 | 64 Rockingham Terrace | Packer | GWR |
| Raymond Way | 59 | 74 Rockingham Terrace | Loco driver | Ironworks |
| Henry Parr | 67 | 15 Grandison Street | Engine cleaner | |
| Alfred Locke | 40 | 25 Grandison Street | Loco driver | Steelworks |
| James Evans | 52 | 9 Vernon Street | Railway inspector | |
| Garnet Massena Waters* | 28 | 10 Vernon Street | Loco driver | Steelworks |
| Thomas Griffiths | 52 | 16 Vernon Street | Loco driver | |
| Thomas Clark | 28 | 25 Vernon Street | Loco driver | |
| William Owen* | 26 | 3 Mansel Street | Shunter | GWR |
| Alfred Jeffs | 57 | 20 Mansel Street | Stationmaster | |
| William David Lynn Pudner* | 20 | 30 Mansel Street | Rail porter | RSBR /Neath |
| Edwin Southcott | 61 | 27 Mansel Street | Railway guard | GWR |
| Augustus Colwill* | 33 | 20 Hoo Street | Shunter | GWR |
| James Jewell | 25 | 20 Hoo Street | Shunter | Steelworks |
| Thomas G Price | 16 | 20 Hoo Street | Rail porter | |
| Morris Johns* | 29 | 13 Osterley Street | Porter | GWR |
| John Allen Thomas | 18 | 25 Osterley Street | Loco driver | Tinplate works |
| David Jenkins | 49 | 14 Middleton Street | Signalman | |
| William James Beer* [4] | 42 | 22 Middleton Street | Railway guard | GWR |
| Thomas James Beer* | 19 | 22 Middleton Street | Railway guard | PTR |
| John Lewis | 33 | 25 Middleton Street | Shunter | GWR |
| John T Read | 22 | 25 Middleton Street | Clerk | GWR |
| Daniel Prosser | 34 | 30 Middleton Street | Wagon repairer | GWR |
| Joseph x | 22 | 30 Middleton Street | Loco driver | Iron works |
| William Lye | 25 | 31 Middleton Street | Painter | GWR |
| Morgan Jenkins | 50 | 4 Swan Street | Engine fitter | |
| Henry Joseph | 26 | Claymill Cottages, Baglan | Loco driver | Steelworks |
| A Cadwallader* | 24 | Ty'r Halen, Baglan | Packer | GWR |
| William T L Collins [5] | 35 | 1 Grove Villas Penrhiwtyn | Loco driver | GWR |
| Benjamin John | 27 | Ex-Goodwick | Signalman | GWR |
| William Williams | 61 | White Gates Lodge, Briton Ferry | Lampman | RSBR |
| James Greener (Boarder) | 23 | Houghton-le-Spring, | Shunter | |
| Thomas Wm James Backshell* | 27 | Ex-Letterston, Haverfordwest | Signalman | GWR |
| George Griffiths* (Boarder) | 45 | 20 Osterley Street, | Bridgeman | RSBR |
| William Thomas* | 45 | 66 Rockingham Terrace | Dock gateman | GWR |
| Robert Maine* (Boarder) | 49 | 19 Albert Road, Melyncrythan | Platelayer | RSBR |
| Frederick R Dare* | 28 | Boarder, Ex-Somerset | Platelayer | RSBR |
| John David* | 38 | | Fireman | SWMR |
| J Reed* | 37 | 62 Regent Street West | Dock gateman | GWR |
| Henry Moses* | 18 | Boarder, ex-Falmouth | Weigher | RSBR |
| William John* | 48 | Llantwit Road workhouse, Neath | Packer | GWR |
| William Weeks* (Boarder) | 19 | Ex Clinton Street, Exeter | Porter | GWR |
| Joseph Shipton* | 23 | 38 Southgate Street, Neath | Checker | GWR |
| Albert John* | 19 | 80 Giant's Grave | Packer | GWR |
| Sam Dunn* | 27 | Siloh Cottages, Baglan | Packer | GWR |
| Willie Evans [6] | 15 | 9 Vernon Street | Apprentice fitter | RSBR |

| | | | | |
|---|---|---|---|---|
| Ed Morgan* (Boarder) | 50 | Cwrt Sart Cottage | Platelayer | RSBR |
| R Adams* | | | Porter | |
| Evan Mark Noot* | 22 | 3 Cornish Court, The Green, Neath | Platelayer | RSBR |
| Arthur Bennett* (Boarder) | 26 | 17 Cresswell Terrace, Neath | Signalman | RSBR |
| Thomas Hedingham* (Boarder) | 38 | 84 Charles Road, Small Heath | Platelayer | RSBR |
| Lawrence H Wyatt* (Boarder) | 21 | Ex Newton Abbott | Porter | RSBR |
| William A Dobson | 50 | Eastleigh House, Penrhiwtyn | Loco driver | GWR |
| Albert L Dobson | 28 | Eastleigh House, Penrhiwtyn | Fireman | |
| William H Dobson | 16 | Eastleigh House, Penrhiwtyn | Engine cleaner | |
| William John Jarrett | 22 | Townhill Road, Swansea, | Booking clerk | GWR |
| John Halliday | 66 | Greenfield Villa, Penrhiwtyn | Fireman | |
| Frank Perry | 23 | 3 Pantyrheol | Rail labourer | |
| William Thomas James | 47 | 4 Pantyrheol | Engine fitter | GWR |
| Richard Lewis Anderson | 46 | 5 Pantyrheol | Wagon painter and letterer | Colliery company |
| William Young | 47 | 11 Pantyrheol | Platelayer | |
| Pat Sullivan (Boarder) | 26 | 11 Pantyrheol | Platelayer | |
| Richard Jenkins | 32 | 12 Pantyrheol | Signalman | |
| David Ivor Cuff | 21 | 16 Pantyrheol | Fitter's mate | GWR |
| William Rees | 48 | 21 Pantyrheol | Engine fitter | GWR |
| William J Rees | 23 | 21 Pantyrheol | Engine fitter | GWR |
| Jesse Turner | 29 | 27 Mansel Terrace, Old Road | Shunter | Melin Tin works |
| William Turner | 55 | 27 Mansel Terrace, Old Road | Labourer | GWR |
| Wm Henry Davies | 41 | 37 Mansel Terrace, Old Road | Storekeeper | GWR |
| John Griffiths | 45 | 42 Mansel Terrace, Old Road | Wagon repairer | GWR |
| William Fear | 64 | 46 Mansel Terrace, Old Road | Platelayer | GWR |
| William K Parry | 23 | 4 Montpellier Terrace, Swansea | Assistant goods clerk | GWR |
| A E A Wheeler | | | Chief goods clerk | GWR |
| Ernest W New | 23 | 5 Brynheulog Street, Port Talbot | Stationmaster | GWR |
| William J E Watts | | | | |

This list includes rail workers who lived in the part of Llantwit Lower parish from Cwrt Sart to Penrhiwtyn

* Names asterisked indicate a trade union member, where known
1. Mayor of Neath, 1951–2
2. Neath Enginemen
3. War casualty
4. Son Robert, killed in Albion works in 1894. Pic of father in Neath Enginemen
5. Collins the pop founder
6. Son of James Evans, Inspector

## Appendix Six

# Intermodal container trains

Chapter Six referred to intermodal container traffic. This involves transporting freight in an intermodal container or vehicle using multiple modes of transport such as rail, ship and lorry, without any handling of the freight itself during changes of mode. It reduces handling, damage, loss and costs, when compared with road transport over longer distances.

The idea is not new because I K Brunel introduced uncovered iron containers to move coal from the vale of Neath to Swansea docks in the mid nineteenth century.

An important concept to be considered in relation to intermodal container traffic is the *loading gauge*. This is to be distinguished from *track gauge*, which is the spacing of the rails on a railway track, measured between the inner faces of the load-bearing rails. The loading gauge defines the maximum height and width for railway vehicles and their loads to ensure safe passage through bridges, tunnels and other structures.

Loading gauges can vary within a network, even though the track gauge is constant. This occurred in Britain because the private Victorian rail companies adopted different standards when the lines were built. However, they all built the tunnel and bridges as arches to accommodate the curved roof structures of passenger carriages. This has implications for the sizes of containers that intermodal container traffic can use. The intermodal containers are not curved and therefore did not fit under many old arched bridges.

The loading gauge can also affect which passenger trains can use the same platform, especially when rolling stock sizes vary. It is also important for overhead electrification, where bridges have to be raised to provide clearances for the pantographs of electric locomotive units.

Under nationalisation a standard loading gauge known as W5 was introduced in 1951. This has been developed by Network Rail into a gauge classification which determines whether or not containers can be conveyed. This is important because containers have increased in both height and width.

W6a  Standard minimum gauge across most of Network

W7  8'0" containers allowed, e.g. over Welsh Marches Route

W8  8'6" containers allowed

W9  8'6" containers allowed on long vehicles with greater distance between bogies

W10  9'6" containers allowed provided they are less than 2500 mm wide

W12  9'6" containers 2600 mm wide allowed

# Locomotives based at Cwrt Sart depot

## 1921

| Class | Wheel arrangement | Numbers | | | | | | | | | | |
|---|---|---|---|---|---|---|---|---|---|---|---|---|
| **Tender Locos** | | | | | | | | | | | | |
| Ex ROD | 2-8-0 | 364 | 407 | 437 | 872 | 997 | 1019 | | | | | |
| Bulldog | 4-4-0 | 1049 | | | | | | | | | | |
| 43xx | 2-6-0 | 1069 | 1077 | 1229 | 1239 | 1393 | 1429 | | | | | |
| Aberdare | 2-6-0 | 1582 | | | | | | | | | | |
| Dean Goods | 0-6-0 | 1583 | 1584 | 1603 | 1605 | | | | | | | |
| **Tank Locos** | | | | | | | | | | | | |
| 42xx | 2-8-0T | 1655 | 1695 | 1706 | | | | | | | | |
| 39xx | 2-6-2T | 1754 | | | | | | | | | | |
| RSB | 0-6-2T | 1762 | | | | | | | | | | |
| Taff Vale | 0-6-2T | 1858 | 1859 | 1920 | | | | | | | | |
| SWMR | 0-6-0ST | 1921 | | | | | | | | | | |
| Ex Cornwall | 0-6-0ST | 2013 | | | | | | | | | | |
| Various | 0-6-0S&PT | 2139 | 2432 | 2447 | 2475 | 2544 | 2606 | 2732 | 2779 | 2782 | 2789 | 3059 | 3060 |
| | | 3063 | 3068 | 3083 | 3091 | 3338 | 3915 | 4205 | 4211 | 4219 | 4314 | 4347 | 4350 |
| | | 4361 | 4364 | 6306 | | | | | | | | |
| 517class | 0-4-2T | 29 | | | | | | | | | | |
| Steam railmotor | | 82 | | | | | | | | | | |
| **Total 57** | | | | | | | | | | | | |

## 1950

| Class | Wheel arrangement | Numbers | | | | | | | | | | |
|---|---|---|---|---|---|---|---|---|---|---|---|---|
| RR | 0-6-2T | 75 | | | | | | | | | | |
| 1854 | 0-6-0PT | 1855 | 1858 | | | | | | | | | |
| BPGV | 0-6-0ST | 2192 | | | | | | | | | | |
| 2301 | 0-6-0 | 2411 | | | | | | | | | | |
| 2721 | 0-6-0PT | 2722 | | | | | | | | | | |
| 57xx | 0-6-0PT | 3611 | 3621 | 3741 | 3757 | 3766 | 3774 | 4621 | 5703 | 5720 | 5746 | 7701 | 7737 |
| | | 7739 | 7742 | 7743 | 7757 | 7767 | 7769 | 7786 | 7799 | 8715 | 8775 | 8782 | 9627 |
| | | 9666 | 9734 | 9750 | 9756 | 9779 | 9783 | 9786 | 9792 | | | |
| 51xx | 2-6-2T | 4169 | | | | | | | | | | |
| 42xx | 2-8-0T | 4221 | 4232 | 4252 | 4259 | 4272 | 4274 | 4279 | 4284 | 4288 | 4293 | |
| | | 4295 | 5225 | 5239 | 5242 | 5254 | | | | | | |
| 81xx | 2-6-2T | 8104 | | | | | | | | | | |
| 94xx | 0-6-0PT | 8420 | | | | | | | | | | |
| **Total 57** | | | | | | | | | | | | |

## June 1961

| Class | Wheel arrangement | Numbers | | | | | | | | | | |
|---|---|---|---|---|---|---|---|---|---|---|---|---|
| 16xx | 0-6-0PT | 1645 | | | | | | | | | | |
| 4073 | 4-6-0 | 4090* | 4093* | 4099* | 5004* | 5013* | 5037* | 5041* | 5044* | 5048* | 5051* | 5062* |
| | | 5074* | 5078* | | | | | | | | | |
| 42xx | 2-8-0T | 4257 | 4282 | 4284 | 5221 | 5222 | 5239 | 5242 | | | | |
| 49xx | 4-6-0 | 4927* | 4988* | 5909* | 5972* | 5989* | 6905* | 6912* | 6918* | | | |
| 51xx | 2-6-2 T | 4134 | 4169 | | | | | | | | | |
| 56xx | 0-6-2 T | 5673 | 6641 | 6649 | 6695 | 9734 | | | | | | |
| 57xx | 0-6-0 PT | 3611 | 3621 | 3687 | 3741 | 3757 | 3766 | 3768 | 3774 | 4621 | 4653 | 5720 |
| | | 5761 | 5773 | 5778 | 7739 | 7786 | 7799 | 8732 | 8760 | 8775 | 8782 | 8784 |
| | | 8788 | 9627 | 9750 | 9777 | 9779 | 9783 | 9786 | 9792 | | | |
| 81xx | 2-6-2 T | 8102 | 8104 | | | | | | | | | |
| 94xx | 0-6-0 PT | 8418 | 8439 | 9430 | 9446 | 9473 | 9478 | | | | | |
| **Total 74** | | | | | | | | | | | | |

## Selected Castle class locos based at Cwrt Sart 1961

| Number | Name | Point of interest |
|---|---|---|
| 4090 | Dorchester Castle | Hauled last up *South Wales Pullman* in September 1961 |
| 4093 | Dunster Castle | Hauled penultimate *South Wales Pullman* |
| 4099 | Kilgerran Castle | Note the Anglicised spelling |
| 5004 | Llanstephan Castle | Note the Anglicised spelling |
| 5013 | Abergavenny Castle | Note the Anglicised spelling |
| 5048 | Earl of Devon | Hauled last down *South Wales Pullman* in September 1961 |
| 5078 | Beaufort | Last *Castle* allocated to Neath. Withdrawn December 1962 |
| 5051 | Earl Bathurst | Now preserved at Didcot Railway Centre |

## August 1964

| Class | Wheel arrangement | Number | | | | | | | | | |
|---|---|---|---|---|---|---|---|---|---|---|---|
| 16xx | 0-6-0 PT | 1669 | | | | | | | | | |
| 28xx | 2-8-0 | 2890 | 3810 | 3814 | 3816 | 3823 | 3836 | 3860 | 3864 | 3866 | |
| 41xx | 0-4-0 T | 4108 | 4110 | | | | | | | | |
| 42xx | 2-8-0 T | 4284 | 4286 | 4292 | 5212 | 5223 | 5245 | 5257 | 5264 | | |
| 49xx | 4-6-0 | 4985* | 5961* | 6932* | 6973* | 7913* | | | | | |
| 57xx | 0-6-0 PT | 3610 | 3615 | 3742 | 3747 | 3754 | 3787 | 3797 | 4612 | 4653 | 4660 | 4669 |
| | | 4695 | 8714 | 9609 | 9615 | 9617 | 9625 | 9637 | 9648 | 9656 | 9660 | 9675 |
| | | 9678 | 9716 | 9780 | | | | | | | |
| 94xx | 0-6-0 PT | 8431 | 8446 | 9442 | 9446 | 9464 | 9473 | 9478 | 9480 | | |
| 41xxx | 0-4-0 T | 41535 | | | | | | | | | |
| 51xxx | 0-4-0 T | 51218 | | | | | | | | | |
| **Total 60** | | | | | | | | | | | |

## Last allocation June 1965

| Class | Wheel arrangement | Numbers | | | | | | |
|---|---|---|---|---|---|---|---|---|
| 57xx | 0-6-0PT | 3642 | 3647 | 3687 | 3690 | 4612 | 6614 | 9617 |
| 56xx | 0-6-2T | 9716 | | | | | | |
| **Total 9** | | | | | | | | |

* Named locomotives

# Locomotives scrapped at Briton Ferry

The majority of the locos were scrapped by T W Ward, Briton Ferry. Some of these, marked with an asterisk in the list below, were cut up at Briton Ferry dock rather than Giant's Grave as they were too big to negotiate the curved branch line to Giant's Grave.

**Scrapped at T W Ward, Briton Ferry** – total 150

| | | | | | | | | | | | | | |
|---|---|---|---|---|---|---|---|---|---|---|---|---|---|
| 1103 | 1104 | 1105 | 1106 | 1401 | 1423 | 1429 | 1437 | 1456 | 1467 | 1623 | 2254* | 3600 | 3604 |
| 3608 | 3617 | 3620 | 3643 | 3644 | 3647 | 3669 | 3678 | 3687 | 3690 | 3696 | 3707 | 3712 | 3716 |
| 3717 | 3735 | 3762 | 3763 | 3777 | 3784 | 3790 | 4142* | 4200* | 4226* | 4261* | 4296* | 4607 | 4611 |
| 4623 | 4630 | 4631 | 4636 | 4638 | 4639 | 4654 | 4655 | 4662 | 4663 | 4666 | 4669 | 4671 | 4672 |
| 4673 | 4675 | 4688 | 4694 | 4698 | 5621 | 5647 | 5655 | 5665 | 5678 | 5680 | 5688 | 5703 | 5743 |
| 6347* | 6614 | 6620 | 6652 | 6653 | 6657 | 6661 | 6664 | 6689 | 6714 | 6721 | 6723 | 6727 | 6737 |
| 6763 | 6772 | 7315* | 7445 | 7738 | 7780 | 8400 | 8403 | 8415 | 8420 | 8433 | 8436 | 8459 | 8471 |
| 8481 | 8484 | 8486 | 8498 | 9404 | 9405 | 9411 | 9415 | 9418 | 9430 | 9437 | 9441 | 9463 | 9464 |
| 9471 | 9477 | 9482 | 9493 | 9495 | 9601 | 9605 | 9617 | 9625 | 9631 | 9644 | 9647 | 9656 | 9659 |
| 9662 | 9666 | 9667 | 9670 | 9676 | 9678 | 9716 | 9726 | 9754 | 9789 | 9790 | 9794 | | |
| 30021 | 30025 | 30029 | 30036 | 30048 | 30052 | 30107 | 30108 | 30111 | 30254 | 31542 | 31551 | | |

**Locos dismantled by other firms at Briton Ferry**

Barlborough Metals: 3847, 7028 *Cadbury Castle*
Slag Reduction: 2219, 6975 *Capesthorne Hall*
Steel Supply: 4137, 4233, 4903 *Astley Hall*, 4919 *Donnington Hall*, 5213, 7205, 9766

The following were stored at Briton Ferry dock but, it seems, were dismantled by Steel Supply at Jersey Marine:
4108, 4292, 6154, 6159, 6368, 6996 *Blackwell Hall*, 7319

The following locos were recorded at Briton Ferry dock in 1965 but details of their dismantling are not known:
6149, 7248, 7249

This makes a total of 161 locos that were known to have been dismantled at Briton Ferry.
(Sources: personal records and Rail UK website.)

# Bibliography

| Author | Year | Title | Publisher |
|---|---|---|---|
| Adams, Philip | 2014 | A most industrious town: Briton Ferry and its people, 1814–2014 | Author |
| Allen, C J | 1974 | Titled trains of the Western Region | Ian Allan Ltd |
| Atkins, T | 2014 | Great Western Docks and Marine | Noodle Books |
| Bradley, Simon | 2017 | The Railways: Nation, Network and People | Profile Books |
| Briton Ferry Photographic and Internet Technology Club (BFP) | 2014 | Briton Ferry: A much loved community | BFP |
| Bryan, Tim | 1995 | The Great Western at War | Patrick Stephens Ltd |
| Butt, R V J | 1995 | The Directory of Railway Stations (1st edition) | Sparkford: Patrick Stephens Ltd |
| Campaign for Better | 2018 | Buses in Crisis: A report on bus funding across England and Wales 2010–2018 | Campaign for Better Transport |
| Cole, Professor Stuart | 2016 | Swansea Public Transport Hubs: Ministerial scoping study | Profile books |
| Cooke, R A | 1988 | Track layout diagrams of the GWR and British Rail WR, S.50A Neath–Port Talbot | R A Cooke |
| Daniel, Haynes *et al* | 2006 | The Red Dragon … and other old friends | LDR Publications |
| Davies, Councillor David | *c*1870 | History of Briton Ferry | Author |
| Department for Transport | 2007 | Delivering a Sustainable Railway | Government White Paper |
| Department for Transport | 2017 | Connecting people: a strategic vision for rail | Government White Paper |
| Furness, Richard | 2011 | Poster to Poster: Railway journeys in Art Vol 3: The Midlands and Wales | JD&F Associates |
| Hale, Michael | 1983 | Steam in South Wales – Vol. 3: Main Line | Oxford Publishing |
| Hale, Michael | 1999 | Steam in South Wales – Vol. 6: The General Scene | Welsh Railway Research Circle |
| Harrison, Ian | 1984 | Great Western Railway Locomotive Allocations for 1921 | Wild Swan |
| Hendy, Sir Peter | 2015 | Report to the Secretary of State for Transport on re-planning of Network Rail's investment programme | Network Rail |
| Hodge, J | 2000 | The South Wales Main Line – Part 1 Cardiff | Wild Swan |
| Hodge, J | 2006 | The South Wales Main Line – Part 4 Bridgend to Swansea | Wild Swan |
| Humphreys, E | 1898 | Reminiscences of Briton Ferry and Baglan | Swansea: Cambria Daily Leader |
| Hutchings, Carol | 2008 | The Railway in 'Memories' | Briton Ferry Older Persons' Forum |
| Jenkins, Elis (Ed.) | 1974 | Neath and District: A Symposium | Editor |
| Jones, S | 2009 | Brunel in South Wales, Vol. 3 | The History Press |

| | | | |
|---|---|---|---|
| Jordan, Arthur and Elizabeth | 1991 | Away for the Day | Silver Link Publishing |
| King, B (Ed.) | 2009 | Neath Enginemen | Oakwood Press |
| Knox, Collie | 1944 | The Unbeaten Track | Cassell & Co |
| Lyons and Mountford | 1986 | Great Western Engine Sheds (1837–1947) | Oxford Publishing Co |
| McNulty, Sir Roy | 2011 | Realising the potential of GB Rail: report of the rail value for money study | DfT/ORR |
| Maggs, C | 1981 | Rail Centres: Bristol | Ian Allan |
| Mitchell and Smith | 2012 | Branch Lines Around Swansea | Middleton Press |
| Morel, J | 1983 | Pullman | David and Charles |
| Morgan, B, and Meyrick, B | 1973 | Behind the steam | Hutchinson |
| Morgan, Cliff | 1977 | Briton Ferry (Llansawel) | Briton Ferry: Cliff Morgan |
| Morgan, Cliff | 1979/ 1985 | A pictorial record of Briton Ferry (Llansawel) Volumes 1/2 | Briton Ferry: Cliff Morgan |
| Morgan, H | 1984 | South Wales Branch Lines | Bibliography |
| Morgan, John M | 2014 | Fifty years within station limits: The life of a south Wales railwayman | Y Lolfa |
| Mountford, E R | 1965 | Caerphilly Works | Roundhouse Books |
| Nicholson, Mavis | 1991 | Martha Jane and me: a childhood in Wales | Seren Books |
| Paige, J | 1979 | Forgotten Railways – South Wales | David and Charles |
| Parker, Richard | 2008 | The railways of Pembrokeshire | Noodle Books |
| Potts, M and Green, G W | 1996 | Idustrial Locomotives of West Glamorgan | Industrial Railway Society |
| RailfutureCymru/Wales | 2016 | On track for the 21st Century: A development plan for the railways of Wales and the Borders | RailfutureCymru/Wales |
| Reynolds, P R | 2018 | The Neath River railway tunnel | *www.derelictplaces.co.uk/ 21043* accessed 3 May 2018 |
| Richards, S | 1976 | The Rhondda and Swansea Bay | Morganwg Cerdydd |
| Simmonds, R | 2012 | The Port Talbot Railway and the South Wales Mineral Railway, Vol 1 and 2 | Lightmoor Press |
| Skidmore, Jonathan | 2018 | Neath and Briton Ferry in the First World War | Author |
| Welsh Assembly Government | 2008 | Wales Transport Strategy | Welsh Assembly Government |
| Williams, Glyn | 2009 | 'The South Wales Mineral Railway' *in* 'The Neath Antiquarian', Volume 1 | Neath Antiquarian Society |
| Williams, Herbert | 1981 | Railways in Wales | Christopher Davies (Publishers) Swansea |
| Wolmar, Christian | 2007 | Fire and Steam: How the railways transformed Britain | Atlantic Books |
| Woodley, Richard | 1996 | The Day of the Holiday Express | Ian Allan Publishing |